In the name of God, the Compassionate, the Merciful

Sayyid Quṭb

IN THE SHADE OF
THE QUR'ĀN

Fī Ẓilāl al-Qur'ān

VOLUME VI

SŪRAH 7

Al-A'rāf

Translated and Edited by
Adil Salahi

THE ISLAMIC FOUNDATION
AND
ISLAMONLINE.NET

Published by

THE ISLAMIC FOUNDATION,

Markfield Conference Centre,
Ratby Lane, Markfield, Leicester LE67 9SY, United Kingdom
Tel: (01530) 244944, Fax: (01530) 244946
E-mail: i.foundation@islamic-foundation.org.uk
Website: www.islamic-foundation.org.uk

Quran House, PO Box 30611, Nairobi, Kenya

PMB 3193, Kano, Nigeria

ISLAMONLINE.NET,
PO Box 22212, Doha, Qatar
E-mail: webmaster@islam-online.net
Website: www.islamonline.net

British Library Cataloguing-in-Publication Data
Qutb, Sayyid, 1903–1966
   In the shade of the Qur'an: fi zilal al-Qur'an,
   Vol. 6: Surah 7: Al-A'rāf translated and edited by Adil Salahi
   1. Koran
   I. Title   II. Salahi, Adil   III. Islamic Foundation
   297.1'227

ISBN 0 86037 377 0
ISBN 0 86037 382 7 pbk

Typeset by: N.A.Qaddoura
Cover design by: Imtiaze A. Manjra

Printed and bound in Great Britain by Antony Rowe Ltd, Chippenham, Wiltshire

Contents

Transliteration Table

Consonants. Arabic

initial: unexpressed medial and final:

ء	ʾ	د	d	ض	ḍ	ك	k
ب	b	ذ	dh	ط	ṭ	ل	l
ت	t	ر	r	ظ	ẓ	م	m
ث	th	ز	z	ع	ʿ	ن	n
ج	j	س	s	غ	gh	هـ	h
ح	ḥ	ش	sh	ف	f	و	w
خ	kh	ص	ṣ	ق	q	ي	y

Vowels, diphthongs, etc.

Short: ﹷ a ﹻ i ﹹ u

long: لَـا ā ـُو ū ﹻي ī

diphthongs: ـَوْ aw

ـَىْ ay

More About the Author

An Introduction by Adil Salahi

After the publication of Volume III, in which I wrote an Introduction about this work and its author, shedding some light about his arrest and the conditions in which he worked in prison, I received many comments and requests for more information. A number of friends and readers have asked me in particular to throw more light on the author's life, especially the period between his release from prison in 1964 and re-arrest in 1965 leading to his trial by military court and execution in 1966. Some asked pointedly whether he could not have left Egypt to lead a more peaceful and comfortable life in another Arab country where he had millions of admirers. On the other hand, one reader objected to my statement that in 1955, Sayyid Quṭb was scheduled to receive the death sentence, but certain circumstances led to this being curtailed to 15 years imprisonment. He argued that this bordered on speculation. I will try here to answer some of these questions.

In 1954, when large numbers of members and sympathizers of the Muslim Brotherhood in Egypt were rounded up and endured a brutal campaign of torture, the authorities' intention of executing most leading figures of this organization was very clear. This was reflected in the pronouncements of several members of the Revolutionary Command Council, which wielded all power in Egypt at the time. Radio broadcasts and newspaper articles were preparing Egyptian and Arab public opinion for very harsh punishments against a large number of people. A study of these would reveal that the ground was being prepared for the summary execution of 30 or 40 leading figures in four or five batches. The first batch of sentences was declared, with seven people being sentenced to death. These included the leader of the Muslim Brotherhood, Justice Hassan al-Hudaybi (later his sentence was commuted to life imprisonment), and six others who were actually executed. Sayyid Quṭb was included in the second batch, together with several members of the Guidance Council, the policy-making body of the Muslim Brotherhood.

It took only a couple of days between the announcement of the first batch of death sentences and their execution. At the same time, the military court was also looking at other cases, which were supposed to be completed quickly. Sayyid Quṭb was scheduled to appear before the military court at that time, but he had contracted a severe chest disease, which meant that when he opened his mouth to talk, he could not do so because blood came from his chest into his mouth. He was put under intensive treatment and his trial was delayed for 24 hours, but the condition persisted. Another 24-hour postponement of the trial ensued, followed by a further postponement of one week.

In the meantime, the first batch of executions, which included four of the leaders of the Muslim Brotherhood, resulted in widespread protests across the Muslim world, with huge demonstrations outside Egyptian embassies from Indonesia to Libya. The military government in Egypt was taken aback by the intensity of the protests. To redress the situation a little, it announced that although the military courts would continue, there would be no more executions.

Thus, his illness on the one hand, and the back down of the Egyptian military government from its policy of executions on the other, were the major factors in saving Sayyid Quṭb from the death sentence early in 1955. This is an example of how God's will overpowers any human design, even by the most powerful of rulers. It was God who wanted Sayyid Quṭb to live so that he could complete his commentary on the Qur'ān, and rewrite nearly the first half of it.

Could he have left Egypt after his release in 1964 to live a more comfortable life? If the opportunity was there, should he have done so?

Yes, an opportunity was there, and indeed offers to leave were extended to Sayyid Quṭb at different times. As I said in the Introduction to Volume III, his release in 1964 was due to the intervention of President Abd al-Salam Arif of Iraq. Iraqi scholars had spoken to their President, making a strong case against the continued imprisonment of many members of the Muslim Brotherhood, particularly Sayyid Quṭb, the scholar writing a commentary on the Qur'ān and placing its treasures before the Arab reading public. Nasser, the Egyptian dictator, was keen not to antagonize his ally, President Arif. Hence, he agreed to his request. It would have been very simple to arrange a trip for our author to Iraq, where he could have lived under the protection of President Arif, who greatly admired his writings.

But Sayyid Quṭb had totally different concerns. A new generation of young men and women were beginning to start small groups on the lines of the Muslim Brotherhood, which was still banned in Egypt. These groups had been in touch with him when he was still in prison, seeking his advice about their programme of study, so that they could develop a proper understanding of Islam and its revival. He wanted to help these young people so that they could avoid clashes with the authorities on the one hand and acquire a proper Islamic perspective on the other. He had devoted his life to the service of the cause of Islam and he felt that setting this new generation of young advocates of Islam on the right course was far more important than leading a life of personal safety and comfort.

In mid 1965, Nasser was visiting Moscow, where he announced that a new Muslim Brotherhood organization had been uncovered by the Egyptian intelligence services. He threatened that this time he would show no mercy whatsoever. It was very unusual for a head of state to announce the 'discovery' of a plot to overthrow him whilst he was visiting another country. It runs against diplomatic traditions which dictate that a leader should avoid giving any impression that his government might be unstable. But Communism considered the Islamic religion its most powerful enemy in Muslim countries, and an announcement like Nasser's in Moscow was calculated to be well received by his Communist hosts.

Immediately after the announcement, all Egyptian media were full of stories about the discovery of the new organization and its plots to destroy Egyptian society. There was a great deal of hype, but little substance in what was said. Salah Nassar, the attorney who headed the prosecution team, declared a few weeks before he published his indictment that 'much of what has been said in the media is baseless. It was no more than a product of a fertile and inconsistent imagination'. But it was evident in all that was published or broadcast that Sayyid Quṭb was the main target.

It was not until the early part of 1966 that new military courts were formed to look into the cases of the Muslim Brotherhood. Once more, the Nasser regime could not put the case to normal civilian courts because no court operating a proper legal system would pronounce the sort of sentences Nasser wanted. Towards the end of August, the military court sentenced a group of 43 Muslim Brothers, giving death sentences to seven and long terms of imprisonment to the others. Sayyid Quṭb was the main figure in this group and he received the death sentence. A few days later, it was announced that Nasser had confirmed three death sentences and commuted four to life imprisonment. Two days afterwards, it was announced that Sayyid Quṭb, Muhammad Yusuf Hawwash and Abd al-Fattah Ismail had been executed.

—•—

We come back to the original question: why did Sayyid Quṭb not flee Egypt when it became clear that things were moving towards a repeat of the earlier wave of persecution?

Towards the end of 1966, I met in Geneva Mr Muhammad Ramadan al-Hawisah, a Libyan diplomat who was based in Cairo at the time when the arrests of the Muslim Brotherhood started. He told me that he had visited Sayyid Quṭb at his home in Helwan, a Cairo suburb, towards the end of July 1965, when Sayyid said that arrests were being made, and that it was expected that a large number of people would be rounded up. Sayyid Quṭb expressed the hope that this time it would not be on the same scale as 1954. He then made a startling revelation when he said: "Their main target this time is none but me."

Mr al-Hawisah said: "Since this is the case, may I suggest that you come with me right now, together with your family, and I will drive you straightaway to Libya. As I have a car with diplomatic registration, no one will stop us. In a matter of a few hours you will be, with God's help, safe in Libya."

The offer was a very practical one, and under King Idris al-Sanousi, Sayyid Quṭb was certain to receive a warm welcome. But his reaction to the offer was totally unexpected by Mr al-Hawisah.

Sayyid Quṭb thanked him warmly and said: "Only a few days ago, I received here a group of Iraqi army officers who brought me a message from President Arif. They said that a plot was being weaved by Egyptian intelligence in which I am the chief target. They conveyed to me President Arif's invitation that I should go with them, on their private plane, to Iraq. They renewed his earlier offer to me to become an adviser to him. To your offer, I give the same answer I gave to them: I realize the seriousness of what is being prepared for me, but there are around 3,000 young men and women who now look at me as their leader. They will be targeted in this new campaign of oppression. If I were to leave Egypt now and abandon them to their destiny, I will be in the same position as a soldier who runs away from the battlefield. I must stay, and I must share with them whatever hardship they may be made to suffer."

Mr al-Hawisah also told me that all his entreaties were in vain. Sayyid Qutb was like a captain who would not abandon his sinking ship until all his men were safe. He emphasized time and again that his place was with his people. Since they could not have the same offer of safety, he would not abandon them, even though this meant his death.

It is not difficult to see why Sayyid Qutb declined the offers of a safe escape at a time when he was certain of re-arrest, with much worse consequences to follow. The theme that he stressed most in his writings, particularly during and after his earlier period of imprisonment (1954-1964) was the need to mould a community with the right understanding of Islam. He believed that a new Islamic revival must follow the arduous track of bringing such a community into existence. Moreover, such a community must be absolutely clear about its role in this life. Its task is not to overthrow a government, gain power, or fight for supremacy. Its task is only to make Islam known to people and to make it clear to them that Islam is God's final message to mankind and that He wants them to believe in it and implement it in their lives. This community of Islamic advocates must not aspire to any gains in this life, not even the triumph of Islam through its own efforts. It seeks its reward from God only, in the life to come.

Sayyid Qutb felt that those young people who formed secret groups which aimed to work for Islam could be the nucleus of a new Islamic movement that had this clear understanding. He felt that he must set them on the right track so that they were not misguided by thoughts or dreams of seizing power. He wanted them to realize that power is easily gained and lost. If advocates of Islam devoted their efforts to gaining power, they might easily slip into dictatorship, because they would try to defend their hold on power. What is worse is that they would be doing so in the name of Islam, describing their opponents as enemies of Islam. Thus, they would come to see Islam through their own interests. This would be a disastrous setback to Islamic revival.

He did not have much time to achieve such a remarkable change of perspective. Nevertheless, he was very successful. The leaders of the new groups accepted his vision and a process was started so as to impart it to the grass roots. But soon the intelligence services were able to infiltrate these groups. The Nasser dictatorship would not tolerate any popular organization, particularly an Islamic-oriented one. Hence, its immediate and brutal strike. The rest is history.

Could Sayyid Quṭb have left Egypt when he had these repeated offers of safety and high position? Many in his place would have jumped at any such offer, and understandably so, but not Sayyid Quṭb. He fully understood the bargain God has made with all true believers, outlined in the following verse: "*God has bought of the believers their lives and their possessions, promising them paradise in return. They fight in God's cause, and slay, and are slain. [This is] a promise which in truth He has willed upon Himself in the Torah, the Gospel and the Qur'ān. Who could be more faithful to his covenant than God? Rejoice, then, in the bargain which you have made with Him; for this is the triumph supreme.*" (9: 111) In declining all these offers, Sayyid Quṭb was indeed faithful to his part of the bargain.

Nor is it difficult to discern why he declined the earlier invitation to become a special adviser to President Arif of Iraq, who admired his writings. To Sayyid Quṭb, personal position was immaterial. What mattered was what he could do if he were to accept such a position. In the circumstances prevailing in Iraq and the Middle East at the time, he felt that he could do very little to help to promote an Islamic revival. President Arif's regime was one in a succession of military governments in which different factions and personalities of the armed forces gained power through plots and counter plots. His was of the more lenient variety, because he himself was religious. But there was nothing in his government to suggest any desire to adopt Islamic values and standards, apart from the appointment of a few religious persons in high government positions. One of these was General Mahmood Sheet Khattab, an Islamic scholar in his own right and an army general. He served as a minister, holding different portfolios in President Arif's government. Indeed, General Khattab himself seized the first opportunity to relinquish his government post as he felt that he could not serve Islam properly in such a position.

———•·■———

What was Sayyid Qutb's attitude when he learnt of his release from prison at the personal request of President Abd al-Salam Arif? It should be remembered that President Arif came to power in February 1963. In October of the same year, he ousted the Baath party and relied on the support of the Arab Nationalists, who wanted to see a union between Iraq and Egypt. President Arif himself was a supporter of this idea. Therefore when he visited Egypt in April 1964, the possibility of such a union was looming and Nasser was very keen to nurture this idea. Hence, President Arif's request for the release of Sayyid Qutb, pressed on him by many Iraqi scholars, was granted by Nasser without hesitation. As a minister accompanying President Arif on this visit, General Khattab was present when the request was made and approved. Nasser also agreed to Khattab's request to be allowed to visit Sayyid Qutb in prison and to break to him the news of his imminent release.

A car from the presidential palace took General Khattab from his hotel to the prison where Sayyid Qutb was delighted to meet him. After a relaxed conversation between the two scholars, Khattab told Sayyid Qutb his news and said that he should expect to be released very shortly. He explained that President Arif admired not only his writings, but also his unyielding stand in support of what he believed to be the truth. Khattab reports that he was very surprised to see an expression of sadness on Sayyid Qutb's face, as he said: "You are telling me that you have already spoken to President Nasser and the matter is settled?" Still in a joyful mood, Khattab said: "Yes. All praise be to God." In a tone of sadness, Sayyid Qutb said: "May God forgive you! I wish you had consulted me before doing so." Surprised, Khattab said: "Would you have objected?" He said: "Yes, I would. Had you consulted me, I would have advised you against speaking to the President, and I would not have left prison in this way." Khattab defended their approach, saying that "to obtain the release of an honourable man unjustly imprisoned is itself an honourable act." Sayyid Qutb said: "Anyway, it is too late to change anything now. May God reward you handsomely for your efforts to secure your brother's release." He requested Khattab to convey his greetings and gratitude to President

Arif. After his release, he presented two complete sets of his books to both President Arif and General Khattab.

Why was Sayyid Quṭb unhappy about the way he was released after being unjustly imprisoned for ten years? We can only try to divine the reasons. He might have felt that he was not alone in enduring such a long imprisonment for his beliefs. He might have felt that the proper way for his release should have been as a part of a general release of all the Muslim Brotherhood members who were still detained. Or he might have taken his lead from the Prophet Joseph, who was imprisoned for several years on the basis of a false accusation. When the King ordered his release, Joseph refused to leave prison until the King had investigated the accusations and his innocence was established. Needless to say, there was no chance that Nasser would climb down and declare that either Sayyid Quṭb or the Muslim Brotherhood were unjustly treated. Nor would he have ordered the release of all the Brotherhood prisoners, as President Sadat did several years later.

London   **Adil Salahi**
Rabī' al-Awwal 1423
June 2002

SŪRAH 7

Al-A'rāf

(The Heights)

Prologue[1]

Like the preceding *sūrah*, al-An'ām, or Cattle, this *sūrah*[2] was revealed in Makkah. Hence, its main subject matter is faith, which runs throughout Makkan revelations. But the two domains in which these two *sūrahs* work are widely different.

Every *sūrah* of the Qur'ān has its unique character and distinctive features. It adopts a special approach, uses a particular style and allows itself a specialized area in explaining its theme, making it clearly understood. All Qur'ānic *sūrahs* have a common theme and share in a common objective. Each, however, has its special characteristics and unique approach. They are similar, in this respect, to human beings who all share the same characteristics and biological and physiological constitution. Apart from that, they exhibit an endless range of variety. We may see similarities between them in certain details, but we find each of them making a special pattern of his or her own which would have made him or her absolutely unique, had it not been for common human qualities and characteristics.

---

1.   This prologue is an amalgamation of the two Introductions the author gives: the first at the beginning of the *sūrah*, and the second at the start of *Sūrah*7. The Arabic edition is arranged on the basis of what is known as the *ajzā'* of the Qur'ān, dividing God's book into 30 parts of equal length. Many of these begin in the middle of a *sūrah*. In the English edition, we have followed the given division into *sūrahs* of different lengths, because every *sūrah* is a unit on its own. (Editor's note.)

2.   In Arabic, this *sūrah* is given the title, al-A'rāf, which most translators render as The Heights. However, the name also connotes 'understanding, or discernment' – Editor's note.

1

I have reflected on, and dealt with, the Qur'ānic *sūrahs* in this light, after having 'lived' with them and recited them over a very long period of time. I have thus been able to identify the distinctive characteristics of each. As a result, I find in the Qur'ānic *sūrahs* a great variety resulting from different patterns, a friendliness which can be attributed to the close personal approach, and an enjoyment that is ever renewed. All of these *sūrahs* are friends imparting an air of friendliness, love and enjoyment. Each gives you a different set of inspirations to impress on you its uniqueness. To take a journey with a *sūrah* from beginning to end involves looking at a great many worlds, contemplating a large number of facts and truisms, and delving into the depths of the human soul as well as contemplating the great scenes of the universe. However, each is a special journey that is bound to give you something unique.

Mankind's Long Journey

As has already been said, the subject matter of both this *sūrah* and the preceding one is faith. However, the preceding *Sūrah*, Cattle or al-An'ām, outlines the nature and essence of faith. It confronts the *jāhiliyyah*, or the state of ignorance which prevailed in Arabia at the time, as well as every type of *jāhiliyyah*, in any community, with the attitude of a person who knows the truth and advocates it. In this confrontation, the *sūrah* makes use of all inspiring indicators available all around us in the universe. These have already been discussed in detail.[3]

On the other hand, the present *sūrah* adopts a totally different approach as it discusses the same question of faith. It provides for it with the panoramic setting of human history. It starts with mankind's journey as it begins in heaven and where it aims to return. Along this great expanse, we see the procession of faith starting with the Prophet Adam (peace be upon him) to the last of all prophets and messengers, Muḥammad (peace be upon him). The procession holds the banner of faith and advocates, throughout human history, that the only way to human happiness is for people to adopt the faith based on God's oneness. The *sūrah* outlines what reception this call received in different periods of history; how the leaders of this procession put the message across to mankind, and the responses they received; how the people in

---

3. See the Prologue to *Sūrah* 6 in Vol. V, pp. 1-32.

power went about conducting their campaigns of opposition and how the procession of believers brushed them aside and went along its way. This *sūrah* also portrays the fate that befell opponents of faith in this life and the different destinies in the hereafter of both believers and unbelievers.

It is a very long journey, but the *sūrah* takes us along, stage by stage, making a stop at every landmark to indicate that the road is clearly demarcated with well-known starting and finishing lines. All mankind travels along, aiming to return to the point where it started, in heaven, with the Supreme society.

Mankind began at the starting point with two individuals, Adam and Eve, the first human beings on earth. Satan also started along with them, having been granted God's permission to try to lead them and their offspring astray. At the same time, Adam and Eve are bound with a covenant with God that applies to their offspring as well. They are given a measure of choice so that they can either fulfil their covenant with God with strong resolve or lean towards Satan, their enemy who drove their parents away from heaven. They either listen to the revelations conveyed to them by the noble group of messengers God sends them, or they listen to Satan's temptation who mobilizes all his power to undermine their position.

Thus, man's march starts with his Lord, before he descends to earth. Here on earth, every human being is supposed to work hard, repair or undermine, build or destroy, compete, fight, and, in general, play his or her part in the toil which no human being can escape. Humanity then returns to its Lord who had set it on its journey. Each individual returns carrying what they have earned on their trip, be it bright or shameful, precious or cheap, good or evil. It is the end of the day at the dawn of which humanity started its march.

As it comes towards the end, we see that humanity carrying a very heavy burden that bends its back. When it arrives at the finishing line, all human beings put their loads on the scales, with a sense of worry, apprehension and expectation. Everyone comes alone, without support. If the burden is too heavy and help is needed in its carriage, no such help is to be found. Everyone receives his or her results on his or her own and realizes what prospect that result signifies for him or her. The *sūrah*, however, continues to follow one group or community of mankind after another, until the doors are closed after the last human beings have completed their journey. They have returned to discover

3

whether their end is in heaven or in hell. After all, on earth they were only visitors and their time there now is up: "*As it was He who brought you into being in the first instance, so also [to Him] you will return: some [of you] He will have graced with His guidance, whereas for some a straying from the right path will have become unavoidable. For, they will have taken Satans for their protectors in preference to God, thinking all the while that they have found the right path.*" (Verses 29-30)

In between the stages of this journey, with humanity going forward or suffering setbacks, the battle between truth and falsehood is portrayed. The fighters include messengers and believers on the one side and arrogant tyrants and their subjugated followers on the other. Of these the *sūrah* portrays similar scenes and similar destinies. The images portrayed show the faithful in a clearly relaxed and highly inspiring situation, while the images of Satans and unbelievers are gloomy, particularly when they show the destruction of certain groups of unbelievers. These are given in the *sūrah* as a reminder to present and future generations.

At the end of each stage we have a suitably placed pause. It is as if the *sūrah* stops to say a couple of words by way of comment, just as a reminder to future generations, before it continues with its message.

This is the story of mankind representing the march of this faith, right from the beginning of human history, and outlining the results it achieves in its endless endeavour. It finally arrives at the finishing line, which was also the starting point. Thus, in presenting the great issue of faith, this *sūrah* moves along a totally different route to that followed by the preceding *Surah*, Cattle, or al-An'ām. The two converge at certain points when they present scenes of how unbelievers receive God's messages, scenes of the Day of Judgement, and others of the universe. However, the methods of image painting used in the two *sūrahs* are completely different.

A few words need to be said about the style employed in both *sūrahs*. In the preceding *Sūrah*, al-An'ām, the style moves in successive waves sometimes presenting an impression of glitter, accompanied by a powerful rhythm that at times reaches a very high pace. In this *sūrah*, the approach is much slower and calmer with a reassuring rhythm that is deliberate and weighted. It is similar to that of one who, with melodious voice, drives a caravan along, step by step, and stage by stage. At times the rhythm is given extra pace, particularly when it comments on certain events, but it soon returns to its original slow lilt. The two *sūrahs* still belong to the same period, for both were revealed in Makkah before the Prophet's migration to Madinah.

Telling a Story to Face Reality

The *sūrah* does not present the history of faith or the journey of mankind from its first origins to its ultimate return in story fashion. Rather, it presents it as a battle with *jāhiliyyah*, the state of ignorance that affects individuals and communities. Hence, its theme is presented in scenes and attitudes, showing us a living community standing in opposition to the Qur'ān. The Qur'ān, therefore, confronts that community with this long story, pointing out the lessons to be drawn from it, reminding and warning people, and engaging them in a real battle. Hence, the comments given after every important stage are addressed in the first instance to those first combatants, as also to all people who adopt the same attitude to faith in every future generation.

The Qur'ān relates a story only to use it as a means of dealing with an existing situation. It only states a truth in order to remove a falsehood. It takes practical measures within a living environment. It neither makes a premise for academic purposes, nor relates a story for intellectual pleasure.

In this *sūrah* we note that, in its comments, it lays special emphasis on reminders and warnings on the one hand, and on the starting and finishing lines in the human journey on the other. It gives accounts of the peoples of Noah, Hūd, Ṣāliḥ, Lot and Shu'ayb, but treats the history of Moses at much greater length and with stronger emphasis.

In this Prologue, we can only give brief examples of the points of emphasis in the *sūrah*. It opens in the following manner: "*Alif. Lām. Mīm. Ṣād. This is a book that has been bestowed on you from on high – so do not entertain any doubt about it – in order that you may warn people with its message, and admonish the believers. Follow what has been sent down to you by your Lord, and follow no masters other than Him. How seldom do you keep this in mind.*" (Verses 1-3) Thus, right from the outset, it takes the form of an address to the Prophet and to the people to whom he directs his efforts, equipped with the Qur'ān. All that is subsequently presented in the *sūrah*, including the historical accounts of past communities, the long human journey and its final destination, the scenes portrayed of the universe and the Day of Judgement, is an indirect address, though it takes at times a direct stance, to the Prophet and his people, serving as a warning and a reminder.

The statement addressed to the Prophet, "*This is a book that has been bestowed on you from on high – so do not entertain any doubt about it,*" describes a practical situation which is only appreciated by one who lives in a state of *jāhiliyyah* and advocates Islam, knowing that his goal is hard and his way full of difficult obstacles. What he aims to achieve is to establish a faith that provides a new set of standards and values, and a social set-up that differs with what exists anywhere in the world. But he encounters *jāhiliyyah* with its lingering concepts, values and standards exercising enormous pressures on people's minds, souls, feelings and social practices. He then discovers that the truth he is advocating sounds strange, objectionable, too demanding, because it seeks a total change in people's ideas, values, laws, traditions, bonds and social relations. Hence, he finds himself reluctant to confront people with this truth and its heavy demands. This reluctance creates that doubt which God tells His Messenger not to entertain. Instead, he should go ahead, warning and reminding, caring little for whatever he meets with of people's surprise, objection, opposition and even active resistance.

Taking into consideration all such objection, opposition, resistance and active hostility to the change faith wants to bring about in human life, the *sūrah* then delivers an early and strong warning. It reminds the addressees of the fate of earlier communities, before it begins to give detailed historical accounts of such communities: "*How many a community have We destroyed, with Our punishment falling upon them by night, or at midday while they were resting. And when Our punishment fell upon them, all they could say was: 'We have indeed been wrongdoers.' We shall most certainly question those to whom a message was sent, and We shall most certainly question the messengers themselves. And most certainly We shall reveal to them Our knowledge [of what they have done]; for never have We been absent. On that day, the weighing will be true and accurate: and those whose weight [of good deeds] is heavy in the balance are the ones who are successful; whereas those whose weight is light in the balance are the ones who have lost their own souls because of their wilful rejection of Our revelations.*" (Verses 4-9)

Having made this introduction, the *sūrah* talks of how mankind has been given power on earth. It is God who has established rules and balances in the universe allowing human life to continue and flourish on earth. He has also given man certain qualities that fit with the universe and which enable man to understand universal laws and phenomena and to utilize them for his benefit: "*We have established you firmly on earth and We have provided you there with means of livelihood. How seldom are you grateful.*" (Verse 10)

On the Starting Line

All this is preliminary to giving an account of how human life came into being, showing its starting point and where it began its long journey. The *sūrah* concentrates on this point. It also uses it by way of reminder and warning, utilizing every element that strikes a strong note in human consciousness. (Verses 11-25)

In this starting point scene, the entire outcome of the journey and the destinies of the travellers are outlined. We see the making of the great fight, which continues with no respite, between all mankind and their declared enemy. We also see man's weaknesses and how Satan tries to exploit these. Therefore, the *sūrah* uses this scene to provide long comments, warning human beings against falling into the same trap set for their first parents by their avowed enemy. Also, in the light of this scene in which we see Satan standing face to face with Adam and Eve, and the results of this first encounter, the *sūrah* addresses its reminders to all mankind, warning people against heading to the same fate.

> *Children of Adam, We have sent down to you clothing to cover your nakedness, and garments pleasing to the eye; but the robe of God-consciousness is the finest of all. In this there is a sign from God, so that they may reflect. Children of Adam, do not allow Satan to seduce you in the same way as he caused your [first] parents to be turned out of the Garden. He stripped them of their garment in order to make them aware of their nakedness. Surely, he and his tribe watch you from where you cannot perceive them. We have made the devils as patrons for those who do not believe. (Verses 26-27) Children of Adam! Whenever there come to you messengers from among yourselves to relate to you My revelations, then those who are conscious of Me and live righteously shall have nothing to fear, nor shall they grieve. But those who deny and scorn Our revelations*

are the ones destined for the fire, where they shall abide. (Verses 35-36)

We note how the scene of nakedness, as a result of disobedience to God, and Adam and Eve's attempt to cover themselves with leaves from the Garden, is followed by a reminder of God's blessing of fine clothing. People are warned that they must not allow Satan to tempt them to uncover themselves as he did with their first parents. We also note that this part of the story and the comments given after it addressed a practical situation in the idolatrous Arabian society. Influenced by certain deviant traditions and myth, some Arabs used to do their *tawāf* around the Ka'bah naked. They prohibited themselves certain types of clothes and food during the pilgrimage period, alleging that this was all part of God's law, and that it was God who enforced such prohibitions. Hence, in this story of mankind and the accompanying comments we find suitable answers to this practical situation in Arabian *jāhiliyyah*, and indeed in every state of *jāhiliyyah*. A common feature of all states of *jāhiliyyah* is to undress, lose one's sense of modesty and to have no fear of God.

This points to an important feature of the Qur'ānic approach. Even when the Qur'ān employs a story, it only does so to deal with an existing situation. Since it always deals with a different situation, the portions of the story related each time are those which fit with the particular situation the Qur'ān is addressing, giving it the sort of emphasis that draws the lesson required. As we said in the Prologue to the preceding *surah*,[4] the Qur'ānic approach does not include anything that is not needed to address an existing situation. It does not store information, rulings, or even stories, so that they may be used when the need arises.

The Ultimate Finish

Before the travellers set out on their long journey; before God's messenger provides them with guidance; before giving any details of the history of faith after Adam and Eve and their first experience; the *sūrah* provides a scene of the ultimate end of the entire journey. This method is often used in the Qur'ān: the two ends of the journey are

---

4. Vol. V, pp. 1-29.

set in contrast, in the life of this world and in the life to come, showing it to be one uninterrupted trek.

Here we have one of the richest and most detailed scenes of the Day of Resurrection given in the Qur'ān. The scene portrays a long succession of images and gives details of dialogues that take place then. This scene, occurring as it does immediately after man's fall from heaven and God's warning to mankind against listening to Satan's promptings, serves as a confirmation of what God's messengers have said to their peoples. Thus, those who obey Satan and do his bidding are forbidden admission into heaven, just like their first parents who were turned out of heaven by Satan. By contrast, those who obey God and turn their backs on Satan are returned to heaven after their long journey. The scene is too long to be quoted here in the Prologue but we will be discussing it in detail at its appropriate place. Nonetheless, the *sūrah* also uses this scene to warn those who disbelieve in the Qur'ān, requiring miracles so that they can accept that it is God's word. It warns them against a greatly miserable end. (Verses 52-53)

After showing this long trip, from first creation to resurrection, the *sūrah* pauses for comments, stating the nature of Godhead and Lordship in the universe with breathtaking scenes. This is all in line with the Qur'ānic method of using the universe as a field in which the truth of Godhead appears in full view, producing its great inspiration to any human heart that warms to it. The aim of this portrayal of universal scenes is to present the central issue of faith, namely that the entire universe submits to, and worships God alone, its only Lord. It behoves man not to be the only jarring note in the superb symphony of faith played by the universe. He must not be the only creature to disclaim himself a servant of God, the overall Lord of the universe, the Lord of all the worlds. (Verses 54-58)

One Message and Many Messengers

So the journey continues and the story unfolds. The long line of noble advocates of faith, formed by God's messengers, call out with compassion to erring mankind, reminding them of the truth and warning them against following a course that is certain to lead to ruin. But those who are deep in error confront this compassionate address with rejection at first and later with force, persecution and tyranny. When God's messengers have fulfilled their duties of reminding and warning, standing up to opposition and persecution by their peoples, ultimately moving away and declaring their allegiance to faith, God Himself takes over the conduct of the fight.

The *sūrah* gives accounts of the prophets Noah, Hūd, Ṣāliḥ, Lot and Shu'ayb with their respective communities. They all present one never-changing truth: "*My people, worship God alone: you have no deity other than Him.*" (Verses 59, 65, 73, 85) Their peoples argued with them, rejecting the very concept of God's oneness and His being the only Lord in the universe. They also wondered about God sending human messengers. Some of them argued that religion had nothing to do with people's lives or with the regulation of financial and business transactions. This is echoed by some people in today's *jāhiliyyah*, despite the passage of many centuries. They describe their old, ignorant and futile argument as 'liberalism,' and 'progress'. At the end of each account, the *sūrah* shows the fate of those who rejected God's message.

When we look carefully at the way these stories are presented, we cannot fail to note that all messengers said the same words to their communities: "*My people, worship God alone: you have no deity other than Him.*" Every messenger presents this central truth to his people in the manner of a caring and honest adviser who fears for his people the inevitable doom of which they remain oblivious. None of these communities appreciated the advice given by their messenger. None thought about their fate. None recognized the profound sincerity of their messenger, nor of his having no personal interest in the matter.

At this point we may refer to the first account of the Prophet Noah (Verses 59-64) and the last one referring to the Prophet Shu'ayb (Verses 85-93). These two show the truth of the single faith which all God's messengers preached, each to his own people. All received the same rejection by people in power and their weak followers. In each account we cannot fail to note the clarity and power of faith in the hearts of the messenger and the believers who follow him, or the messenger's keen desire to guide his people to the truth, or his taking a stand away from them after having completed his mission.

At this point the *sūrah* pauses for comment. It outlines God's law of dealing with people who receive a message from Him but who continue to deny the truth. He tests them first with tribulation and hardship so that they may be alerted to the truth and respond to it. If they continue in their rejection, then He tries them with affluence, which is an even harder test. Thus, they may be confused and mistake God's law. Ultimately, He takes them suddenly, when they are totally unaware. When this law has been outlined, they are strongly alerted to the danger engulfing them. How could they be sure that God's law is not about to strike them while they remain heedless? Should they not reflect on the fate of earlier generations when they are living in the old dwellings of those past communities? (Verses 94-102)

Between Moses and Pharaoh

The *sūrah* then moves on to relate the story of Moses, giving first an account of the events that took place between Moses and Pharaoh, before it gives a detailed account of the struggle Moses had to undertake against his own people, the Children of Israel. The history of Moses related in this *sūrah* is the longest and most detailed of any account given of it in any other *sūrah*. It should be remembered that certain episodes of the story of Moses are given in many places in the Qur'ān, in addition to brief references to it in several other *sūrahs*. It is the story mentioned most frequently in the Qur'ān. The great details of the history of this particular nation are perhaps given in the Qur'ān for the reasons we have already outlined. Let us remind ourselves of these purposes here:

> One purpose relates to the fact that the Children of Israel were the first to confront the Islamic message with wicked designs, plots and open warfare both in Madinah and the whole of Arabia. Their hostile attitude could be traced back to the very early days of the Islamic message. It was they who encouraged and nurtured hypocrisy and the hypocrites in Madinah, providing them with the means to scheme against Islam and the Muslims. They also incited the pagan Arabs to fight the Muslim community and gave them their active support. It was they who started the war of false rumours against the Muslim community raising among them doubts and suspicions about the Muslim leadership and circulating distortions of the Islamic faith before they confronted the Muslim community in open warfare. It was necessary, therefore, to expose them to the Muslim community so that it knew its enemies: their nature, history, methods and means as well as the nature of the battle it had to fight against them.

Another purpose can be seen in the fact that the Israelites were the followers of a Divine faith revealed before the final faith of Islam. They had a long history before Islam, during which distortions crept into their faith and they repeatedly violated their agreement and covenant with God. The practical consequences of these violations and deviations were seen in their lives, their moral values and their traditions. As the Muslim nation is the heir to all divine messages and the custodian of the monotheistic divine faith as a whole, it is necessary that it be made fully aware of the history of the Israelites with all its ups and downs. This gave the Muslim community an accurate knowledge of the way it should follow, what slips lay ahead of it and the consequences of such slips, as these are reflected in the history and morality of the Jews. This enabled the Muslim community to add the experience of the Jews to the total sum of its own experience and to benefit by it in future. It could, thus, avoid the slips and deal effectively with deviation right at the start before it had a chance to develop.

Yet another purpose relates to the fact that over their long history the experience of the Jews was highly varied. God is aware that with the passage of time, people may change, and certain generations may deviate from the right path. As the Muslim nation will continue until the end of life, it is bound to go through certain periods which are not dissimilar to what the Jews have gone through. God has, therefore, chosen to make available to the leaders of the Muslim community and its reformers in different generations, clear examples of what could befall nations so that they may be able to diagnose the disease of their particular generation and administer the proper cure. It is a fact of life that those who deviate after having known the truth are the most resistant to calls and appeals to follow right guidance. Those without any prior knowledge of the truth are more responsive because they find something new which appeals to them and helps them shake off the burden of ignorance. They are most impressed by the first call that makes its appeal to them. Winning over those with an earlier experience requires a much more strenuous effort and a great deal of perseverance on the part of advocates of the Divine faith.[5]

---

5. Vol. IV, pp. 70-72.

Certain episodes in the history of Moses and the Children of Israel are discussed in this commentary on the Qur'ān,[6] which is arranged according to the final order of the Qur'ānic *surahs*, and not the chronological order of their revelation. In looking at the order of revelation, however, we should point out that the parts of the story given in this *surah* were revealed earlier than those given in *surahs* revealed in Madinah, such as *Surahs* 2, 3 and 5, discussed in volumes 1, 2 and 4 respectively. This is evident in the way the story is told here and in the *surahs* revealed in Madinah. Here it is related like a story, while there it confronts the Jews in Madinah, reminding them of its events and the attitudes of their ancestors to each event.

The story is told in more than 30 places in the Qur'ān, but it is given in detail in ten *surahs*, six of which are more detailed than the others. The parts revealed in this *surah* represent the first detailed account, making the longest exposition. However, the episodes related here are less than those in *Surah* 20, Ṭā Hā.

In the present *surah*, the story begins with Moses presenting his message to Pharaoh and his people. In *Surah* 20, it begins with Moses receiving his Lord's call by Mount Sinai, while in *Surah* 28, The Story, or al-Qaṣaṣ, it starts with the birth of Moses during the time when the Children of Israel were exposed to persecution. In perfect harmony with the general ambience of the *surah* and its objectives, the story opens by drawing attention to the fate suffered by Pharaoh and his people as a result of their rejection of God's message: "*Then after those We sent Moses with Our signs to Pharaoh and his people, but they wilfully rejected them. Behold what happened in the end to those spreaders of corruption.*" (Verse 103) Then the story unfolds, showing scenes of Moses confronting first Pharaoh and his clique, then confronting the deviousness and corruption of the Israelites. As we will be discussing the story in detail in due course, we will only refer here very briefly to its main features and general import.

The Central Issue

Moses (peace be upon him) faces Pharaoh and the chiefs of his people, declaring the fact that he, Moses, is a Messenger of God, the Lord of all the worlds: "*Moses said: 'Pharaoh, I am a Messenger from*

---

6. Volumes I-IV.

the Lord of all the worlds, and may say about God nothing but the truth. I have come to you with a clear evidence from your Lord. So, let the Children of Israel go with me.'" (Verses 104-105) The same fact is driven home to Pharaoh when Moses wins the confrontation with Pharaoh's sorcerers and they declare their acceptance of God's oneness: *"The sorcerers fell down prostrating themselves, and said: 'We believe in the Lord of all the worlds, the Lord of Moses and Aaron."* (Verses 120-122) Again when Pharaoh threatens them with severe punishment, they turn to their Lord and declare that they will always turn to Him in life, death and future life: *"They replied: 'To our Lord we shall indeed return. You want to take vengeance on us only because we have believed in the signs of our Lord when they were shown to us. Our Lord, grant us abundance of patience in adversity, and let us die as people who have surrendered themselves to You."* (Verses 125-126)

As Moses teaches his people their faith, we frequently see him emphasizing to them who their true Lord is. This is the case when Pharaoh threatens them with general persecution, and later when they deviate and ask him to make them a deity like those of the people they came across after their salvation from Pharaoh. (Verses 128-129 and 138-140) Such Qur'ānic statements made within the story confirm the true nature of the religion preached by the Prophet Moses (peace be upon him) and the sort of beliefs that result from it. These are the same beliefs Islam calls for and which are advocated by every divine message. Moreover, these Qur'ānic statements prove the fallacy of the theories advanced by Western 'experts' in the history of religion, and the error of anyone who adopts their method and premise about the development of human faith.

These Qur'ānic statements also show the different sorts of deviation that occurred in Jewish history and the perverted nature of the Israelites, even after Moses was given his message. Examples of this are seen in their request: *"Moses, set up a god for us like the gods they have."* (Verse 138); and in their adoption of the calf when Moses went for his appointment with his Lord; and in their demand to see God in order to believe in Him. None of these represents the faith Moses preached. These are deviations which may not be attributed to the faith. The claim that these were part of the Jewish religion which later developed into a monotheistic faith is indeed false.

The confrontation between Moses and Pharaoh illustrates the nature of the battle between the divine faith, in its totality, and *jāhiliyyah*, in all its forms and aspects. It shows how the evil forces look at this faith, feeling the danger it represents to the very existence of these forces. It further shows how believers view the battle between them and tyrannical evil forces.

The *sūrah* reports how Moses said to Pharaoh: "*I am a Messenger from the Lord of all the worlds, and may say about God nothing but the truth. I have come to you with a clear evidence from your Lord. So, let the Children of Israel go with me.*" (Verses 104-105) At that very moment, the aim was clear. It is a call to believe in 'the Lord of all the worlds', which means that all sovereignty belongs to God alone. It was under this clear principle that Moses demanded the release of the Israelites. Since God is the Lord of all the worlds, then it is not up to any servant of His – the tyrant Pharaoh in this case – to impose his authority over them. They submit only to God. Moreover, the declaration that God is the Lord of all the worlds means that all sovereignty, which is a manifestation of Lordship, belongs to Him alone. It is clearly demonstrated when all creatures submit to Him. Hence, people do not truly acknowledge God's Lordship and sovereignty unless they submit to Him alone. Should they accept anyone else's sovereignty, implementing his laws, they deny God's Lordship over them.

Pharaoh and his chiefs realized what danger the message declaring God as the Lord of all the worlds represented. They felt that to accept God as the only Lord meant depriving Pharaoh of his authority and, consequently, the loss of their own authority derived from his. They expressed their fear in this way: "*The great ones among Pharaoh's people said: 'This man is indeed a sorcerer of great skill, who wants to drive you out of your land!' [Said Pharaoh] 'What, then, do you advise?'*" (Verses 109-110) "*The great ones among Pharaoh's people said: 'Will you allow Moses and his people to spread corruption in the land and to forsake you and your gods?'*" (Verse 127) What they really meant is that the only import of this call advocating God's Lordship of all the worlds was that all authority is taken away from people and returned to its rightful owner, God Almighty. To them, this was an act of spreading corruption in the land.

Today, in contemporary forms of *jāhiliyyah*, this same call is described as an attempt to overthrow the government. To such regimes which practically exercise God's sovereignty, even though they may not say so verbally, the success of this call means the overthrow of government. In every *jāhiliyyah* system, government means the assignment of Lordship to one of God's servants, enabling him to rule over others. By contrast, acknowledging God's Lordship over all the worlds means that only God is the Lord of mankind.

Then, the sorcerers were overwhelmed by the truth and declared their belief in God, the Lord of all the worlds, freeing themselves from subjugation to Pharaoh. At this point, Pharaoh accused them of scheming to drive the people out of their land, threatening them with the worst type of torture and persecution: *"Pharaoh said: 'You believe in Him even before I have given you permission! This is indeed a plot you have contrived in this city in order to drive out its people, but you shall soon come to know [the consequences]. I shall have your hands and feet cut off on alternate sides, and then I shall crucify you all."* (Verses 123-124)

On the other hand, those sorcerers, who believed in God, submitting to Him alone and declaring their freedom from subjugation by those who usurped God's authority, realized the nature of the battle between them and the tyrannical forces of falsehood. They knew that it was a battle over faith. Once the declaration of God's Lordship over all the worlds is made, this faith poses a threat to all tyrants, aiming to strip them of their usurped authority. Hence, their reply to Pharaoh's accusation was: *"You want to take vengeance on us only because we have believed in the signs of our Lord when they were shown to us."* (Verse 126) Then they turned to their Lord with this prayer: *"Our Lord, grant us abundance of patience in adversity, and let us die as people who have surrendered themselves to You."* (Verse 126) Thus, when true submission to God took hold of their hearts, it became their distinctive criterion.

Sealed Hearts, Closed Minds

The story also relates how God subjected Pharaoh's people to several trials, allowing different types of hardship to afflict them. Nevertheless, they persist in their rejection of God's message, making all types of excuses. Eventually destruction befalls them. (Verses 130-136)

In this passage we realize how adamantly and persistently tyranny clings to its falsehood, resisting with all its might the message declaring God's Lordship over all the worlds. These tyrants realize, with perfect certainty, that such a message undermines their position. Indeed, it does not recognize their claims to such a position. Tyranny will never allow the declaration of God's oneness, or His Lordship over all the worlds, unless these words lose their true meaning, becoming mere words of little significance. In such a situation, they represent no threat to tyranny. On the other hand, when a group of people adopt these words and take them seriously, in their true meaning, tyranny will not tolerate them. It immediately realizes the threat they represent to its usurped authority which enables it to exercise sovereignty and lordship over its subject people. Thus, Pharaoh could not tolerate that Moses should advocate faith in God, the Lord of all the worlds, or that the sorcerers should declare their belief in Him. He and his chiefs persisted with their rejection of this truth when signs were shown to them, and then when different types of hardship afflicted them, one after another. To them, all this was easier to tolerate than to acknowledge God as the Lord of all the worlds, because that would have ended their usurped authority.

We see also in the way the *sūrah* speaks of the signs and the trials how God deals with those who deny His messages. He first tries them with hardship and tribulation, then with affluence and plenty, before He finally smites them with a severe punishment. The believers, who have been weak and subjugated, are then given power and established in the land. "*We caused the people who were persecuted and deemed utterly low to inherit the eastern and western parts of the land which We had blessed. Thus your Lord's gracious promise to the Children of Israel was fulfilled, because they were patient in adversity; and We destroyed all that Pharaoh and his people had wrought, and all that they had built.*" (Verse 137)

But the Israelites soon succumbed to their deviant nature, and they disobeyed God, as the Qur'ān makes clear. They played tricks on Moses, their Prophet and saviour, remained ungrateful for God's blessings, and turned away from the straight path of faith. This happened time after time, with God forgiving them on each occasion, until eventually they earned God's punishment: "*Then your Lord declared that He would most certainly raise against them people who would cruelly oppress them till the Day of Resurrection. Your Lord is swift indeed in His retribution, yet He is certainly much-forgiving, merciful.*" (Verse 167) God's warnings came true, and they will continue to come true in the future. They may have their day in the cycle of history, but when they spread corruption and resort to injustice, God will raise against them people who will punish them severely. This will continue to be the case until the Day of Judgement.

Our last point in this Prologue on the history of the Israelites is that this *sūrah*, revealed in Makkah, tells us much about the Children of Israel, their deviation, disobedience, and wicked nature. Yet many Orientalists, Christians and Jews alike, allege that Muḥammad, (peace be upon him), did not attack the Jews in the Qur'ān until he had settled in Madinah. These Orientalists claim that the Prophet tried to maintain good relations with the Jews when he was in Makkah and in his early period in Madinah. They further allege that the Qur'ān which Muḥammad preached at that time spoke about their common ancestry as descendants of Abraham, hoping that they would accept his message. But when he gave up on them, he attacked them in no uncertain terms. These Orientalists are certainly lying. Here we have in a Makkan *sūrah* the whole truth about the Jews. It follows the same lines as *Sūrah* 2, The Cow, which was revealed later in Madinah, in stating the truth.

Verses 163-170 of this *sūrah*, which include the warning to the Jews that they would be repeatedly subjected to punishment by other people, are undoubtedly Madinan revelation, while the rest of the *sūrah* was revealed in Makkah. However, the verses that immediately precede and directly follow this Madinan passage state the same truth about the Israelites. They mention their worship of the calf, their demand that Moses should set up a deity for them when they had left Egypt for the sake of God, the only deity in the universe. They also include the punishment inflicted on them because of their declared stand that they would not believe unless they saw God, and their alteration of God's words when they were told to enter the city. All this goes to show these Orientalists distorting history in addition to their fabrication of falsehood against God and His Messenger. Yet some writers who speak about Islam are willing to take such Orientalists for their teachers!

Drawing the Lines

This story of Moses is given in such detail for another purpose. It depicts the nature of faith and unbelief as reflected by the personalities and events of that history. It concludes with the scene of accepting the covenant of the Children of Israel after they have witnessed how God's might strikes. This is followed by the great scene showing human nature making its covenant with God. We then have a scene showing the one who reneges on this covenant as he discards God's revelations after he has learnt them. It is a very powerful scene serving to warn against such a line of action. A comment follows this scene describing the nature of divine guidance and the nature of unbelief, making clear that the latter indicates a failure of man's faculties of perception, leading to utter ruin. (Verses 171-179)

The *sūrah* then turns to the unbelievers in Makkah who were denying the truth of the message of Islam, distorting God's names in order to coin up names for their false deities. It warns them against suffering God's punishment. It also invites them to reflect deeply and clearly on the status of God's Messenger who called on them to follow divine guidance. When they do so, they should remove their prejudices that cause them to accuse the Prophet of madness. They should contemplate the kingdoms of heaven and earth and what they contain of pointers to the truth of divine guidance. A touch is added reminding them of death that could come when they are totally unaware. (Verses 180-186)

The *sūrah* takes on the unbelievers who deny the Last Hour signalling the arrival of the Day of Resurrection and their questions about its timing. It shows that this is a grave matter, but they refer to it lightly. It states the nature of God's message and the role of the Messenger who delivers it. It states the truth of Godhead and that all its attributes belong to God alone, including the knowledge of the realm that lies beyond man's perception, and the bringing about of the Last Hour at its appointed time. (Verses 187-188)

Within the context of this confrontation with the unbelievers, the *sūrah* gives an outline of the nature of idolatry and the story of deviation from the covenant made with human nature to always believe in God's oneness. It shows how such deviation occurs within man, as if it is describing the deviation of that very generation which opposed the Prophet, while their early ancestors followed Abraham's faith. (Verses 189-192)

Since it aims to describe the situation of those particular idolaters whom the Qur'ān was addressing at the time of its revelation, the *sūrah* moves immediately from the case it outlines to a direct address to them. It directs the Prophet to challenge them and their deities. (Verses 193-198)

As the *sūrah* comes to its conclusion, it addresses the Prophet and the Muslim community to deal gently with people as they present God's message to them. They must not give way to anger at people's slackness. They need to seek refuge with God against Satan who tries to fuel their anger. (Verses 199-203) This directive reminds us of what is stated at the beginning of the *sūrah*: "*This is a book that has been bestowed on you from on high – so do not entertain any doubt about it – in order that you may warn people with its message, and admonish the believers.*" (Verse 2) It makes it clear that the task is tough, because it involves calling on all people to accept the faith, putting up with all their impediments, including traces of erroneous beliefs, deviation, desire, negligence, etc. It requires much perseverance and tolerance.

It also requires moving along the road to its final destination. Hence, the *sūrah* reminds us of what helps us to overcome the difficulties involved. Here we are reminded of the need to read the Qur'ān and listen attentively to it, remembering God in all situations and never to be heedless. We should take our cue in this from the angels who do not tire of remembering God and worshipping Him: "*When the Qur'ān is recited, hearken to it, and listen in silence, so that you may be graced with God's mercy. And bethink yourself of your Lord humbly and with awe, and without raising your voice, in the morning and evening; and do not be negligent. Those who are near to your Lord are never too proud to worship Him. They extol His limitless glory, and before Him alone prostrate themselves.*" (Verses 204-206) This is the best equipment along the road. It outlines the manner of worship that good believers should adopt. It is the one followed by God's best servants.

I

The Purpose of the Divine Message

Al-A ʿrāf (The Heights)

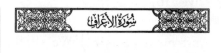

In the Name of God, the Merciful, the Beneficent

بِسْمِ اللّٰهِ الرَّحْمٰنِ الرَّحِيمِ

Alif. Lām. Mīm. Ṣād. (1)

الٓمٓصٓ ۝

This is a book that has been bestowed on you from on high – so do not entertain any doubt about it – in order that you may warn people with its message, and admonish the believers. (2)

كِتَابٌ أُنزِلَ إِلَيْكَ فَلَا يَكُن فِى صَدْرِكَ حَرَجٌ مِّنْهُ لِتُنذِرَ بِهِۦ وَذِكْرَىٰ لِلْمُؤْمِنِينَ ۝

Follow what has been sent down to you by your Lord, and follow no masters other than Him. How seldom do you keep this in mind. (3)

ٱتَّبِعُواْ مَآ أُنزِلَ إِلَيْكُم مِّن رَّبِّكُمْ وَلَا تَتَّبِعُواْ مِن دُونِهِۦٓ أَوْلِيَآءَ قَلِيلًا مَّا تَذَكَّرُونَ ۝

How many a community have We destroyed, with Our punishment falling upon them by night, or at midday while they were resting. (4)

وَكَم مِّن قَرْيَةٍ أَهْلَكْنَاهَا فَجَآءَهَا بَأْسُنَا بَيَاتًا أَوْ هُمْ قَآئِلُونَ ۝

And when Our punishment fell upon them, all they could say was: "We have indeed been wrongdoers." (5)

فَمَا كَانَ دَعْوَىٰهُمْ إِذْ جَآءَهُم بَأْسُنَآ إِلَّآ أَن قَالُوٓاْ إِنَّا كُنَّا ظَٰلِمِينَ ۝

We shall most certainly question those to whom a message was sent, and We shall most certainly question the messengers themselves. (6)

فَلَنَسْـَٔلَنَّ ٱلَّذِينَ أُرْسِلَ إِلَيْهِمْ وَلَنَسْـَٔلَنَّ ٱلْمُرْسَلِينَ ۝

And most certainly We shall reveal to them Our knowledge [of what they have done]; for never have We been absent. (7)

فَلَنَقُصَّنَّ عَلَيْهِم بِعِلْمٍ وَمَا كُنَّا غَآئِبِينَ ۝

On that day, the weighing will be true and accurate: and those whose weight [of good deeds] is heavy in the balance are the ones who are successful; (8)

وَٱلْوَزْنُ يَوْمَئِذٍ ٱلْحَقُّ فَمَن ثَقُلَتْ مَوَٰزِينُهُۥ فَأُوْلَٰٓئِكَ هُمُ ٱلْمُفْلِحُونَ ۝

whereas those whose weight is light in the balance are the ones who have lost their own souls because of their wilful rejection of Our revelations. (9)

وَمَنْ خَفَّتْ مَوَٰزِينُهُۥ فَأُوْلَٰٓئِكَ ٱلَّذِينَ خَسِرُوٓاْ أَنفُسَهُم بِمَا كَانُواْ بِـَٔايَٰتِنَا يَظْلِمُونَ ۝

Issues Spelt Out

The *sūrah* begins with four separate letters, similar to those that occur at the beginning of the second and third *sūrahs*. When we discussed such separate letters in our commentary on these *sūrahs*, we expressed our support of the view that these letters are meant as a reference to the fact that the Qur'ān is composed of words made up of the Arabic alphabet which Arabs use in their language. Nevertheless, it is impossible for them to make up from these letters and sounds a discourse similar to that of the Qur'ān. This in itself proves that the

Qur'ān is not composed by a human being. How else can we explain the fact that these letters, sounds and words were available to the Arabs and yet they could not make of them anything similar to the Qur'ān. There must be, then, some other element which gives the Qur'ān its unique character. We feel that this is perhaps the most likely interpretation of these separate letters occurring at the beginning of some *sūrahs*. God knows best the purpose He has in mind for using them. It is possible, therefore, to consider these four letters together as the subject of a sentence, which is given in the translation as, "this", which means that those letters and what is composed of them and of other letters are "the book bestowed from on high". On the other hand, we may take these letters as sounds serving to alert us to the meaning that follows which suggests that the book has been revealed from on high.

"This is a book that has been bestowed on you from on high." (Verse 2) This book, then, is revealed for warning, so that the Prophet is able to confront with its message all mankind, although they may not like to be so confronted. Its message is thus set in opposition to beliefs, traditions, social norms and set-ups. This is reason enough for entertaining feelings of doubt and hardship with regard to the duty it imposes. This can only be appreciated by those who wish to implement this instruction and raise the message of this book high in society. In so doing, they aim to achieve a complete and total change of the social set-up of the human community, beginning with its foundations and finishing with its outward appearance and points of detail. Hence, the Prophet, the one who was to deliver the message of this book for the first time, must have felt all this when he confronted the state of ignorance, or *jāhiliyyah*, prevailing in Arabia and throughout the world.

This state of affairs is not limited to the situation that prevailed in the Arabian Peninsula at the time, or to what prevailed in surrounding areas. Islam is not a mere event of history which took place at a particular point in time. It is a permanent confrontation that continues to the end of time. Today, Islam puts its message before humanity, as it did the first time, and as it does whenever humanity reverts to *jāhiliyyah* in a repeated 'reactionary' cycle. Whenever this happens, Islam comes forward to pick up humanity from the mud of reaction and to set it along the way to progress and civilization. Every time the advocates of Islam warn people on the basis of the Qur'ānic message, they face the same difficulty and hardship endured by the first advocate of Islam, the Prophet Muḥammad (peace be upon him). It was he who first warned people that their lives were a continuing endurance of the darkness of *jāhiliyyah* which combined the blindness of erring concepts, unrestrained desires, with the oppression of tyranny and subjugation to momentary–whims and fleeting pleasures. Whoever takes up the duty of conveying the Islamic message in order to try to save mankind from the depth of its ignorance will inevitably appreciate the significance of this directive to the Prophet: "*This is a book that has been bestowed on you from on high – so do not entertain any doubt about it – in order that you may warn people with its message.*" (Verse 2)

It is real facts that tell us who the believers to be admonished with the Qur'ānic revelations are and who the unbelievers to whom the warning is addressed are. To the advocate of Islam, the Qur'ān is always a new message, revealed at this moment in time, to confront a situation which is bound to impose on him a very hard struggle.

Today, mankind is in a similar position to that which prevailed when the Prophet Muḥammad (peace be upon him) was instructed by his Lord to start his warning and admonition, entertaining no feeling of anxiety or difficulty, aiming to bring about a very radical change in the life of humanity as a whole. Time has moved full circle since that day, and mankind has reverted to a state of complete ignorance which affects the basis and practical aspects of all its values, norms and practices. In its very concept of faith, humanity has reverted back to some absurdities that prevailed in the past. This applies even to those whose fathers and forefathers used to believe in this religion of Islam, submit themselves to God and associate no partners with Him. The concept of faith held by these new generations has also been distorted.

This religion of Islam has been revealed so that it changes the face of the world, in order to establish a new world order which acknowledges God's absolute authority and removes the authority of all tyrants. In this world order, worship, in its very comprehensive sense, is offered to God alone. When this world order is established, God enables whomever He pleases of His servants to submit himself to God alone instead of submitting to other authorities. In this world order, a new human being is born, who is free and noble, having overcome the tyranny of his desires and the authority of anyone other than God.

This religion of Islam is meant to establish a solid foundation. Indeed, every prophet, in all periods of history, subscribed to this foundation, declaring its motto loud and clear: "There is no deity other than God." This declaration has only one meaning, which is that sovereignty in human life, and indeed in the entire universe, belongs only to God alone. It is He who rules over the universe as He exercises His will, and it is He who controls the lives of human beings in accordance with the law He has laid down and the way of living He has prescribed. On the basis of this rule, a Muslim is a firm believer in God's oneness and that He controls the whole universe. He addresses his worship to God alone. From Him he receives his laws and values. By correlation, he rejects every authority that seeks to replace God's authority in any way.

This is the basic foundation of the religion of Islam. How far away from it does humanity stand today? Mankind can be classified into several groups all of which belong to the realm of *jāhiliyyah*. To start with, there is an atheist group which denies God's existence altogether. Their case needs no elaboration. Another group are idolaters. They recognize the existence of God but associate with Him other partners and deities as we see in India, Central Africa and other parts of the world.

A third group are normally described in the Qur'ān as "the People of the Book", which is a reference to the Jews and Christians. These reverted to polytheism when they claimed that God had begotten a son. They also considered their priests and rabbis as lords alongside God, since they acknowledged their authority to legislate and accepted whatever legislation those priests and rabbis gave them. It is true that the Christians and Jews did not worship those people, but they acknowledged their legislative authority. Today, they deny God's authority to legislate altogether, establishing instead capitalist or socialist systems and adopting democratic or dictatorial styles, etc. By doing so, they abandon the rule of faith altogether and revert to an ignorant system similar to that which prevailed in ancient Rome or Greece.

A fourth group claims to be Muslim, but it nevertheless follows those systems of the "People of the Book" step by step. Thus they remove themselves from the proper Islamic system and adopt a different one. The religion acceptable to God includes a code of living, a law, a system and a complete constitution for life. The religions of human beings include their own systems and laws and their own set-ups.

Time has come full circle, and we are today in a situation similar to that which prevailed when God revealed this religion of Islam. None of these human groupings follows the divine faith. The Qur'ān is now confronting humanity in the same way as it confronted it the first time. It wants humanity to adopt Islam anew as a faith, before it starts to implement its laws and regulations. Hence, any person who advocates such a revival is bound to feel the hardship and difficulty felt by the Prophet as he started his call to mankind. Today the advocates of Islam aim at establishing the faith in the minds of people, so that they can consciously and positively make the declaration: "I bear witness that there is no deity other than God." This will inevitably lead to the establishment of a new social order in which God is worshipped by people. This signals another rebirth for man, where man is liberated from worshipping human beings or worshipping his own caprice and desire and is made free to enjoy the worship of God alone.

A Revelation to Admonish Believers

Islam is not a mere event of history that took place at a particular point in time and completed its role. Today it has a role to play similar to that which it played when it first confronted humanity. Indeed, the circumstances, social systems, beliefs, values and traditions that prevail in the world today are not dissimilar to those which prevailed when Islam first addressed mankind. The term *jāhiliyyah* refers to a state of affairs, not to a particular period in history. Today, it prevails everywhere and applies to all types of beliefs, doctrines, systems and circumstances. It is based on assigning sovereignty and legislative authority to human beings instead of acknowledging that such authority belongs to God alone. The very foundation of this state of ignorance, or *jāhiliyyah*, makes human caprice or desire or thought the ultimate arbiter in human affairs instead of adopting the divine code as the law to implement. *Jāhiliyyah* may take different shapes and forms, adopt different names, follow a variety of creeds, but in all its versions it has the same basic role determining its nature.

Adopting this criterion, it is clear that a state of ignorance, or *jāhiliyyah*, prevails today throughout the world. Islam, on the other hand, has ceased to exist as an entity. Its advocates have the same objective for which the Prophet Muḥammad, God's Messenger (peace

26

be upon him) dedicated himself. They face the same type of opposition he faced. Hence, they should listen to the same reminder contained in this Qur'ānic verse: "*This is a book that has been bestowed on you from on high – so do not entertain any doubt about it – in order that you may warn people with its message, and admonish the believers.*" This fact needs some elaboration.

Human communities today are, generally speaking, overwhelmed by *jāhiliyyah*, and as such, they are 'backward' or 'reactionary', in the sense that they have reverted to a state of ignorance after Islam had saved them from it. It is Islam that is called upon today to save these communities from their backwardness and reaction and to set them along the road to progress and civilization which makes the divine values and standards prevail. It is only when a community acknowledges that the top authority belongs to God, and when this is manifested in practice by the implementation of God's law, that human beings in that community are truly free from subjugation to their own desires or to those of other human beings.

This is indeed the only true image of Islam or civilization, according to the divine standard, because the civilization God wants human beings to enjoy must be based on total freedom and dignity for every individual. How can an individual enjoy such freedom and exercise such dignity if he must submit himself to other human beings? Dignity and freedom cannot truly exist in a community in which some individuals exercise sovereignty and claim to be the ultimate arbiters while others have to submit to them. When we speak of sovereignty in this sense we do not only refer to the authority to legislate and the process of law making. Rather, values, standards, morals and traditions also come under the same heading of legislation, because people submit to them consciously or subconsciously. Such a society can only be described as reactionary and backward, or, to use the Islamic terminology, '*jāhilī*', or unbeliever.

When the bond in a community is that of faith, and when intellectual concepts and the way of life are derived from divine revelations, not subject to the will of any human being, then that community is progressive and civilized, or, to use the Islamic terminology, 'a Muslim community that surrenders itself to God.' The basis of such a community, then, reflects the highest qualities of man which shape his spirit and intellect. On the other hand, when the bond that unites a community is that of race, colour, tribe or geographic area, the community is then backward and reactionary, or, to use the Islamic terminology, an ignorant community. Such bonds do not relate to any of the supreme qualities of man, because a human being retains his human status regardless of his race, colour, tribe, nation or country, while beyond his spirit and intellect, he has no human existence.

On the other hand, by his own free will – which is the highest blessing God has given him – man can change his faith, intellectual concepts or mode of living. He can adopt divine guidance once he has taken care to try to understand it and reflect on its blessings. He can never change his race, colour or nation. He cannot determine beforehand where he will be born or in what nation or to which parents he will belong. A community where people come together on the basis of something they choose by their own free will is much higher and more civilized than one in which people are united on the basis of something over which they have no control.

On the other hand, when materialism in any shape or form, is considered the supreme value, either theoretically as in Marxism, or in the shape of material production as in America, Europe and other capitalist societies, then that community is, in Islamic terminology, both *jāhilī* and idolatrous, or reactionary and backward in the broadest sense. This is due to the fact that such a society sacrifices all human values, particularly moral values, for its supreme bond of materialism.

It is important to remember here that a Muslim community does not despise or deride matter or materialism, either in the form of theory or in that of productivity. What people produce helps man to fulfil the task that has been assigned to him when God made him vicegerent on earth. To enjoy what is wholesome and useful of human production is something that Islam encourages, as this *sūrah* makes clear. However, it cannot be considered the supreme value in society.

It is the values and morals which prevail in a community that determine its character and whether it is civilized and progressive, or, to use the Islamic terminology, Islamic. Such human values and morals are neither vague nor changeable. These are the morals and values that promote the qualities of man which distinguish him from animals, not the ones which he has in common with them. When the question is placed on this basis, we can easily visualize a clear line of demarcation which negates the whole concept of evolution. We will not have then agricultural morals as opposed to industrial ones, or capitalist morals as opposed to socialist ones. Nor can there be pauper values contrasting with those of the bourgeoisie. Morals will not be the product of the environment and the standard of living, treating these as independent factors shaping moral values and traditions, or following an inevitable course of development. There can only be sound human values and morality which Muslims adopt in their civilized community. These may only contrast with morality and values that we may loosely describe as 'animal'. These latter ones can only be adopted by a backward community. To use the Islamic terminology, there can only be Islamic values and morality, and reactionary or ignorant ones, i.e. *jāhiliyyah*.

The communities in which 'animal' values, morality and desires prevail cannot be civilized communities, no matter how scientifically advanced they are. In modern *jāhiliyyah* societies, the concept of morality has become so weak that it is no longer concerned with what distinguishes man from animals. In these communities, for example, illegitimate sexual relationships, and indeed perverted ones, are not considered immoral. Moral values are only confined to personal or economic or political transactions, and even these are sometimes limited to the interest of the country itself. In such communities, writers, journalists, novelists, the media and all sources of education and information make it clear to young people of both sexes that free sex is not immoral. Such communities, then, are, from the human point of view, backward, not civilized. If we are to consider human progress, we describe these communities as non-Islamic as well. The line Islam follows is that of liberating man from his desires, lust, and other animal inclinations in order to enhance and develop within him his human qualities.

Perhaps this is all that we can say for the present in describing such human communities and how they sink deep in *jāhiliyyah*. Indeed, *jāhiliyyah* characterizes all aspects of these communities, from faith to morality and from concepts to practices. What we have said is sufficient to make it clear that these communities are indeed in a state of ignorance or *jāhiliyyah*. It also makes it clear that the objective of the Islamic message today is the same as it was at the beginning: to call on people to adopt Islam as a faith, a moral system and a way of life. It is the objective which the Prophet set for himself when he started to fulfil the task assigned to him by God. The advocates of Islam today have to adopt the same attitude and set themselves the same objective, remembering what God said to the Prophet at the beginning: "*This is a book that has been bestowed on you from on high – so do not entertain any doubt about it – in order that you may warn people with its message, and admonish the believers.*" (Verse 2)

A Sudden Inflection of Punishment

As God assigns this task to His Messenger, He follows it with an order given to the Arabs addressed by the Qur'ān for the first time, and indeed to all nations and communities whom Islam tries to save from the shackles of *jāhiliyyah*. All such communities are ordered to follow what is revealed in this divine scripture and to refrain from following any masters other then God. This is the crux of the matter: whom are we, human beings, to follow in conducting our lives? If we follow divine orders, then we are Muslims who submit ourselves to God. Those who follow the orders of other beings are idolaters. The two situations are diametrically opposed and there cannot be any meeting point between them. This is the central issue in the message of Islam: "*Follow what has been sent down to you by your Lord, and follow no masters other than Him. How seldom do you keep this in mind.*" (Verse 3)

It should be noted here that when the Prophet was addressed in person, the book is described as having been sent down to him personally: "*This is a book that has been bestowed on you from on high.*" (Verse 2) At the same time, when all mankind are addressed, the book is described as having been sent down to them from their Lord: "*Follow what has been sent down to you by your Lord.*" (Verse 3) In the case of the Prophet (peace be upon him), the book is revealed to him so that he believes in it and warns people and reminds them with its message. In the case of other human beings, the book is revealed to them so that they believe in it and follow it to the exclusion of any other source. In both cases, honour is made by this revelation. A human being to whom God sends down a book, choosing him for this task and bestowing on him all this bounty and blessings, should remember and should be thankful. He must also address himself to the task with strength and resolution.

The task is great. It aims to bring about a total change in human communities, encompassing their concepts, ideals, values, moral standards, traditions, social systems, economic set-ups as well as their relationships with God, the universe and other human beings. Hence, the *sūrah* seeks to strongly shake people's consciences so that they wake up to the task and start examining their situation. This is achieved by portraying the destinies of past communities who denied the divine message, how they were destroyed in this life and the sort of destiny awaiting them in the life to come.

> *How many a community have We destroyed, with Our punishment falling upon them by night, or at midday while they were resting. And when Our punishment fell upon them, all they could say was: "We have indeed been wrongdoers." We shall most certainly question those to whom a message was sent, and We shall most certainly question the messengers themselves. And most certainly We shall reveal to them Our knowledge [of what they have done]; for never have We been absent. On that day, the weighing will be true and accurate: and those whose weight [of good deeds] is heavy in the balance are the ones who are successful; whereas those whose weight is light in the balance are the ones who have lost their own souls because of their wilful rejection of Our revelations.* (Verses 4-9)

The destruction of past nations and communities serves as a very good reminder and warner. The fact that they were so severely punished is utilized in the Qur'ān as an inspiring element which should alert human minds that have so far been oblivious of their situation and their duty. Numerous have been those communities which were destroyed because of their rejection of the message of the truth. Invariably, they were taken unawares, either in the dead of the night or at midday when people relax and sleep, feeling a sense of security: "*How many a community have We destroyed, with Our punishment falling upon them by night, or at midday while they were resting.*" (Verse 4)

Both the depth of the night and the middle of the day when people have their siesta are normally thought of as periods of security, when people can relax and sleep. To be punished so severely at this particular time sounds much more horrific. It should also serve as a stronger reminder, helping people to take more heed.

What happened then? Those people who were taken unawares could do nothing other than to own up to their situation and confess to the attitude they had taken: "*And when Our punishment fell upon them, all they could say was: 'We have indeed been wrongdoers.'*" (Verse 5)

Normally a human being makes every sort of claim, but does not confess his crime, particularly if it means that he faces a terrible prospect. But in their situation, those communities could do nothing other than admit their guilt and condemn themselves as 'wrongdoers'. It is a very terrible situation in which they have found themselves, because the maximum they could do to try to alleviate their situation is to make a full confession. Besides, the 'wrongdoing' to which they refer here means the rejection of the faith and the adoption of idolatrous beliefs. This is the most frequent usage of this term in the Qur'ān. To be an idolater or polytheist is to do wrong and to be unjust. The reverse is also true: to do wrong and insist on injustice is to deny God and associate partners with Him. Is there any greater injustice or wrongdoing than the association of partners with God?

When this confession is made, it avails them of nothing, because the time for repentance has lapsed. When God's punishment is administered, there can be no return and no more chance to mend one's ways. When the scene of punishment in this life is portrayed, the *sūrah* immediately moves on with its audience to portray this situation in the life to come. There is no intermission between the two scenes. The move seems to bypass all considerations of time and place in order to link this life with the life to come showing us the punishment in this world strongly linked to the suffering in the hereafter. In no time, we are looking at the scene on the Day of Judgement: "*We shall most certainly question those to whom a message was sent, and We shall most certainly question the messengers themselves. And most certainly We shall reveal to them Our knowledge [of what they have done]; for never have We been absent. On that day, the weighing will be true and accurate: and those whose weight [of good deeds] is heavy in the balance are the ones who are successful; whereas those whose weight is light in the balance are the ones who have lost their own souls because of their wilful rejection of Our revelations.*" (Verses 6-9)

This style which relies on portraying images in succession is peculiar to the Qur'ān. The journey human beings take, representing their life on earth, is thus portrayed in a quick image, taking only a line in a book, so that this life is intertwined with the life to come. Thus the beginning is tied to the end. When those who suffered God's punishment in this life are brought in front of God for questioning, their confession made at the time when they were destroyed in this world is not sufficient. They have to face a new line of questioning which makes their wrongdoing known to all generations of mankind who are gathered together on that great day: "*We shall most certainly question those to whom a message was sent, and We shall most certainly question the messengers themselves. And most certainly We shall reveal to them Our knowledge [of what they have done]; for never have We been absent.*" (Verses 6-7)

This line of questioning is detailed and seeks to throw everything out in the open. It will be directed to those who received messages and to the messengers themselves, so that the whole story, with all its details and hidden aspects is fully publicized. The people who received messengers are asked first and they make their full confession. The messengers themselves are then questioned and they give their full answers. Then the Lord who knows everything and who is fully aware of every detail will relate to them every point they had overlooked but was always well known to Him. He has been witness to it all. This touch is a profound reminder to all mankind, warning them against rejecting God's faith.

"*On that day, the weighing will be true and accurate.*" (Verse 8) There is no room for deception, wrong judgement or arguments. "*Those whose weight [of good deeds] is heavy in the balance are the ones who are successful.*" (Verse 8) This means that what those people bring to weigh on God's accurate scales will be found heavy. Thus they have earned their great reward which ensures their ultimate success. What success can be greater than avoiding Hell and the return to Heaven at the end of a journey that has extended throughout one's life?

"*Whereas those whose weight is light in the balance are the ones who have lost their own souls because of their wilful rejection of Our revelations.*" (Verse 9) This is because what they bring to weigh on God's absolutely accurate scales is seen to be unmistakably light. They have lost their own souls. What gain can they make thereafter? Human beings try to gather wealth and make gains in order to ensure their own future. When they have lost their own souls, what is left for them? This loss has been made "*because of their wilful rejection of Our revelations.*" (Verse 9). Here the Qur'ānic verse uses the same word as 'wrongdoing' which also means 'injustice'. As we have already explained, these two terms are frequently used in the Qur'ān as synonymous with disbelief or associating partners with God: "*To associate partners with God is indeed an act of great injustice.*" (31: 13)

We have no intention of discussing the nature of the weighing that takes place or the nature of the scales with which this weighing is made. There has been much argument about these over the long period of Islamic history, but such argument has been approached in a rather un-Islamic manner. What we know is that what God does cannot be resembled or likened to anything else, because there is simply no one who bears any similarity to God. It is sufficient for us to state the facts mentioned in the Qur'ān, emphasizing that the reckoning on the Day of Judgement will be most fair and accurate, and no one shall suffer any injustice. Every action, little as it may be, shall be taken into account.

2

The Start of Human Life

We have established you firmly on earth and We have provided you there with means of livelihood. How seldom are you grateful. (10)

وَلَقَدْ مَكَّنَّـٰكُمْ فِى ٱلْأَرْضِ وَجَعَلْنَا لَكُمْ فِيهَا مَعَـٰيِشَ قَلِيلًا مَّا تَشْكُرُونَ ۝

We have indeed created you, and then formed you. We then said to the angels: "Prostrate your-selves before Adam!" They all prostrated themselves, except for Iblīs: he was not one of those who prostrated themselves. (11)

وَلَقَدْ خَلَقْنَـٰكُمْ ثُمَّ صَوَّرْنَـٰكُمْ ثُمَّ قُلْنَا لِلْمَلَـٰٓئِكَةِ ٱسْجُدُوا۟ لِءَادَمَ فَسَجَدُوٓا۟ إِلَّآ إِبْلِيسَ لَمْ يَكُن مِّنَ ٱلسَّـٰجِدِينَ ۝

And [God] said: "What has prevented you from prostrating yourself when I commanded you?" Answered [Iblīs]: "I am nobler than he: You created me out of fire, while You created him out of clay." (12)

قَالَ مَا مَنَعَكَ أَلَّا تَسْجُدَ إِذْ أَمَرْتُكَ قَالَ أَنَا۠ خَيْرٌ مِّنْهُ خَلَقْتَنِى مِن نَّارٍ وَخَلَقْتَهُۥ مِن طِينٍ ۝

[God] said: "Off with you hence! It is not for you to show your arrogance here. Get out, then; you will always be among the humiliated." (13)

قَالَ فَٱهْبِطْ مِنْهَا فَمَا يَكُونُ لَكَ أَن تَتَكَبَّرَ فِيهَا فَٱخْرُجْ إِنَّكَ مِنَ ٱلصَّـٰغِرِينَ ۝

Said he: "Grant me a respite until the Day when all will be raised [from the dead]." (14)

قَالَ أَنظِرْنِي إِلَىٰ يَوْمِ يُبْعَثُونَ ۝

God replied: "You shall indeed be among those granted respite." (15)

قَالَ إِنَّكَ مِنَ ٱلْمُنظَرِينَ ۝

[Iblīs] said: "Since You let me fall in error, I shall indeed lurk in ambush for them all along Your straight path, (16)

قَالَ فَبِمَا أَغْوَيْتَنِي لَأَقْعُدَنَّ لَهُمْ صِرَٰطَكَ ٱلْمُسْتَقِيمَ ۝

and I shall most certainly fall upon them from the front and from the rear, and from their right and from their left; and You will find most of them ungrateful." (17)

ثُمَّ لَآتِيَنَّهُم مِّنۢ بَيْنِ أَيْدِيهِمْ وَمِنْ خَلْفِهِمْ وَعَنْ أَيْمَـٰنِهِمْ وَعَن شَمَآئِلِهِمْ ۖ وَلَا تَجِدُ أَكْثَرَهُمْ شَـٰكِرِينَ ۝

[God] said: "Get out of here, despised, disgraced. As for those of them that follow you, I shall fill Hell with you all. (18)

قَالَ ٱخْرُجْ مِنْهَا مَذْءُومًا مَّدْحُورًا ۖ لَّمَن تَبِعَكَ مِنْهُمْ لَأَمْلَأَنَّ جَهَنَّمَ مِنكُمْ أَجْمَعِينَ ۝

And (as for you), Adam: dwell you and your wife in this Garden, and eat, both of you, whatever you may desire; but do not come near this tree, lest you become wrongdoers." (19)

وَيَـٰٓـَٔادَمُ ٱسْكُنْ أَنتَ وَزَوْجُكَ ٱلْجَنَّةَ فَكُلَا مِنْ حَيْثُ شِئْتُمَا وَلَا تَقْرَبَا هَـٰذِهِ ٱلشَّجَرَةَ فَتَكُونَا مِنَ ٱلظَّـٰلِمِينَ ۝

But Satan whispered to them both, so that he might show them their nakedness, of which they had previously been un-aware. He said to them: "Your Lord has only forbidden you this tree lest you two become angels or immortals." (20)

فَوَسْوَسَ لَهُمَا ٱلشَّيْطَـٰنُ لِيُبْدِيَ لَهُمَا مَا وُۥرِيَ عَنْهُمَا مِن سَوْءَٰتِهِمَا وَقَالَ مَا نَهَىٰكُمَا رَبُّكُمَا عَنْ هَـٰذِهِ ٱلشَّجَرَةِ إِلَّآ أَن تَكُونَا مَلَكَيْنِ أَوْ تَكُونَا مِنَ ٱلْخَـٰلِدِينَ ۝

And he swore to them: "I am indeed giving you sound advice." (21)

وَقَاسَمَهُمَآ إِنِّى لَكُمَا لَمِنَ ٱلنَّاصِحِينَ ﴿٢١﴾

Thus he cunningly deluded them. And when they both had tasted the fruit of the tree, their nakedness became apparent to them, and they began to cover themselves with leaves from the Garden. Their Lord called out to them: "Did I not forbid you that tree and tell you both that Satan is your open enemy?" (22)

فَدَلَّىٰهُمَا بِغُرُورٍ فَلَمَّا ذَاقَا ٱلشَّجَرَةَ بَدَتْ لَهُمَا سَوْءَ‍ٰتُهُمَا وَطَفِقَا يَخْصِفَانِ عَلَيْهِمَا مِن وَرَقِ ٱلْجَنَّةِ وَنَادَىٰهُمَا رَبُّهُمَآ أَلَمْ أَنْهَكُمَا عَن تِلْكُمَا ٱلشَّجَرَةِ وَأَقُل لَّكُمَآ إِنَّ ٱلشَّيْطَانَ لَكُمَا عَدُوٌّ مُّبِينٌ ﴿٢٢﴾

Said they: "Our Lord! We have wronged ourselves; and unless You grant us forgiveness and bestow Your mercy upon us, we shall certainly be lost." (23)

قَالَا رَبَّنَا ظَلَمْنَآ أَنفُسَنَا وَإِن لَّمْ تَغْفِرْ لَنَا وَتَرْحَمْنَا لَنَكُونَنَّ مِنَ ٱلْخَٰسِرِينَ ﴿٢٣﴾

Said He: "Get you down hence, [and be henceforth] enemies to one another, having on earth your abode and livelihood for a while." (24)

قَالَ ٱهْبِطُوا بَعْضُكُمْ لِبَعْضٍ عَدُوٌّ وَلَكُمْ فِى ٱلْأَرْضِ مُسْتَقَرٌّ وَمَتَٰعٌ إِلَىٰ حِينٍ ﴿٢٤﴾

"There shall you live," He added, "and there shall you die, and from there shall you be brought forth [on the Day of Resurrection]." (25)

قَالَ فِيهَا تَحْيَوْنَ وَفِيهَا تَمُوتُونَ وَمِنْهَا تُخْرَجُونَ ﴿٢٥﴾

Overview

This is the starting point of the great journey of human life. It begins by giving the human race power so that it can settle on earth. Here the reference is to an absolute fact that precedes the creation of mankind.

"*We have established you firmly on earth and We have provided you there with means of livelihood. How seldom are you grateful.*" (Verse 10) The Creator of both the earth and man is the One who has made it possible for the human race to establish itself on earth. It is He who has given the earth its qualities and characteristics and made all these balances which allow human life to prosper and provide people with sustenance and other means of livelihood.

It is indeed He who has made the earth suitable for sustaining human life, by giving it its atmosphere, its particular size, shape and make-up, its appropriate distance from the sun and the moon. It is He who has set it in its orbit in order to enable it to move round the sun, and given it its particular speed and determined the angle it makes with its axis. All these balances are as important as giving the earth the potential to produce sustenance and sources of energy to enable human life to continue and prosper. It is also God who has made man the master of all creation on earth, giving him the ability to utilize the earth's potential and resources by his ability to identify and use the laws of nature.

Had it not been for the fact that God has established man on earth and given him all these qualities, man, a weak creation as he certainly is, would not have been able to make his 'conquest of nature', as people in *jāhiliyyah* communities, past and present, say. He would not have been able to stand up to the enormous, overwhelming forces that operate in the universe.

It is unfortunate that ancient Greek and Roman concepts continue to impart their colour to present-day *jāhiliyyah*. It is these concepts that portray the universe as hostile to man, and universal forces as opposed to man's existence and action. They try to show man engaged in a fight against natural forces, with every discovery of natural law man makes portrayed as a triumph of man against nature.

All these concepts are both absurd and evil. Had it been true that the natural laws of the universe are hostile to man and that they work in opposition to what man does, and had it been true that these forces operate without any control by a wise will, man would have never come into existence in the first place. How could he have existed? How could he survive in a hostile universe and environment when these are subject to no external will or power whatsoever? How could he have sustained his life, when all these great forces are opposed to him? The question becomes even more forceful if we are to accept the claim that these forces are subject to no control other than their own.

Only the Islamic concept of life provides a coherent concept that relates all these details to their original and consistent line. It is God who has created both man and the universe. His will and wisdom has determined the nature of this universe making it possible for human life to maintain itself and prosper. He has also endowed man with the ability that makes it possible for him to identify certain natural laws and utilize them for his own needs. This perfect coherence and harmony is the one worthy of God's creation, because God's work is characterized by its perfection in every aspect. He does not place His creation on a war footing so that they are always hostile to one another.

Under this concept, man lives in a friendly universe, enjoying the care of a wise, supreme power. He is at peace with himself, reassured, able to move steadily in order to fulfil his task as vicegerent on earth. He feels that he can rely on unfailing help and he deals with the universe in an attitude of mutual friendship. He praises God every time he is able to discover a new secret or a new law of the universe which enables him to fulfil his task and makes it possible for him to make progress and increase his comfort.

This concept does not discourage man from working to discover the secrets of the universe and identify its laws. On the contrary, it encourages him to do so with confidence and reassurance. He is not in confrontation with a hostile universe that guards its secrets from him and withholds its help. He is not in conflict with an enemy who tries to forestall his efforts, his hopes and ambitions.

The great tragedy of the philosophical creed known as existentialism is this ill-conceived principle which describes the universe, and indeed, the collective existence of humanity, as naturally hostile to the existence of the human individual, trying with all its might to crush it. It is a sick concept that is bound to lead to an inward-looking approach giving little value to one's existence, or to a careless, rebellious and self-centred attitude to life as a whole. Both situations cause much worry and misery, both physical and mental. They leave man in total loss, although the sense of loss may differ a little in each situation.

But the tragedy is not that of a single European intellectual creed; it is indeed the tragedy of all European intellectual thought, with all its creeds and doctrines. Furthermore, it is also the tragedy of *jāhiliyyah* as a whole, in all times and environments. Islam stops this tragedy altogether by its comprehensive faith that lays the foundation of a correct concept of this universe and the wise power that controls it.

Man is the son of this earth and this universe. God has created him out of this earth and established him on it, and He has provided him with the means of sustenance and livelihood. Moreover, He has enabled him to acquire knowledge and discover the secrets of the universe. He has made the laws of nature move in harmony with human existence, so that man is able to make use of these laws in order to set his life on the road to progress. What he needs for this is to try to identify these laws with an open mind.

But human beings are seldom grateful, because when they are in the depths of ignorance, they do not know what blessings God has given them. Even those who know are unable to thank God in full for the grace He has bestowed on them. How can they ever thank Him enough? It is an aspect of God's grace that He accepts from them what they can do. In both situations, the Qur'ānic statement is true: "How seldom are you grateful."

The Start of Human Life on Earth

What we are about to learn is the story of human life with all its exciting events. It begins with an announcement of the forthcoming birth of mankind. The announcement is made in a majestic celebration attended by the Supreme Society, a Qur'ānic term that refers to the angels. As a further evidence of honour, no one other than God Almighty makes the announcement when the angels are gathered, and Iblīs is present, though he is not one of the angels. The whole event is witnessed by the heavens and the earth and all that God has created. It is indeed a great event in the history of the universe:

> We have indeed created you, and then formed you. We then said to the angels: "Prostrate yourselves before Adam!" They all prostrated themselves, except for Iblīs: he was not one of those who prostrated themselves. And [God] said: "What has prevented you from prostrating yourself when I commanded you?" Answered [Iblīs]: "I am nobler than he: You created me out of fire, while You created him out of clay." [God] said: "Off with you hence! It is not for you to show your arrogance here. Get out, then; you will always be among the humiliated." Said he: "Grant me a respite until the Day when all will be raised [from the dead]." God replied: "You shall indeed be among those granted respite." [Iblīs] said: "Since you let me fall

in error, I shall indeed lurk in ambush for them all along Your straight path, and I shall most certainly fall upon them from the front and from the rear, and from their right and from their left; and You will find most of them ungrateful." [God] said: "Get out of here, despised, disgraced. As for those of them that follow you, I shall fill Hell with you all." (Verses 11-18)

This is the first scene, which is both exciting and very serious indeed. It is perhaps more appropriate to look properly at the scenes in this story, making our comments at the end when we can better try to understand its importance.

We have indeed created you, and then formed you. We then said to the angels: "Prostrate yourselves before Adam!" They all prostrated themselves, except for Iblīs: he was not one of those who prostrated themselves. (Verse 11)

'Creation' may mean initiation, while 'formation' may mean the assigning of a particular form and special characteristic. These are grades not stages of existence. The conjunction 'then' may signify giving a higher status without having any element of a chronological order. To give something a form is more advanced than its mere existence, for the latter may be limited to the raw material only. Formation, in the sense of giving a special human form and characteristic, is certainly much more significant than mere existence. Hence, the Qur'ānic statement should be understood as not signifying mere existence but also giving that existence a number of higher characteristics. This is akin to the Qur'ānic statement which refers to God Himself as the One "*who has given everything that exists its true form and then guided them.*" (20: 50).

Everything has been given its characteristics and tasks and was guided to its fulfilment at the time of its creation. There was no time gap between the creation of everything and the assigning of its characteristics and duties and then the guidance to the fulfilment of those duties. The meaning remains the same if 'guided' in the above Qur'ānic statement refers to their knowledge of their Lord. Again, that form of guidance has been given to all creation at the time when it came into existence. Adam was also formed and fashioned and given his human characteristics when he was created. Hence, it is much more correct to say that in the Qur'ānic verse which states. "*We have indeed created you and then formed you,*" the conjunction, 'then', signifies enhancement of grade not allowing for a time gap.

The total import of Qur'ānic statements that speak of the creation of Adam (peace be upon him) and the start of human life indicates very strongly that this particular creation was given its human characteristic and special tasks at the time of its coming into existence. Evolution in human history took the form of developing these characteristics and gaining further experience in utilizing them. It is not an evolution of existence which suggests, as Darwinism would like us to believe, that a process of evolution of species has reached its climax with the advent of man.

There might have been stages of advanced animals, with one coming after the other, as evidenced by the theory of natural selection. But this is no more than a theory that does not aspire to any degree of certainty, because the estimation of the ages of rocks in geological strata is again a theoretical process. It is the same as estimating the ages of different stars and planets on the basis of the characteristics of their rays. Future discoveries may amend or change these theories.

But even if we were to learn the ages of rocks with absolute certainty, there is nothing to prevent the existence of different species of animals, some of which are higher than others, in different time periods, and that their advancement makes them particularly suited for the prevailing circumstances. Some of them may disappear when circumstances change drastically to make it difficult for the earth to sustain their existence. That does not make it inevitable that these species have evolved one from the other. All the studies and observations of Charles Darwin and those who followed him cannot prove more than that. They cannot say with any certainty that one species evolved from a preceding one, on the basis of fossils and where they have been found. It simply proves that a subsequent species was higher than a preceding one. This can easily be explained as we have already said: the prevailing circumstances at one particular time allowed the existence of one species. The circumstances subsequently prevailing allowed the existence of another species and the disappearance of the first one.

All this means that the appearance of human beings was independent of other species. It took place at a time when the prevailing circumstances on earth facilitated the existence, development and advancement of this particular type of creation. This is the total sum of the Qur'ānic statements on the creation of man.

The fact that biologically, physiologically, mentally and spiritually, man has unique characteristics is so clear that it has been acknowledged by neo-Darwinists who include a number of atheists. This uniqueness also supports the view that human existence was totally independent of the existence of all other species. It simply has no biological inter-relationship with them.

Be that as it may, God Himself, in all His Majesty, made the announcement of the birth of man in a great gathering of the Supreme Society: "*We then said to the angels: 'Prostrate yourselves before Adam!' They all prostrated themselves, except for Iblīs: he was not one of those who prostrated themselves.*" (Verse 11)

The angels are a different type of God's creation who have their distinctive characteristics and special tasks. We do not know anything about them except what God has told us, which we have stated earlier.[1] Iblīs belongs to yet another type of creation, different from the angels. God states in the Qur'ān, in reference to Iblīs: "*He belonged to the jinn and acted contrary to his Lord's command.*" (18: 50) The *jinn* are also a type of creation different from the angels and we have already summarized earlier [2] what God has told us about them. It will be stated later in this *sūrah*[3] that Iblīs was created out of fire. Hence, most certainly he never was an angel, although he was commanded to prostrate himself to Adam together with the angels in that great event when the Almighty announced the forthcoming appearance of man, the unique creature.

As for the angels, who never disobey God in whatever He may order them and simply do what they are bid, they all prostrated themselves in total obedience to God. None hesitated; none showed any indication of arrogance, because none contemplated disobedience of God for any reason. Such is their nature and such are their characteristics. Here we see clear evidence of the honour God has given to man, and of the total obedience that is always shown by the type of God's servants to whom we refer as the angels.

As for Iblīs, he wilfully disobeyed God, defying His orders. We will soon learn what thoughts were in his mind and what caused him to take this stance although he was perfectly aware that the One who was

---

1. Vol. V, pp. 54-56.
2. Vol. V, p. 313.
3. Verse 12.

giving the orders was his Lord who had created him and who had control of his destiny as also of the destiny of the whole universe. Iblīs never entertained any doubt about all this. Nevertheless, he still disobeyed God.

Three Different Natures

The scene portrays three different types of God's creation: the first is that given to absolute obedience and complete self-surrender. In this scene, its role is completed with the submission it makes which manifested itself in the angels prostrating themselves, one and all, to Adam as commanded by their Lord. The second type is that of absolute disobedience and spiteful arrogance, while the third is that of human nature. We will be discussing shortly the characteristics of these latter types and how they work.

> And [God] said: "What has prevented you from prostrating yourself when I commanded you?" Answered [Iblīs]: "I am nobler than he: You created me out of fire, while You created him out of clay." (Verse 12)

Iblīs here claims for himself a private opinion and a right of discretion to consider whether to comply with an order given by God or not. He wants to base his action on what appears to him to be justifiable. Needless to say, when a clear order is given by God no one has the right of discretion. The only thing that is left is complete obedience and perfect compliance. However, fully aware that God is the Creator and Sustainer of all creation and who controls the universe to the extent that nothing takes place without His permission and consent, Iblīs refuses to comply, justifying his disobedience by his own logic: "*I am nobler than he: You created me out of fire, while You created him out of clay.*" (Verse 12) Immediately, he received the right answer to his arrogance: "*[God] said: Off with you hence! It is not for you to show your arrogance here. Get out, then; you will always be among the humiliated.*" (Verse 13)

Neither his knowledge of God nor his belief in God's existence and attributes were of any benefit to Iblīs. The same applies to anyone who receives a divine order and claims for himself a degree of discretion about whether to accept or refuse that order, or claims the right to refuse God's ruling on any question whatsoever. For this entails disbelief in spite of knowledge and certitude. Iblīs was not at all lacking in either his knowledge of God or his certainty of His attributes. He was expelled from Heaven and deprived of God's grace. He incurred God's displeasure and was condemned to permanent humiliation.

Evil and obstinate as he is, Iblīs does not forget the cause of his expulsion and God's displeasure with him: namely, Adam. He does not want to accept his miserable fate without trying to avenge himself. Furthermore, he wants to fulfil his task in accordance with the evil nature which he has come to symbolize: "*Said he: 'Grant me a respite until the Day when all will be raised [from the dead].' God replied: 'You shall indeed be among these granted respite.' [Iblīs] said: 'Since You let me fall in error, I shall indeed lurk in ambush for them all along Your straight path, and I shall most certainly fall upon them from the front and from the rear, and from their right and from their left; and You will find most of them ungrateful.'*" (Verses 14-17)

His attitude, then, is one of complete determination to follow the evil path, and absolute insistence on trying to lead people astray. Here we see his nature revealing its main characteristic of a deeply entrenched, deliberate evil, and not a passing or temporary one.

We also see here a concrete outline of thoughts, concepts and reactions, all portrayed with exceptional vividness. Iblīs requests his Lord to give him respite until the Day of Resurrection, knowing that what he is asking can only be granted by God's will. God granted his request and gave him respite until the "*Day of the appointed time*" as it is described in another *sūrah*. A number of reports explain that this is a reference to the Day of the blowing of the Trumpet when everything that exists in the heavens and the earth is stunned unconscious, with the exception of whomever God wills. In other words, his respite does not extend to the Day of Resurrection.

As he has been granted prolonged life, Iblīs announces with wicked arrogance that he will concentrate his efforts in leading astray the very creature on whom God has bestowed His honour and who was the cause of Iblīs's own tragedy and rejection. His endeavour to tempt human beings away from the right path is shown here by drawing the practical import of what he declared: "*I shall indeed lurk in ambush for them all along Your straight path, and I shall most certainly fall upon them from the front and from the rear, and from their right and from their left.*" (Verses 16-17)

He wants always to be close to God's straight path watching for Adam and his offspring, trying to turn away any human being who tries to pass along. The way to God cannot be a concrete one, because God is above being confined to a certain place. It is, then, the road of faith and obedience which leads to God's pleasure. Iblīs, then, will have to come at human beings from every direction: "*I shall most certainly fall upon them from the front and from the rear, and from their right and from their left.*" (Verse 17) His aim will always be to try to prevent them from believing in God and obeying Him. This is a very lively portrait of Iblīs falling upon human beings in his never-ending endeavour to tempt them away from God's path so that they cannot believe in God or show their gratitude to Him, except for a small number of them who manage to escape Iblīs's efforts: "*You will find most of them ungrateful.*"

Gratitude is mentioned here because it is in harmony with what was mentioned earlier in this *sūrah*: "*How seldom are you grateful.*" (Verse 10) We have here the reason for this lack of gratitude on the part of human beings. Its real cause is Iblīs's endeavour and the fact that he lurks in ambush for human beings to prevent them from believing in God. Human beings are then alerted to the designs of their enemy who tries to stop them from following divine guidance. They should be on their guard, since now they know the reason for their ingratitude.

Iblīs's request has been granted because God has willed human beings to find their own way since their nature is susceptible to good and evil. Furthermore, man has been given a mind to think, reflect and choose, and he has been given reminders and warnings through God's messengers. Furthermore, he has been given the means to control and correct himself. It is God's will that he receives signals of right guidance and error, and that goodness and evil should have their fight within him so that his faith is determined in accordance with the law God has set in operation. God's will is thus accomplished by testing human beings. Whether they follow right guidance or go astray, God's law is thus accomplished.

The *sūrah* here does not state clearly that any permission has been given to Iblīs to put his threat into effect. At least not in the same way as it clearly states that his request to be given respite has been granted. Rather, we are not told the result of that threat. But we are informed of Iblīs's humiliating expulsion and that he had fallen completely from grace. Furthermore, the *sūrah* tells us that God has warned that He will fill hell with Iblīs's offspring and all those human beings who follow him into error: "*[God] said: 'Get out of here, despised, disgraced. As for those of them that follow you, I shall fill Hell with you all.*" (Verse 18)

His followers among human beings may simply follow him in his knowledge of God and his belief that God is the supreme deity and overall Lord, but they may, nevertheless, reject God's sovereignty and legislative authority. They may follow Iblīs in claiming that they have discretion to look into God's orders and to determine whether to implement them or not. On the other hand, Iblīs's human followers may simply follow his footsteps and thus they are turned away from guidance altogether. Both situations represent following Iblīs and both earn hell as a reward.

God has granted Iblīs and his offspring the chance to lead people away from the right path. He has also given Adam and human beings in general the freedom of choice so that He can put them to the test. It is this choice which makes man a special type of creation: he belongs neither to the realm of angels who obey God in all situations nor to the world of satans who disobey Him all the time. Man has a totally different role to play.

Temptation of the Forbidden Tree

Fast on the heels of the scene ending with Satan's expulsion from Heaven follows a scene in which we see God looking at Adam and his wife. Only at this point do we realize that Adam has a wife of his own species. We do not know how she came to exist. This passage which relates this story of the creation of man and similar passages in the Qur'ān do not tell us anything about the creation of the female human being. All the reports that speak of her being created out of Adam's rib belong to Israelite literature. As such, they are not totally reliable. What we can say without fear of being contradicted is that God created for Adam a spouse of his own type, to make them a couple. Making all species in couples is the law applicable to all creation. God says in the Qur'ān: "*Of all things We have created couples so that you may reflect.*" (51: 49) Keeping this rule in mind, it seems to us that it was not long before Eve was created, and that it must have been in the same manner as Adam's creation.

Be that as it may, both Adam and his wife are now addressed to outline God's commandment to them. They are to be given their experiences so that they are prepared for the fulfilment of their basic role for which they have been created. This is the role of vicegerency on earth, as is stated clearly in the second *sūrah*, The Cow, or, Al-Baqarah, in which we are told: "*Your Lord said to the angels: I am appointing a vicegerent on earth.*" (2: 30)

"*And (as for you), Adam: dwell you and your wife in this Garden, and eat, both of you, whatever you may desire; but do not come near this tree, lest you become wrongdoers.*" (Verse 19) The Qur'ān remains silent about what kind of tree it was, because providing any specific information on this point does not add any particular information about the purpose of its prohibition. Withholding such information lends weight to the view that the prohibition itself was the objective. God has permitted Adam and his wife the enjoyment of what He has made lawful, and commanded them to steer away from what has been forbidden. It was necessary to identify something as forbidden so that the human race could learn that people must not exceed their limits. Thus man's will is restrained such that he controls his desire and caprice. He is thus able to elevate himself above the level of animals who respond involuntarily to their desires and cannot control them. This is indeed the quality that distinguishes man from animals.

Now Satan begins to play the role for which he dedicated himself. This against a unique creation whose birth God so graciously announced Himself before the Supreme Society in grand celebration. Furthermore, He ordered the angels to prostrate themselves to him, and expelled Satan from heaven on his account. We are told how God created man with a dual nature, capable of following both the right and wrong paths. He has inherent weaknesses and desires which can lead him astray, unless he observes God's commandments.

Thus Satan saw his chance and began to play on human desires: "*But Satan whispered to them both, so that he might show them their nakedness, of which they had previously been unaware. He said to them: 'Your Lord has only forbidden you this tree lest you two become angels or immortals.' And he swore to them: 'I am indeed giving you sound advice.'*" (Verses 20-21)

We do not know how the whisperings of Satan took place, because we do not even know Satan's nature or from what he is made, let alone understand how he acts. We cannot say how he establishes his contact with man or how he tempts him. But we know for certain, on the basis of true information given to us by the only source acceptable in connection with such matters known only to God, that temptation to do what is evil does actually happen in order to encourage man to do what he is forbidden. Such temptation relies on the weaknesses in human nature, but such weakness can be transformed into strength through faith and remembrance of God. None of Satan's schemes can be of any effect with a believer who remains conscious of his Lord.

Thus Satan whispered to them in order to show them their nakedness. This was his aim. They certainly had unsightly parts of which they were unaware because they were made not to see them. We will soon learn from the Qur'ānic passage that these were in their physical constitution, requiring to be covered. Hence, we may understand this as a reference to their private parts. Satan did not reveal to them his objective but continued to play on their desires: "*He said to them: 'Your Lord has only forbidden you this tree lest you two become angels or immortals.'*" (Verse 20) He knew the inner desires of man who loves to be immortal or at least to have a very long life. He also loves to be an angel who is not limited to a short lifespan.

The Arabic word in the Qur'ānic text which refers to 'angels' is also read in a different form so as to make it mean 'kings'. Only a change of a short vowel, which is not normally written in Arabic script, is needed to make the word denote either meaning. This second reading is further supported by the statement reporting Satan's word in *Sūrah* 20, "Ṭāhā", when Satan is quoted as saying to them: "*Adam, shall I lead you to the tree of life eternal, and to a kingdom that will never decay?*" (20: 120) According to this reading, the temptation offered by Satan was that of everlasting wealth and immortality. They represent man's two strongest desires. It may be said that sexual desire itself is only a means to fulfil a desire for immortality, perpetuating human existence one generation after another. If we take the first reading which makes Satan's words refer to angels: "*Your Lord has only forbidden you this tree lest you two become angels or immortals*", then the temptation is slightly different. He is tempting them with removal of the limitations of their bodies so that they are like angels and with unending life. Although the first reading, speaking of an everlasting kingdom, is less well-known, it is more in line with the other Qur'ānic statement quoted above and fits more perfectly with Satan's scheming when he tries to play on man's desires.

The Fall from Heaven

Wicked as he is and knowing that prohibition of that tree was firmly rooted in their minds, Satan thought to shaken its effect by assuring them that they had nothing to fear. He coupled that by tempting them with the fulfilment of their desires. He swore to them that he only gave them sound advice and that he was sincere in that advice: "*And he swore to them: 'I am indeed giving you sound advice.'*" (Verse 21).

Upon the influence of their desires and the reassuring effect of his oath, Adam and his wife forgot that Satan was their enemy who would never point out something good to them. They became oblivious of the fact that God had issued a commandment to them which they had to obey, whether they recognized its purpose or not. They further forgot that everything takes place in accordance with God's will. If it is God's will that they should not be immortal or should not have an everlasting kingdom, then they will have neither. They forgot all this and yielded to Satan's temptation. "*Thus he cunningly deluded them. And when they both had tasted the fruit of the tree, their nakedness became apparent to them, and they began to cover themselves with leaves from the Garden. Their Lord called out to them: 'Did I not forbid you that tree and tell you both that Satan is your open enemy?'*" (Verse 22)

The temptation was thus complete and yielded its bitter fruit. With their error, Satan brought them down from the level of obeying God to that of disobeying Him. Thus he caused their delusion: "*Thus he cunningly deluded them.*" (Verse 22) Now they realized that they were naked after they were unaware of those bodily parts which should remain covered. They began to gather leaves from the trees of heaven and patch them together to cover their nakedness. The way all this is expressed in the Qur'ān suggests that it is a reference to the physical private parts which a human being is naturally too shy to expose. He only exposes them when his nature is corrupted under the pressure of traditions and practices that may prevail in *jāhiliyyah* societies.

Their Lord called out to them: "*Did I not forbid you that tree and tell you both that Satan is your open enemy?*" (Verse 22) They heard their Lord's reproach for their disobedience and for taking no heed of His advice. As to how this reproach was made and how they heard it, these are matters of which we have no knowledge other than that they took place. We accept that as we accept the statement that their Lord spoke to them the first time and also spoke to the angels and to Iblīs. God does what He wants.

With this address from on high, the other side of man's nature is revealed. He is liable to forget and to err. He has a weakness which gives Satan the opportunity to delude him. He does not always maintain the right path. However, he recognizes his mistake and regrets it, and seeks God's help and forgiveness. He is ready to turn back to God. He does not insist on his disobedience as Satan did, nor does he request his Lord to help him sink deeper into error: "*Said they: 'Our Lord! We have wronged ourselves; and unless You grant us forgiveness and bestow Your mercy upon us, we shall certainly be lost.'*" (Verse 23) This is one of man's main characteristics, establishing his bond with his Lord. This opening of the doors leading to his Lord involves recognition of his error, repentance, seeking forgiveness, feeling his own weakness, seeking God's help and mercy. He is all the time certain that his own power is of no avail unless God helps him and bestows His mercy on him. Otherwise he is lost.

Thus the first experience is completed. Man's main characteristics are thus outlined. He has become aware of these characteristics and he has gone through this experience. It all provides him with the necessary equipment to fulfil his task as vicegerent on earth. He can now enter into the battle against his enemy which is meant to be an unabating battle: "*Said He: 'Get you down hence, [and be henceforth] enemies to one another, having on earth your abode and livelihood for a while.'*" (Verse 24)

"*There shall you live,*" He added, "*and there shall you die, and from there shall you be brought forth [on the Day of Resurrection].*" (Verse 25) They all fell down, descending to this earth. But where were they? Where is Heaven? All that belongs to the realm which remains unknown to us except in so far as God, who holds the keys to that realm, tells us. Any attempt to discover that realm after revelations have ceased is bound to be futile. Any denial of it based on what is familiar or what is known today to human beings is a mark of arrogance. Man's knowledge certainly falls short of trying to discover this unknown world without the proper tools and means. Man is both conceited and arrogant when he denies the existence of that realm which lies beyond the perception of his senses, when it is all around him. In the world of matter, which is within man's own world, what is unknown is much greater than what is known.

All of them: Adam and his wife, Iblīs and his host, fell down to earth where they began their fight fuelled with hostility. The battle rages between two natures, one of them devoted completely to evil while the other has a dual aspect which responds to good and evil. Thus the test begins and God's will is done.

Adam and his offspring are destined to remain on earth where they have the power to build it and to enjoy its comforts for a while. On earth they live and they die, before they are resurrected, when they return to their Lord at the end of their great journey. He then assigns them either to heaven or to hell.

The first round in the battle is over, but it is to be followed by numerous rounds. Man will also be victorious when he seeks help from his Lord and follows the path He has shown him. He will end up in defeat whenever he defers to his enemy.

Full Harmony in the System of Creation

What we are told in this *sūrah* about Adam's creation is not a mere story. It is a presentation outlining the truth of the creation of man, explaining his nature and origin as well as the world around him and what control he has over his life. It also seeks to explain the code which God wants him to implement, the test to which he is put and the destiny awaiting him. All these are basic elements in the Islamic concept of life. We will tackle these only briefly in our commentary, because they are tackled in greater depth in a separate book.[4]

The first fact which we derive from studying the history of human existence and how man came into being demonstrates that there is full and complete harmony between the nature of the universe and the creation of man. Divine planning, which is characterized by being elaborate and careful, encompasses both man and the universe. It is this planning which makes man's existence the outcome of a deliberate plan, not a mere coincidence. It also makes harmony between man and the universe the norm.

Those who do not have a proper concept of God and do not properly understand His nature or give Him the respect due to Him, apply their own human measures to His will and actions. When they realize that man is only one of numerous creatures which live on earth, and

---

4. This work by the author, in two volumes, is entitled *Khaṣā'iṣ al-Taṣawwur al-Islāmī wa Muqawwimātuh*, or The Main Characteristics and Basic Principles of the Islamic Concept, Dar al-Shuruq, Cairo. – Editor's note.

discover that the earth is no more than a small particle in the ocean of the universe, they claim that "it does not stand to reason" that man's existence has a definite purpose or that man has a role to play in the overall universal system. Some claim that human existence was a mere coincidence and that the universe is hostile to human existence and life in general. These are no more than blind thoughts that result from imposing human standards on God's actions.

Clearly, had man been the owner of this vast universe, he would have paid no attention whatsoever to this earth, or to man, the creature walking here and there on the face of the earth. That is because human concerns cannot be addressed to everything that exists in this great creation or to the establishment of harmony between them. But the Lord of the universe is God (limitless is He in His glory) who does not allow a single particle in any part of the heavens or the earth to escape His attention. He is the sovereign of this great kingdom in which nothing can exist without His will or survive without His care. The problem with man is that when he deviates from divine guidance and follows his own desires, which he may call occasionally as science and knowledge, he forgets what God is like and gives Him a picture of his own making. He then starts to measure His actions by his own standards. As a result, he imposes the dictates of his desire, thereby distorting the truth.

As an example of the many erroneous human concepts let us look at this statement by Sir James Jeans:

> Standing on our microscopic fragment of a grain of sand, we attempt to discover the nature and purpose of the universe which surrounds our home in space and time. Our first impression is something akin to terror. We find the universe terrifying because of its vast meaningless distances, terrifying because of its inconceivably long vistas of time which dwarf human history to the twinkling of an eye, terrifying because of our extreme loneliness, and because of the material insignificance of our home in space – a millionth part of a grain of sand out of all the sea sand in the world. But above all else, we find the universe terrifying because it appears to be indifferent to life like our own; emotion, ambition and achievement, art and religion all seem equally foreign to its plan. Perhaps indeed we ought to say it appears to be actively hostile to life like our own. For the most part, empty space is so

cold that all life in it would be frozen; most of the matter in space is so hot as to make life on it impossible; space is traversed, and astronomical bodies continually bombarded, by radiation of a variety of kinds, much of which is probably inimical to, or even destructive of, life.

Into such a universe we have stumbled, if not exactly by mistake, at least as the result of what may properly be described as an accident.[5]

We have already explained that to assume that the universe is hostile to the emergence of life, together with the assumption that there is no deliberate planning or controlling force, and the fact that life exists in spite of all this cannot be entertained by any man of reason, let alone a scientist. How is it possible that life could appear in a hostile environment assuming there is no controlling power that determines what takes place? Is life stronger than the universe so as to emerge despite its hostility to it? Is it possible to imagine that, even before he comes into existence, man is stronger than the universe which already exists? This is the only meaning of their statement that man existed despite the hostility of the universe.

Such concepts do not deserve a moment's attention. Had those 'scientists' limited their role to telling us about what they see and discover, through the means available to them, in the universe, without venturing into such metaphysical concepts that have no basis whatsoever, they would have played a constructive role, limited as it may be, in making the nature of the universe known to mankind. But they go beyond the area of safe knowledge into the maze of theories and assumptions, without any guidance other than their own whims and caprice.

Praise be to God for His guidance! We, for our part, do not feel any sense of fear when we look at this great universe. We certainly have a sense of awe when we consider the creation of this universe and we feel the greatness of its Creator, and the beauty of His creation. We feel safe and secure with this friendly universe in which God has placed us and with which He made our existence harmonious. We are overawed by its greatness and its elaborate systems, but we fear nothing. Nor do

---

5. Sir James Jeans, *The Mysterious Universe*, Cambridge University Press, 1931, pp. 2-3.

we experience any sense of loss or forthcoming destruction. The Lord of the universe is God, our Lord. With the universe we deal with ease, friendship and confidence. We expect to find in it provisions to sustain our life and comforts to make it more enjoyable. We hope to remain always grateful to God: "*We have established you firmly on earth and We have provided you there with means of livelihood. How seldom are you grateful.*" (Verse 10)

Man's Honour and Role

The second fact to be concluded from the story of the start of human life is that man is not only unique among living creatures, he is also noble and honoured. Moreover, a great task has been assigned to him. He moves within a wide expanse and deals with a variety of worlds, within the framework of his submission to God alone. This concept is diametrically opposed to man-made materialistic philosophies which ignore his role in the universe and give all importance to matter and its inevitable influence. It is also opposed to the theory of evolution which sends man down to the animal world and cares little for his unique and distinctive characteristics. Similarly, it is contrary to the Freudian philosophy which uses psychiatric analysis to depict man as totally lost in the quagmire of sex, to the extent that he can only sublimate himself through sexual behaviour. But the nobility and honour Islam assigns to man does not make of him a god, as he is depicted by the philosophical theories formulated in the Age of Enlightenment. The Islamic concept is distinguished by being factual and balanced at the same time.

Based on the import of all the Qur'ānic statements that speak of man's existence, we are more in favour of the view that man's existence was an independent one, but we cannot say that with absolute certainty. The birth of this unique species was announced in a great gathering witnessed by the Supreme Society. The announcement was made to this noble gathering and to the whole universe by God Almighty. In another account of this event, related in the second *sūrah,* man's mission as vicegerent on earth is also announced at the beginning of his creation. Then he faced his first test in heaven to prepare him for discharging the duties of vicegerency. Qur'ānic statements in other *sūrahs* also make it clear that God has made the whole universe, not only the earth, helpful to him. He has made all things in the heavens and on earth subservient to him.

In this we note the great task assigned to man by his Creator. To build life on a whole planet and to be in charge of it by God's will, regardless of the size of the planet, is certainly a great honour.

What appears from this story and from other statements in the Qur'ān, is that man is a unique creature, not only in respect of this planet of ours but also in the universe. Other worlds of creation like the angels and the *jinn*, and other types known only to God, have other tasks, and have been created with suitable natures that differ from that of man. Man has his own characteristics and tasks giving him a unique position in God's system of creation. This is further supported by God's statement in the Qur'ān: "*We offered Our trust to the heavens, and the earth, and the mountains, but they refused to bear it because they were afraid of it. Yet man took it up, for he has always been prone to be a wrongdoer and foolish.*" (33: 72) This makes man a species on his own, with unique characteristics which include being a wrongdoer and foolish. He has also been given freedom of choice within limits, the ability to learn and acquire progressive knowledge, and a free will of his own. He has the ability to maintain justice and acquire great knowledge in the same way as he has the ability to be unjust and sink into ignorance. This dual ability is indeed his distinctive quality.

All this shows how false is the view of man, based on the very small size of the planet on which we live, compared to other great entities in the universe. Size counts for little. The qualities of a knowledge-absorbing mind, a will that is independent, within the limits of submission to God, the freedom of choice and the ability to weigh up things are all far more important elements than the size of the earth upon which Sir James Jeans and others base their views of man and his role.

The importance which this story and other Qur'ānic statements give to mankind is not limited to man's role as vicegerent on earth, with all his unique characteristics. That importance is complemented by a careful look at the vastness of the world within which man moves to fulfil his task and the worlds with which he deals. To start with, he has a direct relationship with his Lord, limitless is He in His Glory. It is his Lord who made man with His own hand, and it is He who has announced his birth to the Supreme Society and throughout the universe, and then placed him in heaven to eat of its fruit as he pleases, with the exception of the forbidden tree. It is his Lord who then put him in charge of the earth and gave him the basis of knowledge, as related in *Sūrah* 2, The Cow, in which God states: "*He taught Adam the names of all things.*" (2: 31) We understand that statement as referring to man's ability to assign verbal symbols and names to matters and ideas. That is the basis which enables human beings to exchange knowledge and make it available throughout the human race. His Lord then gave him His instructions while still in Heaven and later after he came down to earth. He gave him all the abilities making the human race unique. He then sent him messengers with His guidance, and committed Himself to bestow mercy on man, forgive him his slips and accept his repentance. Indeed the blessings God has bestowed on this unique creation are endless.

Man also deals with the Supreme Society, for God has ordered the angels to prostrate themselves to him. He also assigned angels to guard man, and gave some of them the task of delivering revelations to His messengers. He sends down some of the angels to give happy news to those who declare that God is their Lord and maintain an attitude of obedience to Him. Angels are also sent to support those who fight for God's cause. He gives some angels the task of fighting unbelievers, killing them and taking away their souls. The dealings between angels and human beings continue in this life and in the life to come as well.

And man also deals with the *jinn*, whether believers or unbelievers. The Qur'ān portrays in vivid scenes the first battle between man and Satan. That battle still rages and will continue until the appointed day when the life of this world comes to an end. Man's dealing with the believers among the *jinn* is mentioned in other Qur'ānic statements. Making the *jinn* serve man is also stated clearly in the story of the Prophet Solomon (peace be upon him).

Man also deals with this material world, particularly the earth and the not-too-distant planets and stars. He is God's vicegerent placed in charge of the earth. God has made all potential sources, provisions and latent powers available to him. He has the ability to uncover some of its secrets, and identify some of its laws which help him in discharging his great role. Hence, he deals with all that lives on and in the earth. Finally, with his dual nature and ability, he has an unlimited scope within himself. He can be so sublime as to elevate himself above the rank of angels when he makes his submission to God pure, absolute. And he sinks down far below the level of animals when he makes himself subservient to his desire. For then he sheds his human characteristics and sinks into a bottomless pit. Between these two the gap is far greater than that separating the heavens from the earth in our material sense.

Nothing of all this is available to any creature other than man, as we understand from this story and other Qur'ānic accounts.

The Battle Rages On

The third fact which we can deduce from this story is that despite the uniqueness of man, or because of it, he is weak in certain aspects of his constitution. His weakness makes it possible for him to be led by his desire to evil and to bottomless depths. His two main weaknesses are his love of survival and his possessive desire. He is at his weakest when he leaves God's guidance and submits to his desire or to his sworn enemy who has taken it upon himself to try to seduce him and never let him go.

But God has shown His grace to man by not leaving him alone to carve his path on the basis of the dictates of his nature and reason without any further help. God has sent him messengers to remind and warn him, as we will see in a following verse. This represents man's salvation indeed. He is saved from his caprice and desire by turning to God, and he is saved from his enemy who flies away whenever man remembers his Lord and seeks His mercy and reward.

All these elements strengthen man's resolve and help him elevate himself above his desires and weaknesses. He received his first training in this area whilst still in heaven. He was told then that a particular tree was forbidden him. That training aimed to strengthen his will and to highlight its opposition to temptation and weakness. If he failed in his first experience, that experience should stand him in good stead in the future.

By the grace of God, the door of repentance and return remains open to man at every moment. Should he remember after a slip or a lapse of memory, and should he repent after having fallen into sin, then he finds the door open. God will accept his repentance and forgive him his slips. When he maintains the right path thereafter, God substitutes good deeds for bad ones and multiplies his reward as many times as He pleases. God has not made man's original sin a curse that chases him and his offspring, for there is simply no permanent, everlasting or inherited sin. No one bears the burden of another.

This basic element in the Islamic concept relieves mankind of the burden and the myth of original, inherited sin which forms the basis of Church concepts in Christianity. It also provides the basis for a great mass of rituals and superstitions. It depicts Adam as a sinner whose sin becomes a curse threatening mankind all the time. The only way to save man, according to this concept, is for God to take the form of the son of man, the Christ who, bearing the burden of atonement for this inherited sin, is allegedly crucified. Thus, forgiveness is granted only to those who are in communion with Jesus Christ who sacrificed himself to atone for Adam's sin inherited by his offspring.

The Islamic concept is much simpler and much easier. Adam forgot his instructions and slipped into sin, but he then repented and prayed for forgiveness. God accepted his repentance and forgave him. That puts an end to that first sin. What remains of it is the experience which helps mankind in its ongoing fight against sin and temptation. How simple, how clear and how easy.

The fourth and final conclusion to be derived from this story is that man's battle with Satan is real, serious and unabating. As it is related, the story tells us of the great persistence of this avowed enemy to chase man in all situations and to try to delude him at every moment and attack him from every corner: "*[Iblīs] said: 'Since You let me fall in error, I shall indeed lurk in ambush for them all along Your straight path, and I shall most certainly fall upon them from the front and from the rear, and from their right and from their left; and You will find most of them ungrateful.'*" (Verses 16-17) The evil one has chosen to be given a very long life in which to continue his wicked scheming. He opted for this wickedness in preference to turning to God in sincere repentance, praying to Him to forgive him his sin committed openly in public after he heard His command in person. He made it clear that he would lie in ambush for human beings trying to turn them away from God's path, and attack them from every corner in order to divert them from God's guidance.

Satan can only play on man's weaknesses and tempt him with fulfilling his desires. Man cannot protect himself against Satan except through consolidating his strength with faith and remembrance of God and by raising himself above desires and making these desires subject to the guidance he has received from God.

The battle with Satan is the major encounter, because it is a fight against desire through the following of divine guidance, and a fight against caprice through enhancing will-power, and a fight against evil and corruption to which Satan leads those who befriend him. It is a fight conducted through following the divine law which sets life on earth on the right path. This fight takes place within man's conscience and in his daily life, with the two linked together because Satan continues to stir the fight on both its fronts.

Tyrants who try to subjugate people to their rules, laws, standards and values and exclude those derived from divine faith are evil human beings who listen to the whispering of the evil ones among the *jinn*. The fight against those tyrants is the same as the fight against Satan himself.

This means that the major battle which rages on is that fought against Satan himself and those who befriend him. As a Muslim engages in the fight against his caprice and profane desires, against Satan's friends who tyrannize on earth, their servants and soldiers, and against the evil, corruption and immorality they spread in the land, he realizes that it is all a single, ferocious battle fought in earnest, because his enemy, Satan, is intent to fight him to the bitter end. Thus the fight goes on and *jihād*, or the struggle for God's cause, continues until the Day of Judgement, taking numerous forms and shapes.

Finally, the story and the comments that follow it refer to an intrinsic aspect of human nature, which makes man too shy to willingly appear naked: "*But Satan whispered to them both, so that he might show them their nakedness, of which they had previously been unaware.*" (Verse 20) "*Thus he cunningly deluded them. And when they both had tasted the fruit of the tree, their nakedness became apparent to them, and they began to cover themselves with leaves from the Garden.*" (Verse 22) "*Children of Adam, We have sent down to you clothing to cover your nakedness, and garments pleasing to the eye; but the robe of God-consciousness is the finest of all. In this there is a sign from God, so that they may reflect. Children of Adam, do not allow Satan to seduce you in the same way as he caused your (first) parents to be turned out of the Garden. He stripped them of their garment in order to make them aware of their nakedness.*" (Verses 26-27)

These verses emphasize the importance of this question showing that it touches on something deeply rooted in human nature. Clothing is not merely an adornment to man, but it also covers his physical nakedness, in the same way as fearing God covers his mental nakedness.

Sound, uncorrupted human nature abhors revealing its physical and mental nakedness. Those who try to persuade people to cast off their clothes and the garment of God-consciousness and fearing Him, in order to make them appear naked, unashamed, aim only to deprive man of some of his basic natural qualities. This attempt is supported by many who speak up or write or utilize the media in order to paint this nakedness as normal, using every means for this evil end. Their goal is to deprive man of some aspects of his humanity which distinguishes him from other creatures. They all want to put man at the mercy of his enemy, Satan, who has always wanted to undress him and expose his nakedness. Such people are only putting into practice some evil Zionist schemes, aiming to destroy humanity, and spread promiscuity so that all mankind submits without resistance to the kingdom of Zion, after they have lost their distinctive human characteristics.

Nakedness is a quality of animal nature. Man does not prefer nakedness except when he sinks down to a level below that which befits man. Those who find nakedness beautiful suffer from a distortion of human taste. Some primitive peoples in the heartland of Africa are always nude, but when Islam penetrates into these areas, the first aspect of civilization it imparts to them is that they start to wear clothes. In modern, 'progressive' *jāhiliyyah* people sink into the depths from which Islam rescues those who are backward and puts them on the road to civilization in the Islamic sense, which promotes the distinctive characteristics of man.

Psychological and mental nakedness, which sheds the sense of shame and fear of God, is strongly advocated by many people in the media, but it is simply a step back into *jāhiliyyah*. It is a far cry from the superior level of advancement and civilization, although its advocates try to depict it as so.

The story of the creation of man as told in the Qur'ān emphasizes these values and standards and explains them fully. We praise God for having guided us and saved us from following the whispers of Satan and rescued us from the quagmire of ignorance and *jāhiliyyah*.

3

Man's Finest Garment

Children of Adam, We have sent down to you clothing to cover your nakedness, and garments pleasing to the eye; but the robe of God-consciousness is the finest of all. In this there is a sign from God, so that they may reflect. (26)

يَـٰبَنِىٓ ءَادَمَ قَدْ أَنزَلْنَا عَلَيْكُمْ لِبَاسًا يُوَرِى سَوْءَٰتِكُمْ وَرِيشًا وَلِبَاسُ ٱلتَّقْوَىٰ ذَٰلِكَ خَيْرٌ ذَٰلِكَ مِنْ ءَايَٰتِ ٱللَّهِ لَعَلَّهُمْ يَذَّكَّرُونَ ﴿٢٦﴾

Children of Adam, do not allow Satan to seduce you in the same way as he caused your [first] parents to be turned out of the Garden. He stripped them of their garment in order to make them aware of their nakedness. Surely, he and his tribe watch you from where you cannot perceive them. We have made the devils as patrons for those who do not believe. (27)

يَـٰبَنِىٓ ءَادَمَ لَا يَفْتِنَنَّكُمُ ٱلشَّيْطَٰنُ كَمَآ أَخْرَجَ أَبَوَيْكُم مِّنَ ٱلْجَنَّةِ يَنزِعُ عَنْهُمَا لِبَاسَهُمَا لِيُرِيَهُمَا سَوْءَٰتِهِمَآ إِنَّهُۥ يَرَىٰكُمْ هُوَ وَقَبِيلُهُۥ مِنْ حَيْثُ لَا تَرَوْنَهُمْ إِنَّا جَعَلْنَا ٱلشَّيَٰطِينَ أَوْلِيَآءَ لِلَّذِينَ لَا يُؤْمِنُونَ ﴿٢٧﴾

When they commit a shameful deed, they say, "We found our fathers doing it," and, "God has enjoined it upon us." Say: "Never does God enjoin what is indecent. Would you attribute to God something of which you have no knowledge?" (28)

وَإِذَا فَعَلُوا۟ فَٰحِشَةً قَالُوا۟ وَجَدْنَا عَلَيْهَآ ءَابَآءَنَا وَٱللَّهُ أَمَرَنَا بِهَا قُلْ إِنَّ ٱللَّهَ لَا يَأْمُرُ بِٱلْفَحْشَآءِ أَتَقُولُونَ عَلَى ٱللَّهِ مَا لَا تَعْلَمُونَ ﴿٢٨﴾

Say: "My Lord has enjoined justice, and that you set your whole selves [to Him] at every time and place of prayer, and call on Him, sincere in your faith in Him alone. As it was He who brought you into being in the first instance, so also [to Him] you will return: (29)

قُلْ أَمَرَ رَبِّي بِٱلْقِسْطِ وَأَقِيمُواْ وُجُوهَكُمْ عِندَ كُلِّ مَسْجِدٍ وَٱدْعُوهُ مُخْلِصِينَ لَهُ ٱلدِّينَ كَمَا بَدَأَكُمْ تَعُودُونَ ٢٩

some [of you] He will have graced with His guidance, whereas for some a straying from the right path will have become unavoidable. For, they will have taken satans for their protectors in preference to God, thinking all the while that they have found the right path. (30)

فَرِيقًا هَدَىٰ وَفَرِيقًا حَقَّ عَلَيْهِمُ ٱلضَّلَٰلَةُ إِنَّهُمُ ٱتَّخَذُواْ ٱلشَّيَٰطِينَ أَوْلِيَآءَ مِن دُونِ ٱللَّهِ وَيَحْسَبُونَ أَنَّهُم مُّهْتَدُونَ ٣٠

Children of Adam, dress well when you attend any place of worship. Eat and drink but do not be wasteful. Surely He does not love the wasteful. (31)

يَٰبَنِىٓ ءَادَمَ خُذُواْ زِينَتَكُمْ عِندَ كُلِّ مَسْجِدٍ وَكُلُواْ وَٱشْرَبُواْ وَلَا تُسْرِفُوٓاْ إِنَّهُۥ لَا يُحِبُّ ٱلْمُسْرِفِينَ ٣١

Say, "Who is there to forbid the beauty which God has produced for His servants, and the wholesome means of sustenance? Say, They are [lawful] in the life of this world, to all who believe – to be theirs alone on the Day of Resurrection. Thus do We make Our revelations clear to people of knowledge. (32)

قُلْ مَنْ حَرَّمَ زِينَةَ ٱللَّهِ ٱلَّتِىٓ أَخْرَجَ لِعِبَادِهِۦ وَٱلطَّيِّبَٰتِ مِنَ ٱلرِّزْقِ قُلْ هِىَ لِلَّذِينَ ءَامَنُواْ فِى ٱلْحَيَوٰةِ ٱلدُّنْيَا خَالِصَةً يَوْمَ ٱلْقِيَٰمَةِ كَذَٰلِكَ نُفَصِّلُ ٱلْءَايَٰتِ لِقَوْمٍ يَعْلَمُونَ ٣٢

Say, My Lord has only forbidden shameful deeds, be they open or secret, and all types of sin, and wrongful oppression, and that you should associate with God anything for which He has given no authority, and that you attribute to God anything of which you have no knowledge. (33)

قُلْ إِنَّمَا حَرَّمَ رَبِّيَ ٱلْفَوَاحِشَ مَا ظَهَرَ مِنْهَا وَمَا بَطَنَ وَٱلْإِثْمَ وَٱلْبَغْيَ بِغَيْرِ ٱلْحَقِّ وَأَن تُشْرِكُوا بِٱللَّهِ مَا لَمْ يُنَزِّلْ بِهِۦ سُلْطَانًا وَأَن تَقُولُوا عَلَى ٱللَّهِ مَا لَا تَعْلَمُونَ ﴿٣٣﴾

For every community a term has been set. When [the end of] their term approaches, they can neither delay nor hasten it by a single moment. (34)

وَلِكُلِّ أُمَّةٍ أَجَلٌ فَإِذَا جَآءَ أَجَلُهُمْ لَا يَسْتَأْخِرُونَ سَاعَةً وَلَا يَسْتَقْدِمُونَ ﴿٣٤﴾

Overview

This passage provides a pause for comment, which is one of a few instances in this *sūrah*. It is a long pause after the first scene in the great story of mankind. A similar pause is made at the end of every stage, as if we are told: let us stop here to reflect on the lessons of the previous epoch before we go further on our unique journey.

This pause comes at the beginning of the battle which is about to rage between Satan and man. It is meant as a warning against Satan's schemes and exposes the numerous ways and fashions his scheming may take. But the Qur'ān does not issue any directive unless it is needed to face a practical situation, and does not relate a story unless it is relevant to the day-to-day life of the Islamic movement. It does not relate a story for the sake of literary enjoyment, and does not state a fact only to place it in a theoretical context. Islam is serious and practical, and its statements and directives are meant only to deal with realities which the Islamic movement may have to face.

This comment on the story of man's fall from heaven is given here by way of facing up to the Arabian *jāhiliyyah* when, prior to the advent of Islam, the Quraysh, the major tribe in Arabia, had claimed for itself certain rights against the unbelievers of the rest of Arabia who went to

Makkah for pilgrimage and paid homage to the idols which were placed in the Ka'bah. The Quraysh based its claims on concepts which it alleged to be part of the divine faith. It formulated these in laws, claiming them to be part of the divine law. How else could the Quraysh have won acceptance to its claim by the rest of Arabia? It had to resort to the same tactics followed by priests, chiefs and leaders in every ignorant community. The Quraysh gave itself a special name, al-Ḥums, and claimed for itself special privileges, some of which relate to the ritual of *ṭawāf*, which takes the form of walking round the Ka'bah, the first house ever to be dedicated for worshipping God. They claimed that al-Ḥums, or the Qurayshīs, were the only people to have the privilege of doing *ṭawāf* wearing ordinary clothes. The rest of the Arabs could not do *ṭawāf* wearing clothes that had previously been worn. Instead, they had to borrow clothes from al-Ḥums people, or wear brand new clothing. Otherwise, they had to do *ṭawāf* in the nude, even though they had their women with them.

In his commentary on the Qur'ān, Ibn Kathīr states:

> The Arabs, other than the Quraysh, did not do *ṭawāf* around the Ka'bah wearing clothes that they had already used. Their argument was that they could not do *ṭawāf* wearing clothes that they had worn when committing disobedience to God. The Quraysh, who called themselves al-Ḥums, were the only ones to wear their ordinary garments when they did *ṭawāf*. If anyone was able to borrow a garment from a Qurayshī man, he could use it for *ṭawāf*.
>
> Anyone who had a brand new garment could also use it in *ṭawāf*, provided that he threw it away on finishing his ritual and that no one else used it afterwards. Otherwise, he had to do *ṭawāf* naked. Even women were naked when they did *ṭawāf*, but they could partially cover their private parts. However, women mostly did tawaf at night. This was something they invented, following the footsteps of their fathers, and believing that what their fathers did was based on divine orders. God reproached them for that, saying: "*When they commit a shameful deed, they say, 'We found our fathers doing it,' and, 'God has enjoined it upon us.'*" (Verse 28) In reply God tells His Messenger, Muḥammad, to answer their claims by saying: "*Never does God enjoin what is indecent. Would you attribute to God something of which you have no knowledge?*" (Verse 28)

Thus, he condemns their practice as unacceptable indecency. God would never enjoin anything like that: "*Would you attribute to God something of which you have no knowledge?*" Would you allege that God has said something when you do not know it to be correct? God also instructs His Messenger to tell his people that He only orders justice, the maintaining of the right path and sincere devotion: "*Say: My Lord has enjoined justice, and that you set your whole selves [to Him] at every time and place of prayer, and call on Him, sincere in your faith in Him alone.*" (Verse 29) That is to say that wherever you wish to worship God, you have to be sincere in your worship, following in the footsteps of messengers to whom God gave miracles to endorse the laws they gave you. Moreover, you have to be truly sincere in your worship, because God does not accept any action unless it combines these two essentials: that it is in line with His law and dedicated purely to Him alone:[1]

To deal with this practical state of ignorance and its manifestations in the shape of regulations for worship, *ṭawāf* and dress, as well as similar traditions concerning food, and all that is claimed to be part of God's law, the Qur'ān gives these comments on the first stage in the life of humanity. This stage involves the permission to eat of the fruit of the garden of heaven, except for what God has forbidden, and mentions man's need to have clothes. We have learned how Satan seduced Adam and his wife and persuaded them to eat of the forbidden tree in order to expose their nakedness. Their natural shyness is also mentioned and the fact that they tried to cover their nakedness with leaves.

What is related of the events of the story and the comments made on those events are thus meant as an answer to a particular situation that prevails in an ignorant community. The story is mentioned elsewhere in the Qur'ān, addressing other situations. Every time certain scenes and events are emphasized in order to give comments and statements that relate to those other situations. Everything that is mentioned is true and accurate but the choice is made at each time to confront a relevant situation. Thus harmony is established on every occasion with the subject matter to be emphasized.

Children of Adam, We have sent down to you clothing to cover your nakedness, and garments pleasing to the eye; but the robe of God-

---

1. Ibn Kathīr, *Tafsīr al-Qur'ān al-'Aẓīm*, Beirut, Vol. 2, pp. 193-194

consciousness is the finest of all. In this there is a sign from God, so that they may reflect. (Verse 26)

This address contrasts with the scene of exposed nakedness and the patching up of leaves from the garden to cover that nakedness. That exposure came as a result of disobeying an express order given by God and eating something He had forbidden. It is not the sin mentioned in certain legends which has inspired endless artistic images in the West as also Freud's poisonous suggestions. That sin was not eating the fruits of the tree of knowledge, as claimed in the legend of the Old Testament.

There is no truth in the absurd claim that God felt jealous of man and feared that he would eat of the tree of life and become a God as well. Nor is the sin the sexual pleasure around which much of the European artistic imagery is concentrated in order to interpret all life activities in terms of sexual pleasure as Freud's disciples try to affirm.

A Warning to Be Always Heeded

In contrast to the nakedness that followed Adam's sin we have here a fitting reply to the arbitrary impositions of nakedness practised by the unbelievers in the days of ignorance in Arabia. In His address, God reminds people of His grace as He taught them and made things easy for them, and made it a law for them that they should wear garments to cover their nakedness so that they replace naked ugliness with the beauty of dressing up. In the Arabic text, the term used here for dressing with clothes, "*We have sent down to you clothing*", is often used to denote 'revelation'. This gives the Qur'ānic statement added connotations so as to mean, "We have legislated in the revelations We have sent down to you, etc." The term used in the Arabic text for 'clothing' may denote underwear which covers the private parts, and may also denote general clothing, and the term denoting 'garments' gives the sense of top outfits normally selected for their beautiful appearance. It may also connote wealth and comfortable living. These meanings often go hand in hand:

> *Children of Adam, We have sent down to you clothing to cover your nakedness, and garments pleasing to the eye.* (Verse 26) This is followed by a mention of the robe of piety, described here as 'fine': *But the robe of God-consciousness is the finest of all. In this there is a sign from God, so that they may reflect.* (Verse 26)

'Abd al-Raḥmān ibn Aslam, an early scholar, says: "When a person fears God, he covers his nakedness. Thus he clothes himself with the robe of piety." In divine law, then, there is a close relationship between garments that a person wears to cover his nakedness and to give himself a fine appearance on the one hand and fearing God and being pious on the other. Both are garments, with one covering mental or abstract nakedness and the other physical nakedness. Both give a human being a fine appearance and both go together. When a person is conscious of God and feels ashamed to appear in a way which is unpleasing to Him, he feels physical nakedness to be abhorrent and shies away from it. On the other hand, a person who feels no sense of shame in front of God and does not fear Him is one who does not hesitate to appear naked or to call people to do likewise. Being modest and covering one's body are not matters of social tradition, as claimed by those who try to destroy the humanity of people by attacking their sense of shame and chastity in order to carry out the wicked designs of the Protocol of the Elders of Zion. To have a sense of shame is something that God has implanted in human nature and embodied in His law which He sent down to be implemented in human life. He has made them able to implement this law by giving them talents, abilities and provisions.

God reminds the children of Adam of His grace as He requires them to cover their nakedness with dress in order to protect their humanity against sinking to the level of animals. Everything He has facilitated for them is also an aspect of His grace. He reminds them of it *"so that they may reflect."* (Verse 26) A Muslim, then should never overlook the clear link between the attacks on people's morality and sense of shame while calling for physical nudity in the name of friendliness and civilization, and the Zionist scheme which aims to destroy their humanity and spread immorality as a prelude to forcing them to submit to Zion's power. He should also realize that there is a direct link between all this and the schemes trying to uproot even the vague religious sentiments that remain in the hearts of Muslim people. Even these vague sentiments are not tolerated. The aim is to eradicate them all. Hence, a wicked and shameless campaign advocating physical and mental nudity is launched with the support of writers and media working in the service of world Zionism. Human beauty is that of dress and cover while animal beauty is that of nudity. Human beings in this day and age are sinking into the depth of ignorant reaction that sends them down to the level of animals. Hence they do not remember God's grace which enables them to protect and maintain their humanity.

> *Children of Adam, do not allow Satan to seduce you in the same way as he caused your [first] parents to be turned out of the Garden. He stripped them of their garment in order to make them aware of their nakedness. Surely, he and his tribe watch you from where you cannot perceive them. We have made the devils as patrons for those who do not believe. When they commit a shameful deed, they say, "We found our fathers doing it," and, "God has enjoined it upon us." Say: Never does God enjoin what is indecent. Would you attribute to God something of which you have no knowledge? Say: My Lord has enjoined justice, and that you set your whole selves [to Him] at every time and place of prayer, and call on Him, sincere in your faith in Him alone. As it was He who brought you into being in the first instance, so also [to Him] you will return: some [of you] He will have graced with His guidance, whereas for some a straying from the right path will have become unavoidable. For, they will have taken satans for their protectors in preference to God, thinking all the while that they have found the right path. (Verses 27-30)*

This is the second address to the children of Adam in this passage. It provides comments on the story of their first parents and their experience with Satan, and the scene of nakedness in which he placed them after they had forgotten their Lord's commandment and listened to this wicked whispering. This address becomes easier to understand when we bear in mind the traditions of pagan Arabia, particularly those relating to the nudity imposed by the people of Makkah on the rest of the Arabs in *ṭawāf* rituals. What made their action worse was that they alleged that the practices of their fathers must be part of religion and must have been ordered by God.

The first address to the children of Adam speaks of the affliction caused to their first father, and of God's grace when He ordered human beings to wear clothes, to cover their nakedness, and gave them fine garments pleasing to the eye. In this second address there is a warning to human beings in general and most directly to the pagans whom Islam addressed at the time of its revelation. This warning makes it clear to them that they must not obey Satan in whatever laws they enact for themselves and any traditions they may observe. If they do, he will certainly seduce them just as he seduced their first parents when he caused them to be driven out of heaven and exposed their nakedness showing them what had previously been hidden. Hence revealing much of the body, which is characteristic of all ignorant societies, past and present, is the direct result of listening to Satan's whisperings. He is a most persistent enemy who utilizes nudity to achieve his goal of seducing Adam and his offspring. This is part of the unabating battle that rages on between man and Satan. Human beings, then, should be wise enough not to allow their enemy to seduce them. For his victory means that he will cause hell to be filled with a great many of mankind.

When the Enemy is the Protector

In order to emphasize the urgency of His warning, their Lord tells mankind that Satan and his tribe can see them whereas they cannot see or perceive satans. Satan, then, has a greater ability to seduce them, utilizing his subtle means. They need to be on their guard all the time so that they are not taken unawares: "*Surely, he and his tribe watch you from where you cannot perceive them.*" (Verse 27) Then follows an increased heightening of the effect by saying that God has allowed a relationship of patronage to develop between satans and unbelievers. Doomed indeed is the one whose patron is his enemy. For this enables his enemy to direct him the way he wishes, when he has no real help or support and cannot resort to God's patronage since he is an unbeliever: "*We have made the devils as patrons for those who do not believe.*" (Verse 27)

It is a true fact that Satan is the patronizing friend of the non-believers, while God is the protector of believers.

The effect of this state of affairs is far-reaching, but it is mentioned here in absolute terms before the pagans are given an example of its operation in their real world. We are thus made to feel how Satan's patronage can distort people's concepts and ruin their lives: "*When they commit a shameful deed, they say, 'We found our fathers doing it,' and, 'God has enjoined it upon us.'*" (Verse 28)

That was indeed what the pagan Arabs used to do and say. They performed *ṭawāf* around God's sacred house in the nude, accompanying their women. This they claimed God had ordered them to do, just as He had ordered their fathers: in other words, they inherited the practice from them. Despite their paganism, the Arabs did not make boastful claims similar to those used by people of latter day ignorance who wonder why religion should interfere with human life. They claim that they are the only ones who have any authority to enact laws, develop values and standards, and endorse habits and traditions while the pagan Arabs used to make their false inventions and claim that God ordered them to do so. That may be a more sly and cunning method because it deceives those who still maintain some religious sentiment to the extent that they imagine that their practices are acceptable to God. Nevertheless, it is less impudent than the attitude of those who claim that they have the right to enact legislation in preference to God's.

God commands the Prophet Muḥammad (peace be upon him) to make it clear to them that their inventions are false and that their claims to have God's endorsement are insupportable. He is further ordered to declare that God's law is incompatible with indecency. God would not command anything that is indecent: "*Say: Never does God enjoin what is indecent. Would you attribute to God something of which you have no knowledge?*" (Verse 28)

The word 'indecency' refers to any act which goes beyond the limits of what is acceptable. Nudity is one such act. Hence, God does not enjoin it, for how would He enjoin the transgression of the limits He laid down, and the violation of His orders to cover one's nakedness and to be always modest and God-fearing? Besides, who told them that God enjoined that? What God orders and enjoins cannot be the subject of unsupported claims. These are contained in the Books He has revealed to His messengers. There is simply no other source from which to learn what God says and enjoins. No one can describe any matter as belonging to divine law unless he can rely on a statement in the divine book or by God's Messenger. This is the only way to know for certain what God enjoins. If everyone claims that whatever he sees fit belongs to God's law, then humanity will end up in endless chaos.

Jāhiliyyah is a state of ignorance that always maintains its essential characteristics. Every time people revert to *jāhiliyyah*, they make similar allegations and uphold similar concepts despite the great differences in time and place.

In the *jāhiliyyah* of our contemporary times, we find that every now and then a liar comes up with whatever whims he has and claims that they belong to God's law. Time after time, a shameless impudent person, stands up to deny the clearly stated divine orders and commandments, claiming that divine religion could not order this or that. He has no justification for his claim other than his own prejudices. Hence the rhetorical question: "*Would you attribute to God something of which you have no knowledge?*" (Verse 28)

Having denounced their claims that God has ordered them to follow such indecent practices, God tells them that His commandments run in the opposite direction. God has enjoined justice and moderation in all matters, not indecency. He has also ordered people to follow what He has laid down in matters of worship, and to derive their laws and values from what He has revealed to His Messenger. He has not left matters disorganized, allowing everyone to state what he wants and then claim that his prejudices are endorsed by God. He has also commanded that submission to Him should be pure and complete so that no one submits to anyone else.

> *Say: My Lord has enjoined justice, and that you set your whole selves [to Him] at every time and place of prayer, and call on Him, sincere in your faith in Him alone.* (Verse 29)

This is what God has enjoined. It runs opposite to their practices in which they follow their fathers and implement their man-made laws. It is also contrary to exposing one's nakedness after God has given human beings, out of His grace, clothing to cover themselves and garments with which they appear beautiful. Furthermore, it is contrary to having two different sources of reference in their lives, one for law-making and another for worship; for that is a practical form of associating partners with God.

At this point they are given a reminder and a warning. They should always remember that they will return to God after they have finished their present life which is meant as a test for them. When they return to God they will be in two groups: those who followed God's commandments and those who followed Satan: "*As it was He who brought you into being in the first instance, so also [to Him] you will return: some [of you] He will have graced with His guidance, whereas for some a straying from the right path will have become unavoidable. For, they will have taken satans for their protectors in preference to God, thinking all the while that they have found the right path.*" (Verses 29-30)

This is a remarkable picture showing the starting point and the finishing line in the great journey of life: "*As it was He who brought*

you into being in the first instance, so also [to Him] you will return."
(Verse 29)

When they started the journey, they were in two groups: Adam and his wife in one group, and Satan and his tribe in the other. They will return in the same classification: the obedient will return together with their father, Adam, and their mother, Eve, who were both believers, submitting themselves to God, and following His commandments. In the other group, the disobedient will return together with Satan and his tribe and they will fill Hell because of their mutual patronage of Satan. What is singular is that these people always think that they follow the right path.

God guides whoever seeks His patronage, and He leaves anyone who takes Satan for patron to go astray. In the end they come back to their different destinations: *"some [of you] He will have graced with His guidance, whereas for some a straying from the right path will have become unavoidable. For, they will have taken satans for their protectors in preference to God, thinking all the while that they have found the right path."* (Verse 30)

Forbidding What Is Lawful

A new address is now made to mankind, serving as a pause to comment on the events related earlier before resuming the main theme in the *sūrah*: *"Children of Adam, dress well when you attend any place of worship. Eat and drink but do not be wasteful. Surely He does not love the wasteful. Say, Who is there to forbid the beauty which God has produced for His servants, and the wholesome means of sustenance? Say, 'They are [lawful] in the life of this world, to all who believe – to be theirs alone on the Day of Resurrection.' Thus do We make Our revelations clear to people of knowledge. Say, My Lord has only forbidden shameful deeds, be they open or secret, and all types of sin, and wrongful oppression, and that you should associate with God anything for which He has given no authority, and that you attribute to God anything of which you have no knowledge."* (Verses 31-33)

In this address, we note the emphasis on the basic principle of faith in order to stress the falsehood of the practices of the pagan Arabs. One of the clearest examples is to link their arbitrary prohibition of good wholesome things God has provided for His servants with ascribing partners to God. This is indeed the proper description of anyone who falsely claims the authority to make such a prohibition, attributing to God things of which he has no knowledge.

God tells mankind to don their best clothes, which He has given them and taught them how to make, whenever they attend to any act of worship, including *ṭawāf*, which means walking round the Ka'bah glorifying God, acknowledging His Lordship and asking Him to grant our wishes. Those Arabs used to do *ṭawāf* naked, forbidding themselves the wearing of any garments when God did not forbid them that. On the contrary, He made the provision of such clothes an aspect of His grace. The proper thing to be expected is that they should obey Him and make use of what He has given them, not taking off their clothing in a grossly indecent manner: "*Children of Adam, dress well when you attend any place of worship.*" (Verse 31) He also tells them to enjoy the wholesome provisions He has given them, without being extravagant: "*Eat and drink but do not be wasteful. Surely He does not love the wasteful.*" (Verse 31)

It has been reported that the Arabs also used to forbid themselves certain types of food in a similar manner to their prohibition of certain types of clothing. All these were inventions perpetrated by the Quraysh, the ruling tribe in Makkah.

In an authentic report related by Muslim on the authority of 'Urwah who quotes his father, a companion of the Prophet, as saying: "The Arabs used to do *ṭawāf* around the Ka'bah completely naked with the exception of the Ḥums, a title given to the Quraysh people and their descendants. They would go around the Sacred House in the nude unless they wore clothes given them by the Ḥums. Some of the men of Quraysh might give some of their clothes to other men and their women might give to other women. During pilgrimage, the Ḥums would stay at Muzdalifah, going no further, while the rest of the pilgrims would go as far as 'Arafāt. They justified this by saying: 'We, the Quraysh, are the dwellers of the Ḥaram (i.e. the sacred area). No person from the rest of Arabia may do *ṭawāf* wearing any clothes other than our clothes or eating any food other than ours.' Thus, any Arab who did not have a friend in Makkah to lend him a garment, or did not have the money to hire such a garment, faced the choice of either doing *ṭawāf* naked or wearing his own clothes which he must throw away after he completed his *ṭawāf*. No one else was allowed to touch those clothes after they had been thrown away. Such clothes were considered as discarded clothes, or *liqā*."

In his commentary known as *Aḥkām al-Qur'ān*, al-Qurṭubī, a famous scholar, says: "It has been reported that in pre-Islamic days, the Arabs used not to eat any rich food during their pilgrimage, limiting themselves only to eating very little, and they used to do *ṭawāf* naked. They were told: '*Dress well when you attend any place of worship. Eat and drink but do not be wasteful.*' (Verse 31) This is a clear indication that they must not forbid themselves what is lawful. From the linguistic point of view, the term used for 'being wasteful' could mean extravagance and could also denote the prohibition of what is lawful. In each case, the practice involves going beyond the proper limits."

The *sūrah* does not stop at calling on people to dress well when they attend to any act of worship or to enjoy wholesome food and elegant dress. It censures the prohibitions of such adornment which God has provided for His servants as well as the prohibition of wholesome provisions. The authority to prohibit any thing belongs only to God who has given us the details of what He has forbidden and what He has made lawful in the legal code He has enacted for human life. "*Say: Who is there to forbid the beauty which God has produced for His servants, and the wholesome means of sustenance?*" (Verse 32)

This clear disapproval is followed by a statement making clear that such adornment and means of sustenance are for the enjoyment of believers on account of their belief in God, their Lord, who has produced them for the believers. If such matters are also made available in this life to unbelievers, they will be reserved exclusively for believers on the Day of Resurrection. Unbelievers will have no share in them: "*Say, They are [lawful] in the life of this world, to all who believe – to be theirs alone on the Day of Resurrection.*" (Verse 32) This could not have been the case if such adornments and provisions were forbidden. God would not have given them something forbidden to be theirs alone in the life to come. "*Thus do We make Our revelations clear to people of knowledge.*" (Verse 32) Indeed, those who know the essence of this faith well are the ones to benefit by this explanation.

God has certainly forbidden neither what is reasonable of adornment and clothing nor wholesome food and drink. What He has truly forbidden is what those unbelievers used to practise: "*Say: My Lord has only forbidden shameful deeds, be they open or secret, and all types of sin, and wrongful oppression, and that you should associate with God anything for which He has given no authority, and that you attribute to God anything of which you have no knowledge.*" (Verse 33)

This is in a nutshell the total sum of what God has forbidden. It includes every excess that goes beyond the limits God has laid down, whether committed openly or in secret. It also includes sin, which denotes every disobedience to God, and oppression, which denotes every type of injustice or violation of other people's rights which God has made clear to all. It further includes ascribing the qualities of Godhead to any being other than God. This includes what used to be practised in ignorant Arabia and what happens in every ignorant society when people accept legislation from any source other than God. God has also forbidden that people should attribute to God something of which they have no knowledge. This includes, by way of example, what they used to assert of prohibition and attributing that to God Himself without any true or sound basis.

A most amazing example of the reaction of the unbelievers who were the first to be addressed by these verses, considering the denunciation of their false prohibitions, is given by al-Kalbī, a renowned scholar in the early generations of Islam: "When Muslims went on their *ṭawāf* around the Ka'bah wearing their clothes, the unbelievers criticized their action and ridiculed them. This verse was then revealed to answer their ridicules. This is a most amazing example of how ignorance can twist human logic. Here we have human beings who go around the sacred house of worship in the nude. Their nature has been corrupted and moved far away from sound human nature to which the Qur'ān refers in the story of Adam and Eve and their experience in heaven: *"When they both had tasted the fruit of the tree, their nakedness became apparent to them, and they began to cover themselves with leaves from the Garden."* (Verse 22) But when these unbelievers see the Muslims doing their worship around the Ka'bah wearing their clothes, they criticize and ridicule them. Yet what have the Muslims done except put on their garments which God has given them. He wants them to appear dignified and well covered, so that their sound human qualities are given a chance to grow and be firmly established, and animal nakedness becomes abhorrent to them."

Such is the effect of ignorance, or *jāhiliyyah*, on people. It distorts their nature, taste, concepts and values. If we look at the *jāhiliyyah* prevailing today in our world we find that it affects people in the same way as the pre-Islamic ignorance affected the pagan Arabs, Greeks, Romans, Persians and all other pagan nations. Modern *jāhiliyyah* also fools people so that they take off their clothes and shed their sense of shame. Moreover, it describes that as progress and civilization. Chaste Muslim women are described as reactionary and old fashioned, simply because they maintain their standard of propriety when they appear in public. It is the same twisted logic which distorts human nature and turns values and standards upside down. It is also coupled with the same type of arrogance that insists on adhering to what is false and what is unlawful. It is as the Qur'ān says: "*Have they, perchance, handed down this [way of thinking] as a legacy to one another? Nay, they are filled with overweening arrogance.*" (51: 53)

Distortion of Concepts and Values

The question that arises here concerns the link between such nakedness, twisted logic, overweening arrogance by associating partners with God and accepting laws from deities other than God.

Those pagan Arabs received their notions concerning their nakedness from false lords who were able to fool them and manipulate their ignorance to ensure their supremacy in Arabia remained unchallenged. Other ancient *jāhiliyyah* societies followed the same pattern and received their notions from their priests and chiefs. The same applies to the unbelievers of today who cannot challenge the concepts that false lords are keen to establish.

Fashion houses and designers, and cosmetic manufacturers and sellers are the lords who advocate the stupidity which is blindly followed by men and women in the *jāhiliyyah* societies of today. Those lords have only to set their standards, and they are slavishly obeyed by the multitude of fools throughout the world. Whether this year's fashion or the cosmetics in vogue are suitable to a particular woman or not, she must still obey, or be subjected to the ridicule of other fools who have no say in their own affairs.

It is important to ask who controls those fashion houses and cosmetic companies? Who feeds the campaign promoting nakedness? Who promotes all those films, pictures, novels, magazines and papers that are in the forefront of this campaign? Some of these are nothing less than an epitomized brothel. Indeed it is important to ask, who controls all this? The answer is that the main control is in the hands of Zionism. It is the Zionist Jews who usurp the qualities of God's lordship, subjugating all these fools to their bidding. They achieve their aims, for which they organize sustained campaigns throughout the world, trying to keep the whole world preoccupied with such filth. They try hard to spread immorality and corrupt human nature so that it can be moulded by fashion designers and cosmetic manufacturers. Beyond that, they also have economic objectives which they achieve through the wasteful usage of dress material, cosmetics and other ancillary products.

The question of dress and fashion is not separate from God's law and the way of life He has laid down for mankind. Hence, it is linked in the *sūrah* to the question of faith. There are indeed several aspects linking it to faith and divine law. It has, first of all, a direct relationship with the question of Lordship and the authority which has the power to issue legislation in these matters that have a profound influence on morals, the economy and other aspects of life. Fashion and dress also have a direct bearing on enhancing the human qualities in man and giving them prominence over carnal qualities.

Jāhiliyyah distorts concepts, values and tastes, making nakedness, which is an animal quality, an aspect of progress and advancement, while considering propriety backward and old fashioned. There can be no clearer distortion of human nature.

We find some people advocating such *jāhiliyyah* and protesting: what has religion got to do with fashion, cosmetics and how women dress? This is only the twisted logic that is characteristic of *jāhiliyyah* everywhere and in all generations.

Because this question, which often appears to be only a side issue, has such great importance in the Islamic view – since it relates to the question of faith and to promoting sound human nature and proper human values – the *sūrah* concludes its discussion with a very strong and inspiring comment that is normally used with major issues of faith. The comment reminds human beings that their term on earth is limited, and that when it draws to a close, they cannot delay or hasten it at all: "*For every community a term has been set. When [the end of] their term approaches, they can neither delay nor hasten it by a single moment.*" (Verse 34)

This is a basic concept of faith which serves here as a reminder so that dormant hearts wake up and realize that they must not let themselves be deluded by an apparently unending life.

The term mentioned in this verse could apply to the end of every generation, which is determined by death, or the term that is allowed for every nation to be strong and prosperous. Whichever meaning we apply to the Qur'ānic verse, the term is pre-determined, and they cannot either delay their deadline or hasten it.

Before we finish our commentary on this passage, we better remind ourselves of the great similarity in how the Qur'ān deals with *jāhiliyyah* concepts, whether they relate to slaughtered animals, what is lawful of them and what is forbidden, as explained in the previous *sūrah*, and the way it deals with ignorance and its arbitrary concepts concerning dress and food.

When the previous *sūrah* discussed the question of slaughtered animals and crops that are pledged for certain purposes, it explained the practices of the Arabian *jāhiliyyah* society and its false claims that such practices were sanctioned by God. It then challenged them to produce evidence supporting their claim that God has forbidden what they claimed to be forbidden and made lawful what they considered as such: "*Is it, perchance, that you were witnesses when God gave you these commandments? Who could be more wicked than one who, without any real knowledge, invents lies about God in order to lead people astray? God does not guide the wrongdoers.*" (6: 144) It then confronted them face to face when they tried to evade giving a proper answer, claiming that it all belonged to God's will, and that it was God's will that caused them to maintain their practices: "*Those who associate partners with God will say: 'Had God so willed, neither we nor our fathers would have associated any partners with Him; nor would we have declared anything as forbidden.' In like manner did those who have lived before them deny the truth, until they came to taste Our punishment. Say: 'Have you any certain knowledge which you can put before us? You follow nothing but conjecture, and you do nothing but guess. Say: With God alone rests the final evidence. Had He so willed, He would have guided you all aright. Say: Bring forward your witnesses who will testify that God has forbidden this. If they so testify, do not you testify with them; and do not follow the wishes of those who deny Our revelations, and those who do not believe in the life to come and who consider others as equal to their Lord.*" (6: 148-150)

When *Sūrah* 6 has totally refuted their false claims, it offers to give them a detailed account of what God has ordered them to do and what He has forbidden them. It proceeds to outline such prohibitions in three very clear verses: 151-153.

This *sūrah* follows the same pattern. First it describes their indecent practices, promoting nakedness and associating partners with God.

Thus, they assume for themselves the authority to pronounce certain types of dress and food as lawful or forbidden. It then warns them against these, reminding them of the painful lessons their first parents learned in heaven and their suffering as a result of Satan's scheming against them. It also reminds them of God's grace, as He has provided them with fine garments. It denounces their claims that what they practised was part of God's law: "*Say, Who is there to forbid the beauty which God has produced for His servants, and the wholesome means of sustenance? Say, They are [lawful] in the life of this world, to all who believe – to be theirs alone on the Day of Resurrection. Thus do We make Our revelations clear to people of knowledge.*" (Verse 32) This is coupled with a reference to the absolutely certain knowledge upon which concepts of faith, acts of worship and laws must be established. When all their claims have been refuted, the *sūrah* reiterates what God has actually forbidden: "*Say, My Lord has only forbidden shameful deeds, be they open or secret, and all types of sin, and wrongful oppression, and that you should associate with God anything for which He has given no authority, and that you attribute to God anything of which you have no knowledge.*" (Verse 33) Prior to that, the *sūrah* clarified divine instructions concerning dress and food: "*Children of Adam, dress well when you attend any place of worship. Eat and drink but do not be wasteful.*" (Verse 31)

In both types of confrontation, the whole question is linked directly to the question of faith. This is due to the fact that in essence, the question is that of sovereignty and to whom it belongs, and people's servitude and to whom it should be addressed. It is the same question, treated in the same manner, following the same steps. This unity of approach appears to be much more important when we remember the different natures of the two *sūrahs* and the scope each of them takes in dealing with the question of faith. That difference of scope does not affect the adoption of the same approach in dealing with basic questions and the confrontation with *jāhiliyyah* over these questions. Limitless is God in His glory who has revealed this Qur'ān.

4

Much Pleading, Little Use

Children of Adam! Whenever there come to you messengers from among yourselves to relate to you My revelations, then those who are conscious of Me and live righteously shall have nothing to fear, nor shall they grieve. (35)

But those who deny and scorn Our revelations are the ones destined for the fire, where they shall abide. (36)

Who is more wicked than one who invents lies about God or denies His revelations? These shall have whatever has been decreed to be their lot [in life]. When Our messengers come to carry off their souls, they will say: "Where, now, are those whom you used to invoke besides God?" They will reply: "They have forsaken us!" Thus, they will bear witness against themselves that they had been unbelievers. (37)

يَٰبَنِىٓ ءَادَمَ إِمَّا يَأْتِيَنَّكُمْ رُسُلٌ مِّنكُمْ يَقُصُّونَ عَلَيْكُمْ ءَايَٰتِى فَمَنِ ٱتَّقَىٰ وَأَصْلَحَ فَلَا خَوْفٌ عَلَيْهِمْ وَلَا هُمْ يَحْزَنُونَ ٣٥

وَٱلَّذِينَ كَذَّبُوا۟ بِـَٔايَٰتِنَا وَٱسْتَكْبَرُوا۟ عَنْهَآ أُو۟لَٰٓئِكَ أَصْحَٰبُ ٱلنَّارِ هُمْ فِيهَا خَٰلِدُونَ ٣٦

فَمَنْ أَظْلَمُ مِمَّنِ ٱفْتَرَىٰ عَلَى ٱللَّهِ كَذِبًا أَوْ كَذَّبَ بِـَٔايَٰتِهِۦٓ أُو۟لَٰٓئِكَ يَنَالُهُمْ نَصِيبُهُم مِّنَ ٱلْكِتَٰبِ حَتَّىٰٓ إِذَا جَآءَتْهُمْ رُسُلُنَا يَتَوَفَّوْنَهُمْ قَالُوٓا۟ أَيْنَ مَا كُنتُمْ تَدْعُونَ مِن دُونِ ٱللَّهِ قَالُوا۟ ضَلُّوا۟ عَنَّا وَشَهِدُوا۟ عَلَىٰٓ أَنفُسِهِمْ أَنَّهُمْ كَانُوا۟ كَٰفِرِينَ ٣٧

[God] will say: "Enter into the fire to join the hosts of the *jinn* and humans who have gone before you." Every time a host enters [the fire], it will curse its fellow host. When all are gathered there, the last of them will say of the first: "Our Lord, these are the ones who have led us astray, so give them double suffering in the fire." He will answer: "Every one of you shall have double suffering, although you may not know it." (38)

قَالَ ادْخُلُوا فِي أُمَمٍ قَدْ خَلَتْ مِن قَبْلِكُم مِّنَ ٱلْجِنِّ وَٱلْإِنسِ فِي ٱلنَّارِ كُلَّمَا دَخَلَتْ أُمَّةٌ لَّعَنَتْ أُخْتَهَا حَتَّىٰ إِذَا ٱدَّارَكُوا فِيهَا جَمِيعًا قَالَتْ أُخْرَاهُمْ لِأُولَاهُمْ رَبَّنَا هَٰٓؤُلَآءِ أَضَلُّونَا فَآتِهِمْ عَذَابًا ضِعْفًا مِّنَ ٱلنَّارِ قَالَ لِكُلٍّ ضِعْفٌ وَلَٰكِن لَّا تَعْلَمُونَ ﴿٣٨﴾

And the first of them will say to the last: 'In no wise were you superior to us. Taste, then, this suffering on account of what you have been doing.' (39)

وَقَالَتْ أُولَاهُمْ لِأُخْرَاهُمْ فَمَا كَانَ لَكُمْ عَلَيْنَا مِن فَضْلٍ فَذُوقُوا ٱلْعَذَابَ بِمَا كُنتُمْ تَكْسِبُونَ ﴿٣٩﴾

For those who deny Our revelations and scorn them the gates of heaven shall not be opened; nor shall they enter paradise any more than a thick, twisted rope can pass through a needle's eye. Thus do We reward the evil-doers. (40)

إِنَّ ٱلَّذِينَ كَذَّبُوا بِآيَاتِنَا وَٱسْتَكْبَرُوا عَنْهَا لَا تُفَتَّحُ لَهُمْ أَبْوَابُ ٱلسَّمَاءِ وَلَا يَدْخُلُونَ ٱلْجَنَّةَ حَتَّىٰ يَلِجَ ٱلْجَمَلُ فِي سَمِّ ٱلْخِيَاطِ وَكَذَٰلِكَ نَجْزِي ٱلْمُجْرِمِينَ ﴿٤٠﴾

Hell shall be their resting place, and sheets of fire shall cover them. Thus do We reward the wrong-doers. (41)

لَهُم مِّن جَهَنَّمَ مِهَادٌ وَمِن فَوْقِهِمْ غَوَاشٍ وَكَذَٰلِكَ نَجْزِي ٱلظَّالِمِينَ ﴿٤١﴾

As for those who believe and do righteous deeds, We never burden a soul with more than it can bear. They are destined for paradise, where they will abide. (42)

وَٱلَّذِينَ ءَامَنُوا۟ وَعَمِلُوا۟ ٱلصَّٰلِحَٰتِ لَا نُكَلِّفُ نَفْسًا إِلَّا وُسْعَهَا أُو۟لَٰٓئِكَ أَصْحَٰبُ ٱلْجَنَّةِ هُمْ فِيهَا خَٰلِدُونَ ﴿٤٢﴾

We shall remove any rancour that may be lingering in their hearts. Running waters will flow at their feet; and they will say: "All praise is due to God who has guided us to this. Had He not given us guidance, we would certainly have not found the right path. Our Lord's messengers have certainly brought us the truth." [A voice] will call out to them: "This is the paradise you have inherited by virtue of what you used to do." (43)

وَنَزَعْنَا مَا فِى صُدُورِهِم مِّنْ غِلٍّ تَجْرِى مِن تَحْتِهِمُ ٱلْأَنْهَٰرُ وَقَالُوا۟ ٱلْحَمْدُ لِلَّهِ ٱلَّذِى هَدَىٰنَا لِهَٰذَا وَمَا كُنَّا لِنَهْتَدِىَ لَوْلَآ أَنْ هَدَىٰنَا ٱللَّهُ لَقَدْ جَآءَتْ رُسُلُ رَبِّنَا بِٱلْحَقِّ وَنُودُوٓا۟ أَن تِلْكُمُ ٱلْجَنَّةُ أُورِثْتُمُوهَا بِمَا كُنتُمْ تَعْمَلُونَ ﴿٤٣﴾

The dwellers of paradise will call out to the inmates of the fire: "We have found what our Lord promised to be true. Have you, too, found the promise of your Lord to be true?" They will answer: "Yes," whereupon someone from their midst will proclaim: "Cursed indeed are the wrongdoers (44)

وَنَادَىٰٓ أَصْحَٰبُ ٱلْجَنَّةِ أَصْحَٰبَ ٱلنَّارِ أَن قَدْ وَجَدْنَا مَا وَعَدَنَا رَبُّنَا حَقًّا فَهَلْ وَجَدتُّم مَّا وَعَدَ رَبُّكُمْ حَقًّا قَالُوا۟ نَعَمْ فَأَذَّنَ مُؤَذِّنٌ بَيْنَهُمْ أَن لَّعْنَةُ ٱللَّهِ عَلَى ٱلظَّٰلِمِينَ ﴿٤٤﴾

who turn others away from God's path and try to make it appear crooked, and who reject the truth of the life to come." (45)

ٱلَّذِينَ يَصُدُّونَ عَن سَبِيلِ ٱللَّهِ وَيَبْغُونَهَا عِوَجًا وَهُم بِٱلْآخِرَةِ كَٰفِرُونَ ﴿٤٥﴾

Between the two parties there will be a barrier, and on the Heights there will be men who recognize everyone by their looks. They will call out to the dwellers of paradise: "Peace be upon you", – not having entered it themselves, but longing still [to be there]. (46)

وَبَيْنَهُمَا حِجَابٌ وَعَلَى ٱلْأَعْرَافِ رِجَالٌ يَعْرِفُونَ كُلًّا بِسِيمَاهُمْ وَنَادَوْاْ أَصْحَبَ ٱلْجَنَّةِ أَن سَلَامٌ عَلَيْكُمْ لَمْ يَدْخُلُوهَا وَهُمْ يَطْمَعُونَ ۝

And whenever their eyes are turned towards the inmates of the fire, they will say: "Our Lord, do not place us alongside such wrongdoing people." (47)

وَإِذَا صُرِفَتْ أَبْصَارُهُمْ تِلْقَاءَ أَصْحَبِ ٱلنَّارِ قَالُواْ رَبَّنَا لَا تَجْعَلْنَا مَعَ ٱلْقَوْمِ ٱلظَّالِمِينَ ۝

Then those on the Heights will call out to certain people whom they recognize by their looks, saying: "What have your great throngs and your false pride availed you? (48)

وَنَادَىٰٓ أَصْحَبُ ٱلْأَعْرَافِ رِجَالًا يَعْرِفُونَهُم بِسِيمَاهُمْ قَالُواْ مَآ أَغْنَىٰ عَنكُمْ جَمْعُكُمْ وَمَا كُنتُمْ تَسْتَكْبِرُونَ ۝

"Are these the self-same people whom you swore that God would never show them mercy?" (Now they have been told,) "Enter Paradise. You have nothing to fear, nor will you grieve." (49)

أَهَٰٓؤُلَآءِ ٱلَّذِينَ أَقْسَمْتُمْ لَا يَنَالُهُمُ ٱللَّهُ بِرَحْمَةٍ ٱدْخُلُواْ ٱلْجَنَّةَ لَا خَوْفٌ عَلَيْكُمْ وَلَآ أَنتُمْ تَحْزَنُونَ ۝

And the inmates of the fire will cry out to the dwellers of paradise: "Pour some water on us, or give us some of the sustenance God has provided for you." They will reply: "God has forbidden both to the unbelievers, (50)

وَنَادَىٰٓ أَصْحَبُ ٱلنَّارِ أَصْحَبَ ٱلْجَنَّةِ أَنْ أَفِيضُواْ عَلَيْنَا مِنَ ٱلْمَآءِ أَوْ مِمَّا رَزَقَكُمُ ٱللَّهُ قَالُوٓاْ إِنَّ ٱللَّهَ حَرَّمَهُمَا عَلَى ٱلْكَٰفِرِينَ ۝

who have taken their religion for a pastime and an idle sport, and who have been beguiled by the life of this world." Today We shall be oblivious of them as they were oblivious of the meeting on this day of theirs, and as they used to deny Our revelations. (51)

ٱلَّذِينَ ٱتَّخَذُواْ دِينَهُمْ لَهْوًا وَلَعِبًا وَغَرَّتْهُمُ ٱلْحَيَوٰةُ ٱلدُّنْيَا فَٱلْيَوْمَ نَنسَىٰهُمْ كَمَا نَسُواْ لِقَآءَ يَوْمِهِمْ هَٰذَا وَمَا كَانُواْ بِـَٔايَٰتِنَا يَجْحَدُونَ ٥١

We have indeed given them a Book which We have clearly and wisely spelled out, a guidance and a grace for people who have faith. (52)

وَلَقَدْ جِئْنَٰهُم بِكِتَٰبٍ فَصَّلْنَٰهُ عَلَىٰ عِلْمٍ هُدًى وَرَحْمَةً لِّقَوْمٍ يُؤْمِنُونَ ٥٢

Are they waiting for its final meaning to unfold? On this Day when its final meaning unfolds, those who previously were oblivious of it will say: "Our Lord's messengers have surely told us the Truth. Have we, then, any intercessors who could plead on our behalf? Or could we live our lives again, so that we may act differently from the way we used to act." They have lost their souls and all that which they invented has failed them. (53)

هَلْ يَنظُرُونَ إِلَّا تَأْوِيلَهُۥ يَوْمَ يَأْتِى تَأْوِيلُهُۥ يَقُولُ ٱلَّذِينَ نَسُوهُ مِن قَبْلُ قَدْ جَآءَتْ رُسُلُ رَبِّنَا بِٱلْحَقِّ فَهَل لَّنَا مِن شُفَعَآءَ فَيَشْفَعُواْ لَنَآ أَوْ نُرَدُّ فَنَعْمَلَ غَيْرَ ٱلَّذِى كُنَّا نَعْمَلُ قَدْ خَسِرُوٓاْ أَنفُسَهُمْ وَضَلَّ عَنْهُم مَّا كَانُواْ يَفْتَرُونَ ٥٣

Preview

The previous passage in the *sūrah* provided a long comment on the story of man's creation and the confrontation with the ignorant Arabian society, and indeed all *jāhiliyyah* societies, over the question of propriety and decency. Such values require that bodies be covered with appropriate dress and that souls be adorned with fear of God. The whole question relates directly to the major issue of faith.

This new address to mankind tackles the central issue to which the question of dress was related in the previous passage. It deals with the question of whom to follow in connection with religious rites and practices, as well as in legal issues, and indeed in all matters of life. Mankind must follow the messengers who bring them revelations from their Lord. It is on the basis of their response to those messengers that accountability and reward on the Day of Judgement will be determined. *"Children of Adam! Whenever there come to you messengers from among yourselves to relate to you My revelations, then those who are conscious of Me and live righteously shall have nothing to fear, nor shall they grieve. But those who deny and scorn Our revelations are the ones destined for the fire, where they shall abide."* (Verses 35-36)

It is the covenant God has made with Adam and his children, and the condition that He stipulated for man to be given the task of vicegerency on earth. After all, it is God who has created the earth and made it suitable to support life before assigning the task of building it to mankind and giving them the necessary talents, aptitudes and means to fulfil their obligations in accordance with God's covenant. Unless human beings follow the messengers God sends them, then whatever they do in this life will be rejected. No one who submits himself to God will accept such actions which will become on the Day of Judgement a burden that will inescapably lead to hell: *"Children of Adam! Whenever there come to you messengers from among yourselves to relate to you My revelations, then those who are conscious of Me and live righteously shall have nothing to fear, nor shall they grieve."* (Verse 35)

Fearing God helps human beings to steer away from sin and indecency. Indeed, the most wicked aspect of gross indecency is to associate partners with God and to claim for oneself God's authority and Godhead qualities. Fearing God also helps human beings maintain the path of obedience and to do only what is right. Thus, it brings a sense of security which is totally free from worry about one's eventual destiny. *"But those who deny and scorn Our revelations are the ones destined for the fire, where they shall abide."* (Verse 36) This is only because denying God's revelations and scorning the duty of abiding by God's covenant puts any person in one camp with Satan who most unashamedly scorned his duty of submission to God. Thus, God's warning to Satan and his followers shall come to pass: *"As for those of them that follow you, I shall fill Hell with you all."* (Verse 18)

The *surah* moves on to portray the scene of approaching death, or the term to which the last verse in the previous passage refers: "*For every community a term has been set. When [the end of] their term approaches, they can neither delay nor hasten it by a single moment.*" (Verse 34) This is followed by the scene of resurrection and reckoning, judgement and reward. These come by way of setting in detail what was at first briefly stated. It describes what happens to those who fear God and those who deny His revelations after their term has been completed. The description uses the unique Qur'ānic method of depicting vivid scenes that are held before our eyes as if we see them now and hear what takes place.

The Qur'ān has taken good care in describing the scenes on the Day of Judgement, including resurrection, accountability, eternal bliss and horrifying suffering. What God has promised and warned against is no longer a far-away scene which is described to us in words. Indeed, it is painted before our eyes in a way that brings it to life so that we actually see and feel it. Muslims feel as if they actually experience that world beyond: their hearts warm at one point; they shiver at another. They experience fear at one scene and feel secure at another. They actually feel the heat of the fire and experience the fresh breeze of Heaven. Hence, they are fully aware of what the life to come shall bring, even before their promised day arrives. When you consider what believers say about their feelings concerning the life to come, you will realize that they actually live in that world beyond more than they live their present life. All their feelings move towards the next world in the same way as man moves from one home to another or from one country to another. The life to come is no longer a distant future; it is experienced here and now.

Perhaps the scenes the *surah* portrays are the longest scenes of the Day of Judgement in the Qur'ān. They are perhaps the most vivid, portraying a succession of images coupled with extensive dialogue. Our amazement is endless at how simple words can replace vision and paint with sounds and words a complete scene that we actually visualize.

These scenes of the Day of Judgement are given in the *surah* by way of commentary on the story of Adam and Eve and their fall from Heaven as a result of yielding to Satan's temptation. Human beings are warned by God against temptation from Satan who drove their first parents out of Heaven. They are warned against following their old enemy in whatever he whispers to them. This is coupled with a threat that Satan will be their patron and guardian if they choose to obey him in preference to obeying God's messengers and their proper guidance. The *sūrah* then portrays the scene of approaching death followed by scenes of the Day of Judgement as if these come immediately after that of the approaching death without any time interval. What actually takes place confirms what those messengers have told. Those who obeyed Satan are denied admittance into heaven, because they have been tempted away from it in the same way as their first parents were driven out of it. On the other hand, those who disobeyed Satan choosing instead obedience to God are returned to heaven after they have been addressed from on High: "*This is the paradise you have inherited by virtue of what you used to do.*" (Verse 43) Their entry into heaven is thus a return of a person who had spent a long time away from home.

The harmony between the previous story and the comments on it, on the one hand, and the scenes of the Day of Judgement from start to finish on the other, adds much beauty to this style and to this *sūrah* as a whole. The story begins up there with the Supreme Society, in the presence of angels who witness God's creation of Adam and his wife and their dwelling place in heaven. It was Satan who brought them down from their position of complete obedience and submission to God so as to drive them out of heaven. The story also ends with the Supreme Society in the presence of angels. Thus, the beginning and the end are directly linked. They are separated by this period of human life on earth and the scene of death at its end. Thus the middle part is linked directly with the beginning and the end.

To Testify Against Oneself

We have now a series of scenes portraying the end of this life and the beginning of the next one. We see first a scene of death as it overwhelms those who fabricate false claims against God, alleging that their inherited concepts and philosophies and the traditions and laws they enact for themselves have been sanctioned by God. Such people deny God's revelations when they are conveyed to them by His messengers although these contain a perfect divine code. Thus, they prefer their suspect, unconfirmed knowledge to the confirmed truth of God's revelations. They have already received what was decreed to be their lot of the comforts of this world. They have completed the period of test God had willed them to go through, and received their part of the revelations God has given to His messengers who, in turn, conveyed it to them: *"Who is more wicked than one who invents lies about God or denies His revelations? These shall have whatever has been decreed to be their lot [in life]. When Our messengers come to carry off their souls, they will say: 'Where, now, are those whom you used to invoke besides God?' They will reply: 'They have forsaken us!' Thus, they will bear witness against themselves that they had been unbelievers."* (Verse 37)

Here we see portrayed before our eyes the scene of those who invented lies against God and denied His revelations. The angels come to gather their souls and cause them to die, at which point certain remarks are exchanged between the two groups. The angels ask them: *"Where, now, are those whom you used to invoke besides God?"* (Verse 37) What happened to the fabricated claims you used to emphasize? Where are the gods you invoked and worshipped, which caused you to turn away from the truth conveyed to you by God's messengers? Where are they now at this very critical point in time when your lives have come to an end, and you find no one to give you an extra hour beyond the deadline appointed to you by God?

They have only one answer to make. It is a clear, unambiguous and factual answer: *"They have forsaken us!"* They have simply gone away, far away. We do not know where they are, nor do they have a clear way of returning to us. Lost indeed are those whose gods cannot find them or who cannot help them in their hour of need. Worthless are the gods who know no way to reach their servants when they need them most.

"Thus, they will bear witness against themselves that they had been unbelievers." (Verse 37) This is the same attitude described earlier in the *sūrah* showing their reaction at the time when God's might overwhelms them in this life. Their reply then was a clear acknowledgement of being in the wrong: *"When Our punishment fell upon them, all they could say was: 'We have indeed been wrongdoers."* (Verse 5)

When this scene of approaching death is over, we are immediately presented with another scene showing those who were about to die having been thrown in to hell. The *sūrah* drops completely the period between their actual death and their resurrection and gathering on the Day of Judgement. Thus, it gives the impression that those who are about to die will actually be taken from their homes directly to hell.

[God] will say: "Enter into the fire to join the hosts of the jinn and humans who have gone before you." Every time a host enters [the fire], it will curse its fellow host. When all are gathered there, the last of them will say of the first: "Our Lord, these are the ones who have led us astray, so give them double suffering in the fire." He will answer: "Every one of you shall have double suffering, although you may not know it." And the first of them will say to the last: "In no wise were you superior to us. Taste, then, this suffering on account of what you have been doing." (Verses 38-39)

"Enter into the fire to join the hosts of the jinn and humans who have gone before you." (Verse 38). Join, then, your colleagues and patrons from among the *jinn* and human beings, here in hell. After all, is it not Iblīs who disobeyed his Lord? Is he not the one who drove Adam and his wife out of heaven? Is he not also the one who has led astray so many of Adam's children? It is also he whom God has promised to gather in hell with all those who do his bidding and go astray. Enter, then, all of you, into the fire, whether you belong to the earlier or later generations. All of you are equal and patrons to one another.

In this life of ours all these communities and nations are in the same camp, with the latter ones following in the footsteps of those who preceded them. Those who were in a position of power were able to dictate to those who were weaker.

Let us find out what sort of attitude they take towards one another there, after knowing their fate: *"Every time a host enters [the fire], it will curse its fellow host."* (Verse 38) What a dreadful end is that which makes a son condemn his father and a beneficiary deny his patron!

"When all are gathered there," and the last of them joins the first, and the distant becomes near to the one who is close, arguments and disputes among them become rife. Thus, *"the last of them will say of the first: 'Our Lord, these are the ones who have led us astray, so give them double suffering in the fire.'"* Thus, their comic tragedy begins. We see those who were allies and friends taking a hostile attitude towards one another, exchanging accusations and curses. Each prays to 'Our Lord' to give the other double punishment. Note how they make this appeal to 'Our Lord' about whom they used to fabricate lies and whose revelations and messages they denied. Today they turn to Him alone. The answer is to grant their request, but in a special manner.

"*He will answer: 'Every one of you shall have double suffering, although you may not know it.'*" (Verse 38). The double suffering you have requested will apply both to you and to them.

This shows that those who are condemned maliciously show some rejoicing at the misfortune of those who condemned them as they hear God's answer to them. They speak to them, pleased that they all have the same fate: "*The first of them will say to the last: 'In no wise were you superior to us. Taste, then, this suffering on account of what you have been doing.'*" (Verse 39) Thus the painful scene is concluded. It is followed by an emphatic assertion that this will be the end of all those who turn their backs on God's message and deny His revelations.

> *For those who deny Our revelations and scorn them the gates of heaven shall not be opened; nor shall they enter paradise any more than a thick, twisted rope can pass through a needle's eye. Thus do We reward the evil-doers. Hell shall be their resting place, and sheets of fire shall cover them. Thus do We reward the wrongdoers.* (Verses 40-41)

Reflect as you wish on this remarkable scene, with a very thick twisted rope held opposite to a needle's eye. When that tiny hole allows the twisted rope to go through it, then and only then, will the gates of heaven be opened to those arrogant people and their supplications or repentance be accepted. The fact is that the time allowed to them has lapsed. Hence, until such a rope goes through a needle's eye they will remain in the fire of hell where they are all gathered, cursing one another and trying to get their punishment doubled. Such is the retribution God has in store for the evil-doers. [It should perhaps be noted that the Arabic word used here for 'thick, twisted rope' also means 'camel'. Thus, the scene acquires a sarcastic touch as we visualize a camel trying to go through a needle's eye – Editor.]

Their situation in the fire is then described: "*Hell shall be their resting place, and sheets of fire shall cover them.*" (Verse 41). The fire actually engulfs them from above and from beneath. Thus they have beneath them a raging fire which is sarcastically described as a resting place or a couch, when it bears nothing of such characteristics. Moreover, from above they have sheets of fire drawn over them. "*Thus do We reward the wrongdoers.*" (Verse 41) This last description means the criminals and also refers to unbelievers who deny God's revelations and invent falsehood against God. All these descriptions are synonymous in Qur'ānic usage.

A Scene in Contrast

Let us now look at the opposite scene: "*As for those who believe and do righteous deeds, We never burden a soul with more than it can bear. They are destined for paradise, where they will abide. We shall remove any rancour that may be lingering in their hearts. Running waters will flow at their feet; and they will say: 'All praise is due to God who has guided us to this. Had He not given us guidance, we would certainly have not found the right path. Our Lord's messengers have certainly brought us the truth.' [A voice] will call out to them: 'This is the paradise you have inherited by virtue of what you used to do.*" (Verses 42-43)

Here we have a description of the destiny of those who believe and do righteous deeds as best they can. These return to paradise, because they are, by God's grace, its rightful owners. He has granted it to them as a reward for their good deeds which are motivated by faith. It is they who followed God's messengers, obeyed the commandments of their Lord, the Almighty, the Merciful and disobeyed Satan, their age-old enemy. Had it not been for God's grace, their actions would not have been sufficient, considering their limited ability. The Prophet says in an authentic *ḥadīth* related by Muslim: "No one of you will be admitted into heaven by virtue of his action." His companions asked: "Not even you, Messenger of God?" He replied: "Not even me, unless God bestows His mercy and grace on me."

There is no contradiction or discrepancy between what God says in this regard and what is stated in this *ḥadīth* by His Messenger, who does not say anything related to religion on his own initiative. All scholastic debate that has taken place among Islamic schools of thought concerning this question did not rely on an accurate understanding of this religion. God knows that human beings are too weak to earn admittance into heaven by virtue of their own actions. Indeed, whatever they do is insufficient to repay for a single aspect of His grace which God bestows on them in this life on earth. Therefore, He has committed Himself to bestow His mercy on them and accept from them their meagre efforts and give them heaven as a reward, but only through His grace. Thus they earn it by their action combined with God's mercy and grace.

In contrast to the scene of mutual hatred surfacing among the evil-doers in hell, even against their former close and intimate friends, we see the believers demonstrating their perfect love for one another in heaven. They are brethren who harbour no ill-feeling to anyone. They enjoy perfect peace and bliss: "*We shall remove any rancour that may be lingering in their hearts.*" (Verse 43) They are only human, and they lived the life of human beings. In this life on earth they may have had some disagreements and disputes that brought about ill-feeling. As believers, they tried hard to overcome these feelings and allowed their brotherhood to predominate. Nevertheless, there might have remained some lingering traces of rancour.

Al-Qurṭubī, a leading commentator on the Qur'ān, says: "God's messenger (peace be upon him) says: 'Rancour stays at the doorstep of heaven just like camels are seated outside people's dwellings. God removes it from believers' hearts.' It is also reported that 'Alī said: 'I hope that 'Uthmān, Ṭalḥah, al-Zubayr and myself are among those about whom God says: "*We shall remove any rancour that may be lingering in their hearts.*"'"

As already stated, the people of hell are engulfed by fire that overwhelms them from above and beneath. By contrast, the people of heaven have running waters which give an air of freshness to the whole scene: "*Running waters will flow at their feet.*" (Verse 43). While the former group is always quarrelling and exchanging accusations, the people of heaven praise God and acknowledge their own shortcomings: "*They will say: 'All praise is due to God who has guided us to this. Had He not given us guidance, we would certainly have not found the right path. Our Lord's messengers have certainly brought us the truth.*" (Verse 43).

The former group is strongly rebuked and told: "*Enter into the fire to join the hosts of the jinn and humans who have gone before you.*" (Verse 38). The latter are addressed with respect and given a warm welcome: "*A voice will call out to them: This is the paradise you have inherited by virtue of what you used to do.*" (Verse 43)

Dialogue Across the Divide

The contrast between the two groups is total, but the *sūrah* moves on to raise before our eyes a scene that comes later than the one we have just witnessed. Now we see the people of heaven having settled down comfortably in their dwelling place, while the people of hell are now certain of their doom. The former group calls out to the latter asking them about God's promise: "*The dwellers of paradise will call out to the inmates of the fire: 'We have found what our Lord promised to be true. Have you, too, found the promise of your Lord to be true?' They will answer: 'Yes,' whereupon someone from their midst will proclaim: 'Cursed indeed are the wrongdoers who turn others away from God's path and try to make it appear crooked, and who reject the truth of the life to come.*" (Verses 44-45)

The question itself is full of irony. The believers are absolutely certain that what God has warned against has actually come to pass in the same way as His promise has been fulfilled. Nevertheless, they ask the people of hell about it. The answer is given in a single word: "Yes".

Thus the dialogue that takes place across the great divide between heaven and hell comes to a stop as a voice is heard by the two groups. Someone will proclaim in their midst: "*Cursed indeed are the wrongdoers who turn others away from God's path and try to make it appear crooked, and who reject the truth of the life to come.*" (Verses 44-45) This statement clearly defines the meaning of 'the wrongdoers' which is often used in the Qur'ān as a synonym for 'unbelievers'. It is the ones that are devoid of faith that turn people away from God's path and try hard to make it appear crooked. They do not believe in the life to come.

The description of the wrongdoers as the ones who '*try to make it appear crooked*,' points out the true aim of those who turn people away from God's path. They prefer the crooked way to the straight path. There is simply one straight way which follows what God has revealed and implement His law. Every other way is crooked. As these people prefer it that way, they are in the same line as unbelievers. No one who believes in the Day of Judgement and who ascertains in his mind that he will return to his Lord will ever try to turn people away from God's path or select for himself a path that moves away from it. It is a description that clearly delineates the nature of those who reject God's law.

The Heights

At this juncture, the *sūrah* draws our attention to something additional painted in this scene. We see that the two camps are separated by a barrier over which stand some people who recognize the dwellers of heaven and the inmates of the fire by their looks and features. It is important to find out who these people are and what have they got to do with the two groups destined either for heaven or hell.

> *Between the two parties there will be a barrier, and on the Heights there will be men who recognize everyone by their looks. They will call out to the dwellers of paradise: "Peace be upon you", – not having entered it themselves, but longing still [to be there]. And whenever their eyes are turned towards the inmates of the fire, they will say: "Our Lord, do not place us alongside such wrongdoing people.' Then those on the Heights will call out to certain people whom they recognize by their looks, saying: "What have your great throngs and your false pride availed you? Are these the self-same people whom you swore that God would never show them mercy?" (Now they have been told,) "Enter Paradise. You have nothing to fear, nor will you grieve." (Verses 46-49)*

It has been reported that those people on the Heights which separate heaven and hell are human beings whose good deeds are equal in weight and measure to their bad ones. Hence, their good deeds are not enough to guarantee their admission into heaven, nor have their sins condemned them to the fire. They remain in between, waiting for God's grace to be bestowed on them. They recognize the people of paradise by their looks, probably by the fact that their faces are white and bright, or by the light which accompanies them. They also recognize the people destined to the fire by their features, probably by their dark faces or the marks printed on their noses which they used to raise as a gesture of arrogance. The printing of this mark on their noses is mentioned in *Sūrah* 68, The Pen. They greet the people of heaven with the greeting of peace, clearly entertaining hope that God will bestow His mercy on them and admit them to heaven as well. When their eyes fall on the people of the fire, whom they are deliberately made to see, they plead to be spared their destiny.

> *Between the two parties there will be a barrier, and on the Heights there will be men who recognize everyone by their looks. They will call out to the dwellers of paradise: "Peace be upon you", – not having entered it themselves, but longing still [to be there]. And whenever their eyes are turned towards the inmates of the fire, they will say: "Our Lord, do not place us alongside such wrongdoing people." (Verses 46-47)*

They then see some leading figures among the wrongdoing people and they recognize them by their features. They rebuke them for what they have been doing: "*Then those on the Heights will call out to certain people whom they recognize by their looks, saying: 'What have your great throngs and your false pride availed you?'*" (Verse 48) You see now that you are in Hell, where your armies and great multitude are of no use to you, nor indeed are your arrogance and vain pride.

They remind them of what they used to say about the believers in this life, accusing them of being in error and that they would never be granted God's mercy: "*Are these the self-same people whom you swore that God would never show them mercy? (Now they have been told,) 'Enter Paradise. You have nothing to fear, nor will you grieve.*'" (Verse 49)

Then from the direction of the fire we hear a voice, begging, imploring: "*And the inmates of the Fire will cry out to the dwellers of Paradise: 'Pour some water on us, or give us some of the sustenance God has provided for you.'*" (Verse 50). From the other side comes a reproachful reminder in reply: "*God has forbidden both to the non-believers, who have taken their religion for a pastime and an idle sport, and who have been beguiled by the life of this world.*" (Verses 50-51)

All human voices then die down and the Almighty, the Lord of the universe whose rule is final, gives His judgement: "*Today We shall be oblivious of them as they were oblivious of the meeting on this day of theirs, and as they used to deny Our revelations. We have indeed given them a Book which We have clearly and wisely spelled out, a guidance and a grace for people who have faith. Are they waiting for its final meaning to unfold? On this Day when its final meaning unfolds, those who previously were oblivious of it will say: 'Our Lord's messengers have surely told us the Truth. Have we, then, any intercessors who could plead on our behalf? Or could we live our lives again, so that we may act differently from the way we used to act.' They have lost their souls and all that which they invented has failed them.*" (Verses 51-53)

The scene moves in quick succession, with a glimpse of what happens in the hereafter and a glimpse of what takes place in this world. At one moment we see the sufferers in hell who have been forgotten because they themselves forgot about the meeting on the Day of Judgement and because they denied God's revelations which were given to them in a clearly spelled out book. It is God Himself who has stated it clearly on the basis of His knowledge, but they nevertheless abandoned it and preferred to follow their caprice and held on to their own misconceptions. Then we look at them again when they are still in this world waiting for the final outcome of this book and whether its warnings will come true. But they are warned against this final outcome, because it is exactly what they are made to see in this scene. It is certainly a remarkable scene which cannot be so vividly painted except in this miracle of a book.

Thus this panoramic preview comes to a close, followed by comments that are in complete harmony with the opening. We have a reminder of the Day of Judgement and its awesome scenes, and a warning against denying God's revelations and taking a hostile attitude towards His messengers. There is also a warning against waiting for the full meaning of this book, the Qur'ān, to unfold, because once it is unfolded, there will be no time for repentance, no return for a re-test and there will be no intercession on behalf of anyone to reduce his or her sufferings.

As the panoramic preview is over, we come back to ourselves after having been fully absorbed in contemplation of a spectacular scene. We find ourselves back in this present life, after having made a very long return trip. It is the trip of this whole life, as well as the gathering, resurrection, reckoning and reward that follow it. At the beginning we saw man as he was created and then we witnessed his fall to this world and his life on it.

Thus the Qur'ān makes us travel throughout the universe and across time. It shows us the past, the present and the future in quick snippets so that we may get the warning and heed the reminder: "*This is a book that has been bestowed on you from on high – so do not entertain any doubt about it – in order that you may warn people with its message, and admonish the believers.*" (Verse 2)

5

To Whom All Authority Belongs

Your Lord is God who has created the heavens and the earth in six aeons, and is established on the throne. He covers the day with the night in swift pursuit. The sun, the moon and the stars are made subservient to His command. Surely all creation and all authority belong to Him. Blessed is God, the Lord of the worlds. (54)

إِنَّ رَبَّكُمُ ٱللَّهُ ٱلَّذِى خَلَقَ ٱلسَّمَوَٰتِ وَٱلْأَرْضَ فِى سِتَّةِ أَيَّامٍ ثُمَّ ٱسْتَوَىٰ عَلَى ٱلْعَرْشِ يُغْشِى ٱلَّيْلَ ٱلنَّهَارَ يَطْلُبُهُۥ حَثِيثًا وَٱلشَّمْسَ وَٱلْقَمَرَ وَٱلنُّجُومَ مُسَخَّرَٰتٍ بِأَمْرِهِۦٓ أَلَا لَهُ ٱلْخَلْقُ وَٱلْأَمْرُ تَبَارَكَ ٱللَّهُ رَبُّ ٱلْعَٰلَمِينَ ۝

Call upon your Lord with humility, and in the secrecy of your hearts. He does not love those who transgress the bounds of what is right. (55)

ٱدْعُوا۟ رَبَّكُمْ تَضَرُّعًا وَخُفْيَةً إِنَّهُۥ لَا يُحِبُّ ٱلْمُعْتَدِينَ ۝

Do not spread corruption on earth after it has been so well ordered. Call on Him with fear and hope. Truly, God's grace is ever near to the righteous. (56)

وَلَا تُفْسِدُوا۟ فِى ٱلْأَرْضِ بَعْدَ إِصْلَٰحِهَا وَٱدْعُوهُ خَوْفًا وَطَمَعًا إِنَّ رَحْمَتَ ٱللَّهِ قَرِيبٌ مِّنَ ٱلْمُحْسِنِينَ ۝

He it is who sends forth the winds heralding His coming mercy, and when they have gathered up heavy clouds, We may drive them towards dead land and cause the water to fall upon it, and thus We cause all manner of fruit to come forth. Thus shall We cause the dead to come to life, so that you may keep this in mind. (57)

وَهُوَ ٱلَّذِى يُرْسِلُ ٱلرِّيَٰحَ بُشْرَۢا بَيْنَ يَدَىْ رَحْمَتِهِۦ حَتَّىٰٓ إِذَآ أَقَلَّتْ سَحَابًا ثِقَالًا سُقْنَٰهُ لِبَلَدٍ مَّيِّتٍ فَأَنزَلْنَا بِهِ ٱلْمَآءَ فَأَخْرَجْنَا بِهِۦ مِن كُلِّ ٱلثَّمَرَٰتِ كَذَٰلِكَ نُخْرِجُ ٱلْمَوْتَىٰ لَعَلَّكُمْ تَذَكَّرُونَ ﴿٥٧﴾

Good land brings forth its vegetation in abundance, by its Lord's leave, but from the bad land only poor and scant vegetation comes forth. Thus do We expound Our revelations in various ways for the benefit of those who are grateful. (58)

وَٱلْبَلَدُ ٱلطَّيِّبُ يَخْرُجُ نَبَاتُهُۥ بِإِذْنِ رَبِّهِۦ وَٱلَّذِى خَبُثَ لَا يَخْرُجُ إِلَّا نَكِدًا كَذَٰلِكَ نُصَرِّفُ ٱلْءَايَٰتِ لِقَوْمٍ يَشْكُرُونَ ﴿٥٨﴾

Preview

The *sūrah* has taken us along a trip that extends over epochs and generations, from the very beginning of human life to resurrection after death. Now it takes us along another trip to the depths of the soul of the universe and what appears of it before our eyes. It tells us about the creation of the heavens and the earth after having told us of the creation of mankind. Our attentions are drawn to what the universe contains, its secrets, aspects and phenomena, referring to the night as it follows the day in quick pursuit, and to the sun, moon and stars which are subservient to God's will, and the winds that move along in space, carrying the clouds to a land that is dead, and in no time, it quickens and becomes full of life, yielding all types of fruit.

This reflection on different aspects of God's kingdom comes immediately after relating the story of the creation of mankind and describing both the beginning and the end of man's life journey. The *sūrah* also refers to the attitude of those who follow Satan and who arrogantly refuse to follow God's messengers. It also describes some concepts of *jāhiliyyah*, or ignorance that may prevail in human society, and the traditions people invent for themselves having no sanction by God's law. All this the *sūrah* portrays in order to motivate human beings to return to their Lord who created the universe and made it subservient to His will and who runs it according to His laws and will. Indeed, to Him alone belong all creation and all authority.

This places strong emphasis on the fact that all creation and all existence submit to God's will. In such an atmosphere of complete obedience to God and perfect submission to His will, man's arrogance sounds extremely singular.

When these scenes have been portrayed and its strong rhythm has ensured even greater effectiveness, the *sūrah* calls on human beings to attend to their duties: "*Call upon your Lord with humility, and in the secrecy of your hearts. He does not love those who transgress the bounds of what is right. Do not spread corruption on earth after it has been so well ordered. Call on Him with fear and hope. Truly, God's grace is ever near to the righteous.*" (Verses 55-56)

To submit to God with dedication and to admit complete servitude to Him are no more than the natural correlative of the submission and servitude of the whole universe to God's authority. It is this concept which the Qur'ān seeks to establish in people's minds. Any person who reflects with an open mind on what God has created in the universe, the laws of nature which operate in it along with the physical and apparent outcome of the working of these laws is bound to recognize that it is God who runs, plans and controls this universe and everything that takes place in it. This realization is bound to leave a great effect on him as he acknowledges that all creation and authority in the universe belong to God alone. This is the first step to motivate the human mind to respond positively to God's call, and submit to His authority along with everything else in the universe.

The Qur'ānic method uses the universe as its main domain to explain the nature of Godhead and make people realize the true essence of submission to God. They begin to recognize its full effect with the reassurance generated by their realization that everything else speaks the same language and uses the same wavelength. The Qur'ān does not portray all this in order to provide some rational evidence in support of man's need to submit to God. Indeed, alongside this rational evidence the Qur'ān wants man to feel the reassurance and happiness generated by his sharing the same faith with the whole universe. This gives submission and servitude to God a different colour and taste. A Muslim is happy and content to be God's servant and to submit to Him. There is no compulsion in the matter, no force used to achieve that status. The basic motive for this attitude, even before the divine order, is a believer's love, reassurance and the objective of being in harmony with the rest of the universe. Thus, a Muslim does not try to rebel or avoid compliance with what he has been ordered to do. By his servitude to God, he is only fulfilling a natural need which contributes to his happiness. Submission to God enables man to be free from subjugation by, or servitude to, any other being. He submits with dignity and nobility to God alone, the Lord of the universe.

Such submission gives us the practical meaning of faith and gives belief its distinctive colour and taste. It tells us what Islam really means and imparts to it its nature and spirit. It is the basic rule that must be established before any order is given, before any aspect of worship is laid down, and before any law is enacted. This is the reason for the great importance the Qur'ānic method attaches to this basic rule which is clearly elucidated and firmly established in believers' minds.

A Clear Concept of God

> Your Lord is God who has created the heavens and the earth in six aeons, and is established on the throne. He covers the day with the night in swift pursuit. The sun, the moon and the stars are made subservient to His command. Surely all creation and all authority belong to Him. Blessed is God, the Lord of the worlds. (Verse 54)

The monotheistic Islamic faith allows no room for any attempt by human beings to work out by themselves any particular concept of God: what He is like or how He acts. There is simply nothing similar to God in any way whatsoever. Hence, it is not up to human intellect to try to picture the Supreme Being. A human concept can only be worked out within the framework that the human intellect can define, on the basis of what it makes out of the world around it. Since there is simply nothing similar to God, then the human intellect cannot draw any definite picture of what God is like. Moreover, it simply cannot visualize how His actions take place. The only alternative available to man is to reflect on the effects of God's actions in the universe around him.

Hence, questions like: 'How did God create the heavens and the earth?, 'In what form is He established on the throne?', and 'What sort of throne is this on which He has established Himself?' do not arise in a believer's mind. In fact, all these and similar questions are totally irrelevant and meaningless. To try to give answers to such questions is even more irrelevant and cannot be attempted by a person who properly understands the basic rule we have explained. Unfortunately, some Islamic groups who have tried hard to discuss such questions and wasted much time over them were influenced in their attempts by Greek philosophy.

The Qur'ān uses the expression *yawm*, which means 'day', as it speaks of the span of time in which God created the heavens and the earth. Their creation was over six such *yawm*, or six days. Again, this belongs to the realm that lies beyond the reach of human perception. Nothing of this creation has been witnessed by any human being or indeed by any creature: *"I did not call them to witness at the creation of the heavens and the earth, nor at their own creation."* (18: 51)

Whatever is said about these six days is not based on any certain knowledge. They may be six stages of creation or six epochs, or six of God's days which cannot be measured by our time which is the result of the movement of certain planets and stars. Before these were created, time, as we know it, did not exist. Still, the six days to which the Qur'ānic verse refers may be something totally different. Hence, no one may claim that he has certain knowledge of what this figure truly means.[1]

Any attempt to interpret this statement, and similar ones, on the basis of human theories, and to justify that as being 'scientific' is simply arbitrary. It betrays defeatism under the pressure of 'science' which can do no more in this area than the formulation of theories that cannot be proven.

We, for our part, prefer not to go into such discussion because it contributes nothing to our understanding of the Qur'ānic statement.

---

1. This is the reason for choosing 'aeon', i.e. an extremely long period, in our English rendering of the verse. In his translation of the Qur'ān, Muhammad Asad writes in a footnote: "The word *yawm*, commonly translated as 'day', but rendered above as 'aeon', is used in Arabic to denote any period, whether extremely long (aeon) or extremely short (moment): its application to an earthly 'day' of twenty-four hours is only one of its many connotations." – Editor's note.

We move along with the *sūrah* in its inspiring journey through depicting what we see of the universe and its hidden secrets.

> *Your Lord is God who has created the heavens and the earth in six aeons, and is established on the throne. He covers the day with the night in swift pursuit. The sun, the moon and the stars are made subservient to His command. Surely all creation and all authority belong to Him. Blessed is God, the Lord of the worlds.* (Verse 54)

God, who has created this vast and awesome universe and established His own high position, conducting the operation of the universe and administering its affairs, is the One who throws the veil of the night over the day in swift pursuit. Thus, the night follows the day in quick succession. It is He who has made the sun, the moon and the stars subservient to His will and He is the Creator and the controller of all. It is He, then, who is worthy of being "your Lord", giving you sustenance. He gives you the system which ensures your unity and the legislation which settles your disputes. To Him belongs all creation and all authority. Since He is the only Creator, He is also the only one who has any authority. It is this question of Godhead, Lordship and sovereignty, as well as the fact that all belong to God alone which constitute the theme of this passage, and indeed the whole *sūrah*. Its correlative is the question of submission by human beings to God and their implementation of His law in their lives. This is outlined in this *sūrah* in relation to questions of dress and food, as was discussed in the previous *sūrah*, Cattle, [Volume V], in relation to questions of animals, crops, rituals and pledges.

The great issue that the Qur'ān wants to settle should not make us overlook the remarkable nature of the scenes portrayed, their liveliness and powerful inspiration. Indeed, the greatness of the scene is on the same level as the greatness of the objective.

Our minds move along with the cycle of the day and night as they succeed each other in quick pursuit. Our consciousness cannot just be idle without following this cycle, overwhelmed with awe, almost out of breath, waiting with great interest for what will come next.

There is such finesse as these verses reflect the liveliness and beauty of the movement, portraying the day and the night in the form of persons with a clear aim and with a will to achieve the same. Such finesse of style and expression is far beyond the reach of human artistic talent.

Long familiarity kills the beauty of the majestic scenes of the universe in our minds and makes us look at them in a dull and uninterested way. But this familiarity is easily cast away here to make us look at the scene as if we see it for the first time. The night and day are not simple, natural phenomena that we see in endless repetition. They come alive with feeling, clear direction and a definite purpose. They have sympathy with human beings as they share with them the same movement of life and its essential aspect of struggle and competition.

The same is the case with the sun, the moon and the stars. We see them as living entities that have lives and souls. They receive their orders from God and carry them out in full submission. They are made subservient in the sense that they do what they are bid just as living believers obey God.

All this has its profound effect on the human conscience, motivating it to join the rest of living things that respond to God's call. This gives the Qur'ān its great effect on the human mind which no other literary style can achieve. It addresses human nature with the great authority that belongs to the One who has revealed the Qur'ān and who is fully aware of what touches human hearts and makes them responsive.

Calling on God with Fear and Hope

Thus, the human consciousness is overawed by the lively scenes of the universe which it used to look at in a dull inattentive way. Coupled with this is the realization that all these great creatures submit to the authority of the Creator. At this point, the *sūrah* reminds human beings of their only Lord and directs them to call upon Him with humility and full submission. They must acknowledge His Lordship in order to keep within the limits of their submission to Him, recognizing His authority and refraining from creating or spreading corruption in the land by abandoning His law and following their own capricious desires. *"Call upon your Lord with humility, and in the secrecy of your hearts. He does not love those who transgress the bounds of what is right. Do not spread corruption on earth after it has been so well ordered. Call on Him with fear and hope. Truly, God's grace is ever near to the righteous."* (Verses 55-56)

This directive is made at the most appropriate point, with human beings in the proper frame of mind. They are directed to call upon their Lord and address Him with humility and submission. They should also call on Him in the secrecy of their hearts, not making loud noises. A secret appeal to God is much more befitting because it affirms the close relationship between man and his Lord. Muslim, the renowned *ḥadīth* scholar, relates this authentic *ḥadīth* on the authority of Abū Mūsā who reports: "We were with God's Messenger on one of his travels – (in one version it is stated that this took place when they were on a military expedition) – and people started to glorify God out loud. God's Messenger said to them: O you people, gently and quietly. You are not calling on someone who is deaf or absent. You are calling on the One who hears all and is close at hand. He is indeed with you."

The Qur'ānic drift stresses the consciousness that God, in His Majesty, is so close to man. This is described here in its practical form as we make our supplication to God. A person who is conscious of God's majesty feels too modest to appeal to Him in a loud voice. If we realize that He is so close to us we can have no reason for appealing to Him loudly. Along with this scene of sincere supplication to God and complete humiliation before Him, an order is issued not to try to usurp His authority as the Arabs used to do in their days of ignorance, when they claimed sovereignty for themselves, while all sovereignty belongs to God alone. They are further commanded not to spread corruption in the land by following their capricious desires, after God has set the earth in proper order and laid down the law to govern both the earth and human life. A believing soul, which calls on its Lord with humility and in secrecy, feeling His closeness and ready response, is not given to aggression and corruption. The two attitudes are closely related in the depth of the human soul and feelings. In its approach, the Qur'ān touches on those feelings. It is an approach designed by the Creator who knows His creation and is fully aware of everything.

"*Call on Him with fear and hope,*" (Verse 56), fearing to incur His anger and punishment, and hoping to earn His pleasure and reward. "*Truly, God's grace is ever near to the righteous,*" (Verse 56), who worship God as though they actually see Him. If they do not see him, they are fully aware that He sees them. This is the attitude defined by the Prophet as belonging to the righteous.

Bringing the Dead Back to Life

Once more the *sūrah* gives us a panoramic scene of the universe raising it before our eyes to contemplate, but people often pay little attention to it and remain unaware of what it conveys. The idea that we have just discussed speaks of God's grace, and the new scene provides an example of God's grace in action. We see and feel it in the rain that pours down, the growing vegetation and the life that quickens: "*He it is who sends forth the winds heralding His coming mercy, and when they have gathered up heavy clouds, We may drive them towards dead land and cause the water to fall upon it, and thus We cause all manner of fruit to come forth. Thus shall We cause the dead to come to life, so that you may keep this in mind.*" (Verse 57)

All these are manifestations of what God's Lordship brings about in the universe, in accordance with an elaborate plan. They are all of God's own making. He, then, should be acknowledged by all human beings as their only Lord. It is He who creates and provides sustenance through the operation of the natural laws which He sets in motion as a sign of His mercy which He bestows on His servants. At every moment winds blow and cause the clouds to gather up, prompting a rainfall. But attributing all this to God's action, as it is indeed the case, is the new element outlined most vividly in the Qur'ān as if we actually see it as we contemplate the portrayed scenes.

It is God who sends the winds as heralds of His forthcoming grace. The winds blow according to the natural laws which God has set in place in the universe, for it is a basic fact that the universe could not have initiated itself and set for itself these laws dictating its movement. The Islamic concept of existence, however, is based on the belief that everything that takes place in the universe is the result of a special act of will which brings it into the realm of reality, although it actually happens as a product of the operation of the natural laws God has set in operation. The initial commandments for these laws to operate is in no way contradictory with the belief that every single event that takes place in accordance with these laws is the result of God's will. The blowing of the wind, in accordance with natural laws, is a single event that occurs as a result of a separate act of will.

Similarly, when winds gather up heavy clouds, they do so in accordance with the natural laws God has devised for the universe. Yet, this also happens by a separate act of will. Then God may drive these clouds, by yet another separate act of will, to a land that is dead, such as a barren desert, and He may cause the water in the clouds to fall upon it, by yet again a separate act of will, and thus He causes crops and fruits to come forth, by His own will. Nevertheless all these aspects happen as a result of the operation of the laws God has set in motion to give the universe and life their nature.

The Islamic concept of existence rules out the possibility that anything could happen in the universe involuntarily or by blind coincidence. This applies to the universe coming into existence for the first time, and to every single movement, change or amendment that takes place anywhere in the universe. It also rules out that it could take place in an impulsive, mechanical way, which would imagine the universe as a machine that has been set to operate in a particular method and left to run automatically.

The Islamic concept makes it absolutely clear that creation takes place by God's will and according to a plan. It acknowledges the laws of nature that have been set in operation, but adds to these the conscious will that determines every application and operation of these laws. That divine will is free, unrestrained by the laws it has put in place.

Thus, our hearts are freed from the dullness of the involuntarily mechanical concept of events. They remain always alert and watchful. Whenever something happens in conformity with the divine laws of nature, our minds are quick to see God's hand behind it and His will being done. Thus, we glorify God and we cannot lose sight of His greatness. Thus, the Islamic concept keeps hearts alive and minds alert. We see God's action taking place all the time, and we glorify the Creator whose active hand controls every movement and every event that takes place at any time of the day and night.

The Qur'ānic text links the reality of life that has come into being by God's will and His control of all that takes place on the face of this earth, with the second creation that will also take place by God's will in the same manner as we see in the initiation of this first life: "*Thus shall We cause the dead to come to life so that you may keep this in mind.*" (Verse 57)

The miracle of life with all its forms, aspects and circumstances has the same nature. This is implied in the final comment we have just quoted with which the Qur'ānic verse concludes. Just as God initiates life out of the dead on this planet of ours, He will also bring the dead to life at the end of the journey. The will that blows life into every living thing on earth is the same that causes them to quicken after they have been dead. The analogy is given here so that "*you may keep this in mind.*" (Verse 57). People tend to overlook this reality and lose sight of it, entertaining instead countless misconceptions.

At the end of this journey that encompasses the whole universe and touches on the secrets of existence, the *sūrah* gives an example of good and evil hearts. But the analogy relies heavily on the scene that has just been portrayed in order to maintain harmony between what we see and what is outlined of different natures: "*Good land brings forth its vegetation in abundance, by its Lord's leave, but from the bad land only poor and scant vegetation comes forth. Thus do We expound Our revelations in various ways for the benefit of those who are grateful.*" (Verse 58)

A good heart is often likened in the Qur'ān and the *ḥadīth* to a good land and good soil, while an evil heart is likened to a bad land and soil. For both the heart and the soil can support plants that come forth and yield fruits. The heart is the place where intentions and feelings, reactions and responses, directions and wills are translated into actions that give their results in practical life. The land, on the other hand, supports plants that give fruits of different colours, shapes and tastes.

"*Good land brings forth its vegetation in abundance, by its Lord's leave.*" The vegetation is wholesome, growing easily and giving its goodness in abundance. "*But from the bad land only poor and scant vegetation comes forth.*" (Verse 58) It brings with it harm, difficulty and hardship. Revelation, guidance, good counsel and admonition have the same effect on the heart as rainfall on soil. If the heart is good, it opens up with a newly felt freshness and gives its goodness to its owner and those around, in the same way as good land does. If the heart is evil, it can only harden up and deliver nothing but evil, in the same way as bad land brings forth thorny, harmful plants.

"*Thus do We expound Our revelations in various ways for the benefit of those who are grateful.*" (Verse 58). Gratitude only comes out of a good heart, indicating a welcoming reception and a goodly reaction. It is to those who are grateful and who receive good counsel well that God's revelations are expounded, because it is they who benefit by these revelations and work according to their guidance in order to make their benefits available to all.

Gratitude is often mentioned in this *sūrah*, side by side with warnings and reminders. This is not the first time it has been mentioned in the *sūrah*, but we will have more of it as we move along, in the same way as more reminders and warnings are given.

6

The Qur'ānic Approach to Faith

We sent Noah to his people, and he said: "My people, worship God alone: you have no deity other than Him. I fear lest suffering befall you on an awesome day." (59)

لَقَدْ أَرْسَلْنَا نُوحًا إِلَى قَوْمِهِ فَقَالَ يَقَوْمِ اعْبُدُوا اللَّهَ مَا لَكُم مِّنْ إِلَهٍ غَيْرُهُ إِنِّي أَخَافُ عَلَيْكُمْ عَذَابَ يَوْمٍ عَظِيمٍ ۝

The great ones among his people replied: "We certainly see that you are in obvious error." (60)

قَالَ الْمَلَأُ مِن قَوْمِهِ إِنَّا لَنَرَاكَ فِي ضَلَالٍ مُّبِينٍ ۝

Said he: "My people, I am not in error, but I am a Messenger from the Lord of all the worlds. (61)

قَالَ يَقَوْمِ لَيْسَ بِي ضَلَالَةٌ وَلَكِنِّي رَسُولٌ مِّن رَّبِّ الْعَالَمِينَ ۝

I am delivering to you my Lord's messages and giving you sincere counsel, for I know [through revelation] from God what you do not know. (62)

أُبَلِّغُكُمْ رِسَالَاتِ رَبِّي وَأَنصَحُ لَكُمْ وَأَعْلَمُ مِنَ اللَّهِ مَا لَا تَعْلَمُونَ ۝

Do you think it strange that a reminder from your Lord should come to you through a man from among yourselves, so that he might warn you, and that you may keep away from evil and be graced with His mercy?" (63)

أَوَعَجِبْتُمْ أَن جَاءَكُمْ ذِكْرٌ مِّن رَّبِّكُمْ عَلَى رَجُلٍ مِّنكُمْ لِيُنذِرَكُمْ وَلِتَتَّقُوا وَلَعَلَّكُمْ تُرْحَمُونَ ۝

But they accused him of lying, so We saved him together with all those who stood by him, in the ark, and caused those who rejected Our revelations to drown. Surely they were blind people. (64)

فَكَذَّبُوهُ فَأَنجَيْنَٰهُ وَٱلَّذِينَ مَعَهُۥ فِى ٱلْفُلْكِ وَأَغْرَقْنَا ٱلَّذِينَ كَذَّبُوا۟ بِـَٔايَٰتِنَآ إِنَّهُمْ كَانُوا۟ قَوْمًا عَمِينَ ﴿٦٤﴾

And to 'Ād [We sent] their brother Hūd. He said: "My people, worship God alone, you have no deity other than Him. Will you not, then, be God-fearing." (65)

وَإِلَىٰ عَادٍ أَخَاهُمْ هُودًا قَالَ يَٰقَوْمِ ٱعْبُدُوا۟ ٱللَّهَ مَا لَكُم مِّنْ إِلَٰهٍ غَيْرُهُۥٓ أَفَلَا تَتَّقُونَ ﴿٦٥﴾

Said the great ones among his people who disbelieved: "We clearly see that you are weak-minded, and, truly, we think that you are a liar." (66)

قَالَ ٱلْمَلَأُ ٱلَّذِينَ كَفَرُوا۟ مِن قَوْمِهِۦٓ إِنَّا لَنَرَىٰكَ فِى سَفَاهَةٍ وَإِنَّا لَنَظُنُّكَ مِنَ ٱلْكَٰذِبِينَ ﴿٦٦﴾

Said [Hūd]: "Weak-minded I am not, my people", he said: "I am a Messenger from the Lord of all the worlds. (67)

قَالَ يَٰقَوْمِ لَيْسَ بِى سَفَاهَةٌ وَلَٰكِنِّى رَسُولٌ مِّن رَّبِّ ٱلْعَٰلَمِينَ ﴿٦٧﴾

I am delivering to you my Lord's messages and giving you sincere and honest counsel. (68)

أُبَلِّغُكُمْ رِسَٰلَٰتِ رَبِّى وَأَنَا۠ لَكُمْ نَاصِحٌ أَمِينٌ ﴿٦٨﴾

Do you think it strange that a reminder from your Lord should come to you through a man from among yourselves, so that he might warn you? Do but remember that He has made you successors of Noah's people, and given you a larger stature than other people. Remember, then, God's favours so that you may attain success." (69)

أَوَعَجِبْتُمْ أَن جَآءَكُمْ ذِكْرٌ مِّن رَّبِّكُمْ عَلَىٰ رَجُلٍ مِّنكُمْ لِيُنذِرَكُمْ وَاذْكُرُوٓاْ إِذْ جَعَلَكُمْ خُلَفَآءَ مِنۢ بَعْدِ قَوْمِ نُوحٍ وَزَادَكُمْ فِى الْخَلْقِ بَصْۜطَةً فَاذْكُرُوٓاْ ءَالَآءَ اللَّهِ لَعَلَّكُمْ تُفْلِحُونَ ٦٩

They answered: "Have you come to tell us to worship God alone, and give up what our forefathers used to worship? Bring about, then, whatever you are threatening us with, if you are a man of truth." (70)

قَالُوٓاْ أَجِئْتَنَا لِنَعْبُدَ اللَّهَ وَحْدَهُۥ وَنَذَرَ مَا كَانَ يَعْبُدُ ءَابَآؤُنَا فَأْتِنَا بِمَا تَعِدُنَآ إِن كُنتَ مِنَ الصَّٰدِقِينَ ٧٠

Said [Hūd]: "You are already beset by loathsome evil and by your Lord's condemnation. Are you arguing with me about some names you and your forefathers have invented, and for which God has given no warrant? Wait, then, if you will. I too am waiting." (71)

قَالَ قَدْ وَقَعَ عَلَيْكُم مِّن رَّبِّكُمْ رِجْسٌ وَغَضَبٌ أَتُجَٰدِلُونَنِى فِىٓ أَسْمَآءٍ سَمَّيْتُمُوهَآ أَنتُمْ وَءَابَآؤُكُم مَّا نَزَّلَ اللَّهُ بِهَا مِن سُلْطَٰنٍ فَانتَظِرُوٓاْ إِنِّى مَعَكُم مِّنَ الْمُنتَظِرِينَ ٧١

So, by Our grace, We saved him together with all those who stood by him, and We wiped out the last remnant of those who denied Our revelations and would not believe. (72)

فَأَنجَيْنَٰهُ وَالَّذِينَ مَعَهُۥ بِرَحْمَةٍ مِّنَّا وَقَطَعْنَا دَابِرَ الَّذِينَ كَذَّبُواْ بِـَٔايَٰتِنَا وَمَا كَانُواْ مُؤْمِنِينَ ٧٢

And to Thamūd [We sent] their brother Ṣāliḥ. He said: My people, worship God alone: you have no deity other than Him. Clear evidence of the truth has come to you from your Lord. This she-camel belonging to God is a token for you, so leave her alone to pasture on God's earth and do her no harm, lest grievous punishment befall you. (73)

Remember that He has made you the successors of 'Ād and settled you firmly in the land. You build for yourselves palaces on its plains and carve out houses on the mountains. Remember, then, God's favours and do not go about spreading corruption in the land." (74)

The great ones among his people who gloried in their arrogance towards all who were deemed weak, said to the believers among them: "Do you really know that Ṣāliḥ is a Messenger sent by his Lord?" They answered: "We do believe in the message he has been sent with." (75)

The arrogant ones said: "For our part, we reject what you believe in." (76)

وَإِلَىٰ ثَمُودَ أَخَاهُمْ صَٰلِحًا قَالَ يَٰقَوْمِ ٱعْبُدُوا۟ ٱللَّهَ مَا لَكُم مِّنْ إِلَٰهٍ غَيْرُهُۥ قَدْ جَآءَتْكُم بَيِّنَةٌ مِّن رَّبِّكُمْ هَٰذِهِۦ نَاقَةُ ٱللَّهِ لَكُمْ ءَايَةً فَذَرُوهَا تَأْكُلْ فِىٓ أَرْضِ ٱللَّهِ وَلَا تَمَسُّوهَا بِسُوٓءٍ فَيَأْخُذَكُمْ عَذَابٌ أَلِيمٌ ۞

وَٱذْكُرُوٓا۟ إِذْ جَعَلَكُمْ خُلَفَآءَ مِنۢ بَعْدِ عَادٍ وَبَوَّأَكُمْ فِى ٱلْأَرْضِ تَتَّخِذُونَ مِن سُهُولِهَا قُصُورًا وَتَنْحِتُونَ ٱلْجِبَالَ بُيُوتًا فَٱذْكُرُوٓا۟ ءَالَآءَ ٱللَّهِ وَلَا تَعْثَوْا۟ فِى ٱلْأَرْضِ مُفْسِدِينَ ۞

قَالَ ٱلْمَلَأُ ٱلَّذِينَ ٱسْتَكْبَرُوا۟ مِن قَوْمِهِۦ لِلَّذِينَ ٱسْتُضْعِفُوا۟ لِمَنْ ءَامَنَ مِنْهُمْ أَتَعْلَمُونَ أَنَّ صَٰلِحًا مُّرْسَلٌ مِّن رَّبِّهِۦ قَالُوٓا۟ إِنَّا بِمَآ أُرْسِلَ بِهِۦ مُؤْمِنُونَ ۞

قَالَ ٱلَّذِينَ ٱسْتَكْبَرُوٓا۟ إِنَّا بِٱلَّذِىٓ ءَامَنتُم بِهِۦ كَٰفِرُونَ ۞

They cruelly slaughtered the she-camel, and insolently defied the commandment of their Lord, and said: "Ṣāliḥ, bring about the (punishment) with which you have threatened us, if you are truly one of (God's) messengers." (77)

فَعَقَرُواْ ٱلنَّاقَةَ وَعَتَوۡاْ عَنۡ أَمۡرِ رَبِّهِمۡ وَقَالُواْ يَٰصَٰلِحُ ٱئۡتِنَا بِمَا تَعِدُنَآ إِن كُنتَ مِنَ ٱلۡمُرۡسَلِينَ ۝

Thereupon an earthquake overtook them and the morning found them lying lifeless on the ground in their very homes. (78)

فَأَخَذَتۡهُمُ ٱلرَّجۡفَةُ فَأَصۡبَحُواْ فِى دَارِهِمۡ جَٰثِمِينَ ۝

He turned away from them, and said: "My people, I delivered to you my Lord's message and counselled you sincerely, but you do not like those who give sincere counsel." (79)

فَتَوَلَّىٰ عَنۡهُمۡ وَقَالَ يَٰقَوۡمِ لَقَدۡ أَبۡلَغۡتُكُمۡ رِسَالَةَ رَبِّى وَنَصَحۡتُ لَكُمۡ وَلَٰكِن لَّا تُحِبُّونَ ٱلنَّٰصِحِينَ ۝

And Lot said to his people: "Will you persist in the indecencies none in all the world had ever committed before you? (80)

وَلُوطًا إِذۡ قَالَ لِقَوۡمِهِۦٓ أَتَأۡتُونَ ٱلۡفَٰحِشَةَ مَا سَبَقَكُم بِهَا مِنۡ أَحَدٖ مِّنَ ٱلۡعَٰلَمِينَ ۝

With lust you approach men instead of women. Indeed, you are given to excesses." (81)

إِنَّكُمۡ لَتَأۡتُونَ ٱلرِّجَالَ شَهۡوَةٗ مِّن دُونِ ٱلنِّسَآءِ بَلۡ أَنتُمۡ قَوۡمٌ مُّسۡرِفُونَ ۝

His people's only answer was: "Drive them out of your land; for they are indeed people who would keep chaste." (82)

وَمَا كَانَ جَوَابَ قَوۡمِهِۦٓ إِلَّآ أَن قَالُوٓاْ أَخۡرِجُوهُم مِّن قَرۡيَتِكُمۡ إِنَّهُمۡ أُنَاسٞ يَتَطَهَّرُونَ ۝

117

We saved him together with his household, except his wife: she was one of those who stayed behind. (83)

فَأَنجَيْنَـٰهُ وَأَهْلَهُۥٓ إِلَّا ٱمْرَأَتَهُۥ كَانَتْ مِنَ ٱلْغَـٰبِرِينَ ۝

We let loose a heavy rain upon them. Behold what happened in the end to those criminal people." (84)

وَأَمْطَرْنَا عَلَيْهِم مَّطَرًا فَٱنظُرْ كَيْفَ كَانَ عَـٰقِبَةُ ٱلْمُجْرِمِينَ ۝

And to Madyan [We sent] their brother Shu'ayb. He said: "My people, worship God alone: you have no deity other than Him. Clear evidence of the truth has come to you from your Lord. Give full measure and weight [in your dealings], and do not deprive people of what rightfully belongs to them. Do not spread corruption on earth after it has been so well ordered. That is best for you, if you are true believers. (85)

وَإِلَىٰ مَدْيَنَ أَخَاهُمْ شُعَيْبًا قَالَ يَـٰقَوْمِ ٱعْبُدُوا ٱللَّهَ مَا لَكُم مِّنْ إِلَـٰهٍ غَيْرُهُۥ قَدْ جَآءَتْكُم بَيِّنَةٌ مِّن رَّبِّكُمْ فَأَوْفُوا ٱلْكَيْلَ وَٱلْمِيزَانَ وَلَا تَبْخَسُوا ٱلنَّاسَ أَشْيَآءَهُمْ وَلَا تُفْسِدُوا فِي ٱلْأَرْضِ بَعْدَ إِصْلَـٰحِهَا ذَٰلِكُمْ خَيْرٌ لَّكُمْ إِن كُنتُم مُّؤْمِنِينَ ۝

Do not squat on every road, threatening and turning away from God's path anyone who believes in Him, and trying to make it appear crooked. Remember when you were few and how He caused you to rapidly increase in number. Behold what happened in the end to those who spread corruption. (86)

وَلَا تَقْعُدُوا بِكُلِّ صِرَٰطٍ تُوعِدُونَ وَتَصُدُّونَ عَن سَبِيلِ ٱللَّهِ مَنْ ءَامَنَ بِهِۦ وَتَبْغُونَهَا عِوَجًا وَٱذْكُرُوا إِذْ كُنتُمْ قَلِيلًا فَكَثَّرَكُمْ وَٱنظُرُوا كَيْفَ كَانَ عَـٰقِبَةُ ٱلْمُفْسِدِينَ ۝

If there be some among you who believe in the message with which I am sent, and others who do not believe, then be patient until God shall judge between us. He is the best of all judges." (87)

وَإِن كَانَ طَآئِفَةٌ مِّنكُمْ ءَامَنُوا۟ بِٱلَّذِىٓ أُرْسِلْتُ بِهِۦ وَطَآئِفَةٌ لَّمْ يُؤْمِنُوا۟ فَٱصْبِرُوا۟ حَتَّىٰ يَحْكُمَ ٱللَّهُ بَيْنَنَا وَهُوَ خَيْرُ ٱلْحَٰكِمِينَ ٨٧

Said the great ones among his people, who gloried in their arrogance: "We shall indeed expel you, Shu'ayb, and your fellow believers from our land unless you return to our fold." He said: "Even though we are unwilling? (88)

قَالَ ٱلْمَلَأُ ٱلَّذِينَ ٱسْتَكْبَرُوا۟ مِن قَوْمِهِۦ لَنُخْرِجَنَّكَ يَٰشُعَيْبُ وَٱلَّذِينَ ءَامَنُوا۟ مَعَكَ مِن قَرْيَتِنَآ أَوْ لَتَعُودُنَّ فِى مِلَّتِنَا قَالَ أَوَلَوْ كُنَّا كَٰرِهِينَ ٨٨

We should be guilty of fabricating lies against God, if we were to return to your ways after God has saved us from them. It is not conceivable that we should return to them, unless God, our Lord, so wills. Our Lord has full knowledge of everything. In God we place our trust. Our Lord, lay open the truth between us and our people; for You are the best to lay open the truth." (89)

قَدِ ٱفْتَرَيْنَا عَلَى ٱللَّهِ كَذِبًا إِنْ عُدْنَا فِى مِلَّتِكُم بَعْدَ إِذْ نَجَّىٰنَا ٱللَّهُ مِنْهَا وَمَا يَكُونُ لَنَآ أَن نَّعُودَ فِيهَآ إِلَّآ أَن يَشَآءَ ٱللَّهُ رَبُّنَا وَسِعَ رَبُّنَا كُلَّ شَىْءٍ عِلْمًا عَلَى ٱللَّهِ تَوَكَّلْنَا رَبَّنَا ٱفْتَحْ بَيْنَنَا وَبَيْنَ قَوْمِنَا بِٱلْحَقِّ وَأَنتَ خَيْرُ ٱلْفَٰتِحِينَ ٨٩

The great ones who disbelieved among his people said: If you follow Shu'ayb, you shall indeed be losers." (90)

وَقَالَ ٱلْمَلَأُ ٱلَّذِينَ كَفَرُوا۟ مِن قَوْمِهِۦ لَئِنِ ٱتَّبَعْتُمْ شُعَيْبًا إِنَّكُمْ إِذًا لَّخَٰسِرُونَ ٩٠

Thereupon an earthquake overtook them and the morning found them lying lifeless on the ground in their homes, (91)

فَأَخَذَتْهُمُ ٱلرَّجْفَةُ فَأَصْبَحُوا۟ فِى دَارِهِمْ جَٰثِمِينَ ٩١

as if those that rejected Shu'ayb had never prospered there. Those that rejected Shu'ayb were indeed the losers. (92)

اَلَّذِينَ كَذَّبُواْ شُعَيْبًا كَأَن لَّمْ يَغْنَوْاْ فِيهَا ٱلَّذِينَ كَذَّبُواْ شُعَيْبًا كَانُواْ هُمُ ٱلْخَسِرِينَ ۝

He turned away from them and said: "My people, I delivered to you my Lord's messages and counselled you sincerely. How, then, could I grieve for people who persist in unbelief." (93)

فَتَوَلَّىٰ عَنْهُمْ وَقَالَ يَٰقَوْمِ لَقَدْ أَبْلَغْتُكُمْ رِسَٰلَٰتِ رَبِّى وَنَصَحْتُ لَكُمْ فَكَيْفَ ءَاسَىٰ عَلَىٰ قَوْمٍ كَٰفِرِينَ ۝

Preview

In this long passage we have a glimpse of the history of the procession of faith, with the prophets as its leaders and their actions marking its way. We have a detailed account of what is to be expected along this road. It is the history of faith and how it addresses itself to humanity as it travels along its long journey on this planet. It makes its address every time human beings stray away from the straight path, laid down by God, in order to follow other paths, tempted by the fulfilment of carnal desires. It is indeed Satan who seeks to satisfy his grudge against mankind, fulfil his threats and lead human beings by the collar, through these desires, to hell. In the opposite camp, the noble procession of prophets and messengers hold out guidance for humanity, give it light and present it with the prospect of endless happiness in heaven, warning it against the schemes of its old, accursed enemy, Satan.

It is an awesome scene portraying the age-old struggle that encompasses the whole of life and continues along the whole length of the journey. Human history is so complex because man has a dual nature and a highly sophisticated constitution. He is made of two totally different elements, brought together by God's will: the clay of which he is made and the breath of the divine spirit which made of this clay a human being. This unique being moves along, with his unique nature, and deals with highly complicated and mutually interactive elements, as well as different worlds. He deals with the Divine Being, His will, irresistible might, boundless grace and

120

forthcoming mercy. He also deals with the Supreme Society, the angels, and with Satan and his tribe. Furthermore, he deals with this world and its operative laws, as well as the living things on this earth; and with other human beings. In all his dealings, he relies on this same human nature, served also by his talents and abilities that may pull in one or opposite directions.

It is in this complicated multitude of links and relations that human history is formed, influenced by man's strengths and weakness, the guidance he receives, the righteousness he tries to maintain, his contacts with this world and with the world beyond, and his dealings with the material and the spiritual in this universe, and ultimately with God's will. It is from all these dealings that his history is formed, and in the light of this extreme complexity that his history should be explained.

Those who try to explain human history in either economic, political, biological, spiritual, psychological or rational terms look only at one aspect of the interactive elements that influence man, or the distinctly separate worlds with which he deals. Only the Islamic explanation of human history takes such a broad view which encompasses all this complexity and looks at human history in such a perspective.

Here we have some real scenes of this greatly complex history. In the first scene of creation, at which we have already looked, all the worlds and the elements, apparent and hidden, which man will have to deal with were present right in the first moment. We have seen the essential abilities given to man, and his honour in the Supreme Society, when the angels were ordered to prostrate themselves to him and God Himself announced his birth. We have also seen his weakness and how it has been exploited by his enemy. We have seen his fall to earth and how he has to deal with its elements and the laws of nature as they operate in it.

We then saw that as man fell to earth, he was a believer in his Lord, appealing for forgiveness, and giving the pledge of his vicegerency on earth, which committed him to follow the guidance that he would receive from his Lord and not to follow Satan or his own caprice. In order to help him fulfil that pledge, the first experience was granted to him. Time passed and man had to swim in the sea of the universe, with waves taking him this way and that. All the complicated elements both within him and in the universe continued to have an impact on his life. Here we see him having been led to a state of ignorance, or *jāhiliyyah*. It is true that man may forget or be overcome by his weakness. That gives power to his enemy, Satan, and hence man must be rescued.

When man fell to earth, he repented and sought forgiveness for his sin, pledging to follow guidance and always to believe in God's oneness, but here we find him having strayed far away, associating partners with God. He has been thrown far off course, but he has still the guidance which could bring him back. He has the divine message. Indeed God's mercy has dictated that man is never left without guidance. Here in this *sūrah* we see the procession of faith, with its standard bearers, God's noble messengers, Noah, Hūd, Ṣāliḥ, Lot, Shuʿayb, Moses and Muḥammad peace be upon them all. We see how these noble messengers try, by God's guidance, to rescue mankind from the precipice into which Satan attempts to sink them. Scenes of the struggle between guidance and error, truth and falsehood, the noble messengers and the evil ones from among the *jinn* and humans are portrayed here. We also see at every stage how the unbelievers are destroyed and how the believers are rescued.

It is not always that stories are related in the Qur'ān according to chronological order, but here in this *sūrah* they are, because the *sūrah* gives a glimpse of the line followed by humanity ever since its first creation. It also portrays how those in the procession of faith try to rescue man every time he strays far away from the right path. As we look at this panoramic scene we can detect certain broad lines which deserve to be discussed briefly before we look at the passage in detail.

Fallacy in the Study of Comparative Religion

1. Human beings often stray from the path of guidance from where they started in order to sink into a state of ignorance, or *jāhiliyyah*, that is characterized by associating partners with God. This happens as a result of the interplay of the complex elements that exist in man's own constitution and the elements which he has to deal with. When this state of affairs is reached, God sends a messenger to human beings explaining to them the very same truth they had had before sinking into *jāhiliyyah*. Some of them write their own destruction, while others are able to spare themselves by returning to the truth of faith. These are the ones who accept that they have a single God and submit willingly and totally to Him alone. It is they who

listen to their messenger as he says to them: "*My people, worship God alone: you have no deity other than Him.*" (Verses 59, 65, 73, 85) This is indeed the essence of the divine faith throughout human history. Every messenger preached this same message to his people who had succumbed to Satan's design and associated partners with God, although these partners may differ in different *jāhiliyyah* societies. It is this basic truism that is at the core of the battle between truth and falsehood. It is people's attitudes to this basic fact that puts them in the camp of those who are destroyed, or those who are saved by God. The Qur'ān relates how all these messengers expressed this essential fact in their various languages, using the same wording throughout: "*My people, worship God alone: you have no deity other than Him.*" This serves to emphasize the unity of the divine faith throughout history, even in its verbal expression. The wording itself is so precise in expressing the essence of faith, and its repeated usage portrays in a very tangible way the unity of this faith. This is in itself significant.

This emphasis the Qur'ān places on the unity of the divine faith serves to show the great divide between the Qur'ānic method and the approach of comparative religion. We can see very clearly that there has never been any gradual approach to the basic concept of faith, or development of that concept, which all messengers have preached as they received it from God. Those who speak of the development or progress of human faith and include the divine message in this gradual development make a claim that is at variance with what God states. As we see clearly in the Qur'ān, divine faith has always stressed the same basic concept which the Qur'ān relates in the same wording: "*My people, worship God alone: you have no deity other than Him.*" This God, to whom all messengers refer, is "the Lord of all the worlds" who will gather all human beings for the reckoning on a great day. No messenger sent by God has ever preached a belief in a Lord of a particular tribe, nation or race, and no messenger preached a belief in a duality or multiplicity of Godhead. No messenger urged his people to worship totems, stars, spirits or idols. No religion sanctioned by God omitted to speak of a life to come, as claimed by so-called 'religious experts' who study the different forms of ignorance and claim that such ignorant beliefs were the religions known to humanity in those particular periods of time.

All messengers, one after the other, preached the message of God's absolute oneness and His Lordship over the universe, as well as the reckoning and reward on the Day of Judgement. But the deviation that took place with every new form of *jāhiliyyah* led to a multitude of ignorant concepts. It is these concepts that are studied by 'experts in religion' who claim that they form the line of religious progress.

At any rate, we have here what God states, and it is the truth that we should follow, particularly those of us who tackle this subject when they explain the Islamic faith or defend it. Those who do not believe in the Qur'ān may say what they want, but God tells the truth and His word is final.

2. Every one of God's messengers peace be upon them all came to his people after they had deviated from the principle of monotheism which was already established in their community by their earlier prophet or messenger. The first generation of human beings were monotheists, believing in God, the supreme Lord of the universe. This was the faith in which Adam and his wife believed. When the Prophet Noah (peace be upon him) was sent after humanity had deviated into polytheism, he called on his people to return to the monotheistic faith and to believe in God alone. Then the floods destroyed the unbelievers and only the believers survived to repopulate the earth believing in God alone, as they were taught by the Prophet Noah. Succeeding generations did likewise but after a long period of time, they began to deviate into ignorance as did those who lived earlier. With the Prophet Hūd, the same story happened again with the unbelievers being destroyed by great storms. The story was repeated again and again.

Every one of these messengers was sent to his people and he said to them: "*My people, worship God alone: you have no deity other than Him.*" Every one also said: "*I am giving you honest counsel.*" In this way, every messenger made it clear to his people that the matter was very serious, and that their arrogant refusal to accept the faith could land them in great trouble in this life and expose them to a heavier punishment in the hereafter. He also expressed his keen desire that his people should follow divine guidance. However, on each occasion the notables in the community and those who were in leading positions stood against the truth, refusing to submit themselves to God, the Lord of all mankind. It is submission to God alone which is the central issue in the divine faith in all its forms of expression contained in the messages delivered by God's messengers. Faced with such a stubborn refusal, each one of those messengers declared his stand, totally opposed to tyranny and evil. In the case of each messenger, his people were split into two communities on the basis of faith. Thus, the ties of nationality and family relations were severed to be replaced by the ties of faith. With such a split, God made a judgement between the community following his guidance and the one deviating from the truth. This judgement brought about the destruction of the unbelievers and rescued those who submitted to God. It is God's law that no such judgement be passed until the respective community is divided into two on the basis of faith, with its followers declaring their submission to God alone, disassociating themselves from their compatriots who followed some other faiths and making their own stand very clear. This is endorsed by the history of the divine faith ever since the early days of human life.

3. The central issue in every message was the same: that all people should submit to God alone, their Lord and the Lord of the universe. Such submission and the removal of authority from all its usurpers is the foundation of every good thing in human life. The Qur'ān does not go into any great details of those earlier messages, after explaining this common denominator in all divine messages. The details are based on this basic principle. The importance of this central issue is the reason why the Qur'ān highlights it in this way, and singles it out in painting the main features of the procession of faith. We should remember here what we have said in our Prologue to the sixth *surah*, Cattle, or al-An'ām, [Vol. V], that this central

issue provided the subject matter of all Qur'ānic revelations in Makkah, while the revelations vouchsafed to the Prophet in Madinah outlined Islamic law as it addressed the needs of the community of believers.

This religion of ours has a central truth, and it adopts a very distinctive approach in outlining this truth. The approach is in no way less important than the truth itself. Therefore, we must know the basic truth outlined by Islam and follow the approach in which it is outlined. This approach highlights, frequently repeats and endorses the fact of God's oneness. This is the reason why this basic issue stands out in the stories given in this *sūrah*.

4. These accounts describe the nature of faith and the nature of unbelievers among human beings. It shows two types of hearts: one ready to receive the faith and another ready to deny it. In the case of every messenger, those who believed were willing to submit themselves to God and obey His messenger. They did not find it surprising that God chose one of them to deliver His message warning them against disbelief. The unbelievers in each case were those unwilling to relinquish the authority they had usurped and to acknowledge that it belonged to God alone, to whom all creation and all authority belonged. They were unwilling to listen to a single person among them. Those were the great ones, the chiefs who enjoyed positions of authority and leadership among their people. Thus we can recognize the central point in this faith, namely, that of sovereignty and authority. Those leaders were always aware of the meaning of what each messenger said: "*Worship God alone: you have no deity other than Him*"; and his statement: "*I am only a messenger from the Lord of the universe.*"

They felt that acceptance of God's oneness meant that sovereignty would be acknowledged to belong to its rightful owner, God, the only Lord, in the universe. What they had usurped of it would have to be restored to Him. They were ready to resist that even to the point of their destruction. They were not prepared to learn the lessons of earlier communities. On the contrary, they were prepared to follow in their footsteps to destruction and even to hell. The doom that befell those communities follows the same consistent pattern: a community forgets God's message and moves away from His guidance; a messenger is sent to deliver a message of warning; the same community adopts an arrogant attitude refusing to submit to God; the lure of affluence causes further disregard of the warning and even an invitation to hasten doom; persecution of the believers who are determined to stick to their faith; and finally destruction of the arrogant unbelievers in accordance with God's law that has remained in operation throughout history.

5. Equipped with power, falsehood does not tolerate even the mere existence of the truth. Even when the truth wants to stay well away from falsehood, leaving judgement between them to God, falsehood will not accept this attitude. It will continue to chase the truth and persecute it. The Prophet Shu'ayb said to his people: "*If there be some among you who believe in the message with which I am sent, and others who do not believe, then be patient until God shall judge between us. He is the best of all judges.*" (Verse 87) But they did not accept this offer from him. They could not tolerate seeing the truth in existence, or seeing a group of people freed from the tyranny of evil and submitting to God alone. "*Said the great ones among his people, who gloried in their arrogance: 'We shall indeed expel you, Shu'ayb, and your fellow believers from our land unless you return to our fold.'*" (Verse 88) At this juncture, Shu'ayb declared his commitment to the truth, and refused the tyrants' offer: "*He said: 'Even though we are unwilling? We should be guilty of fabricating lies against God, if we were to return to your ways after God has saved us from them.*" (Verses 88-89)

This will teach the advocates of Islam that the battle against tyranny is imposed on them. They simply cannot avoid it, no matter how they try, because the forces of evil will never let them alone unless they abandon their faith and accept the beliefs of tyrannical forces. They must remember, however, that God has rescued them from those beliefs as soon as they declared their submission to God alone and freed their hearts from submission to tyranny. Hence, they must, by necessity, fight their battle, remaining steadfast, until God grants them victory. They have to say, as the Prophet Shu'ayb said: "*In God we place our trust. Our Lord, lay open the truth between us and our people; for You are the best to lay open the truth.*" (Verse 89) Then, they should let God's law run its course as it has done before in all periods of history.

Putting Human Life Back on the Right Course

The procession of faith, led by the noble messengers God has sent to mankind, is clearly demonstrated in the *sūrah*. This is preceded by the greater procession of faith in the whole universe: "*Your Lord is God who has created the heavens and the earth in six aeons, and is established on the throne. He covers the day with the night in swift pursuit. The sun, the moon and the stars are made subservient to His command. Surely all creation and all authority belong to Him. Blessed is God, the Lord of the worlds.*" (Verse 54)

All messengers sent by God advocated submission to the Supreme Being who created the heavens and the earth, and established Himself on the throne, and who set the night to pursue the day, and set the sun, moon and stars in motion making them subservient to His will. It is He who has created all and possesses authority over all. Indeed, His messengers call on all mankind to submit to God, the Lord of all the worlds, striving to save mankind from Satan's schemes who endeavours to divert humanity away from God and to a state of ignorance. That state has endless forms, but all these forms have in common the characteristic of associating partners with God, claiming that they share Lordship with Him.

The Qur'ānic method often links the submission of the universe to God and the call on people to be in harmony with the universe and to submit to God as the rest of the universe has done and by whose will the universe is set in motion. This universal fact is bound to violently shake man's heart, urging him from within to join in this willing submission, in order not to be the only odd note in the whole universal system.

The noble messengers do not call on mankind to do anything odd. Indeed, they call on mankind to believe in the truth implanted in the universe and forming the basis of its existence. It is the same truth implanted in human nature. When people are swayed by their carnal desires they enable Satan to take them away from the original truth, and it is then that Satan becomes certain that they have blinded their eyes and closed their minds to the truth.

This is a fundamental fact that clearly manifests itself when we listen to historical accounts as they are given in proper order in this *sūrah*.

Noah Rejected by Blind People

We sent Noah to his people, and he said: "My people, worship God alone: you have no deity other than Him. I fear lest suffering befall you on an awesome day." The great ones among his people replied: "We certainly see that you are in obvious error." Said he: "My people, I am not in error, but I am a Messenger from the Lord of all the worlds. I am delivering to you my Lord's messages and giving you sincere counsel, for I know [through revelation] from God what you do not know. Do you think it strange that a reminder from your Lord should come to you through a man from among yourselves, so that he might warn you, and that you may keep away from evil and be graced with His mercy?" But they accused him of lying, so We saved him together with all those who stood by him, in the ark, and caused those who rejected Our revelations to drown. Surely they were blind people. (Verses 59-64)

This first historical account gives us a brief history of Noah. It does not include the details given elsewhere in the Qur'ān where these are required by the main theme under discussion in *Sūrahs*, Hūd and Noah. The main purpose of giving it here is to describe the main features which we have already discussed, the nature of faith, how to deliver God's message, how people receive it and the messenger's reaction to the response he gets, and finally the infliction of the punishment against which they were warned. Hence, only those aspects of the story which outline these points are mentioned here, following the general method of Qur'ānic historical accounts.

This passage opens with the statement, "*We sent Noah to his people.*" (Verse 59) This follows the pattern adopted by God, which meant that a messenger was chosen from among his own people, speaking their own language in order to win over those whose nature remained undistorted and to facilitate discussion and communication. Those whose nature is already distorted wonder at this pattern and feel it beneath them to respond to human beings, demanding that the message be delivered to them by angels. This is no more than an excuse, because they would not have responded positively to divine guidance, whatever its means of delivery.

As Noah was sent to his people, he stressed the central point of all divine messages: "*He said: 'My people, worship God alone: you have no deity other than Him.'*" (Verse 59) This is the solid unchangeable basis of divine faith, the mainstay of human life that guarantees the unity of direction and goal. It ensures that human beings are free from enslavement by their desires or by other human beings. It helps those who accept it to rise above all that they desire and to resist all temptation and threats.

The divine faith is a code for living based on the fundamental principle that all authority in human life belongs to God alone. This is the essential meaning of worshipping God alone and that God is the only deity acknowledged by human beings. When we speak of authority we include the belief that He is the Lord of both the universe and mankind who has originated them and conducts their affairs by His will and power. At the same level, we include belief in God's Lordship over man's day-to-day practical life and that man should conform to God's will and abide by His law, in the same way as worship is offered to Him alone. All this is one integral whole. Otherwise, we come very close to associating partners with God, worshipping others alongside Him, or instead of Him.

Noah conveyed this single message to his people, and warned them against rejecting it, speaking to them as a brother deeply concerned for their well-being and as a herald giving them honest counsel: "*I fear lest suffering befall you on an awesome day.*" (Verse 59) Here we note that the faith preached by Noah, which is the most ancient faith, included belief in the hereafter and the reckoning and reward on an awesome day, with Noah fearing for his people what punishment and suffering may await them. Here we realize the clear divergence between God's system and what it tells us about the origin of faith on the one hand, and, on the other, the system of the 'religious specialists' who grope in the dark and ignore what the Qur'ān says.

How was this clear, straightforward address received by Noah's deviant people? "*The great ones among his people replied: 'We certainly see that you are in obvious error."* (Verse 60) This is also how the idolatrous Arabs responded to the Prophet Muḥammad (peace be upon him) when they accused him of being an apostate who had renounced the faith of Abraham.

Deviation can extend as far as making a person believe that the one who advocates a return to divine guidance is in error! When human nature is corrupted, and standards are perverted and personal desire reigns supreme, then people can be so insolent and describe divine guidance as erroneous. Consider, if you will, what ignorant societies of today say about those who follow God's guidance. They are often described as having gone astray, and they are always offered some temptation to bring them back to the fold. That is, the fold of the filth in which *jāhiliyyah* finds its pleasure. Besides, what does contemporary *jāhiliyyah* say to a young woman who covers her body, and to a young man who looks with contempt at cheap flesh? Their purity is described as reactionaryism, backwardness and primitiveness. Indeed, *jāhiliyyah* employs all means of influence and all media outlets at its command to drag them from their clean standard down into the filth by which it surrounds itself. Again, what does contemporary *jāhiliyyah* say about a person who chooses for himself serious preoccupations and refuses to be football crazy or television and video crazy, or refuses to waste his time in parties and discotheques? He is described as reserved, introvert, inflexible, uncultured, etc. He is offered a variety of temptations to toe the line. All *jāhiliyyah* is essentially the same, although appearances and circumstances may differ.

Noah denies that he is in error, and explains to his people the true nature of his call and its origin. He has not invented it, but he is simply a messenger bearing a message from the Lord of mankind, and delivering it with honest advice, based on the fact that he knows of God what they do not know. He feels that knowledge within himself, because he has his link with God: *"Said he: 'My people, I am not in error, but I am a Messenger from the Lord of all the worlds. I am delivering to you my Lord's messages and giving you sincere counsel, for I know [through revelation] from God what you do not know.'"* (Verses 61-62)

Here we note a gap in the story. It seems that they have wondered that God should choose a human being, one of their number, to bear a message from Him to them, and that this human messenger should find within himself knowledge about his Lord which is not available to those who are not similarly chosen. This gap is indicated by what comes next: "*Do you think it strange that a reminder from your Lord should come to you through a man from among yourselves, so that he might warn you, and that you may keep away from evil and be graced with His mercy?*" (Verse 63)

There is nothing strange about this choice. Indeed, everything about human beings is amazing. Man deals with all the worlds and can have a direct link with his Lord because of what God has imparted to him and settled in his nature as a result of breathing into him of His soul. God certainly knows best whom to choose as His messenger. If God chooses a human being to bear His message, then this honoured person can receive the message through his latent ability to be in contact with God who gives him his special status as a human being receiving honours no other creature receives.

Noah reveals to them the goal of his message: "*That he might warn you, and that you may keep away from evil and be graced with His mercy.*" (Verse 63) There is first the warning so that their hearts respond and steer away from evil, as a prelude to eventually receiving God's grace. Noah himself has no personal interest or purpose other than this noble one.

But when human nature reaches a certain limit of corruption, it ceases to reflect and use its reason. At this stage, no warning or reminder is of any use: "*But they accused him of lying, so We saved him together with all those who stood by him, in the ark, and caused those who rejected Our revelations to drown. Surely they were blind people.*" (Verse 64) We have already seen how blind they are, that they cannot recognize right guidance, honest warning or sincere advice. Indeed, it is their blindness which caused them to reject the truth and let them suffer their inevitable destiny.

When All Argument Is Futile

History moves along and the *sūrah* moves on to another stage. We are now face to face with the people of 'Ād, to whom the Prophet Hūd was sent.

And to 'Ād [We sent] their brother Hūd. He said: "My people, worship God alone, you have no deity other than Him. Will you not, then, be God-fearing.'" Said the great ones among his people who disbelieved: "We clearly see that you are weak-minded, and, truly, we think that you are a liar." Said [Hūd]: "Weak-minded I am not, my people', he said: "I am a Messenger from the Lord of all the worlds. I am delivering to you my Lord's messages and giving you sincere and honest counsel. Do you think it strange that a reminder from your Lord should come to you through a man from among yourselves, so that he might warn you? Do but remember that He has made you successors of Noah's people, and given you a larger stature than other people. Remember, then, God's favours so that you may attain success." They answered: "Have you come to tell us to worship God alone, and give up what our forefathers used to worship? Bring about, then, whatever you are threatening us with, if you are a man of truth." Said [Hūd]: "You are already beset by loathsome evil and by your Lord's condemnation. Are you arguing with me about some names you and your forefathers have invented, and for which God has given no warrant? Wait, then, if you will. I too am waiting." So, by Our grace, We saved him together with all those who stood by him, and We wiped out the last remnant of those who denied Our revelations and would not believe. (Verses 65-72)

It is the same message, the same dialogue and the same end. God's law applies to all people in all generations. The people of 'Ād were descendants of Noah and those who survived with him in the ark. Some reports put their number at only thirteen. There is no doubt that the descendants of those believers, saved in the ark, followed the faith preached by the Prophet Noah (peace be upon him) which is based on complete submission to God. They definitely worshipped God alone, acknowledging no deity other than Him and believing that He is the Lord of all the worlds. That was what Noah told them. Then with the passage of time, their descendants travelled and settled in different parts of the world. Satan continued to try to lead them away from divine guidance, and exploited their desires, particularly for wealth and enjoyment. Thus they abandoned God's law. Those people of 'Ād found it strange that the Prophet sent to them should call on them to worship God alone.

"And to 'Ād [We sent] their brother Hūd. He said: 'My people, worship God alone, you have no deity other than Him. Will you not, then, be God-fearing." (Verse 65) This is exactly what Noah said to his people earlier, and they refused to accept it and suffered their well-known

destiny. God has given power to the people of 'Ād, but the *sūrah* does not mention here where they lived, although we learn from another *sūrah* that they were settled at al-Aḥqāf, which is a reference to the high sand dunes close to the Yemen border between Yamāmah and Ḥaḍramawt. They followed the same pattern as Noah's people, rejected the warnings, and refused to reflect on what happened to those who went along before them. Therefore, Hūd adds in his address to them this sentence: "*Will you not, then, be Godfearing.*" (Verse 65) This implies a strong criticism of their attitude as they show no fear of God and no worry about a terrible destiny.

The elders and the chiefs of his people found it too much that one from among them should call on them to follow divine guidance and denounce them for not fearing God. They found his attitude rather impudent, exceeding the limits and showing them little respect. Hence, they started to accuse their Prophet with being both foolish and a liar, paying him no respect. Without proper reflection, deliberation or sound evidence, they made their accusations: "*Said the great ones among his people who disbelieved: 'We clearly see that you are weak-minded, and, truly, we think that you are a liar.'*" (Verse 66) But he replied decisively: "*'Weak-minded I am not, my people', he said: 'I am a Messenger from the Lord of all the worlds. I am delivering to you my Lord's messages and giving you sincere and honest counsel.'*" (Verses 67-68)

His denial of being foolish or weak-minded combines simplicity with truthfulness, just in the same way as Noah denied that he was in error. Also like Noah before him, Hūd explains to them the source and goal of his message and that as he delivers it to them, he is giving them sound advice and ensuring honesty in its delivery. He says all that to them with the compassion of a person giving advice, and the truthfulness which is the mark of a trustworthy person. But like Noah's people before them, they wondered that he should be chosen as God's messenger, and at the message entrusted to him. Thus, we find Hūd saying to them the same words Noah had said before him, as if the two persons had one soul: "*Do you think it strange that a reminder from your Lord should come to you through a man from among yourselves, so that he might warn you?*" (Verse 69)

He then adds something relevant to their own situation as the successors of the people of Noah and the fact that they had been given greater strength and larger stature which fits with their mountainous area: "*Do but remember that He has made you successors of Noah's people, and given you a larger stature than other people. Remember, then, God's favours so that you may attain success."* (Verse 69) All that they have been given should have made them grateful and should have warned them against being cocky and conceited so that they would not suffer the same fate as earlier nations. They had not made a covenant with God to suspend the laws of nature He had set in operation, in accordance with His design for life on earth. To remember God's favours encourages gratitude for them, and to be grateful for God's blessings requires that what has led to them should be assiduously maintained and preserved. Only in this way can we ensure prosperity in this life as well as in the life to come.

However, when human nature deviates, it ceases to think, reflect and heed warnings. Those elders behaved in the most arrogant of manners. They stopped the argument and precipitated God's punishment, showing boredom with sincere, honest advice and paying little heed to God's messenger's serious warning. Their answer shows that they can hardly tolerate the manner their Prophet spoke to them in. They do not want to even consider it: *"They answered: 'Have you come to tell us to worship God alone, and give up what our forefathers used to worship?'"* (Verse 70)

This is a depressing scene of how familiar traditions exercise a blinding pressure over hearts and minds. This pressure deprives man of one of the most basic of his human qualities: that is, the freedom to think, reflect and choose his beliefs. Thus, man is enslaved by custom and tradition and by what his own and other people's desires impose on him. Every window of knowledge and every light of hope is closed. Those people precipitated their own doom because they did not wish to face the truth or to reflect on the absurdity of their falsehood. They said to their Prophet who gave honest advice: *"Bring about, then, whatever you are threatening us with, if you are a man of truth."* (Verse 70)

The Prophet's answer was quick and decisive, as he said: *"You are already beset by loathsome evil and by your Lord's condemnation. Are you arguing with me about some names you and your forefathers have invented, and for which God has given no warrant? Wait, then, if you will. I too am waiting."* (Verse 71)

He thus told them what fate was about to befall them and which they could no longer avoid. It was his Lord who told him of the suffering they would inevitably endure, together with God's condemnation. He also made it clear to them that their beliefs were absurd: "*Are you arguing with me about some names you and your forefathers have invented, and for which God has given no warrant?*" (Verse 71) What you have associated with God has no reality. They are mere names invented by you or your forefathers. God has never given any sanction for their worship. Hence, they have no power and no proof to support their status.

A short sentence that is often repeated in the Qur'ān is particularly significant. God says, in connection with the worship of anyone or anything other than Him that '*God has given no warrant*' for such worship. This refers to a fundamental principle which tells us that every word, law, tradition or concept which is not sanctioned by God has little or no effect and will soon disappear. Human nature receives all this lightly, but when a word comes from God, it acquires additional weight, causing it to penetrate right through people's minds, because it derives its power from God. Numerous are the theories, doctrines and concepts which received a great deal of publicity backed by strong authority. But once they found themselves face to face with God's word, they soon appeared as they truly are: weak, hollow and insupportable.

With all the confidence of a true believer, Hūd challenges his people: "*Wait then, if you will. I too am waiting.*" (Verse 71) It is this confidence that gives strength to the advocates of faith who are certain that falsehood is truly weak although it may temporarily have the appearance of material power and great following. The advocates of faith are certain that the power and authority of the truth they advocate will eventually triumph because it is derived from God's power.

In the story of Hūd and his people, the waiting is not long: "*So, by Our grace, We saved him together with all those who stood by him, and We wiped out the last remnant of those who denied Our revelations and would not believe.*" (Verse 72) It is total destruction from which no one is saved. This is understood from the expression, "*wiped out the last remnant.*" In the Arabic text, the term used signifies the last person in a caravan who moves a short distance behind it.

Another page of the history of communities denying the truth is thus turned, with the warning given full effect after all reminders have been rejected. This *sūrah* does not go into details of how the destruction took place. This is explained in other *sūrah*s. Therefore, we leave its discussion for now.

Most Flagrant Defiance

And to Thamūd [We sent] their brother Ṣāliḥ. He said: "My people, worship God alone: you have no deity other than Him. Clear evidence of the truth has come to you from your Lord. This she-camel belonging to God is a token for you, so leave her alone to pasture on God's earth and do her no harm, lest grievous punishment befall you. Remember that He has made you the successors of 'Ād and settled you firmly in the land. You build for yourselves palaces on its plains and carve out houses on the mountains. Remember, then, God's favours and do not go about spreading corruption in the land." The great ones among his people who gloried in their arrogance towards all who were deemed weak, said to the believers among them: "Do you really know that Ṣāliḥ is a Messenger sent by his Lord?" They answered: "We do believe in the message he has been sent with." The arrogant ones said: "For our part, we reject what you believe in." They cruelly slaughtered the she-camel, and insolently defied the commandment of their Lord, and said: "Ṣāliḥ, bring about the (punishment) with which you have threatened us, if you are truly one of (God's) messengers." Thereupon an earthquake overtook them and the morning found them lying lifeless on the ground in their very homes. He turned away from them, and said: "My people, I delivered to you my Lord's message and counselled you sincerely, but you do not like those who give sincere counsel." (Verses 73-79)

This is yet another episode in the history of mankind. Yet another sinking into ignorance and a confrontation between the truth and falsehood that ends in another destruction of the unbelievers.

"And to Thamūd [We sent] their brother Ṣāliḥ. He said: 'My people, worship God alone: you have no deity other than Him.'" (Verse 73) It is the same single statement with which the creation of man started and to which humanity will certainly return. It is also the same method of belief, direction, confrontation and delivery of the message. Here we also have an addition referring to the miracle which was given with the Prophet Ṣāliḥ's message when his people demanded it in order to believe in him: *"Clear evidence of the truth has come to you from your Lord. This she-camel belonging to God is a token for you."* (Verse 73)

As the *sūrah* gives a quick presentation of the history of faith, the results of believing in it and the consequences of its rejection, it does not go into the details of the people's request for a miracle. It simply refers to its existence as soon as it has outlined the essence of the message given by the Prophet Ṣāliḥ. Nor does this *sūrah* give us any details about the she-camel other than describing it as "*a clear evidence of the truth ... from your Lord, ... a she-camel belonging to God, ... a token from Him.*" From all this we realize that she was a very special she-camel, or that she was brought up for them in an extraordinary way to make of her a clear proof, and to make its belonging to God particularly significant, confirming Ṣāliḥ's prophethood. We refrain from adding anything about the she-camel which is not mentioned in this most accurate of sources. Indeed, what is mentioned here is more than sufficient.

"*So leave her alone to pasture on God's earth and do her no harm, lest grievous punishment befall you.*" (Verse 73) Since she is God's camel, then she should be left alone to graze on God's earth, or else the warning will take effect.

After having given them the miracle and made the warning clear, Ṣāliḥ begins to counsel his people to remember and reflect, bearing in mind the fate of past nations. He also reminds them that it is their duty to show their gratitude for the power they have been given as successors to those nations: "*Remember that He has made you the successors of 'Ād and settled you firmly in the land. You build for yourselves palaces on its plains and carve out houses on the mountains. Remember, then, God's favours and do not go about spreading corruption in the land.*" (Verse 74)

We are not told here in which area the people of Thamūd lived, but we are told in another *sūrah* that they were at al-Ḥijr, which lies between Hijaz and Greater Syria. From Ṣāliḥ's reminder we realize that the Thamūd were given power and affluence, and we can also visualize the nature of the area in which they lived. It incorporates plains and mountains, and they used to have their palaces in the plains and their homes in the mountains. We can conclude from this short statement that they were a civilized nation that excelled in architecture. Ṣāliḥ also reminds them that they were chosen to succeed the people of 'Ād, although they did not live in the same area. It seems that theirs was the architectural civilization that flourished after that of 'Ād. It also seems that their power extended beyond their own area, giving them added strength and making them feared by other nations. Hence, Ṣāliḥ warns them against being arrogant and conceited. He tells them not to spread corruption in the land, as the lesson of 'Ād and their fate must not be lost on them.

Here again we notice a gap in this story necessitated by the need for brevity. A section of Ṣāliḥ's people have accepted the faith, while another section rejected it with arrogance. Those of high position are the last to believe in a faith which deprives them of personal power and attributes all power to God, the Lord of all the worlds. Hence, they inevitably try to punish the believers who have rebelled against tyranny by declaring their servitude to God alone, submitting to no one other than Him. Thus, we find the proud and arrogant chiefs of Thamūd very clear in their threats to those who have believed, particularly those who are weak: *"The great ones among his people who gloried in their arrogance towards all who were deemed weak, said to the believers among them: 'Do you really know that Ṣāliḥ is a Messenger sent by his Lord?'"* (Verse 75)

It is clear that the question here implies a threat. The elders simply denounce them for their beliefs and ridicule them for accepting his statement that he has been sent by God. But those believers are no longer weak. Their faith has given them strength and self confidence as well as a powerful argument. They are certain of their position. So, what effect will the denunciation and the ridicule by the elders signify? *"They answered: 'We do believe in the message he has been sent with.'"* (Verse 75)

At this moment, the arrogant chiefs clearly identify their attitude which implies a strong warning: *"For our part, we reject what you believe in."* (Verse 76) This is, then, what they say despite the clear proof given to Ṣāliḥ, which leaves no doubt in anybody's mind. It is not the proof which those people needed in order to believe in the message. What turns them away from faith is the fact that their power and authority are threatened when they submit to the only Lord in the universe. It is their lust for power, a deeply rooted desire, which Satan manipulates in order to lead people astray.

They did not wait long before carrying out their threat. They targeted for their assault the she-camel which was a token from God giving support to His Messenger. They slaughtered it despite their Prophet's warnings that they would be severely punished if they harmed her: *"They cruelly slaughtered the she-camel, and insolently defied the commandment of their Lord, and said: 'Ṣāliḥ, bring about the (punishment) with which you have threatened us, if you are truly one of (God's) messengers.'"* (Verse 77)

This is a clear example of the arrogance which goes hand in hand with disobedience, described here as 'insolent defiance' in order to point out those people's frame of mind when they actually slaughtered the she-camel. It is this frame of mind that leads them to adopt their careless attitude, challenging the Prophet Ṣāliḥ to bring about their doom.

The *sūrah* immediately declares the outcome, which is not given here in any detail: "*Thereupon an earthquake overtook them and the morning found them lying lifeless on the ground in their homes.*" (Verse 78) The earth quake and their lying lifeless are shown as a punishment that befits their arrogance. With an earthquake, fear strikes people. The way they laid lifeless shows total powerlessness. It is most fitting that an arrogant and insolent person should tremble with fear, and that an aggressor is deprived of all power. The punishment fits the crime and the image given here of their destiny is highly expressive.

They are left in that position, lifeless on the ground to show us Ṣāliḥ as he saw those who had rejected and challenged him: "*He turned away from them, and said: 'My people, I delivered to you my Lord's message and counselled you sincerely, but you do not like those who give sincere counsel.'*" (Verse 79)

He is simply seeking witnesses for his honesty and sincerity in delivering his message and giving sound advice to his people. He also makes it clear that he could not be blamed for the fate they brought upon themselves by their insolent defiance and rejection of God's message.

Yet another page of the history of the nations that rejected God's message is turned over. Those who reject it anew must heed God's warnings.

Taking the Lead in Perversion

As history moves on we come to the time of the Prophet Abraham (peace be upon him), but the *sūrah* does not refer here to Abraham's history, because it only wants to discuss the fate of those nations who rejected the divine message. This is in line with the fourth verse in the *sūrah* which says: "*How many a community have We destroyed, with Our punishment falling upon them by night, or at midday while they were resting.*" (Verse 4) These stories of earlier communities give some details of what this statement sums up. Abraham's people were not destroyed because the Prophet Abraham (peace be upon him) did not request his Lord to destroy them. Instead, he abandoned them and the deities they worshipped instead of God. We have here a brief account of the story of the people of Lot, who was Abraham's nephew and contemporary, because the story involves giving warnings, rejection by unbelievers, and destruction. It thus fits in with what the *sūrah* is all about.

> *And Lot said to his people: "Will you persist in the indecencies none in all the world had ever committed before you? With lust you approach men instead of women. Indeed, you are given to excesses. His people's only answer was: "Drive them out of your land; for they are indeed people who would keep chaste." We saved him together with his household, except his wife: she was one of those who stayed behind. We let loose a heavy rain upon them. Behold what happened in the end to those criminal people.* (Verses 80-84)

The story of Lot's people tells us about one special aspect of perverted human nature and tackles an issue different from that of Godhead and God's oneness which was the central point in the earlier stories. However, it is not far removed from it. Believing in God, the only Lord in the universe, is bound to lead the believer to accept God's law and conform to the rules of nature He has set in operation. It has been God's will to create human beings in two sexes, male and female, who perfectly complement each other. Survival of this species is effected through reproduction that results from intimate contact between male and female. Hence, it is part of their nature to be physically and psychologically attracted to each other and to make the contact that leads to reproduction. The pleasure they receive from it is profound, and the desire to have that pleasure is deeply rooted. Both desire and pleasure provide the motive for them to seek that contact despite the difficulties they are sure to encounter later with pregnancy, childbirth, breast-feeding, maintenance, and the upbringing and education of children. It also ensures that the male and female remain united in a family where the offspring are reared, because they require fostering over a much longer period than animal offspring. Moreover, it fulfils God's will for human life to continue.

This is the way God has ordained things. To understand it and conform to it is directly related to believing in God and His wisdom in planning and creation. Therefore, to deliberately deviate from this norm is closely related to deviation from faith and from the code of living God has laid down.

Perversion of human nature is presented so clearly in the story of Lot's people. It is clear that Lot, the Prophet, does not mince words about the fact that they are the abnormal ones among God's creation, and that their ugly perversion is unprecedented: "*And Lot said to his people: 'Will you persist in the indecencies none in all the world had ever committed before you? With lust you approach men instead of women. Indeed, you are given to excesses.'*" (Verses 80-81)

The excess to which Lot is referring is that they go beyond the limits of the divine order of things which is reflected in upright human nature. They indeed go to excess with regard to the energy God has given them in order to play their role in the survival and progress of human life, by expending it wastefully in a place other than that of fertilization. It thus becomes no more than a perverted lust. God has made both man and woman derive proper and natural pleasure in the fulfilment of natural law. When a person finds his pleasure in something contrary to this natural law, then that is a mark of the perversion and corruption of nature, let alone its being a corruption of moral values. Indeed, there is no difference between the two, because Islamic morality is an embodiment of natural moral values, free of corruption and perversion.

Just like her psychology, woman's physical constitution is the one that allows the male to have his proper and natural pleasure when the two share contact which is not meant merely to satisfy a desire. Indeed, the pleasure that attends such a contact is an aspect of God's grace and blessing. It is He who has made this activity the source of pleasure, equal to its attendant responsibility. At the same time it fulfils His will that ensures the continuity of life. The male's physical constitution cannot provide uncorrupted human nature with pleasure if this desire is to be fulfilled with another male. Indeed, a feeling of disgust is immediately generated which blocks such a leaning as long as human nature is normal and upright.

The nature of the faith on which a particular system is based has a decisive influence in this respect. We need only to look at contemporary *jāhiliyyah* in Europe and America to find the same sexual perversion rapidly increasing. No justification may be advanced for it other than the fact that people there have deviated from the right beliefs and the way of life that can be based on them. The media, often controlled by Zionist interests, is directed to undermine human life through the spreading of immorality and promiscuity. Hence it has been trying hard to stress the misconception that women's adoption of a position of conservative propriety is the reason for the spread of such abnormal indecencies. But the facts contradict this most glaringly. In Europe and America, there is no longer any impediment to complete social and private contacts between men and women. People there often justify this, taking their lead from the animal world. Nevertheless, perverse sexual practice continues to increase. Indeed, it is no longer limited to homosexuality between males; lesbians are also on the increase. Anyone who still wants to argue in the face of these glaring facts should read first, "Men's sexual behaviour" and "Women's sexual behaviour" in the McKenzie Report. The controlled media nevertheless continues to repeat this falsehood, attributing perversion to women's religious dress. In this way, they are only fulfilling the aims of the protocols of the Elders of Zion and implementing the recommendations of missionary conventions.

Let us now turn our attention to Lot's people to find perversion staring us in the face as we listen to their reply to the Prophet Lot: "*His people's only answer was: 'Drive them out of your land; for they are indeed people who would keep chaste.'*" (Verse 82) How amazing! The person who prefers to be chaste and maintains the path of purity is driven out of town, so that only those immersed in filth remain.

But why should we wonder when we see modern *jāhiliyyah* doing the same thing. It chases those who maintain their chastity and refuse to sink into the filth of *jāhiliyyah* societies, falsely described as progress and as liberation of women from bondage. Such people are exposed to enormous pressures at home and at work and they are condemned personally and intellectually. Their presence in society is hardly tolerated, because only those who are prepared to sink into the filth of ignorance are welcome. The same logic of ignorance wherever and whenever *jāhiliyyah* exists!

The fate of those people is mentioned briefly in the same way as the fate of other nations and communities: "*We saved him together with his household, except his wife: she was one of those who stayed behind. We let loose a heavy rain upon them. Behold what happened in the end to those criminal people.*" (Verses 83-84)

Those who were threatened by the criminals are saved, and the issue is settled on the basis of faith and the way of life it lays down. Lot's wife, the closest person to him, is not saved because she belonged to his people and shared their beliefs and practices. A rain was sent pouring down over them, accompanied by powerful storms. We wonder, was this torrential rain meant to purify the earth from their filth and impurity? It may be so, but another case of rejection of the divine faith was thus settled forever.

Maintaining Justice in All Transactions

The next account of communities rejecting the divine faith in those ancient days is the last given in this *sūrah*. It speaks about the people of Madyan and their Prophet, Shu'ayb.

And to Madyan [We sent] their brother Shu'ayb. He said: "My people, worship God alone: you have no deity other than Him. Clear evidence of the truth has come to you from your Lord. Give full measure and weight [in your dealings], and do not deprive people of what rightfully belongs to them. Do not spread corruption on earth after it has been so well ordered. That is best for you, if you are true believers. Do not squat on every road, threatening and turning away from God's path anyone who believes in Him, and trying to make it appear crooked. Remember when you were few and how He caused you to rapidly increase in number. Behold what happened in the end to those who spread corruption. If there be some among you who believe in the message with which I am sent, and others who do not believe, then be patient until God shall judge between us. He is the best of all judges."

Said the great ones among his people, who gloried in their arrogance: "We shall indeed expel you, Shu'ayb, and your fellow believers from our land unless you return to our fold." He said: "Even though we are unwilling? We should be guilty of fabricating lies against God, if we were to return to your ways after God has saved us from them. It is not conceivable that we should return to them, unless God, our Lord, so wills. Our Lord has full knowledge of everything. In God we place our trust. Our Lord, lay open the truth between us and our people; for You are the best to lay open the truth." The great ones who disbelieved among his people said: "If you follow Shu'ayb, you shall indeed be losers." Thereupon an earthquake overtook them and the morning found them lying lifeless on the ground in their homes, as if those that rejected Shu'ayb had never prospered there. Those that rejected Shu'ayb were indeed the losers. He turned away from them and said: "My people, I delivered to you my Lord's messages and counselled you sincerely. How, then, could I grieve for people who persist in unbelief." (Verses 85-93)

Compared to the other accounts given in this *sūrah*, we note that this one is rather longer because, in addition to the question of faith, it includes a reference to business transactions. Nevertheless, the account follows the same pattern of concentration on the main issues.

"And to Madyan [We sent] their brother Shu'ayb. He said: 'My people, worship God alone: you have no deity other than Him." (Verse 85) It is the same, consistent basis of the divine faith that admits no change or modification. But then we have some details about the message of the new Prophet, starting with a statement: *"Clear evidence of the truth has come to you from your Lord."* (Verse 85)

The *sūrah* does not mention the type of that clear proof or its nature, as it did in the account given of the history of the Prophet Ṣāliḥ. Nor can we ascertain its nature from the other accounts of this history given in other *sūrahs*. We are simply told that clear proof was given to the Prophet Shu'ayb, confirming his statement that he had been sent by God. Clear evidence of the truth has been shown to them as the basis of the commandments given to them by their prophet. These required them to give full and just measure and weight, refrain from spreading corruption on earth and from threatening people as they go about their business, and to stop their efforts to persuade believers to change their faith: *"Give full measure and weight [in your dealings], and do not deprive people of what rightfully belongs to them. Do not spread corruption on earth after it has been so well ordered. That is best for you, if you are true believers. Do not squat on every road, threatening and turning away from God's path anyone who believes in Him, and trying to make it appear crooked. Remember when you were few and how He caused you to rapidly increase in number. Behold what happened in the end to those who spread corruption."* (Verses 85-86)

We understand from these injunctions that Shu'ayb's people were unbelievers who associated partners with God and did not implement in their own dealings the divine law which ensures justice for all. Instead, they devised their own rules and regulations for their business transactions. It may be that in this particular aspect that they associated partners with God, and that made them very unpleasant to deal with in business. In addition, they were the perpetrators of corruption, threatening people and preventing them from attending to their business. They were also wrongdoers, trying to turn those who believe away from their faith, making it difficult for them to follow the right path and trying to show God's straight path as crooked.

Shu'ayb begins by calling on them to worship God alone, submitting to His authority over every aspect of their lives, and attributing Godhead purely to Him alone. Shu'ayb knows that this forms the basis that gives rise to every good system and deals with every situation. It also forms the basis for regulations governing personal behaviour, morals and human dealings. He seeks to give more effectiveness to his admonition by certain reminders which, to them, must have been particularly inspiring, recalling to their minds some of God's blessings: "*Remember when you were few and how He caused you to rapidly increase in number.*" (Verse 86) He also warns them against suffering the fate of corrupt communities that lived before their time: "*Behold what happened in the end to those who spread corruption.*" (Verse 86)

Shu'ayb also wants them to exercise patience and tolerance, and to maintain justice. They must not tempt those who have favourably responded to divine guidance away from their faith, and must not squat on every road, issuing threats and manipulating their might to strike fear in people's hearts. The proper course for them, if they do not wish to accept the faith and believe in God, is to wait until God has judged between the two parties: "*If there be some among you who believe in the message with which I am sent, and others who do not believe, then be patient until God shall judge between us. He is the best of all judges.*" (Verse 87)

This is indeed the fairest plan. Shu'ayb made every reconciliatory move and took his stand at the last position behind which he could not retreat an inch. He called on them to accept a plan of peaceful coexistence, with every party leaving the other to practise their religion and implement their faith, until God judged between the two. Needless to say, God is the fairest of all judges. His is the judgement that shows no favouritism whatsoever.

But the tyrants do not accept that faith should have a following and that believers should form a community that rejects tyranny. The very existence of a community that submits totally to God, acknowledging no authority other than His, and implementing no code of living other than the one He has laid down represents a threat to the authority of those tyrants. Even if this community of believers should mind its own business, leaving the tyrants to God's judgement, its existence is conceived as a threat.

Tyranny will dictate that a battle is fought with the Muslim community, even though it prefers not to engage in such a battle. It is in the nature of things that the very existence of the truth is a source of trouble to falsehood, making a battle between the two inevitable. This is how God has ordained things. Hence, the unbelievers among the people of Shu'ayb rejected his offer and insisted that no mode of peaceful coexistence was acceptable to them: "*Said the great ones among his people, who gloried in their arrogance: 'We shall indeed expel you, Shu'ayb, and your fellow believers from our land unless you return to our fold.'*" (Verse 88) Thus, the battle was set. The believers with Shu'ayb could not avoid a confrontation, because the unbelievers refused every mode of coexistence between the two parties.

No Retreat Contemplated

Threats and warnings cannot shake or intimidate a strong faith. Shu'ayb made his stand taking a position from which he could not budge an inch. That was the position of peaceful coexistence which would allow every individual to adopt the faith of his or her choice and submit to the authority which he or she acknowledged, awaiting God's judgement between the two groups. No advocate of a divine faith can make even the smallest compromise beyond this point, great as the pressures to which he is exposed may be. Otherwise, he would betray the truth he advocates. When the arrogant chiefs of his people responded to his offer by threats of expulsion from their land unless he toed their line, Shu'ayb stood up for the truth, declaring that he would not go back to the false faith after God had rescued him from it. He turned to his Lord and protector, appealing to Him for support against the advocates of evil: "*He said: 'Even though we are unwilling? We should be guilty of fabricating lies against God, if we were to return to your ways after God has saved us from them. It is not conceivable that we should return to them, unless God, our Lord, so wills. Our Lord has full knowledge of everything. In God we place our trust. Our Lord, lay open the truth between us and our people; for You are the best to lay open the truth.'*" (Verses 88-89)

These few words epitomize the nature of faith and its effect on the believers as well as the nature of *jāhiliyyah* and its hateful effects. We also see clearly how the divine truth makes the Prophet's heart come alive: "*He said: 'Even though we are unwilling?'*" (Verse 88) His attitude is one of total denunciation of their despotic threats: "*We shall indeed expel you, Shu'ayb, and your fellow believers from our land unless you return to our fold.*" (Verse 88) He asks them whether they are prepared to go all the way and force him and his fellow believers to return to their faith after God has saved them from it: "*We should be guilty of fabricating lies against God, if we were to return to your ways after God has saved us from them.*" (Verse 89)

A person given guidance by God but who reverts to false beliefs which do not require people to submit themselves totally to God and to obey Him alone makes false testimony against God and His faith. The sum of that testimony is that he could not find anything good in divine faith, so he abandoned it to readopt the creed of the tyrants. Or at least his testimony means that the tyrants' creed also has the right to exist and exercise power, and can exist side by side with divine faith. Thus, he returns to it and recognizes it after he has believed in God. Such a testimony is far more serious than that of a person who has not experienced God's guidance and declared his submission to God. It acknowledges as legitimate the tyrants who usurp God's authority over human life.

Shu'ayb also denounces the tyrants' threats to force him and his followers back into erroneous faith: "*It is not conceivable that we should return to them.*" (Verse 89) It is simply impossible. Shu'ayb makes this statement in the face of threats backed by the might of the tyrants. Indeed, tyranny adopts the same attitude towards every Muslim community, wherever it exists, once it declares its rejection of tyranny and submits at the same time to God alone, associating no partners with Him.

Hard as the cost of rejecting tyranny and submitting to God alone may be, it is far easier to bear than the burden of submitting to tyrants. The latter submission may appear to ensure safety, security and a life of peace where a person can work and earn his living, but its cost is too hard and long lasting. The cost is paid out of man's very humanity, because man does not fulfil himself if he submits to another human being. What submission is worse than yielding to the laws enacted by another human being? What submission is worse than attaching one's destiny to the will of a fellow human being and to his pleasure and capricious desire? What could be worse than a human being with a bridle by which another person leads him wherever he wishes?

But the matter does not rest at this high level of beliefs and authority. It becomes more and more mundane so as to claim, under tyranny, people's property which will not be safeguarded by any law. It claims also their very children who are brought up to accept whatever concept, ideas, morals, traditions and customs, tyranny wishes them to adopt. In addition, tyranny imposes its control over their souls and lives, making of them an offering for its own caprice and erecting of their skulls and remains a monument for its glory. It then claims their honour. Under tyranny, no father can protect his daughter from disgrace, either by being flagrantly raped, as happens throughout history, or through implanting in her mind certain concepts that facilitate for her promiscuity under any guise and make her an easy target for unscrupulous seducers. Whoever imagines that he protects his property, honour, life and the lives of his sons and daughters under tyranny which usurps God's authority is living in self delusion. Under tyranny people lose their sense of reality.

To submit to tyranny is to burden oneself with an extremely heavy cost in terms of personal esteem, honour and property. Whatever burden a person finds himself required to bear for submitting himself to God is far easier and more profitable even by the standards of this present world. This is not to speak of what submission to God is worth by God's own measure.

The Meaning of True Submission

Maulana Mawdūdī says in his scholarly work *The Moral Foundation of the Islamic Movement*:

Even a person with superficial insight into human life cannot fail to realize that the whole question of human well-being depends entirely on who exercises control over human affairs. A train runs only to the destination determined by its driver. All passengers can travel only to the same destination, whether they like it or not. In the same way, the train of human civilization travels to where those who exercise power dictate. It is only too apparent that humanity as a whole cannot refuse the plan imposed by those who are in obvious control of all power throughout the world. It is those who conduct human affairs, and up to whom the masses look for the achievement of their goals and ambitions. Such people have the means of shaping ideas and theories, formulating them in an appealing fashion. They can influence personal habits, control social systems and mould moral values. If such leaders are good believers who fear God and who hope to receive reward from Him on the Day of Judgement, then the whole system of life will inevitably be set on the course of goodness and proper guidance. Evil people will be easily reformed and will realize that the path charted by faith is the proper one. Every good value becomes well established and begins to yield its fruit. The least benefit of social influence is that evil will be contained if not vanquished. On the other hand, if leadership is assumed by people who have deviated from the path laid down by God and His Messenger, and followed instead their own desires, exceeded their limits and led an undisciplined life, then the whole system of life will be based on tyranny, excesses and indecencies. Corruption will creep into concepts, theories, education, morality, politics, culture, civilization, as well as business transactions, law and justice. Evil will spread unchecked...

It is clearly apparent that the first thing divine faith requires of its followers is that they serve God alone, submitting to Him totally, so that they acknowledge no authority other than His and feel themselves to be free of all subjugation. It also requires that they recognize no law in their lives other than that laid down by God Himself and communicated to us and explained by God's Messenger, the Prophet Muḥammad (peace be upon Him). Islam also requires people to ensure the eradication of all corruption and elimination of all evil practices that incur God's displeasure. Nothing of these noble goals can be achieved while the leadership over human beings and the control over their affairs continue to be in the hands of unbelievers. In such a situation those who follow the divine faith are forced to accept the authority of those unbelievers and submit to their tyranny, staying in their own little sanctuaries where they glorify God, isolating themselves from people's lives, benefiting by any pardon or reprieve or guarantee the tyrants may feel pleased to grant them. This shows clearly the importance of good government and how it is instrumental in the implementation of divine law. Hence, the establishment of such good government that undertakes such a task is one of the objectives of faith. It is a fact that man cannot achieve God's pleasure through his own actions if he is to neglect this duty. Consider, if you will, what the Qur'ān and the *ḥadīth* say about being always part of the Muslim community and obeying its leadership. Indeed, people expose themselves to capital punishment if they were to abandon the community of believers, even in a small way, although they may pray, fast and claim to be Muslims. This is because the true aim of faith is the establishment of a proper Islamic system and well-guided leadership. This cannot be achieved except by the unity of the community. Whoever weakens the community does Islam and Muslims a great disservice that cannot be compensated for through prayer or even through the verbal acknowledgement of God's oneness. Consider also the high position Islam gives to *jihād*, so that the Qur'an describes as hypocrite those who are too lazy to join in a campaign of *jihād*. It should be remembered that *jihād* denotes the exertion of continuous effort for the establishment of the system of the truth. The Qur'ān considers this *jihād* the measure which is used to ascertain that a person is a believer. In other words, a person who believes in God and His Messenger cannot accept a system based on falsehood and cannot hesitate to sacrifice his life and property for the establishment of the truth. If a person appears to be reluctant or too weak to join in such an effort, then he lacks strength of faith. How is such a person to benefit by any of his actions?

The establishment of good government in God's earth is of vital importance in the Islamic system. A person who believes in God and His Messenger and submits himself properly to God in accordance with the true faith does not discharge all his obligations if he concentrates his full efforts on moulding his own life in accordance with Islamic teachings. As a believer, he must utilize everything within his power to remove unbelievers, wrongdoers and transgressors from power so that it can be assumed by pious people who fear God and realize that they are going to meet Him when He will hold them to account for what they do in this life. That is the way to ensure that the proper system which God has approved will be implemented, because it is the system which sets this life on its proper course.[1]

No Sorrow for Unbelievers' Fate

As Islam calls upon people to retrieve all authority usurped by human beings in order to return it all to God, it simply calls on them to rescue their humanity and save themselves from submission to fellow creatures. When they make a positive response, they actually save their souls and their property from the designs of tyrants, that serve their desires. In so doing, Islam requires its followers to bear the full burden of fighting tyranny, under its own banner, giving all the sacrifices such a fight may require. But at the same time, it spares them having to give sacrifices that are much more costly and humiliating. It protects their dignity and ensures their own safety at the same time. Hence, the Prophet Shu'ayb [peace be upon him] makes his statement loud and clear: "*We should be guilty of fabricating lies against God, if we were to return to your ways after God has saved us from them. It is not conceivable that we should return to them.*" (Verse 89)

Thus Shu'ayb stands up to the arrogant chiefs of his people, making his attitude absolutely clear and with his head raised high. Yet at the same time, he hangs his head down before his Lord, declaring his submission to Him alone, recognizing that His knowledge encompasses everything in the universe. As he refers to his Lord, he makes no final statement concerning what may happen. He simply declares that he has surrendered himself completely to God: "*It is not conceivable that we should return to them, unless God, our Lord, so wills. Our Lord has full knowledge of everything.*" (Verse 89)

This is an indication of complete submission to God by Shu'ayb and the believers who followed him. He makes clear that he can, at his own behest, refuse what tyrants require him to do of returning to their faith. He declares that he and his followers have no desire for such a return which sounds in principle totally unacceptable. But he, nevertheless, makes no categorical statement concerning what God may do with him or his followers. God's will is free and absolute. Neither he, nor those who have believed with him, have any knowledge of what God may decide to do with them, while their Lord has full

---

1. Mawdūdī's detailed view appear in *The Islamic Movement: Dynamics of Values, Power and Change*, Leicester, Islamic Foundation, 1998.

knowledge of everything. Hence, they submit to God's will and knowledge. This is the mark of good manners which believers are keen to demonstrate in their dealings with God.

At this point, Shu'ayb leaves his people and their threats aside, declaring that he relies totally, and with absolute confidence, on God who is certain to judge between him and his people in accordance with the truth: "*In God we place our trust. Our Lord, lay open the truth between us and our people; for You are the best to lay open the truth.*" (Verse 89)

These few words portray a fascinating scene when the truth of Godhead is clearly seen and properly felt by His friend and Prophet. The Prophet knows the source of all power and the secure refuge that can be found there, and he realizes that it is his Lord who can judge in truth between faith and tyranny. He places his trust completely in his Lord before he goes into the battle that is imposed on him and his followers. He realizes that he cannot win that battle unless his Lord grants him victory.

At this moment, the unbelievers turn to those who have believed with Shu'ayb to warn and threaten them, hoping to turn them away from their faith: "*The great ones who disbelieved among his people said: 'If you follow Shu'ayb, you shall indeed be losers.*" (Verse 90)

The same aspects of the continually raging battle are seen very clearly. The tyrants try first with the advocates of divine faith hoping to stop them. If they stand firm, showing that they trust only in their Lord and that they are determined to fulfil their task and deliver His message, paying little heed to the warnings of unbelievers and to the power they may possess, then the tyrants turn to those who have accepted such advocacy, trying to turn them away from their faith with stern warning and serious threats. Those tyrants have no solid argument to justify their falsehood, but they have brute force. They cannot win hearts over to their *jāhiliyyah*, particularly the hearts of those people who have recognized the truth and no longer pay respect to falsehood. But the tyrants can still persecute those who insist on following the divine faith and submitting to God alone.

But it is a rule that God has established in human life that when truth and falsehood have adopted their respective stands and become clearly distinct, confronting each other on the basis of principle, then God's law will come into operation. This was what took place with Shu'ayb and his people: "*Thereupon an earthquake overtook them and the morning found them lying lifeless on the ground in their very homes.*" (Verse 91)

The earthquake and their lying lifeless clearly contrast with their threats and arrogance and with their persecution of believers. Thus, the punishment seems to perfectly fit the arrogant attitude. The *sūrah* also replies to their earlier warnings to the believers that if they follow Shu'ayb, they will be losers. This was a serious threat that they intended to carry out. But the *sūrah* states with clear derision that it was not Shu'ayb's followers that turned out to be losers. "*As if those that rejected Shu'ayb had never prospered there. Those that rejected Shu'ayb were indeed the losers.*" (Verse 92) It was only a split second and they were lying lifeless, motionless, in their homes, as if they had never lived.

The account is concluded with remonstrations and a declaration of dissociation by the Prophet sent to them. He used to be their brother, but then they parted company and, in consequence, their respective destinies were totally different. He no longer felt any sadness or sorrow for what befell them. "*He turned away from them and said: 'My people, I delivered to you my Lord's messages and counselled you sincerely. How, then, could I grieve for people who persist in unbelief.'*" (Verse 93) They belonged to two different phases, and thus they were two separate communities. Ties of family and nationhood are of no consequence in this faith and of no weight in God's measure. The only solid tie is that of faith. True bonds between human beings can only be established on the basis of their strong ties with God's faith.

7

Lessons to Learn

Never have We sent a prophet to any city without trying its people with tribulations and hardship that they may supplicate with humility. (94)

وَمَآ أَرْسَلْنَا فِى قَرْيَةٍ مِّن نَّبِيٍّ إِلَّآ أَخَذْنَآ أَهْلَهَا بِٱلْبَأْسَآءِ وَٱلضَّرَّآءِ لَعَلَّهُمْ يَضَّرَّعُونَ ٩٤

We then replaced the affliction with good fortune till they throve and said, "Hardship and good fortune befell our forefathers as well.' We then smote them, all of a sudden, while they were totally unaware. (95)

ثُمَّ بَدَّلْنَا مَكَانَ ٱلسَّيِّئَةِ ٱلْحَسَنَةَ حَتَّىٰ عَفَوا۟ وَّقَالُوا۟ قَدْ مَسَّ ءَابَآءَنَا ٱلضَّرَّآءُ وَٱلسَّرَّآءُ فَأَخَذْنَٰهُم بَغْتَةً وَهُمْ لَا يَشْعُرُونَ ٩٥

Yet had the people of those cities believed and been God-fearing, We would indeed have opened up for them blessings out of heaven and earth. But they disbelieved, so We smote them on account of what they had been doing. (96)

وَلَوْ أَنَّ أَهْلَ ٱلْقُرَىٰٓ ءَامَنُوا۟ وَٱتَّقَوْا۟ لَفَتَحْنَا عَلَيْهِم بَرَكَٰتٍ مِّنَ ٱلسَّمَآءِ وَٱلْأَرْضِ وَلَٰكِن كَذَّبُوا۟ فَأَخَذْنَٰهُم بِمَا كَانُوا۟ يَكْسِبُونَ ٩٦

Do the people of these cities feel secure that Our might would not strike them at dead of night when they are asleep? (97)

أَفَأَمِنَ أَهْلُ ٱلْقُرَىٰٓ أَن يَأْتِيَهُم بَأْسُنَا بَيَٰتًا وَهُمْ نَآئِمُونَ ٩٧

Or do the people of these cities feel secure that Our might would not strike them in broad daylight when they are playing around? (98)

أَوَأَمِنَ أَهْلُ ٱلْقُرَىٰ أَن يَأْتِيَهُم بَأْسُنَا ضُحًى وَهُمْ يَلْعَبُونَ ﴿٩٨﴾

Do they feel themselves secure from God's designs? None feels secure from God's designs except those who are losers. (99)

أَفَأَمِنُوا۟ مَكْرَ ٱللَّهِ فَلَا يَأْمَنُ مَكْرَ ٱللَّهِ إِلَّا ٱلْقَوْمُ ٱلْخَٰسِرُونَ ﴿٩٩﴾

Is it not plain to those who have inherited the earth in succession of former generations that, if We so willed, We can punish them for their sins and seal their hearts, leaving them bereft of hearing. (100)

أَوَلَمْ يَهْدِ لِلَّذِينَ يَرِثُونَ ٱلْأَرْضَ مِنۢ بَعْدِ أَهْلِهَآ أَن لَّوْ نَشَآءُ أَصَبْنَٰهُم بِذُنُوبِهِمْ وَنَطْبَعُ عَلَىٰ قُلُوبِهِمْ فَهُمْ لَا يَسْمَعُونَ ﴿١٠٠﴾

We have related to you parts of the history of those communities. Messengers from among themselves came to them with clear evidence of the truth; but they would not believe in what they had formerly rejected. Thus does God seal the hearts of the unbelievers. (101)

تِلْكَ ٱلْقُرَىٰ نَقُصُّ عَلَيْكَ مِنْ أَنۢبَآئِهَا وَلَقَدْ جَآءَتْهُمْ رُسُلُهُم بِٱلْبَيِّنَٰتِ فَمَا كَانُوا۟ لِيُؤْمِنُوا۟ بِمَا كَذَّبُوا۟ مِن قَبْلُ كَذَٰلِكَ يَطْبَعُ ٱللَّهُ عَلَىٰ قُلُوبِ ٱلْكَٰفِرِينَ ﴿١٠١﴾

We found that most of them were untrue to their commitments; indeed We found most of them to be transgressors. (102)

وَمَا وَجَدْنَا لِأَكْثَرِهِم مِّنْ عَهْدٍ وَإِن وَجَدْنَآ أَكْثَرَهُمْ لَفَٰسِقِينَ ﴿١٠٢﴾

Preview

This passage of the *sūrah* comments on the accounts that have just finished of the histories of the communities to whom the Prophets Noah, Hūd, Ṣāliḥ, Lot and Shu'ayb were sent. We have here an explanation of the rule God has laid down which ensures that His will is done when He punishes those who deny His messages. It is the same rule and principle which shapes human history in one very important aspect. God inflicts tribulations and hardship on those who reject His messengers so that their hearts may soften and they turn to God, acknowledging His oneness and recognizing that the only course of action open to them is to submit to His overpowering authority. If they do not respond, then He tries them with affluence and good fortune. He opens up for them all types of blessings and leaves them for a while to enjoy their prosperity. All this, however, is a means of trial. People's prosperity causes them to lead a life of recklessness, negligence and heedlessness, because they tend to think that fortunes change by themselves, and a life of plenty is simply bound to follow a period of hardship, without any particular purpose or design.

When they feel that what they have experienced is the same as was experienced by their forefathers, without any particular purpose in all this design, God's punishment is certain to take them unawares. They do not understand God's purpose when He tries them with affliction and prosperity. They cannot comprehend why people's situations change every now and then. They have not guarded against incurring God's anger, preferring to live like animals until they are smitten by God's punishment. Had they believed in God and followed the right course, their situation would have changed and blessings would have opened up to them. God would have bestowed His grace on them and they would have been made to receive His blessings from everywhere, giving them reassurance and a happy future.

God then warns the new generations against a life of recklessness. He calls on them to be alert and to appreciate the lessons of past generations and how they met their doom. They themselves are also subject to God's laws of nature, which will remain in operation, exercising their influence on human history across all periods and generations.

This short commentary concludes with an address to the Prophet Muḥammad (peace be upon him), telling him that these histories are being related so that he learns how God's law has been given effect. It tells him of the true position of those communities: "*We found that most of them were untrue to their commitments; indeed We found most of them to be transgressors.*" (Verse 102) He is the last Messenger, and his followers are the nation which inherits the divine message in its totality. They are the ones to benefit by past lessons.

Trials of Adversity

Never have We sent a prophet to any city without trying its people with tribulations and hardship that they may supplicate with humility. We then replaced the affliction with good fortune till they throve and said, "Hardship and good fortune befell our forefathers as well."' We then smote them, all of a sudden, while they were totally unaware. Yet had the people of those cities believed and been God-fearing, We would indeed have opened up for them blessings out of heaven and earth. But they disbelieved, so We smote them on account of what they had been doing. (Verses 94-96)

We are not told here of any particular incident, but an important aspect of the natural law God has set in operation is highlighted. We are told how fate is determined. We thus learn that there is a law which sets matters into a particular pattern, dictating events, and shaping human history on earth. We learn that the divine message itself, important as it is, can be regarded as one of the means of implementing the divine constitution, which is far greater in scope than the message. Matters do not simply happen by themselves. Man does not stand alone, as alleged by later day atheists. Whatever takes place in the universe is part of an elaborate scheme, and has a definite purpose, serving an ultimate aim. The law of nature is devised by an absolutely free will which has shaped the constitution. It was in accordance with that law, operated by God's free will, that those communities, whose history was related in this *sūrah*, met their fate.

According to the Islamic concept, man's will and action are factors of great importance in determining the direction of his history and how it is to be interpreted. But man's will and action must be seen within the context of God's free will and absolute power. Within this context, man's will and action come into direct interaction with the entire universe. This means that there are many factors and situations which have a strong bearing on human history giving it greater scope and depth. When we understand this, then, any attempt to explain human history in purely economic, biological or geographical terms is far too narrow and petty.

"*Never have We sent a prophet to any city without trying its people with tribulations and hardship that they may supplicate with humility.*" (Verse 94) Far be it from God to punish His servants physically or cause them to go through adversity that affects their persons or their property for idle play. Such trials could never be motivated by hatred or the desire for revenge, as pagan legends make out. God tries with tribulations and adversity those who deny His message. By nature, such a trial reawakens human hearts and rekindles the light of goodness encouraging weak human beings to turn to God Almighty, their Creator, humbly appealing to Him to grant them forgiveness and bestow His mercy on them. By such humble supplication they declare their submission to Him, which is the ultimate aim of human existence. God does not need that human beings should supplicate humbly to Him and declare their submission: "*I have not created the jinn and human beings to any end other than that they may worship Me. No sustenance do I ever demand of them, nor do I demand that they feed Me. Truly, God Himself is the provider of all sustenance, the Lord of all might, the eternal.*" (51: 56-58)

As clearly stated in a sacred, or *qudsī ḥadīth*, if all human beings and *jinn* were as pious and obedient to God as the most pious and obedient person that ever lived, that would not increase God's kingdom in any way. Conversely, if all human beings and *jinn* were as wicked as the most wicked person that ever lived, that would not decrease God's kingdom in any way. But people's supplication and submission to God is of great benefit to them. It sets their lives on the right course. When human beings declare that they submit to God alone, they actually free themselves from submission to anyone else, particularly to Satan who tries hard to lead them astray, as mentioned earlier in this *sūrah*. They also free themselves from the yoke of their desires. They break the shackles of subjugation to other people and feel too ashamed to follow Satan's guidance or to incur God's displeasure through any action or purpose, particularly when they realize that they seek His help to remove any affliction they may suffer. This helps them follow the right course.

It is because of this that God's will is such that He tries any community who rejects His guidance, provided through His prophets and messengers, causing them to experience physical adversity and loss of property. Such pain may open up the elements of goodness in their nature and awaken their consciences. Thus, they may turn to God, seeking His mercy and appealing to Him to replace their affliction with comfort and reassurance.

But then God may decide to change the type of trial: "*We then replaced the affliction with good fortune.*" (Verse 95) Thus, every aspect of difficulty is replaced by an aspect of comfort and happiness. People begin to enjoy affluence, ease, blessings, good health, fertility, numerical strength and security after they had experienced poverty, hardship, depression, poor health, sterility, numerical weakness and fear. But the change of fortunes is no more than a new trial.

A test exposing people to hardship may be met with perseverance, because hardship may sharpen the elements of determined resistance. It may remind those who are good at heart of God, so they turn to Him with earnest supplication which gives them hope, reassurance and a promise of better things to come. A trial with affluence is withstood by only a few, because affluence makes people forget and riches cause them to feel self-sufficient. Hence, they indulge themselves seeking every type of pleasure. Such a test is passed only by a very small number of people.

"*We then replaced the affliction with good fortune till they throve and said, 'Hardship and good fortune befell our forefathers as well'.*" (Verse 95) This statement indicates that they had increased in numbers and enjoyed an easy life, tasting every pleasure, to the extent that they no longer hesitated to do anything they desired, nor did they feel embarrassed by any action. The Arabic term which is translated here as "they throve" also connotes a certain attitude of mind which is rather careless, even bordering on recklessness. It views everything as easy, and acts on impulse. This attitude is very common among affluent people who enjoy riches for a long period, whether at the individual or community level. It is an attitude that suggests a blunted sensitivity and a care-free attitude. They spend and enjoy themselves with recklessness and they care little for the rights of others. No cardinal sin or ghastly crime seems to worry them. They do not care if they incur God's wrath or people's criticism. They do not reflect on the trials to which other people have been exposed. They think that life just goes on, without a purpose or a definite goal.

"*They throve and said, 'Hardship and good fortune befell our forefathers as well.*'" (Verse 95) They look at it as if it is the turn of a repeated cycle. They have had their turn in adversity and now they are due for some good fortune. This all just happens without any particular consequence. At this moment, when they are totally heedless, indulging themselves in all sorts of transgression, their fate is sealed in accordance with God's law: "*We then smote them, all of a sudden, while they were totally unaware.*" (Verse 95) They had gone so far astray that they no longer felt ashamed of anything they did. To fear God does not occur to them at all.

Thus we see how God's law operates, fulfilling His will. Human history thus moves by human will and human action, within the context of God's will and the laws He has set in operation. The Qur'ān reveals this fact to human beings and warns them that they must prove themselves when they are subjected to a trial of adversity or a test of affluence. It kindles in them a state of alertness which brings back to them a sense of fearing the outcome which befits what they do in this life. Those who do not respond, and continue in their erring ways wrong only themselves because they expose themselves to God's punishment which is certain to engulf them. No one will suffer any injustice.

A Sure Way to Receive God's Blessings

"*Yet had the people of those cities believed and been God-fearing, We would indeed have opened up for them blessings out of heaven and earth. But they disbelieved, so We smote them on account of what they had been doing.*" (Verse 96) This is the other part of the natural law God has set in operation. Had the people of those cities believed instead of denying God's messages, and had they been God-fearing instead of being careless, God would have opened up for them blessings from heaven and earth. They would have been given such blessings in abundance, without restriction. God's blessings would have come to them from above and beneath. The Qur'ānic expression is so general that it imparts a sense of great abundance that is not limited to what is familiar to human beings of provisions and sustenance.

This statement and the one preceding it put in front of our eyes certain facts that relate to faith on the one hand and to human life in this world on the other. They also touch on a factor that has a great influence on human history, even though it is often overlooked and indeed denied by man-made theories and philosophies. That fact tells us that the question of having faith in God and fearing Him is not isolated from the reality of life and the course of human history. To believe in God and to fear Him qualify people to receive blessings from heaven and earth. This is a promise given by God, and God is always true to His promises.

We who believe in God accept this promise as true without having to ask first about its reasons or causes. We have no hesitation in expecting that it will come true. We believe in God, and consequently in what lies beyond human perception; therefore, we believe in the fulfilment of God's promises. But when we reflect on God's promise, as indeed we are ordered to do by our faith, we soon realize its causes. A person who believes in God has an alert nature, sound natural reception, accurate understanding, a healthy human constitution and a keen interaction with the universe. All these elements tend to ensure success in real life.

Moreover, faith in God represents a strong motivation. It streamlines all aspects of the human constitution and directs them to a single goal, allowing them to derive strength from God's power and release them to implement His will in building human life on earth and safeguarding it from all elements of corruption. Again, all this tends to ensure success in practical life.

To believe in God is to be free from being enslaved by desire or by other people. There is no doubt that a human being who achieves his freedom through submission to God is, as a result, better able to fulfil man's task of building human life on earth. To fear God is to combine awareness with wisdom so that we can steer away from rashness, recklessness and conceit as we go about our business in this life. It is a quality that directs human effort sensibly and carefully so that whoever has that quality does not transgress or exceed the limits of acceptable behaviour.

When people maintain a balance between incentives and restraints, working on earth but always looking up to heaven, free from the tyranny of human desire, submitting to God Almighty, human life maintains a steady course and yields wholesome fruits. In this way people deserve God's help after having earned His pleasure. Hence, it will be a blessed life that earns success and prosperity. Viewed from this angle, the whole question is one of visible facts that have their unidentifiable causes, in addition to its being part of God's promise.

The blessings God promises to those who believe in Him and fear Him are given a strong emphasis. They come in a wide variety of shapes and forms but they are not outlined in detail or mentioned in name. The Qur'ānic statement, however, gives an impression of abounding grace that comes from every direction, without any limiting definition. Hence, the reference is to all types and forms of blessings, whether those that are familiar to human beings or those that can only be visualized in their imagination. But they also include what human beings cannot conceive or imagine.

Those who imagine that faith in God and steering away from what incurs His anger are questions of pure worship and have no bearing on practical life have no true knowledge of faith or life. They are better advised to look at this very real relationship which God Himself confirms. Needless to say, His testimony is more than enough to prove anything. Nevertheless, this relationship can be recognized by people if they will only look at different situations in life and recognize their causes: "*Yet had the people of those cities believed and been God-fearing, We would indeed have opened up for them blessings out of heaven and earth. But they disbelieved, so We smote them on account of what they had been doing.*" (Verse 96)

Nevertheless, we see communities and people who claim to be Muslims going through hard times when they experience drought and very poor crops. At the same time, we see communities who are devoid of faith and have no fear of God, yet they enjoy abundance, power and influence. These contrasting situations lead people to ask: where is this unfailing law of nature, and why does it not operate?

But all this is mere delusion based on appearances. The people who claim to be Muslim are not believers in reality, nor do they truly fear God. They do not sincerely submit to God alone, nor do they implement in practical life the basic article of faith which requires them to declare that there is no deity other than God. They submit themselves to fellow human beings who claim for themselves a position of Godhead and begin to legislate laws for them and set values and standards. Such people are not believers, because a believer will never acknowledge that any creature can fill the position of Godhead. He will never allow a fellow human being to determine the laws that shape his life. When the predecessors of those who today claim to be Muslims were true believers, they became the masters of the world. Blessings from heaven and earth were opened up for them in fulfilment of God's promise.

Those others enjoying a life of affluence are only going through a different stage of the operation of the law of nature: "*We then replaced the affliction with good fortune till they throve and said, 'Hardship and good fortune befell our forefathers as well'.*" (Verse 95) It is then a test of plenty, which is far more difficult than a trial of adversity. There is an essential difference between what such people enjoy and the blessings God promises to those who believe in Him and fear Him. Blessings can be given with limited means if people can use those means well and combine them with goodness and a sense of reassurance, security and happiness. Many a rich and powerful community goes through a life of misery, insecurity and hollow ties between its people. The people themselves are worried, apprehensive of losing their power. It is a situation of strength without security, affluence without contentment, plenty without goodness. It is a bright present to be followed by a miserable future. It is a test that is certain to lead to doom.

The blessings that come with faith and a God-fearing attitude can be experienced in all situations, both within the human being himself and in his feelings, as well as within all enjoyable aspects of life. These blessings give growth and elevate life to a higher standard. They are so different from affluence that is combined with misery and immorality.

A False Sense of Security

The *sūrah* has thus established the fact that God's law is set in operation and will never fail, as confirmed by the history of former communities. Now that feelings are high about the doom that befell those who rejected the faith and overlooked the purpose of their test, the *sūrah* addresses those who have so far overlooked these facts of life. It tries to awaken in them a sense of expectation, alerting them to the fact that God's might may strike them at any time of day or night, when they are asleep, at work or having fun: "*Do the people of these cities feel secure that Our might would not strike them at dead of night when they are asleep? Or do the people of these cities feel secure that Our might would not strike them in broad daylight when they are playing around? Do they feel themselves secure from God's designs? None feels secure from God's designs except those who are losers. Is it not plain to those who have inherited the earth in succession of former generations that, if We so willed, We can punish them for their sins and seal their hearts, leaving them bereft of hearing."* (Verses 97-100)

Having been told of God's law that exposes people and communities to tests of adversity and affluence, and having seen the doom that befell those who rejected the divine message in former times, do the people of the present generation feel so secure that they assume that God's might will not strike when they are totally unaware? Do they feel so immune against God's might striking at dead of night when they are fast asleep? They should remember that a sleeping person is powerless, unable to take precautions or even repel a weak, small insect. How could he prevent a mighty strike from God, when no human being, however alert and strong can resist or prevent it?

Or do they feel secure that God's might will not strike in broad daylight when they are engaged in their play? Enjoyable activities, or play and fun, normally preoccupy man and totally distract his attention. A person who is absorbed in his play, having fun, can hardly resist an enemy's strike. How can he resist a strike from God when no human being, at his most alert and highest state of preparedness can avert it?

The fact is that God's might is far too powerful to be resisted by all human beings, whether they are asleep or awake, preoccupied or alert, but the *sūrah* points out the moments of human weakness to shake people and attract their attention. This is the effect of expecting a strike at a moment of weakness when one is totally unaware while realizing that people cannot escape such a strike even at their moments of strength. In both situations, man is totally powerless when confronted by God's might.

"Do they feel themselves secure from God's designs?" (Verse 99) Can they have any immunity against what God plans for human beings when He does not reveal those plans to them so that they can guard against them? If they feel so secure, then the fact is that *"none feels secure from God's designs except those who are losers."* (Verse 99)

Utter loss is indeed the result of an attitude that continues to overlook the facts of history and prefers a sense of false security. Those who adopt such an attitude earn such a loss. How can they feel secure, when they have inherited the earth from people that have been destroyed as a result of their erring ways, and who were punished for adopting the same attitude of disregarding those basic facts? The destiny of those nations should have taught them some good lessons.

Is it not plain to those who have inherited the earth in succession of former generations that, if We so willed, We can punish them for their sins and seal their hearts, leaving them bereft of hearing. (Verse 100)

The laws of nature God has set in operation will never fail, and His will is certain to always be done. So what guarantees people's security against the punishment God may inflict on them for the sins they have committed, in the same way as He punished earlier communities? How can they be safe from having their hearts sealed so that they cannot even listen to divine guidance? For that would ensure that they receive punishment for following the wrong path. The fate of earlier communities and the fact that the laws of nature remain operative should give them sufficient warning to make them fear God and follow His guidance. This would require them to get rid of their sense of false security and to be on their guard. They should benefit by the lessons of earlier communities so that they do not have to suffer the same fate.

In giving this warning in the Qur'ān, God does not want people to always live in fear, worrying that He may cause their immediate destruction at any moment of the night or day. Such a constant fear of the unknown, and permanent worry about the future, and such an expectation of destruction may paralyse people, deprive them of their abilities and lead them to a state of despair. They would then stop working and refrain from fulfilling the task of building human life on earth. What God wants from them is that they should always be on the alert, watching their own actions, paying heed to other people's experience, identifying the elements that shape human history and remain always in touch with God, not allowing prosperity to make them lead an easy, careless life.

God promises human beings a life of security, reassurance and prosperity in this world and in the world to come, if they would only submit to His will and fear Him enough to avoid everything that leaves a stain on human life. He invites them to enjoy security under His protection, trusting to His might, rather than their own material power. They should seek what He has in store for His obedient servants, rather than the luxuries of this world.

Life has known generations of believers who feared God and never thought themselves immune from His will or trusted to anyone other than Him. Such people had a keen sense of their faith, and because they enjoyed God's support they felt reassured, able to overcome Satan and his designs. They lived a goodly life, implementing God's guidance, fearing no human beings, because they feared God alone.

This is how we should understand the constant warnings against the overwhelming might of God and His designs that cannot be foiled. We will then realize that such warnings should not lead us to worry and fear, but to be keenly alert. These warnings do not paralyse life but make sure that it does not sink into a state of carelessness and transgression.

At the same time, the Qur'ānic method addresses all human situations and stages of development, at the individual and community levels, providing the right treatment to each one of them, at the right time. It administers a dose of security, trust and reassurance that God's help will be forthcoming whenever they are threatened by hostile forces. At the same time, it provides a sense of keen apprehension that God's punishment may be forthcoming whenever people yield to worldly forces and temptations. God certainly knows best how His creation responds to all elements and influences.

A History Recorded by God

Having outlined, with highly inspiring touches, the operative rules of nature, the *sūrah* addresses God's Messenger (peace be upon him) informing him of the net outcome of putting those communities to trial, pointing out certain facts about the nature of faith and disbelief, as well as the nature of human beings, as seen in those communities: *"We have related to you parts of the history of those communities. Messengers from among themselves came to them with clear evidence of the truth; but they would not believe in what they had formerly rejected. Thus does God seal the hearts of the unbelievers. We found that most of them were untrue to their commitments; indeed We found most of them to be transgressors."* (Verses 101-102)

This history is clearly stated to have been revealed by God. The Prophet could not have learnt it from any source other than revelation.

"Messengers from among themselves came to them with clear evidence of the truth." (Verse 101) But no evidence was of benefit to them, because they continued to reject the message after having received that

evidence in the same way as they rejected it before such evidence was given them. They simply would not believe in what they had already rejected. No matter how clear the evidence of the truth is, it will not lead such people to adopt the faith. What those people lacked was not plain proof of the truth, but rather open hearts and minds, and a keen desire to receive guidance. They lacked an active nature that receives and responds. When they refused to open their minds to elements of guidance, God sealed their hearts and they could no longer give any proper response: "*Thus does God seal the hearts of the unbelievers.*" (Verse 101)

The history of those communities reveals a predominant fact: "*We found that most of them were untrue to their commitments; indeed We found most of them to be transgressors.*" (Verse 102) The commitment mentioned in this verse may refer to the pledge God has received from human nature and to which reference is made later in the *sūrah*: "*Your Lord brought forth their offspring from the loins of the children of Adam, and called them to bear witness about themselves: 'Am I not your Lord?' – to which they answer: 'Yes, indeed, we do bear witness that You are.*" (Verse 172) It may also refer to the commitment to faith given by their forefathers who followed God's messengers, but subsequent generations deviated, as happens indeed in every community. Successive generations deviate gradually until they go out of the fold altogether and sink back into ignorance, or *jāhiliyyah*.

Whatever the commitment is to which the *sūrah* is referring here, the fact remains that most of those communities were untrue to it. They followed their own fleeting whims and shifting desires. They could not fulfil their pledges.

"*Indeed we found most of them to be transgressors.*" (Verse 102) They deviate from God's faith and from their original commitment. This is the result of following one's capricious desires and taking solemn commitments lightly. Whoever turns away from God's guidance, lacking the determination to fulfil the commitments he has made to Him, is bound to move away from faith into corruption and transgression. That was true of the people of those communities, and that was their end.

8

A Confrontation with Pharaoh

Then after those We sent Moses with Our signs to Pharaoh and his people, but they wilfully rejected them. Behold what happened in the end to those spreaders of corruption. (103)

ثُمَّ بَعَثْنَا مِنۢ بَعْدِهِم مُّوسَىٰ بِآيَٰتِنَآ إِلَىٰ فِرْعَوْنَ وَمَلَإِيْهِ فَظَلَمُواْ بِهَا فَٱنظُرْ كَيْفَ كَانَ عَٰقِبَةُ ٱلْمُفْسِدِينَ ﴿١٠٣﴾

Moses said: "Pharaoh, I am a Messenger from the Lord of all the worlds, (104)

وَقَالَ مُوسَىٰ يَٰفِرْعَوْنُ إِنِّى رَسُولٌ مِّن رَّبِّ ٱلْعَٰلَمِينَ ﴿١٠٤﴾

and may say about God nothing but the truth. I have come to you with a clear evidence from your Lord. So, let the Children of Israel go with me." (105)

حَقِيقٌ عَلَىٰٓ أَن لَّآ أَقُولَ عَلَى ٱللَّهِ إِلَّا ٱلْحَقَّ قَدْ جِئْتُكُم بِبَيِّنَةٍ مِّن رَّبِّكُمْ فَأَرْسِلْ مَعِىَ بَنِىٓ إِسْرَٰٓءِيلَ ﴿١٠٥﴾

He answered: "If you have come with a sign, produce it then if you are so truthful." (106)

قَالَ إِن كُنتَ جِئْتَ بِآيَةٍ فَأْتِ بِهَآ إِن كُنتَ مِنَ ٱلصَّٰدِقِينَ ﴿١٠٦﴾

Moses threw down his staff, and it immediately became a plainly visible serpent. (107)

فَأَلْقَىٰ عَصَاهُ فَإِذَا هِىَ ثُعْبَانٌ مُّبِينٌ ﴿١٠٧﴾

And he drew forth his hand, and it was [shining] white to the beholders. (108)

وَنَزَعَ يَدَهُ فَإِذَا هِىَ بَيْضَآءُ لِلنَّٰظِرِينَ ﴿١٠٨﴾

The great ones among Pharaoh's people said: "This man is indeed a sorcerer of great skill, (109)

قَالَ ٱلۡمَلَأُ مِن قَوۡمِ فِرۡعَوۡنَ إِنَّ هَٰذَا لَسَٰحِرٌ عَلِيمٌ ۝

who wants to drive you out of your land!" [Said Pharaoh] "What, then, do you advise?" (110)

يُرِيدُ أَن يُخۡرِجَكُم مِّنۡ أَرۡضِكُمۡ فَمَاذَا تَأۡمُرُونَ ۝

They said: "Let him and his brother wait a while, and send heralds to all cities (111)

قَالُوٓاْ أَرۡجِهۡ وَأَخَاهُ وَأَرۡسِلۡ فِي ٱلۡمَدَآئِنِ حَٰشِرِينَ ۝

to bring before you every sorcerer of great skill." (112)

يَأۡتُوكَ بِكُلِّ سَٰحِرٍ عَلِيمٍ ۝

The sorcerers came to Pharaoh and said: "Surely there will be a handsome reward for us if it is we who prevail." (113)

وَجَآءَ ٱلسَّحَرَةُ فِرۡعَوۡنَ قَالُوٓاْ إِنَّ لَنَا لَأَجۡرًا إِن كُنَّا نَحۡنُ ٱلۡغَٰلِبِينَ ۝

Answered [Pharaoh]: "Yes; and you will certainly be among those who are close to me." (114)

قَالَ نَعَمۡ وَإِنَّكُمۡ لَمِنَ ٱلۡمُقَرَّبِينَ ۝

They said: "Moses! Either you shall throw [first], or we shall be the first to throw?" (115)

قَالُوٓاْ يَٰمُوسَىٰٓ إِمَّآ أَن تُلۡقِيَ وَإِمَّآ أَن نَّكُونَ نَحۡنُ ٱلۡمُلۡقِينَ ۝

He answered: "You throw [first]." And when they threw [their staffs], they cast a spell upon people's eyes and struck them with awe, making a display of great sorcery. (116)

قَالَ أَلۡقُواْۖ فَلَمَّآ أَلۡقَوۡاْ سَحَرُوٓاْ أَعۡيُنَ ٱلنَّاسِ وَٱسۡتَرۡهَبُوهُمۡ وَجَآءُو بِسِحۡرٍ عَظِيمٍ ۝

We then inspired Moses: "Throw your staff." And it swallowed up their false devices. (117)

وَأَوْحَيْنَا إِلَىٰ مُوسَىٰ أَنْ أَلْقِ عَصَاكَ فَإِذَا هِيَ تَلْقَفُ مَا يَأْفِكُونَ ۝

Thus the truth prevailed and all their doings were proved to be in vain. (118)

فَوَقَعَ الْحَقُّ وَبَطَلَ مَا كَانُوا يَعْمَلُونَ ۝

They were defeated there and then, and became utterly humiliated. (119)

فَغُلِبُوا هُنَالِكَ وَانقَلَبُوا صَاغِرِينَ ۝

The sorcerers fell down prostrating themselves, (120)

وَأُلْقِيَ السَّحَرَةُ سَاجِدِينَ ۝

and said: "We believe in the Lord of all the worlds, (121)

قَالُوا آمَنَّا بِرَبِّ الْعَالَمِينَ ۝

the Lord of Moses and Aaron." (122)

رَبِّ مُوسَىٰ وَهَارُونَ ۝

Pharaoh said: "You believe in Him even before I have given you permission! This is indeed a plot you have contrived in this city in order to drive out its people, but you shall soon come to know [the consequences]. (123)

قَالَ فِرْعَوْنُ آمَنتُم بِهِ قَبْلَ أَنْ آذَنَ لَكُمْ إِنَّ هَٰذَا لَمَكْرٌ مَّكَرْتُمُوهُ فِي الْمَدِينَةِ لِتُخْرِجُوا مِنْهَا أَهْلَهَا فَسَوْفَ تَعْلَمُونَ ۝

I shall have your hands and feet cut off on alternate sides, and then I shall crucify you all." (124)

لَأُقَطِّعَنَّ أَيْدِيَكُمْ وَأَرْجُلَكُم مِّنْ خِلَافٍ ثُمَّ لَأُصَلِّبَنَّكُمْ أَجْمَعِينَ ۝

They replied: "To our Lord we shall indeed return. (125)

قَالُوا إِنَّا إِلَىٰ رَبِّنَا مُنقَلِبُونَ ۝

You want to take vengeance on us only because we have believed in the signs of our Lord when they were shown to us. Our Lord, grant us abundance of patience in adversity, and let us die as people who have surrendered themselves to You." (126)

وَمَا تَنقِمُ مِنَّا إِلَّا أَنْ ءَامَنَّا بِـَٔايَٰتِ رَبِّنَا لَمَّا جَآءَتْنَا ۚ رَبَّنَا أَفْرِغْ عَلَيْنَا صَبْرًا وَتَوَفَّنَا مُسْلِمِينَ ١٢٦

The great ones among Pharaoh's people said: "Will you allow Moses and his people to spread corruption in the land and to forsake you and your gods?" He replied: "We shall put their sons to death and shall spare only their women. We shall certainly overpower them." (127)

وَقَالَ ٱلْمَلَأُ مِن قَوْمِ فِرْعَوْنَ أَتَذَرُ مُوسَىٰ وَقَوْمَهُۥ لِيُفْسِدُوا۟ فِى ٱلْأَرْضِ وَيَذَرَكَ وَءَالِهَتَكَ ۚ قَالَ سَنُقَتِّلُ أَبْنَآءَهُمْ وَنَسْتَحْىِۦ نِسَآءَهُمْ وَإِنَّا فَوْقَهُمْ قَٰهِرُونَ ١٢٧

Moses said to his people: "Turn to God (alone) for help and remain steadfast. The whole earth belongs to God. He allows it to be inherited by whomever He wills of His servants. The future belongs to those who are God-fearing." (128)

قَالَ مُوسَىٰ لِقَوْمِهِ ٱسْتَعِينُوا۟ بِٱللَّهِ وَٱصْبِرُوٓا۟ ۖ إِنَّ ٱلْأَرْضَ لِلَّهِ يُورِثُهَا مَن يَشَآءُ مِنْ عِبَادِهِۦ ۖ وَٱلْعَٰقِبَةُ لِلْمُتَّقِينَ ١٢٨

They said: "We have been oppressed before you came to us and since you have come to us." He replied: "It may well be that your Lord will destroy your enemy and leave you to inherit the earth. He will then see how you conduct yourselves." (129)

قَالُوٓا۟ أُوذِينَا مِن قَبْلِ أَن تَأْتِيَنَا وَمِنۢ بَعْدِ مَا جِئْتَنَا ۚ قَالَ عَسَىٰ رَبُّكُمْ أَن يُهْلِكَ عَدُوَّكُمْ وَيَسْتَخْلِفَكُمْ فِى ٱلْأَرْضِ فَيَنظُرَ كَيْفَ تَعْمَلُونَ ١٢٩

We afflicted Pharaoh's people with drought and poor harvests, so that they might take heed. (130)

وَلَقَدْ أَخَذْنَآ ءَالَ فِرْعَوْنَ بِٱلسِّنِينَ وَنَقْصٍ مِّنَ ٱلثَّمَرَٰتِ لَعَلَّهُمْ يَذَّكَّرُونَ ۝

Whenever something fine came their way, they would say: "This is our due", but whenever affliction befell them, they attributed their ill omen to Moses and those who followed him. Surely, whatever befalls them has been decreed by God, though most of them do not know it. (131)

فَإِذَا جَآءَتْهُمُ ٱلْحَسَنَةُ قَالُوا۟ لَنَا هَٰذِهِۦ وَإِن تُصِبْهُمْ سَيِّئَةٌ يَطَّيَّرُوا۟ بِمُوسَىٰ وَمَن مَّعَهُۥٓ أَلَآ إِنَّمَا طَٰٓئِرُهُمْ عِندَ ٱللَّهِ وَلَٰكِنَّ أَكْثَرَهُمْ لَا يَعْلَمُونَ ۝

They said [to Moses]: "Whatever sign you may produce before us in order to cast a spell on us, we shall not believe in you." (132)

وَقَالُوا۟ مَهْمَا تَأْتِنَا بِهِۦ مِنْ ءَايَةٍ لِّتَسْحَرَنَا بِهَا فَمَا نَحْنُ لَكَ بِمُؤْمِنِينَ ۝

So We plagued them with floods, and locusts, and lice, and frogs, and blood: clear signs all; but they gloried in their arrogance, for they were evil-doing folk. (133)

فَأَرْسَلْنَا عَلَيْهِمُ ٱلطُّوفَانَ وَٱلْجَرَادَ وَٱلْقُمَّلَ وَٱلضَّفَادِعَ وَٱلدَّمَ ءَايَٰتٍ مُّفَصَّلَٰتٍ فَٱسْتَكْبَرُوا۟ وَكَانُوا۟ قَوْمًا مُّجْرِمِينَ ۝

Whenever a plague struck them, they would cry: "Moses, pray to your Lord for us on the strength of the covenant He has made with you. If you lift the plague from us, we will truly believe in you, and we will let the Children of Israel go with you." (134)

وَلَمَّا وَقَعَ عَلَيْهِمُ ٱلرِّجْزُ قَالُوا۟ يَٰمُوسَى ٱدْعُ لَنَا رَبَّكَ بِمَا عَهِدَ عِندَكَ لَئِن كَشَفْتَ عَنَّا ٱلرِّجْزَ لَنُؤْمِنَنَّ لَكَ وَلَنُرْسِلَنَّ مَعَكَ بَنِىٓ إِسْرَٰٓءِيلَ ۝

But when We had lifted the plague from them, for a term they were sure to reach, they broke their promise. (135)

فَلَمَّا كَشَفْنَا عَنْهُمُ ٱلرِّجْزَ إِلَىٰ أَجَلٍ هُم بَٰلِغُوهُ إِذَا هُمْ يَنكُثُونَ ﴿١٣٥﴾

So We inflicted Our retribution on them, and caused them to drown in the sea, because they denied Our signs and were heedless of them. (136)

فَٱنتَقَمْنَا مِنْهُمْ فَأَغْرَقْنَٰهُمْ فِى ٱلْيَمِّ بِأَنَّهُمْ كَذَّبُوا۟ بِـَٔايَٰتِنَا وَكَانُوا۟ عَنْهَا غَٰفِلِينَ ﴿١٣٦﴾

We caused the people who were persecuted and deemed utterly low to inherit the eastern and western parts of the land which We had blessed. Thus your Lord's gracious promise to the Children of Israel was fulfilled, because they were patient in adversity; and We destroyed all that Pharaoh and his people had wrought, and all that they had built. (137)

وَأَوْرَثْنَا ٱلْقَوْمَ ٱلَّذِينَ كَانُوا۟ يُسْتَضْعَفُونَ مَشَٰرِقَ ٱلْأَرْضِ وَمَغَٰرِبَهَا ٱلَّتِى بَٰرَكْنَا فِيهَا وَتَمَّتْ كَلِمَتُ رَبِّكَ ٱلْحُسْنَىٰ عَلَىٰ بَنِىٓ إِسْرَٰٓءِيلَ بِمَا صَبَرُوا۟ وَدَمَّرْنَا مَا كَانَ يَصْنَعُ فِرْعَوْنُ وَقَوْمُهُۥ وَمَا كَانُوا۟ يَعْرِشُونَ ﴿١٣٧﴾

Preview

This passage relates much of the history of Moses with Pharaoh and his people. It starts when Pharaoh and the leading figures among his people are confronted with the fact that God is the Lord of all the universe, and ends with the drowning of Pharaoh and his army. In between these events, the *surah* tells us of the contest between Moses and the magicians which ends up with a triumph for the truth, and the declaration by the sorcerers that they believe in the Lord of all the worlds, according to the concept preached by Moses and his brother Aaron. The *surah* tells us of Pharaoh's threats to punish those magicians and to put them to death. Nevertheless, the truth had taken such a hold of their hearts that they no longer cared for Pharaoh. They were prepared to sacrifice their lives for their faith.

The *sūrah* also tells us of the persecution to which the Children of Israel were subjected and how God punished Pharaoh and his people with poor harvests and also inflicted on them floods, and pests of locusts, ants, frogs and blood. Each time, they appealed to Moses to pray to his Lord to lift the punishment. However, whenever a punishment was lifted, they reverted to their erring ways, declaring that they would not believe, no matter what signs they were shown. Eventually, God's law overtook them and they were drowned because of their rejection of the clear evidence shown to them and because they overlooked the purpose of the tests to which God may subject any community. According to God's law, He tests unbelievers with hardship and affluence before destroying them. Then, power in the land was given to Moses's people as a reward for their perseverance through the test of hardship. That meant a new test with affluence.

We have chosen to divide the story of Moses, as related in this *sūrah*, into two passages, devoting the second passage to the events that took place after the Israelites were saved and Pharaoh and his people were drowned.

The story opens here with a brief outline of its beginning and end, highlighting the purpose for which it is related in this *sūrah*: "*Then after those We sent Moses with Our signs to Pharaoh and his people, but they wilfully rejected them. Behold what happened in the end to those spreaders of corruption.*" (Verse 103)

Thus, we are clearly told the purpose behind relating this history here. It is to tell us about the end faced by the spreaders of corruption. Having made this brief outline, the *sūrah* goes on to relate one episode after another, in clear and detailed scenes that serve the overall purpose.

The story is divided into a number of vivid scenes, each of which is full of life, employing significant dialogue. Each is clearly inspiring, with certain distinctive features. In between, we have some relevant instructions pointing out the lessons that should be learned from the story. In essence, the passage demonstrates in sharp relief the nature of the battle between the call to faith, which declares that God is the Lord of all the worlds, and the tyrants who impose their authority on mankind, claiming to have lordship over the world. We also see how faith asserts itself, paying little heed to tyrannical power and caring nothing for threats of impending punishment.

As the Story Begins

"Then after those We sent Moses with Our signs to Pharaoh and his people, but they wilfully rejected them. Behold what happened in the end to those spreaders of corruption." (Verse 103) We first learn that Moses's mission came after those communities to whom earlier prophets were sent. The *sūrah* has given us an account of each of those communities and what happened to their people who rejected the messages of those Prophets.

The *sūrah* now begins the story of Moses from when he confronted Pharaoh and the leaders of his government with the divine message. It then tells us very briefly the sum of their response, and refers to the fate they suffered. Pharaoh's people wilfully and wrongfully rejected the signs shown to them by God, without proper consideration or reflection. We find that the Qur'ān often uses terms like, 'wrongful, unjust, oppression or transgression' in place of 'disbelief' or 'associating partners with God'. Here the Arabic text uses the phrase 'resorted to injustice' for what is rendered in the translated text as 'wilful rejection'. The fact is that the association of partners with God or rejecting divine faith is the worst type of injustice and the most ghastly transgression. Those who reject faith adopt a wrongful attitude towards the basic truism of God's oneness. They also wrong themselves by exposing themselves to destruction in this life, as well as severe punishment in the life to come. They are also unjust to other human beings because they try to take them away from submission to God, the only Lord in the universe, in order to force them to submit to different deities and authorities. There can be no worse injustice than this. Hence, to disbelieve in God is to be unjust, and, as the Qur'ān states, *"Truly, the unbelievers are the wrongdoers."* (2: 254) Similarly, a person who rejects faith is a transgressor, because he turns away from the straight path leading to God in order to follow other paths that lead only to hell.

Pharaoh and his people certainly took a wrongful and oppressive attitude, rejecting God's signs and revelations. Hence, *"Behold what happened in the end to those spreaders of corruption."* (Verse 103) Their fate will be presently outlined in the *sūrah*. Let us for now reflect on the import of the term, 'spreaders of corruption', which is used here as a synonym for 'unbelievers' and 'wrongdoers'.

Here they are described as 'spreaders of corruption' because of their wrongful rejection of God's signs. The fact is that to disbelieve is the worst type of corruption and indeed a wilful spreading of such corruption. Human life cannot flourish and prosper unless it is built on the foundation of believing in God as the only deity in the universe, and on submission to Him alone. Life on earth will certainly suffer corruption when people refrain from such submission, which means that there is only one master for mankind, to whom they address their worship. They will then submit to His law alone which frees their lives from submission to fleeting human desires. When human beings acknowledge the Lordship of several deities in preference to that of God alone, corruption does not affect merely their social lives, but also their concepts and beliefs. The fact is that human life on earth was not set on the proper footing and did not prosper except when they declared that they submit only to God in faith, worship and law. Man did not achieve his liberation except under the single Lordship of God. Hence, God says in reference to Pharaoh and his people: "*Behold what happened in the end to those spreaders of corruption.*" (Verse 103) Every tyrant who imposes his law on human beings in preference to God's law is a spreader of corruption.

The Truth, the Whole Truth

This opening of the story represents a particular Qur'ānic method of relating historical accounts. It is certainly the most appropriate method for this *sūrah*, because it fits in well with its central theme. It tells us the outcome right at the beginning. It then moves on to give the details, so that we may follow the events right up to their conclusion. What happened, then, between Moses and Pharaoh?

> *Moses said: "Pharaoh, I am a Messenger from the Lord of all the worlds, and may say about God nothing but the truth. I have come to you with a clear evidence from your Lord. So, let the Children of Israel go with me."* He answered: *"If you have come with a sign, produce it then if you are so truthful."* Moses threw down his staff, and it immediately became a plainly visible serpent. And he drew forth his hand, and it was [shining] white to the beholders. The great ones among Pharaoh's people said: "This man is indeed a sorcerer of great skill, who wants to drive you out of your land!" [Said Pharaoh] "What, then, do you advise?" They said: "Let him and his brother wait a while, and send heralds to all cities to bring before you every sorcerer of great skill." (Verses 104-112)*

Here is the first encounter between truth and falsehood, faith and rejection. It is a scene which brings the Messenger, who calls on people to believe in the Lord of all the worlds, face to face with the tyrants who claim, and indeed practise, lordship over their people.

"*Moses said: 'Pharaoh, I am a Messenger from the Lord of all the worlds, and may say about God nothing but the truth. I have come to you with a clear evidence from your Lord. So, let the Children of Israel go with me.'*" (Verses 104-105) He addresses him with his plain title, "Pharaoh". He does not call him, "My lord", as do those who do not really know who the true Lord is. Moses combines good manners with self assurance, addressing Pharaoh with his simple title in order to point out to him his true position while asserting at the same time the greatest fact in the universe: "*I am a Messenger from the Lord of all the worlds.*" (Verse 104)

Moses reasserts the fact stated by every messenger that preceded him. It is the fact that God is the only Lord of the universe: just one God and one Lord, and total submission by the whole universe to Him alone. This is contrary to what is advanced by 'comparative religion' specialists and their disciples who grope in the dark as they make their claims about the development of religion, making no provision for the messages given by God to all His messengers. The faith preached by all those messengers is the same, repeated by every single one of them, stating that God is the Lord of all the worlds. This faith has not developed from a primitive pagan one which believed in numerous deities, progressing then to dualism, before eventually reaching its highest form of belief in one god. For when people deviate from divine faith and sink into a state of ignorance, or *jāhiliyyah*, there is no end to chaos. They then have a multitude of erring beliefs, ranging from the worship of totems, spirits, multiple gods to the worship of the sun and stars, to dualism, and to a monotheism that retains traces of paganism. No such deviant form of belief could ever be placed on the same level as the divine messages which consistently preached clear monotheism.

Moses (peace be upon him) confronted Pharaoh and his powerful clique with this basic truth which every Prophet before or after him proclaimed in the face of all types of deviant beliefs. He stated it clearly to his face, knowing that it meant revolution against Pharaoh, his regime and government. A primary result of God's Lordship of the universe and all the worlds is that every regime and form of government, which exercises power over human beings without following God's law or abiding by His commandments, is illegitimate. It also means the removal of every form of tyranny that seeks to subjugate people to its own laws. Moses confronted Pharaoh with this great fact in his own capacity as a Messenger from the Lord of the universe, committed to stating the truth about God who gave him his message: "*I am a Messenger from the Lord of all the worlds, and may say about God nothing but the truth.*" (Verses 104-105) A messenger who knows the true nature of God can only say the truth about Him. How can he say anything else when he knows God's power and authority?

"*I have come to you with a clear evidence from your Lord.*" (Verse 105) It tells you that I am truly a Messenger from the Lord of the universe. In his capacity as a Messenger, and under the authority of the Lord of the universe, Moses demanded that Pharaoh should release the Children of Israel to him.

The Children of Israel are God's own servants. It is not up to Pharaoh, then, to proclaim himself as their master. Human beings must not serve any masters other than God. Whoever is God's own servant cannot serve anyone beside Him. Because Pharaoh subjugated the Children of Israel to his own will, Moses declares to him that God is the only Lord of the universe. Such a declaration renders Pharaoh's action invalid.

The declaration that God is the Lord of all the worlds implies that man is free from subjugation and servitude to anyone other than God. He is released from the tyranny of man-made laws, traditions and from human desires and authority. This declaration of God's Lordship over the universe is incompatible with submission by any human being to anyone other than God. It is also diametrically opposed to the assigning of sovereignty to anyone who may implement any law other than divine law. Those who think themselves to be Muslims while submitting to man-made laws only delude themselves. They cannot be believers in divine faith for a single moment while acknowledging the sovereignty of anyone other than God or implementing any law other than His. They would be followers of their ruler, whoever that ruler may be. It is on this basis that Moses was commanded to demand that Pharaoh should release to him the Children of Israel: "*Pharaoh, I am a Messenger from the Lord of all the worlds... so let the Children of Israel go with me.*" (Verses 104-105) The first statement is the preamble to the logical conclusion given in the second. The two go hand in hand and cannot be separated.

Pharaoh and the leaders of his government were fully aware of the import of the declaration that God is the Lord of all the worlds. They were aware that the declaration implied the termination of Pharaoh's authority, the overthrow of his government and the end to his tyranny. They felt, however, that they had a chance to denounce Moses as a liar. Hence, Pharaoh demands a sign to prove Moses's claim: "*If you have come with a sign, produce it then if you are so truthful.*" (Verse 106)

Confrontation and Mobilization

Pharaoh felt that if he could prove that Moses was a liar, then all his claims could be refuted and all danger would be removed. But Moses had the complete answer: "*Moses threw down his staff, and it immediately became a plainly visible serpent. And he drew forth his hand, and it was [shining] white to the beholders.*" (Verses 107-108) This came as a complete surprise to Pharaoh and the elders of his people. The staff became a real serpent which was "plainly visible". It is described in another *sūrah* as "a scurrying snake".[1] (20: 20) Moreover, Moses was a man of dark complexion, but when he took his hand out of his pocket, it was seen as very white, without any sign of illness. This in itself was a miraculous sign, because he only had to put his hand in his pocket again for it to regain its original dark complexion.[2]

So, Moses had the signs and proofs to confirm his statement that he was a Messenger from the Lord of the universe, but would Pharaoh and his people accept such a dangerous claim and acknowledge God, the Lord of all the worlds? What basis would Pharaoh then have for his rule as the king of Egypt? What justification would his aides have for occupying such influential positions when these were given them by Pharaoh himself? How could the whole system be justified if all authority in the universe belonged to its Lord, the only God? If this Lordship is acknowledged, then God's law must prevail, and God would be the only one to be obeyed. What then would be Pharaoh's position when his rule is neither based on God's law nor relies on His commandments? When people acknowledge God's Lordship, they can

---

1. Animal specialists differentiate between serpents and snakes, but they belong to the same species.

2. This means that the transformation of Moses's hand was only temporary, as his hand would resume its original colour until he needed to show God's sign again. – Editor's note.

have no other lord who imposes on them his rule and legislation. They submit to Pharaoh's law when Pharaoh is their lord. Whoever can impose his legislation on a community is the Lord of that community, and they simply accept his religion whatever he tells them.

It is not in the nature of falsehood to surrender easily or to admit that it has no legitimacy. Pharaoh and the great ones among his people were certainly aware of the import of the great truth declared by Moses. They indeed declared it plainly, but they also tried to divert attention from it by accusing Moses of sorcery: "*The great ones among Pharaoh's people said: 'This man is indeed a sorcerer of great skill, who wants to drive you out of your land!' [Said Pharaoh], 'What, then, do you advise?'*" (Verses 109-110) The net result of this clear declaration is thus stated openly: it is to be driven out of the land, to relinquish power, or, to use modern terminology, to overthrow the government.

The whole earth belongs to God, and so do all creatures. So, if sovereignty in God's land is acknowledged to belong to God alone, then no shred of sovereignty will belong to those who impose a law other than that of God. In real terms, this means that not a particle of sovereignty can belong to claimants of lordship who exercise Godhead by subjugating people to their own laws. Thus, people given high positions by Godhead claimants have no real authority. After all, they are given such positions in order to ensure that people acknowledge the lordship of their deities.

Pharaoh and his aides were aware of the danger represented by Moses's message. Indeed, tyrants always recognize that danger. As a simple bedouin Arab, totally unsophisticated, remarked after hearing the Prophet Muḥammad calling on people to accept that there is no deity other than God and that Muḥammad is His Messenger: "This is something that kings dislike." Another similarly unsophisticated bedouin said to the Prophet: "You will be opposed by Arabs and non-Arabs alike." Both of them were keenly aware of what those words signified. They understood that the declaration of God's oneness means a rebellion against every ruler who does not implement God's law. The Arabs felt the seriousness of this declaration. They realised that to make this declaration and accept a rule based on any law other than that of God was a contradiction in terms. Their understanding of the declaration of God's oneness was totally different from that of those who today claim to be Muslims. The understanding of later day Muslims cannot be supported.

181

Hence, the great ones began their consultations with Pharaoh: "'*This man is indeed a sorcerer of great skill, who wants to drive you out of your land!' [Said Pharaoh], 'What, then, do you advise?*'" (Verses 109-110) Their consultations were concluded with agreement on a certain procedure: "*Let him and his brother wait a while, and send heralds to all cities to bring before you every sorcerer of great skill.*" (Verses 111-112)

At that time Egypt was full of priests in all types of temples, and those priests actually practised sorcery. In all pagan beliefs, religion was closely linked with sorcery. Hence, those who specialize in comparative religion speak of magic and sorcery as a stage in the development of human faith. Those among them who are atheists claim that religious beliefs will one day be abandoned in the same way as sorcery was abandoned. They claim that science will put an end to the reign of faith just as it put an end to the reign of sorcery. Their confusion knows no limit, yet they call it science.

Pharaoh's aides determined, after their lengthy discussions, that Pharaoh should gain time and fix an appointment with Moses. Meanwhile, he would send heralds to summon to his presence all skilful sorcerers, so that they could overpower what they claimed to be Moses's sorcery. Despite all that we know about Pharaoh's tyranny, his action in this regard was much milder than what twentieth-century tyrants did when they confronted the advocates of divine faith who proclaimed that God is the only Lord in the universe, and thereby threatened the authority of self-proclaimed rulers.[3]

Squaring Up to Sorcery and Falsehood

The Qur'ānic account skips over all the measures taken by Pharaoh and his aides in gathering all the sorcerers from every corner of the kingdom. The curtain falls after the first scene to be raised again with the contest progressing in full view in order to show this history as if it is happening now, in front of us. This is a characteristic of the inimitable style of the Qur'ān.

"*The sorcerers came to Pharaoh and said: 'Surely there will be a handsome reward for us if it is we who prevail.' Answered [Pharaoh]: 'Yes; and you will certainly be among those who are close to me.'*" (Verses

---

3. The author was writing in the second half of the twentieth century. Needless to say, his remark about contemporary dictators applies today in the same manner. – Editor's note.

113-114) They are mere professionals. To them, both sorcery and priesthood are professions. Their ultimate aim in carrying on with both vocations is to enjoy a handsome financial reward. Being in the service of rulers and overpowering tyranny is the task undertaken by professional clergy. Whenever the general situation in a country or a community moves away from pure submission to God, acknowledging all sovereignty to Him alone, and whenever a form of false, arbitrary authority replaces God's law, those exercising such an authority find themselves in need of such professional clergy. The false authority is always ready to remunerate such clergy for their services. It is a deal which serves the mutual interests of both parties; the clergy acknowledge that false authority in the name of religion, and those exercising power provide them with wages and give them high positions.

Pharaoh assured them that they would be paid for their services, and promised them positions in the circle closest to him to increase the temptation and to encourage them to make their best efforts. Neither Pharaoh nor the sorcerers realized that the situation did not call for any professional expertise, skill or deception. They were placing themselves in confrontation with a miracle given by God who has power over all things, and a message revealed by Him. No sorcerer or tyrant can stand up to these.

Pharaoh's sorcerers were reassured that they would have a generous reward, and they looked forward to be in positions close to Pharaoh. They came ready for the match, and began by an open challenge to Moses. Little did they realize that God was storing for them something far better than their promised wages: "*They said: 'Moses! Either you shall throw [first], or we shall be the first to throw?' He answered: 'You throw [first].'*" (Verses 115-116) It is a clearly apparent challenge. As they gave Moses the choice, they demonstrated their confidence that they would triumph. But we also see Moses unperturbed by the challenge, full of confidence as he answered: "*You throw first.*" That short answer reveals how completely assured Moses was. We often find the Qur'ān using a single word to impart such rich connotations.

But then the *sūrah* delivers a surprise. Indeed, Moses himself was surprised as he found himself face to face with very skilful sorcery that strikes awe in people's hearts: "*And when they threw [their staffs], they cast a spell upon people's eyes and struck them with awe, making a display of great sorcery.*" (Verse 116)

It is sufficient for us that the Qur'ān describes their work as "great sorcery" to imagine how skilful they truly were. It is also enough that we should know that they could "cast a spell upon people's eyes", in order to be able to imagine the nature of the situation. Indeed, the Qur'ān uses here a very vivid term to describe that the sorcerers were able to create a very real feeling of fear among all beholders. We also learn from another Qur'ānic statement that Moses himself felt fear creeping into his heart.

But something totally unexpected takes place to surprise Pharaoh and his aides, these sorcerers and the masses gathered in the large square which served as a stage for this contest: "*We then inspired Moses: 'Throw your staff.' And it swallowed up their false devices. Thus the truth prevailed and all their doings were proved to be in vain. They were defeated there and then, and became utterly humiliated.*" (Verses 117-119)

Falsehood may appear powerful. It may dazzle people's eyes, strike fear in their hearts and give the majority of people the impression that it is unstoppable and that it has its own rights. But once it comes into confrontation with the truth, with its intrinsic characteristics of calmness and self confidence, falsehood's bubble bursts and its fire dies down. The truth is thus seen to be much weightier, with firmer roots and a more solid foundation. The Qur'ānic expression here makes all these connotations clear as it describes the triumph of the truth as an accomplished fact, solid and stable. Everything else disappears and all the sorcerers' doings prove to be in vain. Falsehood and its advocates are vanquished, humiliated. This contrasts with the great display they tried to put out: "*They were defeated there and then, and became utterly humiliated.*" (Verse 119)

But the surprise is not over yet. The scene brings yet another, even greater surprise: "*The sorcerers fell down prostrating themselves, and said: 'We believe in the Lord of all the worlds, the Lord of Moses and Aaron.'*" (Verses 120-122)

How does this happen? It is simply the truth exercising its authority over people's feelings and consciences. It opens up hearts to prepare them to receive its light and accept its reassurance. The sorcerers are the best people to know how far their skill can go, and they are the best to evaluate the nature of what Moses worked out and whether it was an act of skilful sorcery or something brought about by a power far greater than any human being can have. A learned specialist in any field is the first to acknowledge the truth in that field whenever it appears clearly to him, because he can recognize the truth much quicker than those who have only superficial knowledge of his specialty. This explains how the sorcerers moved from open challenge to total submission, after having recognized the truth with open minds.

No Permission to Believe in God

No tyrant enjoying absolute power can ever understand how light penetrates human hearts, or how people can enjoy the reassurance of faith and experience the happiness it imparts. Tyrants continue to exercise power for a long time, seeing that people accept whatever they say. With the passage of time they come to believe that their authority extends over people's minds, hearts and souls, when these actually submit only to God. Hence, Pharaoh was totally surprised to see the sorcerers accept the faith so quickly, especially as he could not see the faith penetrating into their hearts and could not realize how their minds worked. But he was quick to recognize how serious this development was and that it threatened his very authority. Those sorcerers, who were actually the attendants in temples throughout Egypt, were gathered in order to prove Moses's and Aaron's message as false. It was those same sorcerers who accepted that message and declared their submission to God, the Lord of the universe and of Moses and Aaron.

Pharaoh felt his throne shake, and it is well known that the throne and the crown represent all that is in the life of a tyrant. Tyrants are always ready to commit any crime, without hesitation, in order to retain power: *"Pharaoh said: "You believe in Him even before I have given you permission! This is indeed a plot you have contrived in this city in order to drive out its people, but you shall soon come to know [the consequences]. I shall have your hands and feet cut off on alternate sides, and then I shall crucify you all."* (Verses 123-124)

He haughtily exclaims: *"You believe in Him even before I have given you permission!"* (Verse 123) He really expects them to seek his permission before their hearts, consciences and souls open up to receive the truth, when they themselves have no control over these and cannot prevent anything from touching or penetrating them. Perhaps Pharaoh wanted them to repel the truth as it penetrated their souls, or to stifle their faith as its shoots began to spring up and blossom inside their souls, or to cover their eyes so that they could not see the light. That is tyranny: ignorant and stupid, but at the same time arrogant and conceited.

There is another element which influences Pharaoh's attitude: namely, fear that his power is threatened. "*This is indeed a plot you have contrived in this city in order to drive out its people.*" (Verse 123) Elsewhere in the Qur'ān where the history of Moses and Pharaoh is related, Pharaoh is quoted as saying to the sorcerers in reference to Moses: "*He is your chief who has taught you sorcery.*" (20: 71)

The whole question is absolutely clear. It is the fact that Moses calls on people to believe in 'God, the Lord of all the worlds' that causes all this worry and fear. The tyrants realize that they can have no peace of mind if they allow that message to be preached. Their power relies on dismissing God's Lordship of mankind through ignoring His law. Instead, they appoint themselves as deities enacting legislation for human society and forcing people to submit to the laws they enact. These two methods can have no meeting point, because they move in opposite directions. They are two contradictory religions addressing worship to different lords. Pharaoh and the elders among his people were aware of this, and they were frightened when they realized that Moses and Aaron advocated submission to the Lord of the universe. Now that the sorcerers prostrated themselves in submission to God, Pharaoh and his elders were increasingly alarmed. Those sorcerers were the clergy in a pagan faith that attributed Godhead to Pharaoh himself. They were the ones who ensured that he exercised absolute power in the name of religion.

Hence, it was only expected that Pharaoh should issue his fearful warning: "*You shall soon come to know [the consequences]. I shall have your hands and feet cut off on alternate sides, and then I shall crucify you all.*" (Verses 123-124) Torture, disfigurement and unabating persecution: these are the methods to which tyranny resorts when it finds itself in confrontation with the truth. The tyrants realize that they cannot refute the argument of the truth, therefore they have to suppress it by force.

But when the truth of faith takes hold of a human being, he looks with contempt at the tyrants and their power. Faith takes over as the top priority, even ahead of life itself. A firm believer feels this life contemptible when it is compared to the eternal life of the hereafter. A human being who believes in the message of the truth does not stop to inquire: "What shall I gain and how much will I benefit?" He will not even think of what cost he will have to incur or what sacrifices he is called upon to give. The bright horizon opens up for him right in front of his eyes, so he does not look to anything along the way: "*They* replied: '*To our Lord we shall indeed return. You want to take vengeance on us only because we have believed in the signs of our Lord when they were shown to us.*'" (Verses 125-126) It is the unshakeable faith that will not submit to any worldly power. It is the faith which is reassured about the future, in the knowledge that all human beings will return to their Lord. With faith, people have the reassurance of being close to Him: "*To our Lord we shall indeed return.*" (Verse 125)

When a person realizes the nature of the battle against tyranny, and that it is a battle over the central issues, he takes his stand firmly, without hesitation. He would never seek the clemency of an enemy who is not prepared to accept anything from him short of abandoning his faith altogether, because, after all, that is the issue over which the fight takes place: "*You want to take vengeance on us only because we have believed in the signs of our Lord when they were shown to us.*" (Verse 126) When anyone realizes what the battle is all about and to whom he should turn for help, he will not ask his enemy to ensure his own safety. He will only pray to his Lord to give him patience and perseverance in times of adversity, and to help him to continue in an attitude of submission to God until he dies: "*Our Lord, grant us abundance of patience in adversity, and let us die as people who have surrendered themselves to You.*" (Verse 126)

Tyranny stands helpless as it finds itself in confrontation with faith based on clear understanding. Tyranny realizes that it can do nothing to human hearts although it used to think that even hearts and consciences were subject to its power as human bodies are. Now it discovers that only God can have power over people's hearts and consciences. What can human power do to any heart or soul that seeks God's protection and prefers to wait for God's reward?

As attitudes were shaping up between Pharaoh and his elders on the one side and Moses and those who believed with him on the other, human history was witnessing one of its most decisive moments. It was a moment when faith triumphed over life and when souls became stronger than pain, and man overpowered Satan. It was a moment when true freedom was born. What does freedom mean if not defeating tyranny with the power of faith? When a person is free, he thinks very lightly of a brute force that cannot subjugate his heart and soul, although it can inflict physical pain and cause death. When brute force is unable to subjugate hearts, true freedom is actually born.

A Decisive Victory

It was a decisive moment in the history of mankind because it witnessed the bankruptcy of brute force. Those free individuals who only a few moments earlier were asking Pharaoh for their reward and hoping to win favour with him were now able to rise above Pharaoh's standard, having no fear of him, paying little attention to his threats and preparing themselves to face persecution. Nothing in their lives or in the material world around them had changed. Only a subtle touch that connects a mortal human being to the power of immortality. Hearts and souls were now able to feel God's power, and consciences were ready to receive divine guidance and its light. That subtle touch brings about a fundamental change in the material world and elevates man to a standard he could never have dreamed possible. Warnings and threats, then, sound hollow, meaningless. Faith goes along its way steadily, unhesitatingly and with complete reassurance.

At this point the curtain falls and the Qur'ānic account of this encounter is over. The scene has reached its climax. Its powerful description serves the psychological purpose behind relating this account. It is the method of the Qur'ān that addresses hearts and souls with the message of faith and the language of artistic expression in a degree of harmony that only the Qur'ān can achieve.

The first point to be made as we conclude our discussion of the scene that witnessed how the sorcerers declared their submission to God is that Pharaoh and his top aides recognized immediately that this represented a threat to their system of government. This is due to the fact that the foundation of faith is in conflict with the basis upon which Pharaoh established his authority. We have discussed this previously, but we wish to restate here this fundamental principle. There can be no coexistence either in one person's mind or in the same land or under the same regime between the two concepts of God's Lordship over all the worlds and the exercise of power by a human being who proceeds to enact his own legislation for his people. These are aspects of two different faiths that have no common ground.

We should also note that once the sorcerers felt the light of faith penetrating their hearts, they began to recognize that the ensuing battle between them and Pharaoh's regime was over faith. He had nothing to take against them except the fact that they believed in God, the Lord of the universe, a faith representing a threat to his power, and the position and authority he confers on his aides. In other words, it threatened Pharaoh's claimed lordship and the values of that pagan community. It is imperative that advocates of divine faith, who call on people to believe in God as the only Lord in the universe, should be fully aware of the nature of the battle. Such awareness enables believers to think little of all that they may be forced to endure for the sake of their faith. They will be able to face death with fortitude because they are certain that they are the ones who believe in the Lord of the universe while their enemy follows a different religion. Indeed the very way that their enemy exercises power and subjugates people to his will is a denial of God's lordship. Thus, the enemy is an unbeliever. It is not possible for believers to advocate the divine message, with all that awaits them of persecution along the way, unless they have both these issues clear in their minds: that they are the believers while their enemies are unbelievers, and that they are being so persecuted because of their faith, which is the only issue taken against them.

We also have to note how remarkable and fascinating is the scene which describes the triumph of faith over life, human will over agony and man over Satan. Indeed, it is a breathtaking scene which we simply cannot adequately describe in human language. Let us, then confine ourselves to admiring its description in God's own language as He paints it in the Qur'ān.

What Constitutes Corruption

Let us now pick up the thread of the story as the curtains are drawn back to reveal a fourth scene where conspiracy is taking place. Pharaoh's advisers felt that they simply could not allow Moses and those who believed with him, a small minority as they were, to go unpunished. They began to plot and instigate. They wanted Pharaoh to take strong action against Moses and his followers, raising before him the spectre of losing all his power and position, should he take a lenient attitude. They warned him against the possibility that the new faith, based on God's oneness and Lordship of the universe, could be allowed to establish roots in society. Pharaoh was furious and began to issue his warnings feeling that he had the power to suppress the rebellion: "*The great ones among Pharaoh's people said: 'Will you allow Moses and his people to spread corruption in the land and to forsake you and your gods?'*

189

He replied: 'We shall put their sons to death and shall spare only their women. We shall certainly overpower them.' (Verse 127)

Pharaoh did not claim Godhead in the sense that he was the creator and controller of the universe, or that he had power over natural forces. He simply claimed to be the god of his subjugated people, in the sense that he ruled them according to his own law and that they were subject to his will in all their affairs. This is still claimed by every ruler who enforces his own law and imposes his own will. This is lordship in both its linguistic and practical senses.

Nor did the Egyptians serve Pharaoh in the sense that they addressed their worship rituals to him. They had their own deities as did Pharaoh himself. This is clearly understood from his aides' statement where he is warned against being abandoned by Moses and his followers: *"And to forsake you and your gods."* (Verse 127) This is also confirmed by what we know of the history of ancient Egypt. They served Pharaoh in the sense that they accepted his authority and never violated his law or disobeyed his orders. This is the practical and linguistic meaning of worship. Hence, if people in any community receive their laws from a human being and obey him, then they actually worship him. Indeed this is what the Prophet himself indicated when he interpreted the Qur'ānic verse which says in reference to the Jews and Christians: *"They make of their clerics and monks lords besides God."* (9: 31) 'Adiy ibn Ḥātim, who was formerly a Christian tribal chief, heard this verse at the time he accepted Islam. He said to the Prophet: "Messenger of God, they did not worship them." The Prophet said to him: "Yes, indeed they did. They permitted them what was forbidden and forbade them what was lawful, and they accepted that. This is their worship of those clerics and monks." (Related by al-Tirmidhī)

At one time, Pharaoh says to the elders of his nation: *"Nobles, you have no other God that I know of except myself."* (28: 38) But this statement is interpreted by yet another reported in the Qur'ān: *"My people, is the kingdom of Egypt not mine, and are these rivers which flow at my feet not mine also? Can you not see? Am I not better than this despicable wretch, who can scarcely make his meaning plain? Why have no bracelets of gold been given him, or angels sent down to accompany him?"* (43: 51-52) It is clear that he was comparing his authority and the gold that he had as a king with Moses's plain appearance. His proclamation, *"You have no other God that I know of except myself,"* (28: 38) was simply an assertion that he was the only one to have the

190

authority to make any order, and that he was the one to be obeyed at all times. Exercising such power is, in the linguistic sense and in practical terms, a claim to Godhead. The one who legislates for people and imposes his will on them exercises Godhead, whether he claims it verbally or not. It is in this light that we should understand the instigation of Pharaoh's aides as they said to him: *"Will you allow Moses and his people to spread corruption in the land and to forsake you and your gods?"* (Verse 127)

In their view, to declare that God is the only Lord in the universe is to spread corruption, because it entails that Pharaoh's regime is illegitimate and his rule invalid. That regime was founded on giving all sovereignty to Pharaoh, or, to use a synonymous term, making him lord of his people. Hence, to them, corruption is spread in the land by overthrowing that regime and destroying the social set-up based on the lordship of human beings in order to establish a totally different situation which assigns lordship only to God. It is for this reason that they equated Moses' forsaking of Pharaoh and his gods with spreading corruption in the land.

How the Truth Unnerves Tyrants

Pharaoh used to derive his authority from the religion based on the worship of those gods, making out that he was the favourite son of those gods. It was not a physical parenthood, because people knew very well that Pharaoh was born to a human couple. It was a symbolic relationship, which ensured for him the authority to exercise his power. If Moses and his people were to worship God, the Lord of all the worlds, forsaking those deities worshipped by the Egyptians, then they are practically destroying the foundation of Pharaoh's spiritual authority over his people. We must remember here that the people themselves were transgressors, and hence their obedience to Pharaoh, as God Himself states: *"Thus did he make fools of his people, and they obeyed him. They were indeed transgressors."* (43: 54)

This is indeed the correct interpretation of history. Pharaoh could not have been obeyed by his people when he made fools of them, had they not been transgressors. A believer simply does not allow tyranny to fool him and will not obey tyranny in any respect, because he knows such obedience cannot be endorsed by true faith. This was what represented a threat to Pharaoh's regime and power, as Moses called on people to believe in God, the Lord of all the worlds. The threat was embodied by the sorcerers' positive response, coupled with the acceptance of the new faith by a minority of Moses's own people. Similarly, every social set-up established on the lordship of some human beings over others feels threatened by any call that aims to acknowledge the Lordship of God alone, or declaring that there is no deity other than God. We are speaking here of the true sense of this declaration which brings people into the fold of Islam, not its watered-down sense that prevails these days.

We can now understand why Pharaoh was enraged by these words, feeling that his whole regime was seriously threatened. Hence, he made his brutal intentions clear: "*We shall put their sons to death and shall spare only their women. We shall certainly overpower them.*" (Verse 127)

The Children of Israel suffered persecution on a similar scale by Pharaoh and his clique, as stated in *Sūrah* 28, The Story, in which we read: "*Pharaoh made himself a tyrant in the land. He divided his people into casts, one group of which he persecuted, putting their sons to death and sparing only their daughters. Truly, he was an evildoer.*" (28: 4) This is characteristic of tyranny everywhere, in all periods of history. It still resorts today to the same methods it employed centuries ago.

To Whom the Future Belongs

The *sūrah* leaves Pharaoh and his clique to cook up their conspiracy and portrays a new scene that imparts to us the impression that Pharaoh put his threats and warnings into effect. Now we see the Prophet Moses speaking to his people in the language and with the passion of a prophet who truly knows His Lord and how His will works. He impresses on them the need to endure adversity with patience and to seek God's help to overcome it. He enlightens them about the rules God has put in place in the universe, making it clear to them that the whole earth belongs to God alone and that He causes it to be inherited by any group of His servants according to His will. The ultimate trial will inevitably be given to those who fear none other than God. They complain to him that before he came they endured a wave of persecution and torture similar to that which they now suffer after his arrival. They feel that such persecution is endless. He declares that he sincerely hopes that God will destroy their enemy and cause them to be the heirs of the land to see how they conduct themselves when they are given the trust of building human life on earth: "*Moses said to his people: 'Turn to God (alone) for help and remain steadfast. The whole earth belongs to God. He allows it to be inherited by whomever He wills of His servants. The future belongs to those who are God-fearing.' They said: 'We have been oppressed before you came to us and since you have come to us.' He replied: 'It may well be that your Lord will destroy your enemy and leave you to inherit the earth. He will then see how you conduct yourselves.'*" (Verses 128-129)

This is how a prophet sees the nature of Godhead and how it enlightens his heart. He is aware of what takes place in the universe, the forces operating in it, the laws God has established in it and what those who remain steadfast, holding firmly to their faith, may hope for the future. The advocates of the true faith have only one safe haven and one protector who is God Almighty. They have to be patient in adversity until God, their protector, in His perfect wisdom, determines the time when He grants them victory. They may not precipitate matters because they cannot foretell the future and they do not know what will work for their own good.

The whole earth belongs to God; while Pharaoh and his people are there only for a transitory period. God will allow, in His wisdom and according to the rules He has established, the earth to be inherited by whomever He chooses of His servants. Hence, the advocates of the true faith may not judge by appearances, which could give the impression that tyranny is firmly established on earth and cannot be driven out. It is the owner of the earth who decides when to kick those tyrants out. The God-fearing will sooner or later be triumphant. Hence, the advocates of the true faith must not worry about the future or consider for a moment that those unbelievers will continue to have the upper hand for ever.

Such is a prophet's vision of the essential facts that govern what happens in the universe. But the Children of Israel have their typical characteristics: "*They said: 'We have been oppressed before you came to us and since you have come to us.'*" (Verse 129) These words carry an implicit complaint. They are telling him that his coming to them as a Prophet has not changed anything. Their oppression seems to be everlasting.

But the noble Prophet does not change his characteristic attitude: he continues to remind them of God. He counsels them to put all their trust in Him and raises before them the prospect that God may destroy their enemy and grant them victory. He couples this with a warning that victory brings to them a new test, which they have to take in order to prove themselves: *"He replied: 'It may well be that your Lord will destroy your enemy and leave you to inherit the earth. He will then see how you conduct yourselves.'"* (Verse 129)

Moses's vision is that of a Prophet who recognizes the laws of nature God has established, and how they operate in line with what He has promised both to those who remain steadfast and to those who deny Him. He can see as a reality that tyranny will be destroyed and that those who show steadfastness and who turn to God alone for help will be given victory. He thus points out the way to his people, which is sure to give them what they want. He tells them right at the outset that when they are allowed to inherit the earth, they are actually being put to a test. They will not be given it because they claim to be God's favourite sons. Nor should they assume that He will not punish them for their sins, or that their power will continue for ever. It is all a test in which they have to prove themselves: *"He will then see how you conduct yourselves."* (Verse 129) Needless to say, God knows what is going to happen even before it happens. But His justice determines that He does not put human beings to account until they have actually done what He already knows they will do. He is certainly the One who knows all, and He is the most fair of judges.

Who Brings Bad Omen

We afflicted Pharaoh's people with drought and poor harvests, so that they might take heed. Whenever something fine came their way, they would say: "This is our due", but whenever affliction befell them, they attributed their ill omen to Moses and those who followed him. Surely, whatever befalls them has been decreed by God, though most of them do not know it. (Verses 130-131)

Here we have another scene in the story whereby Pharaoh and his people begin to taste the fruits of injustice and tyranny, while the promises Moses has given to his people, based on his trust in his Lord, come true. The warnings, stressed in the entire *sūrah* and endorsed throughout the story, are also seen to be true.

The scene starts on a quiet note, but we can feel the storm gathering slowly. When the curtains are about to fall, the storm is at its highest, wreaking destruction and wiping the tyrants out. We also learn that the Children of Israel have been well rewarded for their steadfastness, while Pharaoh and his people were punished for their transgression. Both God's promises and warnings have come true. The law of nature which He has established, sentencing unbelievers to destruction after testing them with hardship and affluence, has also operated in full:

> We afflicted Pharaoh's people with drought and poor harvests, so that they might take heed. Whenever something fine came their way, they would say: "This is our due", but whenever affliction befell them, they attributed their ill omen to Moses and those who followed him. Surely, whatever befalls them has been decreed by God, though most of them do not know it. They said [to Moses]: "Whatever sign you may produce before us in order to cast a spell on us, we shall not believe in you." So we plagued them with floods, and locusts, and lice, and frogs, and blood: clear signs all; but they gloried in their arrogance, for they were evil-doing folk. Whenever a plague struck them, they would cry: "Moses, pray to your Lord for us on the strength of the covenant He has made with you. If you lift the plague from us, we will truly believe in you, and we will let the Children of Israel go with you." But when We had lifted the plague from them, for a term they were sure to reach, they broke their promise. So We inflicted Our retribution on them, and caused them to drown in the sea, because they denied Our signs and were heedless of them. We caused the people who were persecuted and deemed utterly low to inherit the eastern and western parts of the land which We had blessed. Thus your Lord's gracious promise to the Children of Israel was fulfilled, because they were patient in adversity; and We destroyed all that Pharaoh and his people had wrought, and all that they had built. (Verses 130-137)

The shift in the sequence of the story suggests that Pharaoh and his group actually put their warnings into effect, killing men and sparing women. Moses and his followers where patient when this adversity befell them, proving that they were true believers hoping for intervention by God to lift their affliction. Thus, the whole situation was clearly identified: faith versus rejection of God's message, tyranny against steadfastness, and human force opposing God.

At this stage in the conflict, the Supreme Power intervenes to settle the issue between the two camps. "We afflicted Pharaoh's people with *drought and poor harvests, so that they might take heed.*" (Verse 130) This was a first warning given in the form of drought and poor harvests. In the richly fertile land of Egypt, this was a highly worrying situation that called for reflection and reconsideration. But the tyrants, and those who are fooled by tyrants because of their own transgression, do not wish to reflect or reconsider. They simply do not accept that poor harvests and drought came in fulfilment of God's warnings. They do not wish to admit the close relationship between the values of faith and practical life, because that relationship belongs to the realm that lies beyond human perception. They have been too hardened in their ignorant ways to be able to see anything beyond the material world. When they see some aspect of a world beyond, they cannot recognize God's hand in it, or His free will. They attribute everything to blind coincidence.[4]

Similarly, Pharaoh's people preferred to overlook the early signs that should have awakened them as they pointed to the fact that God's mercy is bestowed on people, even when they continue to disbelieve in Him. Paganism and its superstitions had corrupted their nature, so that they could not recognize or understand the elaborate laws maintaining the fine order of the universe and influencing human life. These are only recognized and appreciated by true believers; for they realize that the universe has not been created in vain, and that it is governed by strict and well-defined laws. This is indeed the correct scientific mentality, which does not deny what lies beyond our perception, because there is simply no conflict between scientific facts and such a world beyond. Nor does it deny the relationship between the values of faith and practical life, because these have been set by God Himself who wants His servants to believe in Him and to build human life on earth. He lays down for them laws that are in harmony with those operating in the universe so that there is no conflict between their existence and their world.

So, Pharaoh's people did not see the connection between their transgression and the oppression they wreaked on God's servant on

---

4. When the former Soviet Union and the Communist Bloc suffered poor harvests, Khrushchev could find no explanation other than to say, "nature is opposing us." This came from the man who insisted on denying any unseen force and claimed to believe in scientific socialism. His attitude was one of deliberate blindness. Otherwise, what is this "nature" which has a will to oppose human beings?

the one hand, and their affliction with drought and poor harvests in the richly fertile land of Egypt on the other. It was a gesture of God's mercy to raise this fact before their very eyes, so that they could reflect. They should have remembered that the land of Egypt could always feed its people, except at times when God decided to try them with poor harvests after they had transgressed. Pharaoh's people considered every good fortune that came their way as their due. Affliction and poor harvests were attributed to Moses and his followers as people who brought bad omen: "*Whenever something fine came their way, they would say: 'This is our due', but whenever affliction befell them, they attributed their ill omen to Moses and those who followed him.*" (Verse 131)

When human nature turns away from faith, it cannot see God's hand conducting its affairs, or His will initiating events. At this stage, it loses all its appreciation of the constant laws of the universe. It starts to give events isolated, disjointed interpretations and accepts all sorts of superstition, which lack even the slightest degree of coherence. A simple example is the statement made by Khrushchev, the advocate of scientific socialism, explaining poor harvests in the Soviet Union as the opposition of nature to the socialists. Those who try to explain events in allegedly 'scientific' terms, while denying God's will, provide another example. What is singular is that some of them still claim to be Muslims when they deny the foundations of faith altogether.

It was in the same vein that Pharaoh and his people interpreted events. Good fortune was their due, and it came to them because they deserved it, while affliction was the ill-omen Moses and his followers brought about. The word used here for "ill-omen" has the same root as a "flying bird". The connection originates from an Arabian pagan practice. When an Arab wanted to choose a course of action, he came to a bird's nest and frightened the bird inside. If the bird flew to the right, the man felt that was a good omen and he followed his chosen line of action. If the bird flew to the left, the man considered that a bad omen and he stopped short. Islam stopped all this superstition and replaced it by a truly scientific line of thinking. It attributed matters to the laws God operates in the universe, and to God's will ensuring the operation of all these laws. Events are valued on a scientific basis, which takes note of man's intention, action and effort. All these are placed within the context of God's free will: "*Surely, whatever befalls them has been decreed by God, though most of them do not know it.*" (Verse 131)

Whatever happens to human beings has the same source, because it is decreed by God. It is to this source that their trial with affliction is attributed, as well as their trial with affluence: "*We test you all with evil and good by way of trial. To Us you all must return.*" (21: 35) The same source causes their punishment when they are punished for their misdeeds. But most of them do not recognize this. These ancient unbelievers were the same as those who in our present day claim for themselves 'scientific pragmatism' in order to justify their denial of God's will and His control of what lies beyond our world. Similar to them are those 'scientific socialists' who attribute their poor harvests to an antagonistic nature! All of them are ignorant, devoid of knowledge.

The Promises of Unbelievers

But Pharaoh's people were too arrogant, always persisting with their evil ways and paying no heed to God's signs or to any test to which they were put. They said to Moses: "*Whatever sign you may bring before us in order to cast a spell on us, we shall not believe in you.*" (Verse 132) It is an attitude of arrogance that will heed no reminder and will not respond to any proof. It is the attitude of a person who does not want to look or evaluate, because he declares his insistence on rejecting the message, even before proof is shown to him. Thus, he feels able to dismiss the proof altogether. This is an attitude which is frequently demonstrated by unbelievers after they have been overwhelmed by the truth and its clear proofs, while they recognize that their interests, wealth, authority and power belong elsewhere and are better served by denying the truth altogether.

At this juncture, the supreme power of God intervenes: "*So We plagued them with floods, and locusts, and lice, and frogs, and blood: clear signs all.*" (Verse 133) All these clear signs were meant as a test and a warning. Their import was very clear, and all of them gave the same message, with each subsequent one endorsing what had gone beforehand. These clear signs were shown to them separately, but the *sūrah* mentions them altogether here. Each time one of these plagues afflicted them, they rushed to Moses imploring him to pray to his Lord to save them. Every time they promised to let the Children of Israel go with him, if he would only relieve their affliction. They recognized that they themselves had no means of lifting their hardship: "*Whenever a plague struck them, they would cry: 'Moses, pray to your Lord for us on the strength of the covenant He has made with you. If you lift the plague from us, we will truly believe in you, and we will let the Children of Israel go with you.'"* (Verse 134) Every time they broke their promise and resorted to their same ways and practices before the plague had smitten them. But the plague was lifted only in accordance with God's will so as to let them alone for a while until their appointed term had come: *"When We had lifted the plague from them for a term they were sure to reach, they broke their promise."* (Verse 135)

As we have already said, the *sūrah* groups all these signs together, as if they came all at once, and as if they broke their promises once only. The fact remains that all these trials were essentially one, and their ultimate result was the same as well. This is a method of presentation often employed in the Qur'ān in relating different events and their consequences to indicate that they are the same. It is in the nature of a sealed heart that it will always look at various experiences as one, benefiting nothing from them and learning no lesson.

Now, how did these miraculous signs take place? We have only the Qur'ānic statement, and we have not found in authentic *ḥadīths* any further details. We maintain our method that we have followed in this work, going only as far as the Qur'ānic or authentic *ḥadīths* go. This ensures that we steer away from any superstition or unfounded report. Many of these have found their way into some older commentaries on the Qur'ān. Indeed, the commentary written by Imām al-Ṭabarī and the one written by Ibn Kathīr, valuable indeed as they are, have not escaped such pitfalls.

Al-Ṭabarī includes in his work on history and in his commentary on the Qur'ān several reports attributed to earlier scholars, explaining these signs. We will mention only one of these, given on the authority of Saʿīd ibn Jubayr, a famous scholar from the generation that followed the Prophet's companions:

> When Moses asked Pharaoh to release to him the Children of Israel, Pharaoh refused. God plagued Pharaoh's people with flooding rain. When they feared that it might have been a penalty, they said to Moses: "Pray to your Lord to cause this rain to cease, and we will send the Children of Israel with you." He prayed to his Lord, and the rain stopped, but they, nevertheless, refused to believe in him. And did not let the Children of Israel go with him.

God gave them that year plentiful harvests which gave them fruits and crops as they had never known before. They said: "We now have all that we ever wished for." God then plagued them with the locusts which started ruining their meadows. When they saw what the locusts were doing to their meadows, they realized that they would also ruin all their harvest. Therefore, they appealed to Moses to pray to his Lord to lift the plague of locusts and promised that they would believe in him and let the Children of Israel go with him. He prayed to his Lord and the locusts went away. Nevertheless, Pharaoh's people refused to believe in him or to release the Children of Israel.

Thus, they had their harvest safe, and stored all their crops at their homes and storehouses. When they completed their work, they were very pleased with themselves. God then sent on them lice. A person would take out ten full sacks of his grains to the mill, but he would not get even one sack of flour. Once again, they rushed to Moses, imploring him to pray to his Lord to lift this plague. They again promised to believe in him and to release the Children of Israel. Once more, he prayed to his Lord and He lifted their hardship, but they nevertheless rejected his message and refused to release the Children of Israel.

Moses was sitting with Pharaoh when he heard the sound of a frog. He said to Pharaoh: "You and your people will soon suffer from this." Pharaoh said: "What harm could this one do?" They hardly reached the evening when the frogs were all over them. A man would be up to his neck in frogs. If he opened his mouth to speak, frogs would jump into it. They again appealed to Moses to pray to his Lord to make the frogs go away. They again promised solemnly to believe in him and release the Children of Israel. When that plague was lifted, they reverted to their hardened attitude.

Now, God plagued them with blood. Every time they collected water from any river or any well, and indeed all the water they had in their containers, it turned into blood. They complained to Pharaoh and said that they had nothing to drink. He suggested that Moses had cast a spell on them. They said: "How could he have done that, when we find every drop of water that has been in our containers has turned into blood?" Again, they rushed to

Moses and implored him to pray to his Lord, making the same solemn promises. He prayed as they had requested, and God answered his prayer and lifted the plague of blood off them. Nevertheless, they continued to refuse to believe in Moses and would not release the Children of Israel.[5]

God knows best which of these stories corresponded to fact, and in what form each one of these signs was given. Any differences that might have occurred would not affect the message of these verses. God sent these signs by His own will, at a time He had determined, in order to test a particular people according to His law which punishes the rejecters so that they may turn to Him.

Wreaking Vengeance on Hardened Unbelievers

Despite their pagan religion, their total ignorance, and their transgression which enabled Pharaoh to take them as fools, they still rushed to the Prophet Moses, time and again, beseeching him to pray to his Lord on account of the covenant he had with Him. They felt that was the only way for the plague to be lifted. But those in power refused to honour their promises because their whole authority was based on their claim that Pharaoh was the Lord of his people. They feared what would have happened if God's Lordship was to be recognized. That would have meant that the entire system, which assigned sovereignty and legislative authority to Pharaoh, would collapse, giving way to a system which recognized sovereignty as belonging only to God.

In present-day *jāhiliyyah*, God may allow pests to threaten harvests, but people do not turn back to God at all. If the farmers experience the natural feeling which occurs to human beings, even unbelievers, in times of hardship, that it is God who sends these plagues, and if they turn to God praying to Him to lift this affliction, the advocates of false 'science' tell them that their action is deeply rooted in superstition and metaphysics. They adopt a very sarcastic attitude in order to turn them back to a state of rejection that is far worse than that of ancient pagans.

The end then takes place in accordance with God's law of punishing unbelievers after having tested them both with affliction and affluence.

---

5. Al-Ṭabarī, Ibn Jarīr, *Jāmi' al-Bayān*, Beirut, Vol. 6, p. 34

Having given Pharaoh and his people every chance, and assigned for them a term which they were certain to reach, God destroyed Pharaoh and his clique. He also fulfilled His promise to the oppressed who remained patient in adversity: "*So We inflicted Our retribution on them, and caused them to drown in the sea, because they denied Our signs and were heedless of them. We caused the people who were persecuted and deemed utterly low to inherit the eastern and western parts of the land which We had blessed. Thus your Lord's gracious promise to the Children of Israel was fulfilled, because they were patient in adversity; and We destroyed all that Pharaoh and his people had wrought, and all that they had built.*" (Verses 136-137)

The *sūrah* refers very briefly here to the drowning of Pharaoh and his people. The details are not given here in a relaxed pattern as they are given in other *sūrahs*. What happens here instead is to give an air of swift punishment after the unbelievers have had a long time to reconsider. Hence, the details are overlooked. The swiftness of the punishment has its effect which fills us with awe. "*So We inflicted Our retribution on them, and caused them to drown in the sea.*" (Verse 136) Just one strike and they are all destroyed. Proud, arrogant and despotic they certainly were, and suddenly they sink right to the bottom of the sea. It is certainly a fitting recompense, "*Because they denied Our signs and were heedless of them.*" (Verse 136) The compatibility is made clear between their attitude of denying God's signs, choosing to remain heedless of them and this fitting destiny. We are clearly told that events do not come as a result of coincidence. They do not just happen haphazardly, as simple people tend to think.

To enhance the atmosphere of swiftness and decisiveness, the *sūrah* also portrays the opposite picture of giving power to the oppressed. This is brought forward because the Children of Israel were not given power in Egypt, where Pharaoh and his people lived. Instead, they were given power when they were at their best in following divine guidance, before they deviated and incurred the punishment of humiliation and dispersal. Their kingdom was in Palestine, several decades after the drowning of Pharaoh, and long after the Prophet Moses had passed away, and indeed after their forty years in the wilderness which is mentioned elsewhere in the Qur'ān. But the *sūrah* glides over all these events and shifts from one period of time to another in order to highlight the fact that they were established and given power to be free to conduct their own affairs. This provides a clear contrast with their state of weakness when they endured Pharaoh's persecution: *"We caused the people who were persecuted and deemed utterly low to inherit the eastern and western parts of the land which We had blessed. Thus your Lord's gracious promise to the Children of Israel was fulfilled, because they were patient in adversity; and We destroyed all that Pharaoh and his people had wrought, and all that they had built."* (Verse 137)

Restricted by the limitations of time as we are, we, human beings, speak of a time order because we record events in accordance with their occurrence and the moment when we note their happening. For this reason, we say that the power that was given to those who were oppressed came after the event of Pharaoh's drowning. That is our own understanding of events. What could "before" and "after" signify to God in His absolute knowledge, we cannot tell. All that takes place clearly appears to Him in full vision, with nothing partially or totally screened by limitations of time and place. To Him everything is known absolutely perfectly, while our knowledge remains scanty indeed.

Thus the curtain falls with the scene of total destruction on the one side and that of a new power to build a new civilization on the other. Pharaoh, yesterday's tyrant, is drowned with his people. All that they had built in this life, and all the edifices and towers they raised on great pillars, and all their construction, vineyards and riches lie in ruin. All this takes place in a fraction of a moment, and all is portrayed in a few short words.

This is an example given by God to the small band of believers in Makkah who suffered persecution by the pagan Arabs. It also provides a wider perspective to every group of believers suffering persecution at the hands of the new pharaohs of this world. They can always look at the oppression they suffer in the same light as those believers suffered at Pharaoh's hands. They remained steadfast and showed patience in adversity, so God caused them to inherit the blessed land to see how they would conduct themselves.

9

Relapse into a State of Ignorance

We led the Children of Israel across the sea; and thereupon they came upon people who were dedicated to the worship of some idols of theirs. Said [the Children of Israel]: "Moses, set up a god for us like the gods they have." He replied: "You are indeed an ignorant people. (138)

وَجَٰوَزْنَا بِبَنِىٓ إِسْرَٰٓءِيلَ ٱلْبَحْرَ فَأَتَوْا۟ عَلَىٰ قَوْمٍ يَعْكُفُونَ عَلَىٰٓ أَصْنَامٍ لَّهُمْ قَالُوا۟ يَٰمُوسَى ٱجْعَل لَّنَآ إِلَٰهًا كَمَا لَهُمْ ءَالِهَةٌ قَالَ إِنَّكُمْ قَوْمٌ تَجْهَلُونَ ۝

As for these people: their method will inevitably lead to destruction, and worthless is all that they have been doing." (139)

إِنَّ هَٰٓؤُلَآءِ مُتَبَّرٌ مَّا هُمْ فِيهِ وَبَٰطِلٌ مَّا كَانُوا۟ يَعْمَلُونَ ۝

[And] he said: "Am I to seek for you a deity other than God, although He has favoured you above all other people?" (140)

قَالَ أَغَيْرَ ٱللَّهِ أَبْغِيكُمْ إِلَٰهًا وَهُوَ فَضَّلَكُمْ عَلَى ٱلْعَٰلَمِينَ ۝

We have indeed saved you from Pharaoh's people, who oppressed you cruelly: they slew your sons and spared your women. Surely that was an awesome trial from your Lord. (141)

وَإِذْ أَنجَيْنَٰكُم مِّنْ ءَالِ فِرْعَوْنَ يَسُومُونَكُمْ سُوٓءَ ٱلْعَذَابِ يُقَتِّلُونَ أَبْنَآءَكُمْ وَيَسْتَحْيُونَ نِسَآءَكُمْ وَفِى ذَٰلِكُم بَلَآءٌ مِّن رَّبِّكُمْ عَظِيمٌ ۝

We appointed for Moses thirty nights, to which We added ten, whereby the term of forty nights set by His Lord was complete. Moses said to his brother Aaron: "Take my place among my people and act righteously. Do not follow the path of those who spread corruption." (142)

وَوَٰعَدْنَا مُوسَىٰ ثَلَٰثِينَ لَيْلَةً وَأَتْمَمْنَٰهَا بِعَشْرٍ فَتَمَّ مِيقَٰتُ رَبِّهِۦٓ أَرْبَعِينَ لَيْلَةً وَقَالَ مُوسَىٰ لِأَخِيهِ هَٰرُونَ ٱخْلُفْنِى فِى قَوْمِى وَأَصْلِحْ وَلَا تَتَّبِعْ سَبِيلَ ٱلْمُفْسِدِينَ ﴿١٤٢﴾

When Moses came for Our appointment and his Lord spoke to him, he said: "My Lord, show Yourself to me, so that I may look at You." Said [God]: "You shall not see Me. But look upon the mountain; if it remains firm in its place, then, only then, you shall see Me." When his Lord revealed His glory to the mountain, He sent it crashing down. Moses fell down senseless. When he came to himself, he said: "Limitless You are in Your glory. To You I turn in repentance. I am the first to truly believe in You." (143)

وَلَمَّا جَآءَ مُوسَىٰ لِمِيقَٰتِنَا وَكَلَّمَهُۥ رَبُّهُۥ قَالَ رَبِّ أَرِنِىٓ أَنظُرْ إِلَيْكَ قَالَ لَن تَرَىٰنِى وَلَٰكِنِ ٱنظُرْ إِلَى ٱلْجَبَلِ فَإِنِ ٱسْتَقَرَّ مَكَانَهُۥ فَسَوْفَ تَرَىٰنِى فَلَمَّا تَجَلَّىٰ رَبُّهُۥ لِلْجَبَلِ جَعَلَهُۥ دَكًّا وَخَرَّ مُوسَىٰ صَعِقًا فَلَمَّآ أَفَاقَ قَالَ سُبْحَٰنَكَ تُبْتُ إِلَيْكَ وَأَنَا۠ أَوَّلُ ٱلْمُؤْمِنِينَ ﴿١٤٣﴾

He said: "Moses, I have chosen you of all mankind and favoured you by entrusting My messages to you and by My speaking to you. Take then what I have given you and be thankful." (144)

قَالَ يَٰمُوسَىٰٓ إِنِّى ٱصْطَفَيْتُكَ عَلَى ٱلنَّاسِ بِرِسَٰلَٰتِى وَبِكَلَٰمِى فَخُذْ مَآ ءَاتَيْتُكَ وَكُن مِّنَ ٱلشَّٰكِرِينَ ﴿١٤٤﴾

We wrote for him on the tablets all manner of admonition, clearly spelling out everything, and (said to him): "Implement them with strength and determination, and bid your people to observe what is best in them. I shall show you the abode of the transgressors. (145)

"I will turn away from My revelations those who, without any right, behave arrogantly on earth: for, though they may see every sign, they do not believe in it. If they see the path of righteousness, they do not choose to follow it, but if they see the path of error, they choose it for their path; because they disbelieve in Our revelations and pay no heed to them. (146)

"Those who deny Our revelations and the certainty of the meeting in the hereafter will see all their works collapse. Are they to be rewarded for anything other than what they have done?' (147)

In his absence, the people of Moses took to the worship of the effigy of a calf made of their ornaments, which gave a lowing sound. Did they not see that it could neither speak to them nor give them any guidance? Yet they took to worshipping it, for they were evildoers. (148)

وَكَتَبْنَا لَهُ فِي ٱلْأَلْوَاحِ مِن كُلِّ شَيْءٍ مَّوْعِظَةً وَتَفْصِيلًا لِّكُلِّ شَيْءٍ فَخُذْهَا بِقُوَّةٍ وَأْمُرْ قَوْمَكَ يَأْخُذُوا۟ بِأَحْسَنِهَا سَأُو۟رِيكُمْ دَارَ ٱلْفَٰسِقِينَ ﴿١٤٥﴾

سَأَصْرِفُ عَنْ ءَايَٰتِيَ ٱلَّذِينَ يَتَكَبَّرُونَ فِي ٱلْأَرْضِ بِغَيْرِ ٱلْحَقِّ وَإِن يَرَوْا۟ كُلَّ ءَايَةٍ لَّا يُؤْمِنُوا۟ بِهَا وَإِن يَرَوْا۟ سَبِيلَ ٱلرُّشْدِ لَا يَتَّخِذُوهُ سَبِيلًا وَإِن يَرَوْا۟ سَبِيلَ ٱلْغَيِّ يَتَّخِذُوهُ سَبِيلًا ذَٰلِكَ بِأَنَّهُمْ كَذَّبُوا۟ بِـَٔايَٰتِنَا وَكَانُوا۟ عَنْهَا غَٰفِلِينَ ﴿١٤٦﴾

وَٱلَّذِينَ كَذَّبُوا۟ بِـَٔايَٰتِنَا وَلِقَآءِ ٱلْءَاخِرَةِ حَبِطَتْ أَعْمَٰلُهُمْ هَلْ يُجْزَوْنَ إِلَّا مَا كَانُوا۟ يَعْمَلُونَ ﴿١٤٧﴾

وَٱتَّخَذَ قَوْمُ مُوسَىٰ مِنۢ بَعْدِهِۦ مِنْ حُلِيِّهِمْ عِجْلًا جَسَدًا لَّهُۥ خُوَارٌ أَلَمْ يَرَوْا۟ أَنَّهُۥ لَا يُكَلِّمُهُمْ وَلَا يَهْدِيهِمْ سَبِيلًا ٱتَّخَذُوهُ وَكَانُوا۟ ظَٰلِمِينَ ﴿١٤٨﴾

When they were later afflicted
with remorse, having realized that
they had gone astray, they said:
"If our Lord does not have mercy
on us and forgive us, we shall
certainly be losers." (149)

وَلَمَّا سُقِطَ فِىٓ أَيْدِيهِمْ وَرَأَوْا أَنَّهُمْ
قَدْ ضَلُّوا۟ قَالُوا۟ لَئِن لَّمْ يَرْحَمْنَا
رَبُّنَا وَيَغْفِرْ لَنَا لَنَكُونَنَّ مِنَ
ٱلْخَٰسِرِينَ ۝

When Moses returned to his
people, full of wrath and sorrow,
he said: "What an evil thing you
have done in my absence! Have
you tried to hurry up your Lord's
command?" He put down the
tablets and, seizing his brother by
the head, he pulled him to
himself. Cried Aaron, "Son of my
mother, the people felt I was weak
and they almost killed me. Do not
let our enemies rejoice over my
affliction, and do not count me
among the evil-doing folk." (150)

وَلَمَّا رَجَعَ مُوسَىٰٓ إِلَىٰ قَوْمِهِۦ غَضْبَٰنَ أَسِفًا
قَالَ بِئْسَمَا خَلَفْتُمُونِى مِنۢ بَعْدِىٓ أَعَجِلْتُمْ
أَمْرَ رَبِّكُمْ وَأَلْقَى ٱلْأَلْوَاحَ وَأَخَذَ بِرَأْسِ
أَخِيهِ يَجُرُّهُۥٓ إِلَيْهِ قَالَ ٱبْنَ أُمَّ إِنَّ ٱلْقَوْمَ
ٱسْتَضْعَفُونِى وَكَادُوا۟ يَقْتُلُونَنِى فَلَا
تُشْمِتْ بِىَ ٱلْأَعْدَآءَ وَلَا تَجْعَلْنِى مَعَ
ٱلْقَوْمِ ٱلظَّٰلِمِينَ ۝

Said [Moses]: "My Lord, forgive
me and my brother, and admit
us to Your grace: for You are
indeed the most merciful of
those who are merciful." (151)

قَالَ رَبِّ ٱغْفِرْ لِى وَلِأَخِى وَأَدْخِلْنَا
فِى رَحْمَتِكَ وَأَنتَ أَرْحَمُ
ٱلرَّٰحِمِينَ ۝

Those who took to worshipping
the calf have surely incurred their
Lord's wrath, and disgrace [will
be their lot] in this life. Thus do
We reward those who invent
falsehood. (152)

إِنَّ ٱلَّذِينَ ٱتَّخَذُوا۟ ٱلْعِجْلَ سَيَنَالُهُمْ
غَضَبٌ مِّن رَّبِّهِمْ وَذِلَّةٌ فِى ٱلْحَيَوٰةِ
ٱلدُّنْيَا وَكَذَٰلِكَ نَجْزِى ٱلْمُفْتَرِينَ ۝

But those who do evil deeds and
later repent and truly believe will
surely, after such repentance, find
your Lord to be much-forgiving,
most merciful. (153)

وَٱلَّذِينَ عَمِلُوا۟ ٱلسَّيِّئَاتِ ثُمَّ تَابُوا۟ مِنۢ
بَعْدِهَا وَءَامَنُوٓا۟ إِنَّ رَبَّكَ مِنۢ بَعْدِهَا
لَغَفُورٌ رَّحِيمٌ ۝

Then when his wrath had subsided, Moses took up the tablets, upon which was inscribed a text of guidance and grace to those who stood in awe of their Lord. (154)

وَلَمَّا سَكَتَ عَن مُّوسَى ٱلْغَضَبُ أَخَذَ ٱلْأَلْوَاحَ وَفِي نُسْخَتِهَا هُدًى وَرَحْمَةٌ لِّلَّذِينَ هُمْ لِرَبِّهِمْ يَرْهَبُونَ ﴿١٥٤﴾

Moses chose out of his people seventy men to come at a time set by Us. Then, when they were seized by violent trembling, he said: "My Lord, had it been Your will, You could have destroyed them, and myself too, long ago. Would You destroy us because of what the weak-minded among us have done? This is only a trial You have ordained, whereby You allow to go astray whom You will, and You guide aright whom You will. You alone are our guardian: grant us, then, forgiveness and bestow mercy on us. You are the best of all those who do forgive. (155)

وَٱخْتَارَ مُوسَىٰ قَوْمَهُۥ سَبْعِينَ رَجُلًا لِّمِيقَٰتِنَا فَلَمَّآ أَخَذَتْهُمُ ٱلرَّجْفَةُ قَالَ رَبِّ لَوْ شِئْتَ أَهْلَكْتَهُم مِّن قَبْلُ وَإِيَّٰىَ أَتُهْلِكُنَا بِمَا فَعَلَ ٱلسُّفَهَآءُ مِنَّا إِنْ هِيَ إِلَّا فِتْنَتُكَ تُضِلُّ بِهَا مَن تَشَآءُ وَتَهْدِى مَن تَشَآءُ أَنتَ وَلِيُّنَا فَٱغْفِرْ لَنَا وَٱرْحَمْنَا وَأَنتَ خَيْرُ ٱلْغَٰفِرِينَ ﴿١٥٥﴾

Ordain for us what is good, both in this world and in the life to come. To You alone we turn." [God] answered: "I afflict anyone I wish with My torment while My grace encompasses all things; so I will confer it on those who steer away from evil, and spend in charity, and who believe in Our signs— (156)

وَٱكْتُبْ لَنَا فِي هَٰذِهِ ٱلدُّنْيَا حَسَنَةً وَفِي ٱلْأَخِرَةِ إِنَّا هُدْنَا إِلَيْكَ قَالَ عَذَابِى أُصِيبُ بِهِۦ مَنْ أَشَآءُ وَرَحْمَتِى وَسِعَتْ كُلَّ شَىْءٍ فَسَأَكْتُبُهَا لِلَّذِينَ يَتَّقُونَ وَيُؤْتُونَ ٱلزَّكَوٰةَ وَٱلَّذِينَ هُم بِـَٔايَٰتِنَا يُؤْمِنُونَ ﴿١٥٦﴾

209

those who follow the Messenger, the unlettered Prophet whom they shall find described in the Torah and the Gospel that are with them. He commands them to do what is right and forbids them to do what is wrong, and makes lawful to them the good things of life and forbids them all that is foul. He lifts from them their burdens and the shackles that weigh upon them. Those, therefore, who believe in him, honour and support him, and follow the light that has been bestowed from on high through him shall indeed be successful." (157)

ٱلَّذِينَ يَتَّبِعُونَ ٱلرَّسُولَ ٱلنَّبِيَّ ٱلْأُمِّيَّ ٱلَّذِي يَجِدُونَهُۥ مَكْتُوبًا عِندَهُمْ فِي ٱلتَّوْرَىٰةِ وَٱلْإِنجِيلِ يَأْمُرُهُم بِٱلْمَعْرُوفِ وَيَنْهَىٰهُمْ عَنِ ٱلْمُنكَرِ وَيُحِلُّ لَهُمُ ٱلطَّيِّبَٰتِ وَيُحَرِّمُ عَلَيْهِمُ ٱلْخَبَٰئِثَ وَيَضَعُ عَنْهُمْ إِصْرَهُمْ وَٱلْأَغْلَٰلَ ٱلَّتِي كَانَتْ عَلَيْهِمْ فَٱلَّذِينَ ءَامَنُوا بِهِۦ وَعَزَّرُوهُ وَنَصَرُوهُ وَٱتَّبَعُوا ٱلنُّورَ ٱلَّذِي أُنزِلَ مَعَهُۥٓ أُو۟لَٰئِكَ هُمُ ٱلْمُفْلِحُونَ ﴿١٥٧﴾

Say: Mankind, I am indeed God's Messenger to you all. It is to Him that sovereignty over the heavens and the earth belongs. There is no deity other than Him. He alone grants life and causes death. Believe, then, in God and His Messenger, the unlettered Prophet, who believes in God and His words. And follow him, so that you may be rightly guided. (158)

قُلْ يَٰٓأَيُّهَا ٱلنَّاسُ إِنِّي رَسُولُ ٱللَّهِ إِلَيْكُمْ جَمِيعًا ٱلَّذِي لَهُۥ مُلْكُ ٱلسَّمَٰوَٰتِ وَٱلْأَرْضِ لَآ إِلَٰهَ إِلَّا هُوَ يُحْيِۦ وَيُمِيتُ فَـَٔامِنُوا بِٱللَّهِ وَرَسُولِهِ ٱلنَّبِيِّ ٱلْأُمِّيِّ ٱلَّذِي يُؤْمِنُ بِٱللَّهِ وَكَلِمَٰتِهِۦ وَٱتَّبِعُوهُ لَعَلَّكُمْ تَهْتَدُونَ ﴿١٥٨﴾

Yet among the folk of Moses there are some who guide (others) by means of the truth and act justly in its light. (159)

وَمِن قَوْمِ مُوسَىٰٓ أُمَّةٌ يَهْدُونَ بِٱلْحَقِّ وَبِهِۦ يَعْدِلُونَ ﴿١٥٩﴾

We divided them into twelve tribes, each a community. And when his people asked Moses for water to drink, We inspired him: "Strike the rock with your staff." Twelve springs gushed forth from it, and each tribe knew its drinking-place. We caused the clouds to draw their shadow over them and sent down for them manna and quails, [saying]: "Eat of the good things We have given you as sustenance." Yet they could do Us no wrong, but they certainly wronged themselves. (160)

وَقَطَّعْنَٰهُمُ ٱثْنَتَىْ عَشْرَةَ أَسْبَاطًا أُمَمًا وَأَوْحَيْنَآ إِلَىٰ مُوسَىٰٓ إِذِ ٱسْتَسْقَىٰهُ قَوْمُهُۥٓ أَنِ ٱضْرِب بِّعَصَاكَ ٱلْحَجَرَ فَٱنۢبَجَسَتْ مِنْهُ ٱثْنَتَا عَشْرَةَ عَيْنًا قَدْ عَلِمَ كُلُّ أُنَاسٍ مَّشْرَبَهُمْ وَظَلَّلْنَا عَلَيْهِمُ ٱلْغَمَٰمَ وَأَنزَلْنَا عَلَيْهِمُ ٱلْمَنَّ وَٱلسَّلْوَىٰ كُلُواْ مِن طَيِّبَٰتِ مَا رَزَقْنَٰكُمْ وَمَا ظَلَمُونَا وَلَٰكِن كَانُوٓاْ أَنفُسَهُمْ يَظْلِمُونَ ۝

It was said to them: "Dwell in this city and eat of its food whatever you may wish, and say: "Lord, relieve us of our burden," and enter the gate in humility. We will forgive you your sins, and We will richly reward those who do good." (161)

وَإِذْ قِيلَ لَهُمُ ٱسْكُنُواْ هَٰذِهِ ٱلْقَرْيَةَ وَكُلُواْ مِنْهَا حَيْثُ شِئْتُمْ وَقُولُواْ حِطَّةٌ وَٱدْخُلُواْ ٱلْبَابَ سُجَّدًا نَّغْفِرْ لَكُمْ خَطِيٓـَٰتِكُمْ سَنَزِيدُ ٱلْمُحْسِنِينَ ۝

But the wrongdoers among them substituted other words for those which they had been given. Therefore We let loose against them a scourge from heaven in requital for their wrongdoing. (162)

فَبَدَّلَ ٱلَّذِينَ ظَلَمُواْ مِنْهُمْ قَوْلًا غَيْرَ ٱلَّذِى قِيلَ لَهُمْ فَأَرْسَلْنَا عَلَيْهِمْ رِجْزًا مِّنَ ٱلسَّمَآءِ بِمَا كَانُواْ يَظْلِمُونَ ۝

Ask them about the town which stood by the sea: how its people profaned the Sabbath. Each Sabbath their fish appeared before them breaking the water's surface, but they would not come near them on other than Sabbath days. Thus did We try them because of their disobedience. (163)

وَسْـَٔلْهُمْ عَنِ ٱلْقَرْيَةِ ٱلَّتِي كَانَتْ حَاضِرَةَ ٱلْبَحْرِ إِذْ يَعْدُونَ فِي ٱلسَّبْتِ إِذْ تَأْتِيهِمْ حِيتَانُهُمْ يَوْمَ سَبْتِهِمْ شُرَّعًا وَيَوْمَ لَا يَسْبِتُونَ لَا تَأْتِيهِمْ كَذَٰلِكَ نَبْلُوهُم بِمَا كَانُوا۟ يَفْسُقُونَ ۝

When some among them asked: "Why do you preach to people whom God is certain to destroy, or at least to punish severely?" [others] replied: "So that we may be free from blame in the sight of your Lord, and that they may become God-fearing." (164)

وَإِذْ قَالَتْ أُمَّةٌ مِّنْهُمْ لِمَ تَعِظُونَ قَوْمًا ٱللَّهُ مُهْلِكُهُمْ أَوْ مُعَذِّبُهُمْ عَذَابًا شَدِيدًا قَالُوا۟ مَعْذِرَةً إِلَىٰ رَبِّكُمْ وَلَعَلَّهُمْ يَتَّقُونَ ۝

When they had forgotten all the warnings they had been given, We saved those who had tried to prevent evil, and overwhelmed the transgressors with dreadful suffering for their iniquitous deeds. (165)

فَلَمَّا نَسُوا۟ مَا ذُكِّرُوا۟ بِهِۦٓ أَنجَيْنَا ٱلَّذِينَ يَنْهَوْنَ عَنِ ٱلسُّوٓءِ وَأَخَذْنَا ٱلَّذِينَ ظَلَمُوا۟ بِعَذَابٍ بَـِٔيسٍۭ بِمَا كَانُوا۟ يَفْسُقُونَ ۝

And when they insolently persisted in doing what they had been forbidden to do, We said to them: "Turn into despicable apes." (166)

فَلَمَّا عَتَوْا۟ عَن مَّا نُهُوا۟ عَنْهُ قُلْنَا لَهُمْ كُونُوا۟ قِرَدَةً خَٰسِـِٔينَ ۝

Then your Lord declared that He would most certainly raise against them people who would cruelly oppress them till the Day of Resurrection. Your Lord is swift indeed in His retribution, yet He is certainly much forgiving, merciful. (167)

وَإِذْ تَأَذَّنَ رَبُّكَ لَيَبْعَثَنَّ عَلَيْهِمْ إِلَىٰ يَوْمِ ٱلْقِيَـٰمَةِ مَن يَسُومُهُمْ سُوٓءَ ٱلْعَذَابِ إِنَّ رَبَّكَ لَسَرِيعُ ٱلْعِقَابِ وَإِنَّهُ لَغَفُورٌ رَّحِيمٌ ۝

We dispersed them all over the earth as separate communities; some of them were righteous, and some far from that, and We tried them with blessings and misfortunes, so that they might mend their ways. (168)

وَقَطَّعْنَٰهُمْ فِي ٱلْأَرْضِ أُمَمًا مِّنْهُمُ ٱلصَّٰلِحُونَ وَمِنْهُمْ دُونَ ذَٰلِكَ وَبَلَوْنَٰهُم بِٱلْحَسَنَٰتِ وَٱلسَّيِّئَاتِ لَعَلَّهُمْ يَرْجِعُونَ ۝

They were succeeded by generations who inherited the Book. Yet these are keen to enjoy the fleeting pleasures of this lower world and say, "We shall be forgiven." Should some similar pleasures come their way, they would certainly be keen to indulge them. Have they not solemnly pledged through their Scriptures to say nothing but the truth about God? And have they not studied well what is in [the Scriptures]? Surely the life in the hereafter is better for all who are God-fearing. Will you not use your reason? (169)

فَخَلَفَ مِنۢ بَعْدِهِمْ خَلْفٌ وَرِثُوا۟ ٱلْكِتَٰبَ يَأْخُذُونَ عَرَضَ هَٰذَا ٱلْأَدْنَىٰ وَيَقُولُونَ سَيُغْفَرُ لَنَا وَإِن يَأْتِهِمْ عَرَضٌ مِّثْلُهُ يَأْخُذُوهُ أَلَمْ يُؤْخَذْ عَلَيْهِم مِّيثَٰقُ ٱلْكِتَٰبِ أَن لَّا يَقُولُوا۟ عَلَى ٱللَّهِ إِلَّا ٱلْحَقَّ وَدَرَسُوا۟ مَا فِيهِ وَٱلدَّارُ ٱلْأَخِرَةُ خَيْرٌ لِّلَّذِينَ يَتَّقُونَ أَفَلَا تَعْقِلُونَ ۝

As for those who hold fast to the Scriptures and attend regularly to their prayers, We shall not fail to reward those who enjoin the doing of what is right. (170)

وَٱلَّذِينَ يُمَسِّكُونَ بِٱلْكِتَبِ وَأَقَامُواْ ٱلصَّلَوٰةَ إِنَّا لَا نُضِيعُ أَجْرَ ٱلْمُصْلِحِينَ ﴿١٧٠﴾

We suspended the mountain over them as if it were a shadow, and they thought that it would fall down on them [We said]: Hold fast with all your strength to what We have given you and bear in mind all that it contains, so that you may remain God-fearing. (171)

وَإِذْ نَتَقْنَا ٱلْجَبَلَ فَوْقَهُمْ كَأَنَّهُۥ ظُلَّةٌ وَظَنُّواْ أَنَّهُۥ وَاقِعٌ بِهِمْ خُذُواْ مَآ ءَاتَيْنَكُم بِقُوَّةٍ وَٱذْكُرُواْ مَا فِيهِ لَعَلَّكُمْ تَتَّقُونَ ﴿١٧١﴾

Preview

This passage discusses a new episode in the history of Moses and the Children of Israel, after God has saved them from their enemy. In the previous passage we see how Pharaoh and his people were drowned in the sea and all that they had done and built was destroyed. In this episode, Moses does not confront the tyranny of Pharaoh and his people, for that battle is over. He fights a different sort of battle, which may be longer and more ferocious. He is fighting against the human self. Traces of ignorance and humiliation still had their effects on the nature of the Children of Israel, allowing traits of deviousness, cruelty, cowardice and weakness to reveal themselves in their attitude. These traits are bound to take their toll on human nature, because nothing corrupts human nature more than living for a long while under tyranny and in an atmosphere of terror and fear that compels people to resort to devious scheming in order to avoid trouble.

The Children of Israel lived under this type of suffering for a long while. They endured a reign of terror, coupled with Pharaoh's idolatrous faith. At first, Pharaoh killed their sons but spared their women. When this type of brutal tyranny abated, it only gave way to a life of humiliation and subjugation. A long life in these conditions was certain to corrupt their nature, leading them to wrong concepts and filling them with cowardice and a cruel bitterness.

Equipped with the fine insight granted by God to His best servants, 'Umar ibn al-Khaṭṭāb, recognized the interactions of human nature when he gave his instructions to those whom he appointed as governors of various provinces, urging them to take good care of their subjects, and saying: "Do not thrash them, because that would humiliate them." He realized that a physical beating is likely to humiliate people. His Islamic faith wanted him to make sure that people living under an Islamic government should have their integrity preserved. They must never be beaten by rulers, because they are not slaves to be subjugated by their rulers. They are servants of God only and their integrity is clearly evident when they deal with anyone else.

The Children of Israel were beaten and thrashed under Pharaoh's rule until they became too humble and submissive. Indeed, physical beating was the mildest type of humiliation they suffered in peaceful times. The Egyptians were also beaten and thrashed until they also became submissive and Pharaoh could make fools of them. They were beaten under Pharaoh's tyranny as also under Roman tyranny. It was under Islam that they were saved from all this humiliation, because Islam granted them their freedom and made them serve only the Lord of all mankind. During 'Amr ibn al-'Āṣ's reign, who liberated Egypt and brought it under the rule of Islam, his own son thrashed a young Coptic Egyptian who probably still bore the marks of flogging by the agents of the Byzantine authority. The Copt's father was furious because his son had suffered one lash from the whip of the governor's son. He travelled for a month on camel's back to put his complaint to 'Umar ibn al-Khaṭṭāb, the Caliph, who was the overall ruler of the Muslim state. Yet only a few years earlier the father endured endless flogging under the Byzantines.

This transformation was a miracle achieved by Islam when it reawakened the feeling of integrity in the hearts of the Egyptian Copts and all those who came under Islamic rule wherever they were. Even those who did not come to accept Islam regained their integrity. This was indeed a miracle, reclaiming those hearts and souls after they had endured centuries of humiliation and submissiveness. Their rediscovered integrity could only have been given back to them by Islam.

It is within this reclamation process of the hearts and minds of the Children of Israel that we will witness sin in this forthcoming passage of the *sūrah*. It represents Moses's task in this new episode, after he has crossed the sea with the Children of Israel, leaving Egypt behind them. In the Qur'ānic account we will see how the Israelites had to cope with the responsibilities of freedom and the divine message after having endured submissiveness and ignorance for a very long time. We will see them dealing with Moses with all the deviousness, ignorance and transgression that had left their marks on their nature. We will also see how Moses (peace be upon him) faced up to this mammoth task, and the troubles he had to endure as he tried to reform their natures.

These troubles are encountered by every advocate of the divine message when he tries to reform people that have for long lived under tyranny and acquired a submissive nature. The situation is even worse if those people have known the divine faith but have forgotten it following years of abandonment. In such a situation, the message of the divine faith appears lifeless to such people. Hence, the advocate of divine faith needs to double his efforts and his patience. He needs an inexhaustible wealth of patience in order to cope with such people's deviousness, transgression, rigid nature and petty concerns. He also needs to be able to cope with sudden setbacks that will jolt him at every stage as he finds those people trying time and again to relapse into ignorance.

This is perhaps one reason why the Qur'ān frequently relates to the Muslim community the history of the Children of Israel in such detail. Their history and experience are of benefit to the advocates of the divine faith in every generation.

Trampling Over God's Favours

We led the Children of Israel across the sea; and thereupon they came upon people who were dedicated to the worship of some idols of theirs. Said [the Children of Israel]: "Moses, set up a god for us like the gods they have." He replied: "You are indeed an ignorant people. As for these people: their method will inevitably lead to destruction, and worthless is all that they have been doing." [And] he said: "Am I to seek for you a deity other than God, although He has favoured you above all other people?" We have indeed saved you from Pharaoh's people, who oppressed you cruelly: they slew your sons and spared your women. Surely that was an awesome trial from your Lord. (Verses 138-141)

This picture of the Children of Israel after having crossed the sea is the seventh scene in this story. We clearly see here the deviant, incorrigible nature of those people encumbered by their long history. It has not been long since they were subjected to cruel oppression under the paganism of Pharaoh and his people. A short while earlier, they were saved from that oppression at the hands of their Prophet and leader, Moses, in the name of God, the only Lord in the universe, who destroyed their enemy and parted the sea for them to cross. Yet hardly had they crossed the sea than they came upon pagan people, dedicated to the worship of idols. At that moment, they asked Moses, the Prophet sent by the Lord of the universe preaching self-surrender to the One God, to set up for them a deity to worship. *"We led the Children of Israel across the sea; and thereupon they came upon people who were dedicated to the worship of some idols of theirs. Said [the Children of Israel]: 'Moses, set up a god for us like the gods they have.'"* (Verse 138)

Diseases of the soul are contagious just like diseases of the body, yet the infection cannot be passed on except to souls that are ready to receive it. As accurately and faithfully portrayed in the Qur'ān, the nature of the Children of Israel is weak, totally lacking in resolve. It hardly begins to follow proper guidance when it relapses into deviation. Scarcely does it begin to elevate itself before it tumbles again. When it has gone only a short distance along the straight path, it suffers a sudden setback. All this is accompanied by a rigid and hardened attitude that will not abide by the dictates of the truth. Here we see their nature brought out in full relief. Hardly had they come across people engaged in worshipping deities than they began to overlook what they had been taught over a period extending more than twenty years since Moses first called on them to believe in God's oneness. Some reports mention that Moses spent twenty-three years in Egypt from the day when he first put his message to Pharaoh and his people to the day when he crossed the sea with the Children of Israel. They even forgot the miracle that had only a short while ago saved them from Pharaoh and drowned him and his army. Those who were with Pharaoh subjugated and oppressed the Children of

Israel in the name of idolatry. Pharaoh's aides tried to provoke him so that he would punish Moses and his followers. They said to him: "*Will you allow Moses and his people to spread corruption in the land and to forsake you and your gods?*" (Verse 127) Yet those very Children of Israel forgot all this and made their singular request of Moses, the messenger sent by the Lord of the universe, to set up a god for them! Had they themselves made such gods, the matter would appear less strange than asking Moses to provide them with one. But such is the nature of the Israelites.

Motivated by his faith in God, the Lord of the universe, Moses was very angry. He could not understand how his people could relapse into paganism. He said to them: "*You are indeed an ignorant people.*" (Verse 138) He did not specify what they were ignorant of, because he wanted this description to apply in its fullest sense. In the Arabic original, the term "ignorant" is used in two senses, contrasting with knowledge and wisdom. Such a request betrays a total lack of both. This tells us that deviation from the faith based on God's oneness into paganism can only happen to those who are both ignorant and stupid. Knowledge and wisdom will inevitably lead to believing in God's oneness. No true knowledge or true wisdom can lead anywhere else. When science and reason look at this universe and the laws that operate in it they understand that all these laws point to the single Creator who has set everything in motion. These laws do not reflect only God's careful planning, but also the unity, the complementarity and coherence between these laws and the effects of their operation. All this would readily appear to anyone who reflects properly on the universe and what takes place in it. No one will turn a blind eye to all that except ignorant and stupid people, although they may claim to have knowledge, as they often do.

Moses explains to his people what may result out of their request, pointing to the terrible end that awaits those whom they wanted to imitate, making gods similar to theirs: "*As for these people: their method will inevitably lead to destruction, and worthless is all that they have been doing.*" (Verse 139)

Their idolatry, and the type of life they lead on the basis of such beliefs are in vain. The large army of functionaries and clerics, and the rulers who derive their authority from such a chaotic mess and all the erroneous concepts and corrupted life that result from deviating away from belief in one God are of no avail. They will all end in ruin.

But Moses's anger at his people's attitude takes an even stronger expression and in a higher pitch that also wonders at how they could so quickly forget God's grace when its manifestations are still there: "*Am I to seek for you a deity other than God, although He has favoured you above all other people?*" (Verse 140)

That they were favoured above all mankind in their own time was reflected in the fact that they were chosen to be the bearers of the divine message of God's oneness. This is the greatest favour of all. They were also chosen to be the heirs to inherit the blessed land, which was at that time in pagan hands. How could they, after all this, request their Prophet to seek for them a deity other than God, when they were at that very moment enjoying God's grace? As typical of the Qur'ān, the *sūrah* follows the argument made by Moses with an address by God Himself: "*We have indeed saved you from Pharaoh's people, who oppressed you cruelly: they slew your sons and spared your women. Surely that was an awesome trial from your Lord.*" (Verse 141) Such a direct link between the two speeches is a gesture of sublime honour to those prophets and advocates of the divine message.

This favour given to the Children of Israel was still present in their minds at that time. It should have been enough to remind them of their duty to be grateful to God for His blessings. God draws their attention to the lessons that they should have learnt from their suffering and trials, followed by their salvation. It was a trial of affliction followed by a trial of peace and security: "*Surely that was an awesome trial from your Lord.*" (Verse 141) None of this happened aimlessly. It was all a lesson which should equip them for a great test. If the test fails to set their minds and hearts on the right course and they incur, as a result of that failure, God's punishment, then they know that the punishment is well deserved.

An Appointment with the Supreme Lord

Now we move on to witness the eighth scene in the story when Moses is preparing himself for a meeting with his great Lord in this life. He gives specific instructions to his brother, the Prophet Aaron, before he leaves for that meeting: "*We appointed for Moses thirty nights, to which We added ten, whereby the term of forty nights set by His Lord was complete. Moses said to his brother Aaron: 'Take my place among my*

219

people and act righteously. Do not follow the path of those who spread corruption.'" (Verse 142)

The first stage of the mission assigned to Moses had been completed. He had saved the Children of Israel from a life of affliction, humiliation and subjugation by Pharaoh and his people. He crossed over with them from the land of tyranny and humiliation into the open desert, on the way to the Holy Land. They, however, were not yet prepared to undertake the great task awaiting them, which was the implementation of God's law on earth. We have seen how they wanted to revert to paganism once they saw a group of people dedicated to the worship of their idols. The faith preached by Moses, based on God's absolute oneness, was shaken in their hearts after only a short while. It was necessary for those people to have a detailed message to prepare them to shoulder their forthcoming responsibilities. It was to give Moses that detailed message that God appointed those nights for him. The appointment would prepare Moses himself for the great meeting ahead.

The period of preparation was thirty nights, to which ten more were added in order to complete forty nights during which Moses would be completely free from all preoccupations of this world in order to concentrate on dedicating himself to God alone. Thus, his soul would achieve purification and refinement, and his resolve would be strengthened to fulfil the great trust which was about to be given to him.

Just before leaving for his period of seclusion and dedication, Moses gave his instructions to the man who was to deputize for him: *"Moses said to his brother Aaron: 'Take my place among my people and act righteously. Do not follow the path of those who spread corruption.'"* (Verse 142) Moses was aware that his brother, Aaron, was also a Prophet sent alongside him by his Lord. But a believer always gives good counsel to other believers. This is the right and duty of Muslims. Moses was aware of the heavy burden Aaron was about to shoulder, and of the nature of the Children of Israel. Aaron welcomed the good advice given him by his brother. Advice is felt to be a burden only by wicked people who want to break loose, or by arrogant people who feel that to take advice is beneath them. It is a small man who refuses to take a supporting hand in order to show that he can cope on his own.

As regards the thirty nights and the addition of ten more, Ibn Kathīr states in his commentary on the Qur'ān: "God mentions in His book that He appointed thirty nights for Moses. Commentators say that

Moses (peace be upon him) fasted during these days and ate practically nothing. When the term was over, Moses took the skin of a tree and rubbed his teeth with it. God commanded him then to continue for ten more days."

A Request to See the Lord

Then we come to the ninth scene which is unique. In this scene we find that God has chosen His Prophet Moses [peace be upon him] to talk to him directly, without any intermediary. It is a scene where an insignificant mortal makes contact with the everlasting existence, without any catalyst or intermediary. A human being is thus able to receive instructions directly from God, the eternal, when that human being is still on earth. As for us, we do not know how this took place. We do not know how God spoke to His servant Moses, nor do we know with what sense or organ Moses received God's commandments. To try to describe this for certain is impossible for us, human beings, because we are limited by our own experience and confined within our own practical world. What we can do is to utilize that aspect of our constitution which results from the fact that God has breathed of His soul into man in order to look up to that great horizon. When we do this, we must not ruin that experience by asking how it all took place, trying to limit it to our own experience.

> When Moses came for Our appointment and his Lord spoke to him, he said: "My Lord, show Yourself to me, so that I may look at You." Said [God]: "You shall not see Me. But look upon the mountain; if it remains firm in its place, then, only then, you shall see Me." When his Lord revealed His glory to the mountain, He sent it crashing down. Moses fell down senseless. When he came to himself, he said: "Limitless You are in Your glory. To You I turn in repentance. I am the first to truly believe in You." He said: "Moses, I have chosen you of all mankind and favoured you by entrusting My messages to you and by My speaking to you. Take then what I have given you and be thankful." We wrote for him on the tablets all manner of admonition, clearly spelling out everything, and (said to him): "Implement them with strength and determination, and bid your people to observe what is best in them. I shall show you the abode of the transgressors. I will turn away from My revelations those who,

without any right, behave arrogantly on earth: for, though they may see every sign, they do not believe in it. If they see the path of righteousness, they do not choose to follow it, but if they see the path of error, they choose it for their path; because they disbelieve in Our revelations and pay no heed to them. Those who deny Our revelations and the certainty of the meeting in the Hereafter will see all their works collapse. Are they to be rewarded for anything other than what they have done?" (Verses 143-147)

We need to concentrate all our mental ability into visualizing this great and unique scene in order to begin to understand what Moses must have felt: *"When Moses came for Our appointment and his Lord spoke to him, he said: 'My Lord, show Yourself to me, so that I may look at You.'"* (Verse 143) In that awesome scene when Moses was receiving his Lord's commandments, his soul was looking up to something greater, eager to reach out to what is most desirable. He forgets himself and his nature, and requests what no one can have or can tolerate while on earth. He requests to see the Lord Himself, prompted by his hope, genuine love and keenness to have the greatest prize of all. But he is brought back to reality by a decisive word: *"Said [God]: 'You shall not see Me.'"* (Verse 143)

But then the great Lord is kind to him, so He explains to him why he cannot see Him. His constitution cannot tolerate it: *"But look upon the mountain; if it remains firm in its place, then, only then, you shall see Me."* (Verse 143) A mountain is certainly much firmer and less affected by outside powers than a human being. But what happened? *"When his Lord revealed His glory to the mountain, He sent it crashing down."* (Verse 143) How did God reveal His glory to the mountain? We simply cannot describe or understand this. We can only have a feeling of it when we use that secret aspect of our constitution which holds a bond between us and God, when our souls are purified, with all filth purged away, and we concentrate all our thinking and understanding on God and His power. Simple words cannot express it at all. Therefore, we will not try to describe with words how God revealed His glory to the mountain. We prefer to discount all the reports that try to explain it, because none of them is authentically attributed to the Prophet himself, while the Qur'ān has said nothing on it.

"When the Lord revealed His glory to the mountain, He sent it crashing down." (Verse 143) The whole mountain was thus levelled down with

no obtrusions on the surface of the earth. Moses was overawed and "*Moses fell down senseless.*" (Verse 143) He was completely unconscious.

"*When he came to himself,*" realizing the limits of his ability, and recognizing that he overstepped his limits when he made his request, "*he said: 'Limitless You are in Your glory.'*" He thus realized that God is too glorious to be seen by the naked human eye. "*To You I turn in repentance,*" for having overstepped my limit in making such a request. "*I am the first to truly believe in You.*" (Verse 143) God's messengers are always the first to believe in the greatness of their Lord and in His revelations. God commands them to declare that they are the first to believe. The Qurʾān reports in several instances that they comply and make that declaration.

Once more God's grace was bestowed on Moses in abundance. He soon received the happy news of his being chosen to carry God's message to his people after they had been saved. His message to Pharaoh and his people focused on that deliverance: "*He said: 'Moses, I have chosen you of all mankind and favoured you by entrusting My messages to you and by My speaking to you. Take then what I have given you and be thankful.'*" (Verse 144)

We understand from this statement that Moses was favoured over all his contemporaries. Messengers were sent before Moses and other messengers were sent after his time. It is, then, a favour over a whole generation of mankind. What was unique to Moses alone was the fact that God spoke to him directly. Moses was also commanded by God to take what he was given and to be grateful for being favoured and for having been given God's message. Thus he was instructed how to react to God's favour. All messengers [peace by upon them] provide guidance to people and present them with a good example. Hence, all people should accept whatever is given to them by God and show their gratitude for it so that they can receive more blessings and guard against arrogance and conceit, and maintain a good relationship with God.

A Serious Approach to Divine Law

The *sūrah* then tells us how Moses was given the message and its contents: "*We wrote for him on the tablets all manner of admonition, clearly spelling out everything.*" (Verse 145) Reports and commentators give different accounts of these tablets. Some of them give very detailed descriptions which we imagine to have been taken from Jewish sources. Such accounts have found their way into commentaries on the Qur'ān. None of these details is authentically reported to have been given by God's Messenger (peace be upon him). Therefore, we confine ourselves to the true Qur'ānic statement, not going an inch beyond it. Those descriptions neither add to, nor detract anything from the nature of those tablets. What were these tablets and how they were written are matters that do not concern us, since no authentic report has provided us with any details. What is important is the contents of those tablets. They included all aspects that were of the essence of the divine message, its aim of providing a true concept of God and details of His law, and the instructions needed to reform the Israelite community whose nature had been corrupted by enduring tyranny and humiliation for a long time.

"Implement them with strength and determination, and bid your people to observe what is best in them." (Verse 145) This is a divine order to Moses (peace be upon him) to take those tablets and implement their contents with strength and determination. Moreover, he was to bid his people to fulfil their tough obligations because these were the best for them and the most certain to bring about a great transformation in their situation. The way this order is given suggests that this was the proper approach to reform the nature of the Israelites. They needed to show seriousness and determination to fulfil their obligations outlined to them in God's message. But the order given to Moses also suggests that this is the approach to be followed by every community towards divine faith.

Faith is a matter of great importance in God's view, and in as far as this universe is concerned and how God conducts its affairs by His will. It is also a matter of great importance in human history, man's life on earth, and in the hereafter as well. The code of living detailed by the divine faith is based on the basic concept of God's oneness, the only Lord in the universe, to whom all mankind are servants. It thus transforms human life in general, giving it a direction that is totally different from all courses chartered by ignorance that assign lordship in the universe to beings other than God.

What is viewed so seriously by God and enjoys such importance in the universe, human life and history must be taken seriously and cannot but have a strong effect on people. It simply cannot be trifled with or taken lightly. It is a serious matter in itself, and it demands serious action. But such seriousness cannot be tolerated by people who, by their nature, take everything very lightly. This does not mean any rigidity, complexity or extremism. None of these have anything to do with divine faith. It simply means that the approach must be serious and the implementation must be carried out with strength and determination.

The nature of the Children of Israel in particular required such a serious instruction after it had been corrupted by a long period of humiliation in Egypt. It is noted that all commandments given to the Children of Israel were coupled with added emphasis in order to train them to be serious, straightforward and determined. This applies to any community that may have suffered a long period of subjugation, humiliation and tyranny. After such a period, it is only natural that people should become devious in the way they approach all matters, because their priority has been to avoid trouble and do only that which is easy. We can see this very clearly in many contemporary communities which try to evade faith in order not to fulfil its obligations. They simply join the crowd, because being one of a crowd does not cost much.

In return for carrying out God's orders, God promises Moses and his people to establish them in the land and to cause them to inherit the land which was then in the hands of a transgressor community: "*I shall show you the abode of the transgressors.*" (Verse 145)

Most probably this is a reference to the Holy Land which was at the time in the hands of a pagan community. Thus, this was happy news given to the Israelites that they were certain to take over the Holy Land. It is true that the Children of Israel did not enter the Holy Land in Moses's lifetime, but that was because their reformation was as yet incomplete, and their nature not yet straightened. We should remember that they stood at its borders, saying to their Messenger: "*Mighty people dwell in that land, and we will surely not enter it unless they depart from it. If they do depart, then we will enter.*" (5: 22) When two believers who truly feared God urged them to force their way into the Holy Land, they spoke to Moses with all the rudeness only cowards can command, just like a mule that kicks its driver, saying: "*We will never go in so long as they are in it. Go forth, then, you and your Lord, and fight, both of you. We shall stay here.*" (5: 24) This describes their cowardly nature which cannot stand up to any serious obligation. The faith and the law given to the Prophet Moses (peace be upon him) and

From the point of view of faith, we believe that God's warnings will certainly come true, regardless of any contrary appearances. Whoever denies God's revelations and the certainty that all people will be gathered to Him in the hereafter will have all his works ruined. In practice, we find that this is truly the case in human life. Those who deny the signs God has placed all over the universe or deny the revelations He has vouchsafed to His Messenger, and consequently deny the certainty of meeting God on the Day of Judgement, have gone astray. They continuously move away from the nature of the universe, because the universe submits to God's law. They have no link with the universe and have no motivation to link themselves with the action that fulfils the purpose of universal existence. Hence, every action that such people perpetrate will certainly collapse, even though it may appear to be flourishing. This is because such action is not linked to the motives that are deeply rooted in the very basis of the universe or its goal. It is just like a little stream that gets cut off from the main spring. It will eventually dry out.

Those who see no close relationship between the values of faith and the movement of human history, and those who overlook God's will which defines the destiny of everyone that denies such values are indeed the ones who continue to pay no heed to God's signs and revelations. It is to those that God's declaration applies. They are the ones whom God will turn away from His revelations and leave them to their inevitable destiny.

Those who admire the apparent success achieved by some unbelievers, unaware that it is only a short term success, are like those who admire the swollen belly of a she-camel that has eaten poisonous plants, thinking it to be indicative of good health, unaware that its death is so close. Past nations provide very clear examples. Those who have succeeded them should learn the lessons to be derived from their experience and watch how God's law never fails. God's will is certain to be done.

Miserable Return to Old Ways

When Moses was on this unique trip, attending with all his faculties to his meeting with his Lord, something else was happening with his people. He was fully engaged with a mission that our minds can only contemplate but we cannot visualize; a mission our thoughts cannot conceive, but to which our spirits warm. But at that very same time, his people were relapsing into paganism, and taking to themselves a lifeless calf that issues a lowing sound, making of it a deity for worship in place of God. There is, then, a wide gulf between the ninth and tenth scenes of the story. The former took us into a sublime horizon in which we look up to the resplendent glory of God, while the latter brings us to a low depth of deviation, superstition and disbelief:

> In his absence, the people of Moses took to the worship of the effigy of a calf made of their ornaments, which gave a lowing sound. Did they not see that it could neither speak to them nor give them any guidance? Yet they took to worshipping it, for they were evildoers. When they were later afflicted with remorse, having realized that they had gone astray, they said: "If our Lord does not have mercy on us and forgive us, we shall certainly be losers." (Verses 148-149)

That was typical of the nature of the Israelites who could hardly move one step along the straight path before they deviated. They were hardly able to elevate themselves, in their beliefs and concepts, above what is physical and tangible. Even a short lull in exhortation and reminders could see them relapsing into disbelief.

We saw earlier how they tried to persuade their Prophet to set up a deity for them to worship. They did so only because they saw pagan people worshipping idols. Their Prophet rebuked them severely for entertaining such thoughts. But when they were left to themselves and saw a mere body of a calf of gold made by the Sāmirī in a way that allowed the calf to make a lowing sound, they were so excited and addressed their worship to it. The Samirī said to them: "This is your and Moses's God, whom Moses has gone to meet, but has forgotten his appointment." Perhaps this was said because of the ten extra nights that were added to the period appointed for Moses, of which his people were not aware. When Moses did not return after the thirty original nights, the Samirī said to his people: "Moses has forgotten his appointment with his God, so now his God is here. This is it." The strange thing is that those people forgot all the teachings of their Prophet who had repeatedly told them that they must only worship their Lord, the Lord of the universe, who cannot be seen by the naked human eye. They did not even reflect on the nature of that calf which was shaped and fashioned by a man among them. They belonged to a disgraceful type of people. The Qur'ān wonders at such people as they are presented to the unbelievers in Makkah who worshipped idols and statues.

"*Did they not see that it could neither speak to them nor give them any guidance? Yet they took to worshipping it, for they were evildoers.*" (Verse 148) Who is a worse evildoer than one who worships something made by a human hand, when it is God who has created human beings and all that they do?

Aaron, the Prophet (peace be upon him) was still among them, but he was unable to stop them from sinking into this stupid idiocy. There were also a few wise people, but these could not restrain the masses who scrambled to touch the golden calf, particularly because it was made of gold, the true idol of the Israelites.

Eventually, the farce died down, the truth was clear to all, and it was plain to everyone how far into stupid error they had sunk. Error gave way to remorse: "*When they were later afflicted with remorse, having realized that they had gone astray, they said: 'If our Lord does not have mercy on us and forgive us, we shall certainly be losers.'*" (Verse 149)

The original Arabic statement gives an impression that they were at a total loss, unable to determine how to get out of the trouble in which they had landed themselves. They realized that this relapse could not be corrected, because it had actually taken place. Hence, their admission: "*If our Lord does not have mercy on us and forgive us, we shall certainly be losers.*" (Verse 149) This statement suggests that they had still retained some willingness to follow the right guidance. Their hearts had not yet hardened to the extent of their being harder than stones, as God describes them in the Qur'ān (2: 74). When they recognized their error, they were afflicted with remorse and realized that they could only be saved by God's mercy.

A Sad Return for Moses

All this took place when Moses was with his Lord, addressing his appeal to Him. He was unaware of what his people had done in his absence. At this point, scene eleven is raised before our eyes: "*When Moses returned to his people, full of wrath and sorrow, he said: 'What an evil thing you have done in my absence! Have you tried to hurry up your Lord's command?' He put down the tablets and, seizing his brother by the head, he pulled him to himself. Cried Aaron, 'Son of my mother, the people felt I was weak and they almost killed me. Do not let our enemies rejoice over my affliction, and do not count me among the evil-doing folk.' Said [Moses]: 'My Lord, forgive me and my brother, and admit us to Your grace: for You are indeed the most merciful of those who are merciful.'"* (Verses 150-151)

We see how terribly angry Moses was. Anger can be felt in both what he said and did, particularly seizing his brother by the head and dragging him: "*What an evil thing you have done in my absence! Have you tried to hurry up your Lord's command?'" Seizing his brother by the head, he pulled him to himself.*" (Verse 150)

Yet is was only right that Moses should feel very angry. He had received a terrible shock and a painful surprise. Hence he exclaimed: "*What an evil thing you have done in my absence!*" (Verse 150) I left you following right guidance, and you relapsed into error. Before I left, you were worshipping God alone, and while I was away you took to the worship of a mere lifeless calf that gave a lowing sound. "*Have you tried to hurry up your Lord's command?*" (Verse 150) This could mean that they were trying to hurry God's judgements and punishment, or it could mean that they tried to hasten his appointment.

"*He put down the tablets and, seizing his brother by the head, he pulled him to himself.*" (Verse 150) This is a very strong reaction. Those tablets contained the law God had given him. Moses would not put those tablets down except in a state of extreme anger which caused him to lose control of himself. Again, dragging his brother by the head is indicative of the same reaction, because Aaron was a noble Prophet, full of faith and piety.

Aaron appeals to the bond of brotherhood that he had with Moses, in order to cool his temper. He explained his attitude and that he spared no effort in trying to give good counsel to his people: "*Cried Aaron, 'Son of my mother, the people felt I was weak and they almost killed me.'*" (Verse 150)

This statement gives us an impression of how the Israelites scrambled to worship the golden calf. They almost killed Aaron when he tried to restrain them. "*Son of my mother!*" That address is an appeal to a bond of compassion. "*The people felt I was weak and they almost killed me.*" (Verse 150) That is a vivid description of his own attitude. "*Do not let our enemies rejoice over my affliction.*" (Verse 150) Again, Aaron is appealing to a bond that should ensure mutual support between the two brothers, because their enemies would gloat over his affliction.

"*And do not count me among the evil-doing folk.*" (Verse 150) I did not share in their error or evil deeds. I dissociated myself from their action.

At this point, Moses begins to cool down, because his brother did not meet anger with anger. He simply explained himself and his attitude. Therefore, Moses turns to his Lord and seeks forgiveness for himself and his brother from the most merciful. "*Said [Moses]: 'My Lord, forgive me and my brother, and admit us to Your grace: for You are indeed the most merciful of those who are merciful..'*" (Verse 151)

A Fitting Judgement

At this point, the final judgement is passed by the One who has the authority to give such a judgement. God's words follow directly on what the Qur'ān relates of the words in the familiar Qur'ānic fashion: "*Those who took to worshipping the calf have surely incurred their Lord's wrath, and disgrace [will be their lot] in this life. Thus do We reward those who invent falsehood. But those who do evil deeds and later repent and truly believe will surely, after such repentance, find your Lord to be much-forgiving, most merciful.*" (Verses 152-153)

This is a judgement and a promise. The people who worshipped the calf were certain to incur God's anger and were certain to be at the receiving end of disgrace in this life. At the same time, God's rule remains valid: those who repent after having misbehaved are certain to receive God's forgiveness and His mercy. This means that God is fully aware that those who worshipped the calf would never turn back to God in sincere repentance. They were sure to do enough to make that permanent rule inapplicable to them. History shows that this was the case. The Children of Israel continued to do one sinful act after another, and God continued to forgive them time after time, until eventually they incurred God's permanent rejection: "*Thus do We reward those who invent falsehood.*" (Verse 152) This applies to all the inventors of falsehood. Whenever the crime is repeated, time after time, whether by the Children of Israel or any other people, then its punishment is certain to apply.

God's promise will certainly come true. He has condemned those who took to worshipping the calf to be subject to His anger and to be disgraced. The last part of His condemnation was that He would be sending them, time after time, until the Day of Judgement, people who would inflict on them great suffering. It may happen that in a certain period of history they appear to exercise so much power and influence which enables them to behave arrogantly towards the Gentiles. They may appear to have enormous wealth which gives them so much power. They may be able to control the world's media; and they may even have a decisive say in bringing in governments, in different countries, that do their bidding. We may see all this and a great deal more, but this does not contradict God's warning to them or His condemnation. All these actions will work against them, as people will nurture their hatred which will eventually destroy them.

They can overcome the people in Palestine, for example, because those people have abandoned their faith and are no longer Muslims. They do not rally under the banner of the Islamic faith, but instead they hoist a nationalist or racist banner. Their efforts end in failure and Israel is able to overcome them. But this state of affairs will not last forever. These Arab people have been in a state of total unawareness of the only method, weapon and banner which saw them victorious for a thousand years, and which is certain to make them victorious again. When they abandon them, they are sure to be defeated. Such lack of awareness comes as a result of the poison injected in the Muslim community by Zionist and Christian imperialist forces, which try to perpetuate such a state of affairs through the regimes they establish in the Muslim world. But all this will not last. There will be a re-awakening of the Muslim community. Future Muslim generations will equip themselves with the same weapons as their forefathers. Who knows, but humanity will one day wake up to recognize the tyranny of the Zionist Jews. They will then act to make God's warnings come true and return the Zionist Jews to the state of humiliation and disgrace to which God has condemned them. If humanity will not wake up, then certainly future Muslim generations will. We are absolutely certain of this.

Those two verses serve as a pause in order to comment on the ultimate destiny of those who worshipped the calf inventing falsehood against God. They come in the middle of this scene, but then the *sūrah* picks it up again: "*Then when his wrath had subsided, Moses took up the tablets, upon which was inscribed a text of guidance and grace to those who stood in awe of their Lord.*" (Verse 154)

The Qur'ānic style personifies anger as if it is a living thing that exercises control over Moses, dictating his actions. But when it subsides and its promptings die down, Moses regains his self-control. He picks up the tablets, which, as we are told again, contain the guidance and mercy for those who fear God and open their hearts to receive His guidance and mercy. Indeed, the very provision of guidance is an act of grace. No one is more miserable than a deviant person who cannot see the light, or a soul that is lost without faith and without guidance. It is the fear of God that opens hearts to receive guidance and prepares them to respond properly. It is God, the Creator of hearts, who states this fact. Who knows these hearts better than the Lord who created them?

The Seventy Chosen Israelites

The *sūrah* then begins a new scene, in which we see Moses selecting seventy men from among his people: "*Moses chose out of his people seventy men to come at a time set by Us. Then, when they were seized by violent trembling, he said: 'My Lord, had it been Your will, You could have destroyed them, and myself too, long ago. Would You destroy us because of what the weak-minded among us have done? This is only a trial You have ordained, whereby You allow to go astray whom You will, and You guide aright whom You will. You alone are our guardian: grant us, then, forgiveness and bestow mercy on us. You are the best of all those who do forgive. Ordain for us what is good, both in this world and in the life to come. To You alone we turn. [God] answered: 'I afflict anyone I wish with My torment while My grace encompasses all things; so I will confer it on those who steer away from evil, and spend in charity, and who believe in Our signs — those who follow the Messenger, the unlettered Prophet whom they shall find described in the Torah and the Gospel that are with them. He commands them to do what is right and forbids them to do what is wrong, and makes lawful to them the good things of life and forbids them all that is foul. He lifts from them their burdens and the shackles that weigh upon them. Those, therefore, who believe in him, honour and support him, and follow the light that has been bestowed from on high through him shall indeed be successful.'*" (Verses 155-157)

Reports differ as to the reason for this appointment. It may have been set so that they would declare their repentance and pray to God to forgive the Children of Israel after they had sunk back into error and disbelief. In the second *sūrah*, The Cow, we learn that the penance imposed on the Israelites was that they should kill themselves, which means that the good ones among them should kill those who were disobedient. They did just that until God told them to stop and accepted their penance. Those seventy men were the best among them. The way the choice is expressed in Arabic makes them stand out from the whole community of Israelites.

Nevertheless, what happened to this choice group? They were seized by a violent trembling and dropped unconscious. The reason for this, as mentioned in another *sūrah*, was that they asked Moses to show them God so that they would believe him and accept the law He has given them in the tablets. This is typical of the nature of the Children of Israel. It applies to all of them, whether good or bad, in different measures. The most singular thing is that they should make such a request when they were supposed to declare their repentance and seek God's forgiveness.

Moses, on the other hand, turned to his Lord imploring Him to bestow His forgiveness and mercy, declaring his total submission to Him: "*When they were seized by violent trembling, he said: 'My Lord, had it been Your will, You could have destroyed them, and myself too, long ago.'*" (Verse 155) That is the mark of total submission to God's power. Moses makes sure to declare his own submission as he addresses his supplication to God to forgive his people, end their test and to spare them from destruction because of the deed perpetrated by some fools among them: "*Would You destroy us because of what the weak-minded among us have done?*" (Verse 155) Moses puts his appeal in a questioning form to emphasize his request that God does not destroy them. It is as if he is saying: my Lord, Your grace makes it absolutely unlikely that You should destroy us on account of what some fools among us have done. "*This is only a trial You have ordained, whereby You allow to go astray whom You will, and You guide aright whom You will.*" (Verse 155)

Thus Moses declares his understanding of what was taking place, that it was all a trial. In every trial, God guides those who understand its nature and recognize it as a test. He also lets those who ignore it to go deeper into error. Moses reiterates his recognition as a prelude to an appeal to God for His help to enable him and his people to pass the trial successfully: "*You alone are our guardian.*" (Verse 155) Give us your help so that we pass the test, and earn Your forgiveness and Your grace: "*Grant us, then, forgiveness and bestow mercy on us. You are the best of all those who do forgive.*" (Verse 155)

"*Ordain for us what is good, both in this world and in the life to come. To You alone we turn.*" (Verse 156) We are returning to You in repentance. We seek Your protection and support.

We see here how the appeal for forgiveness and mercy by Moses was preceded by a declaration of full submission to God and recognition of the purpose of his trial. It is concluded with a declaration of a return to God to seek His protection. Thus, it serves as an example for supplication to be followed by every good servant of God, the glorious, the beneficent.

This is followed by God's reply: "*God answered: 'I afflict anyone I wish with My torment while My grace encompasses all things.'*" (Verse 156) This is a statement of God's free will which chooses a rule and implements it as a matter of free choice. It is true that the rule is always enforced in accordance with the truth and justice, but this is also a matter of choice. Justice is an attribute of God which is seen in every aspect of the working of His will, because this is His choice. His punishment is visited only on those who deserve it, as a matter of will. His mercy encompasses all, but it is given only to those who deserve it; again as a matter of choice. He does not will to punish or show mercy to anyone in a haphazard manner. Far be it from God to do so.

The Recipients of God's Mercy

Having thus informed His Prophet, Moses, of this rule, God then tells him something about the future and the community which will advocate the final version of His message and who will earn His mercy that encompasses everything. The expression here shows that God's grace and mercy is far greater than the whole universe whose dimensions are impossible for human beings to visualize. Great indeed is the mercy whose measure is only known to God Himself.

> *My grace encompasses all things; so I will confer it on those who steer away from evil, and spend in charity, and who believe in Our signs – those who follow the Messenger, the unlettered Prophet whom they shall find described in the Torah and the Gospel that are with them. He commands them to do what is right and forbids them to do what is wrong, and makes lawful to them the good things of life and forbids them all that is foul. He lifts from them their burdens and the shackles that weigh upon them. Those, therefore, who believe*

in him, honour and support him, and follow the light that has been bestowed from on high through him shall indeed be successful. (Verses 156-157)

This is an extremely important piece of news confirming that the Children of Israel had been given, most emphatically, confirmed information of the advent of the unlettered Prophet. This was given them by their Prophets Moses and Jesus (peace be upon them both) a long time ago. Both informed them of his mission, description, the method his message would follow and the distinctive features of his faith. He is 'the unlettered Prophet' who enjoins people to do what is good and forbids them what is evil. He will also lift off the shoulders of those among the Children of Israel who will believe in him the burdens and shackles God knew would be imposed on them because of their disobedience. They will continue to apply to them until the unlettered Prophet lifts them from those who believe in him. His followers fear their Lord, steer away from evil, pay zakāt and believe in God's signs. The Children of Israel have also received the most certain news that those who believe in this unlettered Prophet, honour and support him and follow the light that has been sent down with him "*shall indeed be successful.*"

This early information given to the Children of Israel by their Prophet Moses (peace be upon him) makes it clear what future form God's message will take, who will bear its banner, who will follow that standard bearer and what course of action will ensure receiving His mercy. Thus, there is no excuse for the followers of earlier religions not to follow the message of Islam, having received such an early warning of it.

This absolutely true piece of information, given by the Lord of the universe to Moses (peace be upon him) when he and the seventy chosen people were at their appointment with their Lord, reveals the extent of the crime perpetrated by the Jews and their attitude to the unlettered Prophet and the religion revealed to him. They adopted an uncompromisingly hostile attitude to him and his message in spite of what it contained of reducing their burden and giving his followers the certain promise of success. They have perpetrated this crime despite their being fully aware of the facts. They have spared no effort in pursuing their hostility. History records that the Children of Israel have been the most hardened opponents of this Prophet and his religion.

The Jews come first, followed closely by extremist Christians. The war they have launched against this Prophet, his faith and followers is an ugly, wicked, determined and cruel war.

We need only refer to what the Qur'ān mentions about the way the people who received earlier Scriptures fight Islam and Muslims. There are detailed accounts of this in *Sūrahs* 2, 3, 4 and 5. Such references give us a glimpse of the broad front over which they have conducted their wicked war with this religion. Reference to historical events, ever since the first day Islam established its state in Madinah, to the present moment is sufficient to reveal their unhesitating and obstinate resolve to fight this religion and to try to exterminate it altogether.

Zionism and Christian Imperialism have employed in these modern times various methods of combat, scheming and plotting against this religion which are far superior to what they used over past centuries. In our modern time, they are trying to put an end to the Islamic faith altogether, thinking that they are fighting their final decisive battle. Therefore, they re-employ the methods and schemes they used in the past, in addition to what the present advancements enable them to use. At the same time, some naïve people, who claim to belong to Islam, call in a most simplistic and naïve way for cooperation between Muslims and the followers of other religions against the tide of atheism and materialism. They overlook the fact that those followers of other religions are slaughtering Muslims everywhere and waging against them a war that combines all the ugliness of the Crusades and the Spanish Inquisition, either using their own forces in their colonies in Asia and Africa, or through the regimes they support in so-called independent states. They try hard to replace Islam with secular creeds which claim to be 'scientific', in order to deny everything that lies beyond the reach of common perception. These creeds also call for the 'modernization' of moral values in order to adopt animal 'freedom' and a standard of 'morality' that only fits animals. They want also to 'modernize' Islamic law, convening Orientalists' seminars and conferences for this purpose, with the aim of finding ways to legalize usury, promiscuity and other practices that Islam forbids.

All these are aspects of the ferocious war fought against this religion by those who claim to follow earlier Scriptures, although they are the ones who were given the news of this final religion and the Prophet who calls for it.

That news was given to them a very long time ago, but they nevertheless have chosen to oppose this religion with evil and hardened determination.

God's Messenger to All Mankind

The *sūrah* pauses at this point in its relating of Moses and the Children of Israel's story to address the unlettered Prophet himself, giving him God's order to declare that his message applies to all mankind, in fulfilment of God's promise: "*Say: Mankind, I am indeed God's Messenger to you all. It is to Him that sovereignty over the heavens and the earth belongs. There is no deity other than Him. He alone grants life and causes death. Believe, then, in God and His Messenger, the unlettered Prophet, who believes in God and His words. And follow him, so that you may be rightly guided.*" (Verse 158)

This is, then, the final, universal message that is not confined to a particular community, area or generation. Earlier messages were limited to a certain community or a certain period of time which extended until the appearance of a new messenger. Mankind made certain limited progress in the light of those messages, in preparation for this last message. Every new message incorporated certain modifications of the divine law that took into account human progress. The final message is complete and perfect in essence leaving room for flexibility in the implementation of its details. It is meant for all mankind, and there will be no subsequent local messages for any particular community or generation. It responds to basic human nature, which means that it is suitable for all mankind. Hence, it was conveyed by the unlettered Prophet whose nature remained pure, refined only by the care he received from God. Hence, the Prophet's pure nature conveyed the naturally pure message, addressing the very nature that is common to all mankind: "*Say: Mankind, I am indeed God's Messenger to you all.*" (Verse 158)

This Qur'ānic verse which commands God's Messenger (peace be upon him) to address his message to all mankind was revealed in Makkah. It thus provides the perfect answer to the falsehood alleged and promoted by some followers of earlier divine religions who claim that Muḥammad could not have contemplated, when he was in Makkah, to address his message to anyone outside it. They further claim that he only started to go beyond the tribe of Quraysh, and then to move to a larger area in order to address his message to the followers of earlier religions, and then to go beyond the Arabian Peninsula after the successes he was fortunate to achieve. This is merely a lie that serves them in their age-long war against his religion and its followers, and which continues unabating even today.

It is not surprising that the followers of earlier religions should mobilize their forces against Islam, or that the Orientalists who write such lies take the lead in the unabating onslaught against the followers of Islam. What is surprising and most unfortunate is that many simple-minded and naïve people among those who claim to be Muslims are happy to be students to those who invent falsehood against the Prophet of Islam and who continue to fight Muslims and the Islamic faith itself. They are happy to accept their ideas about Islam and to quote them on the history of this faith. Those naïve people have the audacity to describe themselves as 'intellectuals'.

Having commanded the Prophet to declare that his message applies to all mankind, the Qur'ānic verse continues to make it clear that the Prophet's role is to make people fully aware of who is their true Lord: "*It is to Him that sovereignty over the heavens and the earth belongs. There is no deity other than Him. He alone grants life and causes death.*" (Verse 158)

The Prophet, then, is a Messenger to all mankind from their Lord who is the Sovereign of the whole universe to which they themselves belong. He is the only God to whom everything in the universe submits. The clearest manifestation of His Godhead and His power is seen in the fact that He alone grants life and causes death. His religion, which His Messenger conveys to mankind, is the one that deserves to be accepted by all humanity because it is the religion that makes people fully aware of the true nature of their Lord. Thus, their submission to Him is an enlightened one, entailing complete obedience to God's Messenger: "*Believe, then, in God and His Messenger, the unlettered Prophet, who believes in God and His words. And follow him, so that you may be rightly guided.*" (Verse 158)

This final address makes some important, though subtle, points which should be outlined. To start with, this address implies an order to believe in God and His Messenger. This is the same implication as the declaration that there is no deity other than God and that Muḥammad is God's Messenger. This is certainly the essence of faith. This order is preceded by an outline of God's essential attributes: "*It is to Him that sovereignty over the heavens and the earth belongs. There is no deity other than Him. He alone grants life and causes death.*" (Verse 158) Hence, it is an order to believe in God, having learnt His true and essential attributes, and learnt that this message applies to all mankind.

It also implies that the unlettered Prophet (peace be upon him) believes in God and His word. While this goes without saying, drawing attention to it here is quite important. Before a person advocates a certain cause, he himself must believe in it and must have its essentials clear in his mind so that he knows the true nature of what he advocates. Hence, the Prophet sent as God's Messenger to all mankind is described as one "*who believes in God and His words.*" (Verse 158) This is exactly what he calls on people to believe.

The address also refers to the practical requirements of the faith which the Prophet calls on people to accept. When they have accepted faith, they are required to abide by its law and to follow its teachings. This is stated clearly in God's own words: "*And follow him, so that you may be rightly guided.*" (Verse 158) There is simply no way that people can benefit by the guidance given to them through God's Messenger unless they follow in practice what that Messenger says. It is not sufficient that they should believe in it, unless that belief is endorsed by practice. This is the essence of Islam.

This faith of Islam makes its own nature clear at every occasion. It is not simply a set of beliefs that find their way into people's minds and hearts. Nor is it merely a set of rituals that have to be observed. It means the complete adherence in practice to everything that God's Messenger has conveyed to us as part of his message. The Prophet has not confined himself to telling people to believe in God and His Messenger, or merely to do the various aspects of worship, but he has also conveyed to them, in word and deed, God's law which must be implemented in human life. There is no way that people can have full guidance unless they follow the Prophet in all these aspects, which, together, form the religion God has given them. This religion of Islam has no version other than that indicated by the command to believe in God and His Messenger, coupled with this order: "*And follow him, so that you may be rightly guided.*" (Verse 158) Had the Islamic faith been merely a matter of beliefs only, it would have been sufficient to say: "*Believe, then, in God and His Messenger.*" (Verse 158) But God has followed this by the order to follow the Prophet in everything that he has given us.

Straying Away from God's Commandments

The *sūrah* resumes its account of the certain aspects of the history of the Israelites, picking it up after the violent trembling that seized the seventy people Moses had chosen for the appointment set by God. Moses was absorbed in a heartfelt supplication to his Lord to save them. We know from the accounts given in other *sūrahs* that these seventy people were resurrected and returned to their folk, full of faith. The *sūrah* picks up the thread of this story, but begins first by stating that not everyone among the Israelites was in error: "*Yet among the folk of Moses there are some who guide (others) by means of the truth and act justly in its light.*" (Verse 159)

This describes their situation at the time of Moses, and after him, which meant that there was among them a group who were keen to follow the truth and show its guidance and maintain justice. It was such people who received the Prophet Muḥammad's message with ready acceptance, since they were informed in the Torah of his forthcoming appearance. The most notable of these was 'Abdullāh ibn Sallām (may God be pleased with him), a companion of the Prophet who stood up to the Jews in Madinah pointing out to them what the Torah says about the unlettered Prophet as well as the fact that Islamic law endorsed a number of Jewish laws.

The *sūrah* then resumes its account of the historical events: "*We divided them into twelve tribes, each a community. And when his people asked Moses for water to drink, We inspired him: 'Strike the rock with your staff.' Twelve springs gushed forth from it, and each tribe knew its drinking-place. We caused the clouds to draw their shadow over them and sent down for them manna and quails, [saying]: 'Eat of the good things We have given you as sustenance.' Yet they could do Us no wrong, but they certainly wronged themselves.*" (Verse 160)

These are aspects of God's care which continued to be extended to Moses and his people, even after they strayed away and worshipped the calf, then atoned for their error as God told them and He accepted their repentance. This also comes after they demanded to see God Himself and were stunned by the trembling, before God brought them back to life in answer to Moses's prayers. God's care is demonstrated here in organizing them into twelve communities, according to their ancestry. Each community traced their ancestry to one of the children of the Prophet Jacob, who was also known as Israel. They confirmed their allegiance on tribal lines: "*We divided them into twelve tribes, each a community.*" (Verse 160)

God's care is also manifest in assigning a spring to each community so that none of them would try to take what belonged to others: "*When his people asked Moses for water to drink, We inspired him: 'Strike the rock with your staff.' Twelve springs gushed forth from it, and each tribe knew its drinking-place.*" (Verse 160)

Another aspect of God's care was to send clouds to give them shade from the burning desert sun, and to bestow on them from on high manna, a kind of wild honey, and quails to provide them with food after their drink had been guaranteed: "*We caused the clouds to draw their shadow over them and sent down for them manna and quails.*" (Verse 160) A further aspect of God's care was the fact that all these good things were made lawful to them, as nothing had been forbidden them yet in punishment for their disobedience: "*Eat of the good things We have given you as sustenance.*" (Verse 160)

God's care is manifest in all that, but the Israelite nature continued to be rebellious, unwilling to keep to the path of guidance, as clearly appears from the final comment of this verse which mentions all these blessings that gave them water out of the rock, shade in the burning desert sun and wholesome, delicious food: "*Yet they could do Us no wrong, but they certainly wronged themselves.*" (Verse 160) Disobedience to God and straying away from His path were the manifestations of their wronging themselves. Such disobedience could cause God no harm, because God has no need of the Israelites or anyone else. Indeed, His kingdom is not affected at all even if they and all creatures were to unite in total disobedience to Him. Nor is His kingdom increased in any way, if all creatures were to continue to obey Him without fail. People simply wrong themselves by disobedience to God and straying away from His path.

Response to God's Care

How did the Children of Israel respond to God's care? What steps did they take on the long road pointed out to them? "*It was said to them: 'Dwell in this city and eat of its food whatever you may wish, and say: "Lord, relieve us of our burden," and enter the gate in humility. We will forgive you your sins, and We will richly reward those who do good.' But the wrongdoers among them substituted other words for those which*"

243

they had been given. Therefore We let loose against them a scourge from heaven in requital for their wrongdoing." (Verses 161-162)

God forgave them their sin of worshipping the calf, and He also forgave them after they were seized by the trembling when they were on the mountain. He has given them all His blessings; yet again their nature takes them away from the straight path. Again they disobey and change God's words. They are told to enter a particular city, the name of which is not given in the Qur'ān because knowing its name does not add to the significance of the story, and God makes lawful for them all its fruits and provisions, provided that as they enter they say a particular supplication and prostrate themselves on entry. That last gesture was required as a declaration of their submission to God at the time of victory when they felt very powerful, just as the Prophet Muḥammad (peace be upon him) prostrated himself many centuries later, on the back of his camel, when Makkah fell to Islam. In return for their obedience, God promised to forgive them their sins and to increase the reward of those among them who did well. But why would they disobey? There is no explanation other than the fact that deviation was in their nature: *"But the wrongdoers among them substituted other words for those which they had been given."* (Verse 162)

At this point, God let loose against them a scourge from heaven. It was the same heaven from which He sent down manna and quails, and which carried the clouds that gave them shade and comfort: *"Therefore We let loose against them a scourge from heaven in requital for their wrongdoing."* (Verse 162) Thus, the fact that a group of them disbelieved constituted what is termed in the Qur'ān as 'wronging themselves' and made them liable to God's punishment. The Qur'ān does not tell us exactly the nature of the suffering to which they were subjected, because the purpose of this account is achieved without specifying it. All that is needed here is to explain that disobedience entails the enforcement of the threats, giving the guilty their fair punishment.

Temptation Overcomes Willpower

Once more the Children of Israel are guilty of sinful disobedience. In this particular case, they do not openly contravene God's law, but they try to find loopholes to evade what the law requires. They cannot remain steadfast in the face of the trial to which they are exposed, because steadfastness requires a nature that can control desires and ambitions: *"Ask them about the town which stood by the sea: how its people profaned the Sabbath. Each Sabbath their fish appeared before them breaking the water's surface, but they would not come near them on other than Sabbath days. Thus did We try them because of their disobedience. When some among them asked: 'Why do you preach to people whom God is certain to destroy, or at least to punish severely?' [others] replied: 'So that we may be free from blame in the sight of your Lord, and that they may become God-fearing.' When they had forgotten all the warnings they had been given, We saved those who had tried to prevent evil, and overwhelmed the transgressors with dreadful suffering for their iniquitous deeds. And when they insolently persisted in doing what they had been forbidden to do, We said to them: 'Turn into despicable apes.' Then your Lord declared that He would most certainly raise against them people who would cruelly oppress them till the Day of Resurrection. Your Lord is swift indeed in His retribution, yet He is certainly much forgiving, merciful."* (Verses 163-167)

There is a change of style here as the method of reporting historical events is dropped in preference for confronting the descendants of the Israelites who opposed the Prophet Muḥammad (peace be upon him) in Madinah. The passage beginning with this verse up to verse 171 was revealed in Madinah to give answers to its Jewish population. However, it is incorporated in this Makkan *sūrah* to complete the history of the Israelites with their Prophet Moses.

Here God orders His Messenger (peace be upon him) to ask the Jews about this well-known event in their former history. They are questioned about it here because they were keen to assert their ancestry and that they belonged to a nation with a history extending over many generations. It reminds them of their old disobedience and the fact that their disobedience doomed a group of them to a complete change of form in this life, and condemned them all to a long history of humiliation. The only exceptions are those ready to follow the last Prophet who would certainly relieve them of the burdens and the shackles that tied them down.

The name of the city by the sea is not mentioned, because it was well known to the addressees. The event itself was perpetrated by a group of Jews who were living in a coastal city. The Children of Israel had requested that a day should be assigned to them for rest and total devotion, so that none of them would need to work on that day. Hence the appointment of the Sabbath for them. They were then subjected to a test so that they would learn how to demonstrate their willpower and resist temptation. They certainly needed to learn how to fulfil their commitments, particularly in the case of a conflict between duty and desire. That was absolutely necessary for the Children of Israel whose characters were badly weakened as a result of the humiliation they had long suffered. Their will needed to be liberated after such a long history of subjugation, so that they could get used to facing challenges and resisting temptations.

Besides, this is needed by everyone who aspires to be an advocate of God's message, and to fulfil the trust God has given to human beings on earth. Indeed, the test of willpower was the first to which Adam and Eve were subjected. They could not stand up to it, and were tempted by Satan to eat of the fruit of the tree, which he described to them as the tree of everlasting life and imperishable wealth. Every community of advocates of God's cause must go successfully through this test before they can be trusted with the task assigned to mankind as they are placed in charge of the earth. The nature of the test remains the same, but its methods may vary.

A group of the Children of Israel were unable to face the challenge and pass the test this time. This was the result of their repeated disobedience. Fish of different types used to come very close to the shore on Sabbath days, appearing to be so easy to catch. Yet they could do nothing to catch them because of the sanctity of the Sabbath, which they needed to observe. When the Sabbath day ended the fish were no longer there. They had gone deep into the sea. This is the event which the Prophet Muḥammad was ordered to remind them of, in addition to giving them a reminder of what they did and what happened to them as a result: "*Ask them about the town which stood by the sea: how its people profaned the Sabbath. Each Sabbath their fish appeared before them breaking the water's surface, but they would not come near them on other than Sabbath days. Thus did We try them because of their disobedience.*" (Verse 163)

How did all this happen? What made the fish behave in this way? How could the fish out-manoeuvre them? This is a miracle that takes place by God's will at the time He chooses. Those who are devoid of knowledge are keen to deny that God's will can operate in any way other than what they describe as 'the laws of nature'. But the Islamic concept, endorsed by the facts of life, has a different view. It is God (limitless is He in His glory) who has created this universe and set its laws in operation, in accordance with His absolute, free will. This means that God's law is not restrained by those laws of nature, or that it must operate within them. God's will remains free and absolute after these laws have come into operation, just as it was before them. This is the fact ignored by those who are devoid of knowledge. It is certainly an aspect of God's grace which He bestows on His servants that these laws of nature remain constant, but that does not mean that His will becomes subject to them or restrained by them. Whenever He, in His wisdom, wants something to take place in a fashion that breaks these laws of nature, His will is certainly done. Moreover, every time these constant laws operate, their operation takes place by a new act of God's will, which is specific to that particular instance. These laws do not operate automatically, of their own accord, or without God's will. This is indeed the case, despite the fact that the laws of nature remain constant, unless God determines otherwise. Whether the constant laws of nature operate or some other laws operate in their place, whatever actually happens in the universe is subject to a special act of God's will. Hence, the operation of the laws of nature and the accomplishment of something supernatural are equal and at the same level. There is nothing in the system of the universe that happens automatically, not even once, as those who are devoid of knowledge are keen to assert. In fact, they have recently started to recognize this.

Be that as it may, the temptation was too strong for those people of the city facing the sea. A group of them found the temptation irresistible, and all their willpower collapsed. They forgot their covenant with their Lord and began, as is typical of the Jews, to try to find subtle ways of fishing on the Sabbath. When faith is weak in people's hearts, many a deviant way can be found, since people start to deal with the law as a mere restriction which they need to evade. No law can be properly enforced by its mere statements, or by a police force. A law is safeguarded by God-fearing hearts who are keen to please God and to avoid His punishment. People will continue to try to evade the law when they have an interest in evading its provisions. Therefore, a law cannot be safeguarded by material power or a police force. No strong-handed tactics can give a government enough power to appoint a policeman to watch every individual to ensure observance of the law. That can only be achieved through faith, when people are God-fearing, keen to abide by God's law in public and private.

Abundant Grace, Swift Punishment

Hence, all situations which do not rely on the inner motivation of God-fearing hearts are bound to fail. Also doomed to failure are all man-made theories and regimes which do not rely on God's authority. Hence, all human systems to ensure the enforcement of the law remain ineffective, because no police force can watch over all people, all the time.

In this particular case mentioned in the *sūrah*, the inhabitants of that city began to seek ways and means to get around the prohibition of fishing on the Sabbath day. It has been reported that they put up certain barriers on the Sabbath day so that the fish could not return to the sea, and on the Sunday they would be quick to take their catch. They claimed that they did not do the fishing on the Sabbath, because the fish remained in the water, behind the barriers. A second group recognized the deviousness in all this, and warned those people who perpetrated it against God's punishment, dissociating themselves from their schemes.

A third group said to the ones urging their community to comply with God's orders: what use is your admonition to those erring people, when they persist in their erring ways? God is certain to destroy them or to inflict severe punishment on them: "*When some among them asked: 'Why do you preach to people whom God is certain to destroy, or at least to punish severely?'*" (Verse 164) Warnings and admonition are no longer of use, after they have condemned themselves to destruction or severe punishment by violating God's law. The second group replied: "*So that we may be free from blame in the sight of your Lord, and that they may become God-fearing.*" It is a duty on us to enjoin what is right and warn against what is evil and against violating God's law. When we have done our duty, we hope to be free from blame. Besides, it may be that our admonition will touch a sensitive heart and cause at least some disobedient people to repent.

Thus, the inhabitants of that city were divided into three groups, or three communities. In Islamic terminology, a nation or a community is a group of people who believe in one faith, have the same concept, and admit allegiance to a single leadership. It is thus different from the definitions given to it in non-Muslim societies, ancient and modern, which make a nation any group of people living in a particular area and governed by a particular regime. This concept is alien to Islam.

Hence, we say that the inhabitants of that city were divided into three groups: a clearly disobedient one, and one opposed to the sly schemes of disobedience to God, taking a positive action or denouncing disobedience and giving admonition. A third group adopted a negative attitude, disapproving of those disobedient schemes but taking no positive action to repel them. Each group had its own concept and line of action, which made each of them a separate nation.

When warnings and admonition were apparently useless, and the disobedient group persisted with their erring ways, God's warnings had to be fulfilled. Those who admonished them were saved, while the disobedient community suffered a very severe punishment, as will be explained presently. The *sūrah* does not mention what happened to the third group or community, perhaps in order to indicate that they were of no consequence, because they refrained from taking positive action and were satisfied to disapprove of God's disobedience only in a negative way. Hence, they deserved to be ignored although they did not incur punishment: *"When they had forgotten all the warnings they had been given, We saved those who had tried to prevent evil, and overwhelmed the transgressors with dreadful suffering for their iniquitous deeds. And when they insolently persisted in doing what they had been forbidden to do, We said to them: 'Turn into despicable apes.'"* (Verses 165-166)

We note here how the Qur'ān equates disobedience with denying the faith, and refers to this as 'wrongdoing', or 'transgression'. This occurs very frequently in the Qur'ān, which gives these terms a different concept to what is used in the works of scholars of later generations. The dreadful suffering inflicted on those scheming people who disobeyed God was to transform them into despicable apes. They forfeited their humanity when they abandoned their will, which could control their desires. They simply sank into the world of animals. Hence, it was a befitting punishment that they should be given the appearance of apes.

How did they become apes, and what happened to them thereafter? Did they perish, as would every creature that is transformed into another shape? Or did they procreate in the form of apes? There are so many different reports in books of Qur'ānic commentary. However, none of these questions is given an answer in the Qur'ān, and we do not have any authentic statement by the Prophet to give answers to them. Hence, we will not delve into these areas.

249

The same order which initiates creation and gives creatures their forms and shapes was given in order to bring about a change of form or a transformation. The word used in all these cases is, "Be", and whatever God desires immediately takes place. "*We said to them: 'Turn into despicable apes,'*" with the Arabic text using the formula, "*Be despicable apes*". (Verse 166) That was sufficient for them to be apes that are despicable, and to live in humiliation. That was the order that no power could repel, issued by the One who always accomplishes His purpose.

This was followed by an everlasting curse, which spared only those who would believe in the unlettered Prophet and follow him. This curse was also earned because of their long persistence in disobeying God. Hence, God issued the verdict that was certain to be implemented: "*Then your Lord declared that He would most certainly raise against them people who would cruelly oppress them till the Day of Resurrection. Your Lord is swift indeed in His retribution, yet He is certainly much forgiving, merciful.*" (Verse 167)

That declaration will last for ever, although its fulfilment started the day it was issued. In different periods of history, there were those who dealt very severely with the Jews and were ready to oppress them. The declaration will continue to operate, and there will from time to time be those who will deal cruelly with them. Whenever the Jews gain power and tyrannize in disobedience of God, they will certainly come to suffer at the hands of people whom God will raise against them. This is because they will continue to move from one act of disobedience of God to another, and will not mend their ways before they start with new erring ways.

At times we may think that the curse is no longer operative, and that the Jews have gathered so much power and influence. The fact is that this will only be for a limited period of history. It is God alone who knows whom He will raise against the Jews in the next round, and the round to follow that, until the Day of Resurrection. God has made this declaration, and informed His Messenger of it in His own book, the Qur'ān, and concluded this declaration with a statement outlining the two attributes of God that He is at the same time swift in retribution, much forgiving and merciful: "*Your Lord is swift indeed in His retribution, yet He is certainly much forgiving, merciful.*" (Verse 167) With His swift punishment, He overwhelms those who earn that punishment, as happened to those dwellers of that city by the seaside. With His forgiveness and mercy He accepts the repentance of those of the Israelites who are ready to follow the unlettered Prophet who is clearly described in the Torah and the Gospel. His punishment is not the result of any grudge, but it is the fitting retribution for those guilty of disobedience. God's mercy and forgiveness are always there to be extended to those who earn them.

A Strong Motivation for Believers

The Qur'ānic account follows the historical events after Moses. It refers to succeeding generations up to the Jewish generation that lived in Madinah at the time when the Prophet Muḥammad (peace be upon him) established the first Muslim community there.

> We dispersed them all over the earth as separate communities; some of them were righteous, and some far from that, and We tried them with blessings and misfortunes, so that they might mend their ways. They were succeeded by generations who inherited the Book. Yet these are keen to enjoy the fleeting pleasures of this lower world and say, "We shall be forgiven." Should some similar pleasures come their way, they would certainly be keen to indulge them. Have they not solemnly pledged through their Scriptures to say nothing but the truth about God? And have they not studied well what is in [the Scriptures]? Surely the life in the hereafter is better for all who are God-fearing. Will you not use your reason? As for those who hold fast to the Scriptures and attend regularly to their prayers, We shall not fail to reward those who enjoin the doing of what is right. We suspended the mountain over them as if it were a shadow, and they thought that it would fall down on them. [We said]: Hold fast with all your strength to what We have given you and bear in mind all that it contains, so that you may remain God-fearing. (Verses 168-171)

These verses, revealed in Madinah and added to this Makkan *sūrah*, serve as a complement to the history of the Children of Israel after the Prophet Moses had passed away. The Jews were dispersed across the earth, divided into groups of varying concepts and different schools, trends and leanings. Some of them were righteous indeed, while others were not. In His wisdom, God continued to set them one test after another, trying them at times with ease and comfort, and at others with affliction and misfortune. All these tests were meant to help them see things in the right perspective and choose the path of righteousness: *"We tried them with blessings and misfortunes, so that they might mend their ways."* (Verse 168) It is an act of divine mercy that God puts His servants to one test after another, because these tests serve as reminders to them so that forgetfulness will not let them think too highly of themselves. Such thoughts can easily lead people to self-condemnation.

"They were succeeded by generations who inherited the Book. Yet these are keen to enjoy the fleeting pleasures of this lower world and say, 'We shall be forgiven.' Should some similar pleasures come their way, they would certainly be keen to indulge them." (Verse 169) This new generation of Israelites have certain characteristics that are described in the Qur'ān. They have inherited the Scriptures and learned them well. However, they did not take the Scriptures to heart, so that they would bring their behaviour and practices in line with their dictates. In other words, their approach to faith was an academic one, taking their faith as mere knowledge to be learned, but having no practical purpose. Whenever a worldly pleasure offered itself to them, they took it up and indulged in it. They then claimed that they would be forgiven by God.

This state of affairs was repeated time after time. Hence, the Qur'ān poses this rhetoric question: *"Have they not solemnly pledged through their Scriptures to say nothing but the truth about God? And have they not studied well what is in [the Scriptures]?"* (Verse 169) In their very Scriptures they pledged never to try to manipulate the provisions of divine law, or give them a false interpretation. They also vowed not to say anything about God but the plain truth. How is it possible, then, for them to claim that they will be forgiven when they are keen to indulge in every worldly pleasure that presents itself to them? How can they justify such indulgence by making a false statement about God, assuring themselves of His forgiveness, when they are well aware that God forgives only those who truly repent of their mistakes and resolve not to repeat them? This does not apply to them, because having studied the Scriptures well and known everything they contain, they remain ready to indulge in every fleeting pleasure of this low world.

A mere academic study of religion is of little benefit, as long as faith does not establish itself in the heart of the person studying it. Many of those who study religion let their hearts drift away from it. They simply study it in order to find justification for their deeds by twisting the meaning of religious statements. Thus they try to find loopholes to justify their indulgence in worldly pleasures. Indeed, the true enemies of religion are those who have an academic approach to it, without truly believing in it and without fearing God.

"*Surely the life in the hereafter is better for all who are God-fearing. Will you not use your reason?*" (Verse 169) Indeed, the abode of the hereafter is the one to seek. Its value, as it is recognized by those who are God-fearing, is bound to tilt the scales. Seeking it provides the determination to resist the fleeting pleasures that present themselves now, in the life of this world. It is the motivation to gain admission into that abode of the hereafter that mends hearts and sets life on the proper footing. Without observing the requirements for such future life, this present life will go awry. How else can a human being resist the great pressure of indulging the immediate pleasures of this life? What stops a human being from indulging his greed or taking away what belongs to others? What can tame people's urges, cravings and powerful aspirations? What can give people the reassurance that what is lost in this life struggle will not have been totally lost at the point of death? Rather, there is still more to come in a future, everlasting life. What gives the believers support in the battle between good and evil, truth and falsehood, when they see life's pleasures slipping away from their hands, and find evil gaining increased power and imposing tyrannical authority?

Nothing can give such strength and help to believers to remain steadfast in the face of misfortunes and changing circumstances during an unabating battle with falsehood except the firm belief in the life to come and that it is far better and superior for those who are God-fearing. That abode belongs to those who forgive, rise above the fleeting pleasures of this world, show determination to follow the truth and to do what is good, remain unshakeable, as they go along the way, reassured that what God has for them is infinitely better than what they may have in this world.

This abode of the hereafter is something that lies beyond the reach of our human perception. The advocates of 'scientific socialism' want to obliterate the belief in it from our hearts, faith and life in order to replace it with an ignorant, atheistic concept, which they describe as 'scientific'. But their attempt relates to the corruption of hearts and souls, and the corruption of life itself. So many social ills, such as bribery, greed, oppression, negligence, apathy and treachery break loose, but nothing can check them except faith. To place what is 'scientific' in opposition to what is 'imperceptible' is no more than an ignorant phenomenon that spread in the eighteenth and nineteenth centuries, but human knowledge has abandoned it altogether. In the twentieth century, it has only been upheld by a small minority. This whole phenomenon is in conflict with human nature. Hence, it corrupts lives to the extent that it exposes all mankind to the risk of destruction. It is part of the Zionist plan, which tries to rob humanity of the most important factors that give it health and strength. In this way, they hope to eventually make the whole world submissive to the kingdom of Zion. Such flimsy ideas are repeated by some human parrots, scattered here and there, while the regimes that Zionism has put in power in most parts of the world continue to implement the wicked Zionist plan. What is worse is that they implement it knowing its aim and purpose.

Unfailing Reward

Because the questions of the hereafter and fearing God are central to faith and life, the Qur'ān tells those who are keen to indulge in the fleeting pleasures of this world to use their minds: "*Surely the life in the hereafter is better for all who are God-fearing. Will you not use your reason?*" (Verse 169) Had reason had the final say, and had the final verdict been that of true knowledge, rather than ignorance given the guise of knowledge, the hereafter would have been seen as far superior to the fleeting pleasures of this lower world. Fearing God would have been seen as strengthening faith and achieving success in this life: "*As for those who hold fast to the Scriptures and attend regularly to their prayers, We shall not fail to reward those who enjoin the doing of what is right.*" (Verse 170)

Clear criticism of those who have given their pledges through the Scriptures and who have studied them thoroughly is implied. That is because they do not hold fast to the Scriptures they studied, and do not implement their teachings, or refer to them in formulating their concepts and deciding their behaviour. However, this verse remains general in its import, addressing all generations and all situations.

The very expression, "*hold fast to the Scriptures*", gives a vivid image that we can almost see and feel. It is the image of holding the book with strength and seriousness. This is how God likes His book to be approached, without rigidity or narrow-mindedness. Strength and seriousness are totally different from rigidity and narrow-mindedness. They are not opposed to ease, broad vision and compatibility with day-to-day life, but they are opposed to looseness, carelessness, and giving human practices precedence over God's law. Indeed, what people do must always be subject to God's law.

Holding fast with strength and seriousness to what God has revealed and attending regularly to prayers, which is here a reference to all aspects of worship, are the twin essential factors of the divine method that aims at setting human life on the right footing. The way this Qur'ānic verse clearly links holding fast to the Scriptures with attending to worship is significant. It shows that implementing divine revelations in human life gives it the right basis, and that proper worship reforms human rights. Thus, the two operate in everyday life as well as in human hearts and set them both aright. This is further emphasized by the reference to doing right at the conclusion of the Qur'ānic verse: "*As for those who hold fast to the Scriptures and attend regularly to their prayers, We shall not fail to reward those who enjoin the doing of what is right.*" (Verse 170)

The plain fact is that all human life suffers as a result of abandoning these two essential factors of the divine method. When the revealed message is taken lightly, it has no effect on everyday life, and when worship is abandoned, people's hearts become prone to corruption. This leads to evading the law, as was the practice of the people of earlier Scriptures. The same applies to the followers of any Scripture when their hearts take worship lightly, and in consequence, their fear of God weakens.

The divine system is a complete whole, which establishes life on the basis of a divine writ, and reforms hearts through worship. Thus, hearts are healthy and human life is also wholesome. That is the divine method, which is abandoned in preference for another only by those who are bound to suffer misery in this world and punishment in the life to come.

At the end of the story, as related in this *sūrah*, an account is given of how God accepted the pledges of the Children of Israel: "*We suspended the mountain over them as if it were a shadow, and they thought that it would fall down on them. [We said]: Hold fast with all your strength to what We have given you and bear in mind all that it contains, so that you may remain God-fearing."* (Verse 171) That covenant cannot be forgotten, because it was taken in unforgettable circumstances. It was taken at a time when God suspended the mountain over the Children of Israel's heads, just as though it was a shadow. For all intents and purposes, they thought it was going to fall on them. Just prior to that, they were reluctant to give any pledges, but when they experienced that supernatural event, they hastened to make their pledges. That in itself should have prevented any relapse on their part. With such a miracle taking place before their eyes, they were ordered to take their pledges seriously, and to fulfil them conscientiously. They were warned against any slackness or complacency. They must always remember their pledges and work for their fulfilment, so that their hearts soften and remain conscious of God. But the nature of the Israelites remains the same. They soon broke their pledges and sank into disobedience. Thus, they incurred God's wrath. They proved that they could not be grateful for God's favours and the grace He had bestowed on them. Hence, they incurred God's punishment on account of breaking their pledges to Him. God never deals unjustly with anyone.

10

Bearing Witness

Your Lord brought forth their offspring from the loins of the children of Adam, and called them to bear witness about themselves. [He said]: "Am I not your Lord?" They replied: "Yes, indeed, we bear witness to that." [This He did] lest you should say on the Day of Resurrection, "We were truly unaware of this;" (172)

وَإِذْ أَخَذَ رَبُّكَ مِنۢ بَنِىٓ ءَادَمَ مِن ظُهُورِهِمْ ذُرِّيَّتَهُمْ وَأَشْهَدَهُمْ عَلَىٰٓ أَنفُسِهِمْ أَلَسْتُ بِرَبِّكُمْ قَالُوا۟ بَلَىٰ شَهِدْنَآ أَن تَقُولُوا۟ يَوْمَ ٱلْقِيَٰمَةِ إِنَّا كُنَّا عَنْ هَٰذَا غَٰفِلِينَ ﴿١٧٢﴾

or lest you say, "It was our fore-fathers who, in times gone by, associated partners with God, and we were only their late offspring. Will You destroy us on account of what those inventors of falsehood did?" (173)

أَوْ تَقُولُوٓا۟ إِنَّمَآ أَشْرَكَ ءَابَآؤُنَا مِن قَبْلُ وَكُنَّا ذُرِّيَّةً مِّنۢ بَعْدِهِمْ أَفَتُهْلِكُنَا بِمَا فَعَلَ ٱلْمُبْطِلُونَ ﴿١٧٣﴾

Thus We make plain Our revelations so that they may return [to the right path]. (174)

وَكَذَٰلِكَ نُفَصِّلُ ٱلْءَايَٰتِ وَلَعَلَّهُمْ يَرْجِعُونَ ﴿١٧٤﴾

Tell them of the man to whom We give Our revelations, and who then discards them. Satan catches up with him and he strays, like many others, into error. (175)

وَٱتْلُ عَلَيْهِمْ نَبَأَ ٱلَّذِىٓ ءَاتَيْنَٰهُ ءَايَٰتِنَا فَٱنسَلَخَ مِنْهَا فَأَتْبَعَهُ ٱلشَّيْطَٰنُ فَكَانَ مِنَ ٱلْغَاوِينَ ﴿١٧٥﴾

Had We so willed, We would have exalted him by means of those (revelations), but he clings to the earth and succumbs to his desires. He may be compared to a dog: no matter how you drive him off, he pants on away, and if you leave him alone, he still pants on. That is what the people who reject Our revelations are like. Tell them, then, such stories, so that they may take heed. (176)

وَلَوْ شِئْنَا لَرَفَعْنَٰهُ بِهَا وَلَٰكِنَّهُۥٓ أَخْلَدَ إِلَى ٱلْأَرْضِ وَٱتَّبَعَ هَوَىٰهُ فَمَثَلُهُۥ كَمَثَلِ ٱلْكَلْبِ إِن تَحْمِلْ عَلَيْهِ يَلْهَثْ أَوْ تَتْرُكْهُ يَلْهَثَّ ذَّٰلِكَ مَثَلُ ٱلْقَوْمِ ٱلَّذِينَ كَذَّبُوا۟ بِـَٔايَٰتِنَا فَٱقْصُصِ ٱلْقَصَصَ لَعَلَّهُمْ يَتَفَكَّرُونَ ١٧٦

A dismal example is that provided by those who reject Our revelations; for it is against their own selves that they are sinning. (177)

سَآءَ مَثَلًا ٱلْقَوْمُ ٱلَّذِينَ كَذَّبُوا۟ بِـَٔايَٰتِنَا وَأَنفُسَهُمْ كَانُوا۟ يَظْلِمُونَ ١٧٧

He whom God guides is on the right path; whereas those whom He lets go astray are indeed losers. (178)

مَن يَهْدِ ٱللَّهُ فَهُوَ ٱلْمُهْتَدِى وَمَن يُضْلِلْ فَأُو۟لَٰٓئِكَ هُمُ ٱلْخَٰسِرُونَ ١٧٨

We have destined for Hell many of the *jinn* and many human beings; they have hearts they cannot understand with, and they have eyes with which they fail to see, and ears with which they fail to hear. They are like cattle; indeed, they are even further away from the right way. They are the truly heedless. (179)

وَلَقَدْ ذَرَأْنَا لِجَهَنَّمَ كَثِيرًا مِّنَ ٱلْجِنِّ وَٱلْإِنسِ لَهُمْ قُلُوبٌ لَّا يَفْقَهُونَ بِهَا وَلَهُمْ أَعْيُنٌ لَّا يُبْصِرُونَ بِهَا وَلَهُمْ ءَاذَانٌ لَّا يَسْمَعُونَ بِهَآ أُو۟لَٰٓئِكَ كَٱلْأَنْعَٰمِ بَلْ هُمْ أَضَلُّ أُو۟لَٰٓئِكَ هُمُ ٱلْغَٰفِلُونَ ١٧٩

God has the finest names, so appeal to Him by these and stay away from those who blaspheme against His names. They shall be requited for all they do. (180)

وَلِلَّهِ ٱلْأَسْمَآءُ ٱلْحُسْنَىٰ فَٱدْعُوهُ بِهَا وَذَرُوا۟ ٱلَّذِينَ يُلْحِدُونَ فِىٓ أَسْمَٰٓئِهِۦ سَيُجْزَوْنَ مَا كَانُوا۟ يَعْمَلُونَ ١٨٠

Among those whom We have created there is a community who guide others by means of the truth and with it establish justice. (181)

وَمِمَّنْ خَلَقْنَا أُمَّةٌ يَهْدُونَ بِالْحَقِّ وَبِهِ يَعْدِلُونَ ۝

As for those who deny Our revelations, We will lead them on, step by step, from whence they cannot tell; (182)

وَالَّذِينَ كَذَّبُوا بِآيَاتِنَا سَنَسْتَدْرِجُهُم مِّنْ حَيْثُ لَا يَعْلَمُونَ ۝

for although I may give them respite, My subtle scheme is mighty. (183)

وَأُمْلِي لَهُمْ إِنَّ كَيْدِي مَتِينٌ ۝

Have they not thought things over? Their companion is no madman; he is only a plain warner. (184)

أَوَلَمْ يَتَفَكَّرُوا مَا بِصَاحِبِهِم مِّن جِنَّةٍ إِنْ هُوَ إِلَّا نَذِيرٌ مُّبِينٌ ۝

Have they not considered [God's] dominion over the heavens and the earth, and all that God has created, and [reflected] that it may well be that their own term is drawing near? In what other message after this will they, then, believe? (185)

أَوَلَمْ يَنظُرُوا فِي مَلَكُوتِ السَّمَوَاتِ وَالْأَرْضِ وَمَا خَلَقَ اللَّهُ مِن شَيْءٍ وَأَنْ عَسَى أَن يَكُونَ قَدِ اقْتَرَبَ أَجَلُهُمْ فَبِأَيِّ حَدِيثٍ بَعْدَهُ يُؤْمِنُونَ ۝

Those whom God lets go astray will have no guide; and He leaves them in their overweening arrogance to stumble along blindly. (186)

مَن يُضْلِلِ اللَّهُ فَلَا هَادِيَ لَهُ وَيَذَرُهُمْ فِي طُغْيَانِهِمْ يَعْمَهُونَ ۝

They ask you about the Last Hour: "When will it come to pass?" Say: Knowledge of it rests with my Lord alone. None but He will reveal it at its appointed time. It will weigh heavily on the heavens and the earth; and it will not fall on you except suddenly. They will ask you further as if you yourself persistently enquire about it. Say: Knowledge of it rests with God alone, though most people remain unaware. (187)

يَسْتَلُونَكَ عَنِ السَّاعَةِ أَيَّانَ مُرْسَىٰهَا قُلْ إِنَّمَا عِلْمُهَا عِندَ رَبِّي لَا يُجَلِّيهَا لِوَقْتِهَا إِلَّا هُوَ ثَقُلَتْ فِي السَّمَوَٰتِ وَالْأَرْضِ لَا تَأْتِيكُمْ إِلَّا بَغْتَةً يَسْتَلُونَكَ كَأَنَّكَ حَفِيٌّ عَنْهَا قُلْ إِنَّمَا عِلْمُهَا عِندَ اللَّهِ وَلَٰكِنَّ أَكْثَرَ النَّاسِ لَا يَعْلَمُونَ ۝

Say: It is not within my power to bring benefit to, or avert evil from, myself, except as God may please. Had I possessed knowledge of what lies beyond the reach of human perception, I would have availed myself of much that is good and no evil would have ever touched me. I am no more than one who gives warning, and a herald of good news to people who believe. (188)

قُل لَّا أَمْلِكُ لِنَفْسِي نَفْعًا وَلَا ضَرًّا إِلَّا مَا شَاءَ اللَّهُ وَلَوْ كُنتُ أَعْلَمُ الْغَيْبَ لَاسْتَكْثَرْتُ مِنَ الْخَيْرِ وَمَا مَسَّنِيَ السُّوءُ إِنْ أَنَا إِلَّا نَذِيرٌ وَبَشِيرٌ لِّقَوْمٍ يُؤْمِنُونَ ۝

It is He who has created you all from a single soul, and out of it brought into being its mate, so that he might incline with love towards her. When he has consorted with her, she conceives a light burden, which she carries with ease. Then, when she grows heavy, they both appeal to God, their Lord: "Grant us a goodly child and we will be truly grateful." (189)

هُوَ الَّذِي خَلَقَكُم مِّن نَّفْسٍ وَاحِدَةٍ وَجَعَلَ مِنْهَا زَوْجَهَا لِيَسْكُنَ إِلَيْهَا فَلَمَّا تَغَشَّاهَا حَمَلَتْ حَمْلًا خَفِيفًا فَمَرَّتْ بِهِ فَلَمَّا أَثْقَلَت دَّعَوَا اللَّهَ رَبَّهُمَا لَئِنْ آتَيْتَنَا صَٰلِحًا لَّنَكُونَنَّ مِنَ الشَّٰكِرِينَ ۝

Yet when He has granted them a goodly child, they associate with Him partners, particularly in respect of what He has granted them. Exalted is God above anything people may associate with Him as partners. (190)

فَلَمَّآ ءَاتَىٰهُمَا صَٰلِحًا جَعَلَا لَهُۥ شُرَكَآءَ فِيمَآ ءَاتَىٰهُمَا فَتَعَٰلَى ٱللَّهُ عَمَّا يُشْرِكُونَ ۞

Do they associate with Him those that can create nothing, while they themselves have been created, (191)

أَيُشْرِكُونَ مَا لَا يَخْلُقُ شَيْـًٔا وَهُمْ يُخْلَقُونَ ۞

and neither can they give them any support nor can they even help themselves. (192)

وَلَا يَسْتَطِيعُونَ لَهُمْ نَصْرًا وَلَآ أَنفُسَهُمْ يَنصُرُونَ ۞

If you call them to guidance they will not follow you. It is all the same whether you call them or keep silent. (193)

وَإِن تَدْعُوهُمْ إِلَى ٱلْهُدَىٰ لَا يَتَّبِعُوكُمْ سَوَآءٌ عَلَيْكُمْ أَدَعَوْتُمُوهُمْ أَمْ أَنتُمْ صَٰمِتُونَ ۞

Those whom you invoke beside God are God's servants, just like you. Invoke them, then, and let them answer you, if what you claim is true. (194)

إِنَّ ٱلَّذِينَ تَدْعُونَ مِن دُونِ ٱللَّهِ عِبَادٌ أَمْثَالُكُمْ فَٱدْعُوهُمْ فَلْيَسْتَجِيبُوا۟ لَكُمْ إِن كُنتُمْ صَٰدِقِينَ ۞

Have they, perchance, feet on which they could walk, or hands with which to grasp things, or eyes with which to see, or ears with which to hear? Say: Appeal to those you claim to be partners with God, and scheme against me, and give me no respite. (195)

أَلَهُمْ أَرْجُلٌ يَمْشُونَ بِهَآ أَمْ لَهُمْ أَيْدٍ يَبْطِشُونَ بِهَآ أَمْ لَهُمْ أَعْيُنٌ يُبْصِرُونَ بِهَآ أَمْ لَهُمْ ءَاذَانٌ يَسْمَعُونَ بِهَا قُلِ ٱدْعُوا۟ شُرَكَآءَكُمْ ثُمَّ كِيدُونِ فَلَا تُنظِرُونِ ۞

My guardian is God who has bestowed this Book from on high. It is He who is the guardian of the righteous. (196)

إِنَّ وَلِيِّـﻲَ ٱللَّهُ ٱلَّذِى نَزَّلَ ٱلْكِتَٰبَ وَهُوَ يَتَوَلَّى ٱلصَّٰلِحِينَ ۞

Those whom you invoke beside Him cannot give you any support, nor can they even help themselves. (197)

وَٱلَّذِينَ تَدْعُونَ مِن دُونِهِۦ لَا يَسْتَطِيعُونَ نَصْرَكُمْ وَلَآ أَنفُسَهُمْ يَنصُرُونَ ۞

If you pray to them for guidance, they will not hear you. You may see them looking at you but they do not see. (198)

وَإِن تَدْعُوهُمْ إِلَى ٱلْهُدَىٰ لَا يَسْمَعُوا۟ وَتَرَىٰهُمْ يَنظُرُونَ إِلَيْكَ وَهُمْ لَا يُبْصِرُونَ ۞

Preview

The historical accounts given in this *sūrah* have centred on the theme of God's oneness. In all these accounts, God's messengers emphasized the truth of God's oneness to their peoples, and warned them against associating partners with Him. In each account we see how the warnings of those messengers came to pass. Now the *sūrah* moves on to deal with the central issue of God's oneness from a different angle, which refers particularly to human nature as created by God. It speaks of a firm pledge with far-reaching implications for human nature and its constitution. Indeed, acknowledging God as the only Lord in the universe is ingrained in human nature, which admits to it by its very existence and by what it feels deeply at heart. Divine messengers bring reminders and warnings to those who deviate from their essential nature. Believing in God's oneness is the basic issue of a covenant between human nature and the Creator of human beings. Therefore, they have no justification for breaking this covenant, even if God did not send them any messenger to remind and warn them. But it is God's grace that dictates that human beings should not be left to their nature alone, because it may deviate, or to their minds because they may err. Hence, He sends them messengers to bring them happy news and to warn them so that people may not have an argument to press against God after He sent them those messengers.

Tackling the question of God's oneness from this angle the *sūrah* follows several lines. The first of these is a narrative speaking of a situation that, according to some reports, took place in the past history of the Children of Israel. More accurately, its speaks of a type of people that may exist at any time or place. In any society or generation, we come across those who have enough knowledge to lead them to the truth and to follow guidance, but they nevertheless defy their own knowledge and sink into error just as those who are devoid of all knowledge. Indeed, their own knowledge adds to their misery and deviation because they remain devoid of the faith, which makes knowledge a guiding light.

Another narrative line describes how nature moves gradually away from believing in God's oneness to associating partners with Him. Here we have a married couple who are full of hope with respect to the child they are expecting. By nature, they turn to their Lord making all pledges to Him to be very grateful if He would give them a healthy and dutiful child. When their wishes are granted, they begin to deviate and associate partners with God.

A third line is descriptive, showing how receptive human systems stop functioning until people go a very long way into error so as to sink below the level of animals. This deservedly turns them into fuel for Hell. They have minds, eyes and ears, but they understand, see and hear nothing. This leaves them hardened in error.

A further line is inspirational, trying to resuscitate those receptive systems so that people may think and reflect. They are encouraged to look at what is in the heavens and the earth and to contemplate God's creation. It also reminds them of the predetermined moment of death and invites them to reflect on the position of the noble Messenger who calls on people to follow guidance. Yet those who have gone astray describe him as mad. And we have a line that disputes their claims about their alleged deities, which lack all qualities of Godhead, and indeed lack the essential qualities of life.

All this ends with a directive to the Prophet to challenge them and their deities, and to declare that he dissociates himself from their community, beliefs, deities and worship, and turns to the only true patron and guardian *"who has bestowed this Book from on high. It is He who is the guardian of the righteous."* (Verse 196)

The previous passage concluded the story of the Children of Israel with the scene of the pledges they gave to God in the shadow of the suspended mountain. This new passage follows on that final scene and begins with a discussion of the broader covenant God has taken from human nature. The scene is even more awesome and splendid than that of the suspended mountain.

A Scene to Defy All Imagination

Your Lord brought forth their offspring from the loins of the children of Adam, and called them to bear witness about themselves. [He said]: "Am I not your Lord?" They replied: "Yes, indeed, we bear witness to that." [This He did] lest you should say on the Day of Resurrection, "We were truly unaware of this;" or lest you say, "It was our forefathers who, in times gone by, associated partners with God, and we were only their late offspring. Will You destroy us on account of what those inventors of falsehood did?" Thus We make plain Our revelations so that they may return [to the right path]. (Verses 172-174)

In this short passage we have the central issue of faith and human nature portrayed in a uniquely vivid scene that shows the generations of the faraway future, as they are still in the loins of human beings, before they make their appearance in this visible world. All of them are gathered in front of their Creator who asks them: *"Am I not your Lord?"* (Verse 172) They all acknowledge His Lordship, admit their position as obedient servants and His status as the only Lord. They are no bigger than small atoms held in the hand of the great Creator.

This is a sublime scene with no equivalent in human language or its imaginative portraits. Its remarkable nature becomes even greater when our minds try, as hard as we can, to visualize it, looking at all these countless cells being gathered together and brought forth. They are then addressed as rational beings, on account of the innate qualities God has placed in them. They respond like rational beings, acknowledging their position and status and giving their pledges when they are still in the loins of their ancestors. We are filled with awe as we contemplate this splendid scene, looking at these tiny cells, each holding a potential life. Each is the seed of a complete human being, with unique qualities, waiting for permission to grow and appear in its special form reserved for it in the world beyond. It gives its pledge and enters into a covenant before it appears into this world of ours.

The Qur'ān portrays this splendid scene describing a great truth, which is deeply established in human nature. This Qur'ānic description was made fourteen centuries ago, when no human being had any vision of the reality of human creation, apart from myth that had no foundation. Now after all these centuries, human beings have come to know some rudimentary elements of that truth. Today, biological science tells us that genes keep a record for every human being, showing his or her qualities or characteristics when they are still in the loins of their ancestors. These genes, which keep the records of no less than three thousand million human beings, may be pooled together in a space not exceeding one cubic centimetre. Had this fact been stated at that time, it would have been met with derision and incredulity. But God certainly says the truth, as He states: *"In time We shall make them see Our signs in the utmost horizons (of the universe) and within themselves so that it will become clear to them that this revelation is the truth."* (41: 53)

Ibn 'Abbās, a companion of the Prophet who is renowned for his scholarship, reports: "Your Lord went over Adam's back with His hand, and out came every human being He would be creating until the Day of Resurrection. He took their pledges and made them bear witness about themselves, saying to them: *"Am I not your Lord? They replied 'Yes, indeed.'"* (Verse 172)

How did this event take place? How did God take the offspring of Adam's children from their loins to make them testify? How did He ask them, "Am I not your Lord?" And how did they reply, "Yes, indeed." The answer to all these questions is that our human perception cannot understand how God acts, since it cannot perceive God's own nature. Perceiving the 'how' is subsequent to perceiving the nature of the one who does. There are numerous actions that the Qur'ān attributes to God, such as the following few examples: *"He then applied His design to the skies, which were yet but smoke"* (41:11); *"He is established on the throne of His Almightiness"* (10: 3); *"God annuls or confirms whatever He pleases"* (13: 39); *"The heavens will be folded up in His right hand"* (39: 67); *"Your Lord comes down with the angels, rank upon rank"* (89: 22); and *"Never can there be a secret confabulation between three persons without His being the fourth of them."* (58: 7) All these actions and many others reported in authentic *ḥadīths* as having been done, or will be done by God must be accepted as perfectly true, without any attempt on our part to understand how. It is just as we have mentioned that the perception of 'how' is subsequent to perceiving the nature of the one who does it. There is simply nothing that resembles God in any way. Hence, there is no way that we can perceive His nature or how He accomplishes His deeds. There is no possibility that we can resemble His action to anything we know, since there is nothing that resembles God in any way. Any attempt to do so will end in error and failure. All philosophers who tried to describe how God acts could do no more than come up with theories of endless confusion.

One interpretation of this statement suggests that the pledge God has taken from the offspring of Adam's children relates to their nature. He has established in their nature the tendency to acknowledge His Lordship as the only God in the universe. They grow up with this tendency until they deviate as a result of external factors of one sort or another.

In his commentary on the Qur'ān, Ibn Kathīr reports that many scholars are of the view that this testimony from the offspring of Adam's children refers to the fact that in their very nature, they have a tendency to accept God's oneness. This is why the Qur'ānic statement says, "*Your Lord brought forth their offspring from the loins of the children of Adam*", rather than saying, "from the loins of Adam himself or from his loins." And the statement speaks of "their offspring", to indicate the succession of their generations, one after another. This is similar to the Qur'ānic statement: "*It is He who has given you the earth to inherit.*" (27: 62) God also says: "*He brought you into being out of other people's seed.*" (6: 133) Here, in the verse we are discussing, God goes on to say: "*And called them to bear witness about themselves. [He said]: 'Am I not your Lord?' They replied: 'Yes, indeed'.*" (Verse 172) This means that He has created them admitting this fact, testifying to it at the very moment of their existence. Scholars also say that testimony is sometimes given verbally as in the Qur'ānic verse: "*They will reply: 'We bear witness against ourselves.' The life of this world has beguiled them. So they will bear witness against themselves that they were unbelievers.*" (6: 130) At other times, the testimony can be made by adopting a certain position or attitude, as that described in the Qur'ānic verse stating: "*It is not for the idolaters to visit or tend God's houses of worship, while they bear witness against themselves for being unbelievers.*" (9: 17) This means that their situation testifies against them, not that they make a statement

266

to this effect. The same applies to the Qurʾānic verses: *"Man is surely ungrateful to his Lord, and of this he himself is a witness."* (100: 6-7)

Requests also can be made verbally or by adopting a particular position. This is evidenced by the Qurʾānic verse stating: *"He gives you of everything you ask Him for."* (14: 34) Scholars say that a factor that supports this view is the fact that this testimony is counted against them as they associate partners with God. Had this taken place in the way some people suggest, then everyone would have remembered it, and it would have been taken against them. It is suggested that its being reported by the Prophet is sufficient as a proof of its taking place. This is true, but we should remember that those unbelievers rejected everything that God's messengers have stated. Since this is stated as an argument against them, it must be a reference to their nature, which admits God's Lordship and oneness. For this reason, the Qurʾānic passage goes on to say: *"[This He did] lest you should say on the Day of Resurrection, 'We were truly unaware of this;' or lest you say, 'It was our forefathers who, in times gone by, associated partners with God.'"* (Verses 172-173)

A Pledge Given by Human Nature

The *ḥadīths* to which Ibn Kathīr refers as confirming this Qurʾānic statement are quoted here. Both al-Bukhārī and Muslim relate in their authentic collections, the *Ṣaḥīḥ*, a *ḥadīth* narrated by Abū Hurayrah who quotes the Prophet as saying: "Every human being is born with upright nature. [One version puts the statement as: every human being is born believing in this faith.] His parents then make him a Jew, a Christian, or a Magian."

A *ḥadīth* related by Muslim quotes the Prophet as saying: "God says I have created My servants following the pure faith. Satans then assaulted them and removed them from their faith, forbidding them what I have made lawful."

Al-Aswad ibn Sarīʿ, one of the Prophet's companions who belonged to the Saʿd clan reports: "I joined God's Messenger in four expeditions. Once, when our people had killed enemy fighters, they also attacked their children. On hearing this, the Prophet was very angry and rebuked them, saying: 'How is it that some people attack children?' One man said: 'Messenger of God, are they not the children of unbelievers?' He said: 'The best among you have been born to unbelievers. Let it be known that every human being is born following the right faith. He will continue to do so until he is able to express himself. His parents then make of him a Jew or a Christian.'"

For our part, we do not exclude the possibility that the event related in this Qur'ānic verse took place as is described, i.e. literally: "*Your Lord brought forth their offspring from the loins of the children of Adam, and called them to bear witness about themselves.*" (Verse 172) We believe that it could easily happen as God has described, because there is nothing to stop it happening when God wills. But at the same time we do not exclude the interpretation outlined by Ibn Kathīr and approved by other scholars. At any rate, we can conclude that there is a pledge made by human nature to God Himself, declaring that human nature believes in His oneness and will continue to do so. This means that the essence of God's oneness is well established in human nature, and every human child is born with this clear tendency. It deviates from it only when an external factor corrupts its nature by the manipulation of the dual susceptibility of human beings to follow right guidance or to deviate from it. This is a latent susceptibility which can be influenced by external factors and circumstances.

We go beyond this to say that the truth of God's oneness is also well established in the nature of all existence, of which human nature forms only a part. It continues to be a part of that whole existence, governed by the same laws and reacting to whatever takes place. The great truth of God's oneness is acknowledged by the nature of the whole universe, as it is also established within human nature itself.

The law of unity which governs the whole existence is clearly evident in the outer appearance of the universe as well as its coherence, the perfect compatibility between its different parts and components, as well as its consistent movement and action. It is also reflected in the complete absence of conflict between the various rules and laws operating in the universe and their practical effects. Furthermore, we see it in the unity of the essence of atoms, according to the latest findings of human knowledge. That essence is radiation that results from all matters when their atoms are made to split and release their charge.

As human knowledge advances, it uncovers more and more of the law of unity that applies to this whole universe, and the rules that dictate its actions and reactions, not automatically, but by God's free will that operates consistently at every moment and every turn. However, we do not rely merely on what is uncovered by human knowledge, which can never be absolute, considering the means available to human beings. We simply take this human knowledge as supporting evidence. Our foremost basis in establishing any universal truth is what is stated by the Creator Himself who knows perfectly what He has created. The Qur'ān leaves no room for doubt that the law which governs this whole universe is the law of unity, set in operation by the consistent will of the single Creator who is limitless in His glory. Nor does the Qur'ān leave any room for doubt that this whole universe submits to its Lord, acknowledges His oneness and worships Him in the way and fashion known to God. Of these we only know what God has told us. We certainly see the effects of this worship in the consistency and coherence that we observe in the universe and its operation.

This same law also applies to man who is, after all, a creature living in this universe. It is firmly rooted in human nature, which feels it instinctively and acts in consistency with it, as long as it remains sound, far from corrupting influences. When human nature suffers corruption, it becomes less instinctively aware of this law and allows fleeting desires to dictate its action, instead of following its perfect law that is well established within its own constitution.

This law is a covenant that has been made between human nature and its Creator. It is established in every single living cell from the moment it comes into existence. It predates God's messages and messengers. According to this covenant every cell testifies to the Lordship of the one God who has a consistent will that has established a single law to govern the whole universe as well as its own actions and reactions. With such a covenant made with human nature, no one can argue that he is unaware of God's revelations that explain the divine faith or that he knows nothing of God's messages that call on people to believe in His oneness. There is no validity in the argument advanced by anyone who says: "I was born into a family of unbelievers. Therefore, I had no chance of knowing the faith based on belief in God's oneness. I had to follow the footsteps of my forefathers who had erred and caused me to err. Therefore, the responsibility is theirs, not mine". Hence, the Qur'ānic comment on the testimony given by the offspring of Adam's children is stated most clearly: "*[This He did] lest you should say on the Day of Resurrection, 'We were truly unaware of this;' or lest you say, 'It was our forefathers who, in times gone by, associated partners with God, and we were only their late offspring. Will You destroy us on account of what those inventors of falsehood did?"'* (Verses 172-173)

But God knows that human nature is likely to go astray when subjected to the pressures exercised by satans, whether human or *jinn,* who manipulate human weaknesses. He is fully aware that human beings can go far astray once they are set on the way to error. Hence, He has determined, out of His grace, not to hold them to account merely on the basis of this covenant with their nature or the reason He has given them to judge and evaluate matters. He has determined to send them messengers who are given plain revelations, and to make His signs clear so that human nature can be saved from the effects of pressure. In the same way, the human intellect is freed from the shackles of its weaknesses and desires. Had God's knowledge shown that nature and reason were sufficient for people to follow the right path without sending them messengers and messages, He might have made these the basis of accountability. But God's grace has dictated that this basis must be His message: *"Thus We make plain Our revelations so that they may return [to the right path]."* (Verse 174)

They may turn back to their nature and honour their covenant with God. When they operate the faculties of perception and understanding God has established within their souls and constitution, the reality of God's oneness becomes so clear in their minds and causes them to adhere firmly to the faith based on that reality. Hence, we have to look on those messages and messengers sent by God as an aspect of His grace.

An Analogy to Leave Everyone Speechless

The *sūrah* then gives an example of the practical effects of deviation from sound human nature, betraying its covenant and abandoning God's revelations after having learnt them. The example is shown through a person who has been given God's revelations, plain, direct and easy to grasp. However, he discards them, turning away, clinging to the life of this world and following his desire. This means that he neither fulfils his first covenant nor follows the revelations providing him with clear guidance. Hence, Satan overpowers him and he stands rejected by God, unable to enjoy security or peace.

In its inimitable style, the Qur'ān does not describe this example in such terms. It brings it within a very lively scene, with violent movement, distinctive lines, clear reactions combining both the effect of a bustling life with that of a highly inspiring style: "*Tell them of the man to whom We give Our revelations, and who then discards them. Satan catches up with him and he strays, like many others, into error. Had We so willed, We would have exalted him by means of those (revelations), but he clings to the earth and succumbs to his desires. He may be compared to a dog: no matter how you drive him off, he pants on away, and if you leave him alone, he still pants on. That is what the people who reject Our revelations are like. Tell them, then, such stories, so that they may take heed. A dismal example is that provided by those who reject Our revelations; for it is against their own selves that they are sinning.*" (Verses 175-177)

This is a remarkable scene, absolutely new to all that human language knows of vocabulary, expression and image. Here we see a man on whom God bestows His grace, giving him His revelations and favouring him with knowledge to give him a perfect chance to follow the right path and to exalt himself. But he discards it all. The Qur'ānic description shows this man's action as if he is peeling God's guidance off his own body, as if those revelations form a skin that gives him his appearance. Therefore, discarding them requires a very strong action and the exercise of much effort. It is like taking the skin off of a person who is still alive. But this is an apt description, because believing in God is so essential to human existence as a skin to a living creature. Nevertheless, this man, given God's revelations, is exercising a strong effort to take off his protective shield in order to follow his desire and deviate from God's guidance. Thus he falls from the bright and sunny horizon in order to cling to the dark clay. He becomes easy prey for Satan, without any protection from his designs. Satan thus catches up with him and exercises his power over him.

We then look at a miserable and horrific scene in which this creature appears covered with mud, clinging to the earth, taking the shape of a dog that pants away whether he is driven off or left alone. All these scenes follow in quick succession and we follow the rapid change from one scene to the other with complete amazement. When the last scene of a dog always panting away is raised before our eyes, we have the highly significant comment on the whole panorama: "*That is what the people who reject Our revelations are like. Tell them, then, such stories, so that they may take heed. A dismal example is that provided by those who reject Our revelations; for it is against their own selves that they are sinning.*" (Verses 176-177)

That example is certainly applicable to them. Signs indicating guidance and pointers guiding to faith have been provided for them in such a way that these are felt within their own nature and constitution as well as the whole universe around them. They, nevertheless, discard all these to corrupt their own souls and to fall from the position of man to the position of animals. They find themselves just like a dog covered with mud. Faith would have provided them with wings to fly up to an elevated position, and their nature would have ensured for them the fairest form and the best position, but they have chosen instead to come down and occupy a position that can only be described as 'the lowest of the low.'

"*A dismal example is that provided by those who reject Our revelations; for it is against their own selves that they are sinning.*" (Verse 177) Can there be a more dismal example than that? Can there be a worse action than discarding guidance and pulling oneself away from divine revelations? Is there anything more disgraceful than clinging to the lowly life of this earth and succumbing to desires? Can any human being cause himself more wrong than the one who does this? By so doing, he tears apart that protective shield which could have ensured his safety. Instead, he leaves his soul easy prey for Satan and sinks to the level of animals, with all that it entails of worry and uncertainty. He is soon seen as a dog constantly panting away.

Can we think of a more vivid, lively and inspiring description of this case? The Qur'ānic style is at its most effective when it gives such descriptions and examples.

It is pertinent to ask here whether these verses tell a story that actually took place or whether they refer to a particular case that happens frequently. If it is the latter, then it is perfectly right to tell it as a story.

The Example and Its Application

There are reports which tell that these verses speak of a man from Palestine who used to lead a very pious life, prior to the arrival of the Children of Israel in the Holy Land. These reports describe in great detail how he deviated from the truth and then rejected it altogether. No one who has studied the numerous reports that have been derived from the books of Jewish history, some of which found their way into the commentaries on the Qur'ān, could discount the possibility that the story of this person is just another of these unauthentic reports. It is impossible to be certain of all the details that are given in this story. Moreover, these reports suffer from a great deal of contradiction, compelling us to approach them very cautiously. Some reports suggest that the man belonged to the Children of Israel, and that his name was Bel'am ibn Bā'ūrā'. It is also reported that he belonged to the powerful Philistines. Yet in some other reports he is said to have been an Arab named Umayyah ibn al-Ṣalt. It is even suggested that the description applies to a man who was contemporary with the Prophet and that his name was Abū 'Āmir who earned the title, 'al-Fāsiq', which means 'the transgressor'. Other reports suggest that he was a contemporary of the Prophet Moses, while still others mention that he lived at the time of Joshua, who, with the Israelites, fought the Philistines and defeated them. This took place when the Children of Israel had completed forty years in the wilderness after having refused to enter Palestine with Moses. The Qur'ān reports that they said to the Prophet Moses, at that time: "*Go forth, then, you and your Lord, and fight, both of you. We shall stay here.*" (5: 24) It is mentioned also that the revelations which this man was given included the greatest name of God which ensures the answering of any supplication. On the other hand, it is mentioned that he was given scriptures and that he himself was a prophet. More conflicting details are given.

For our part we have chosen not to go into the details of any of these reports, since there is nothing in the Qur'ānic text itself to support any of them and there is no authentic *ḥadīth* attributing to the Prophet any statement to give any of them more probability. This is in line with our approach which we have chosen in this commentary. We concentrate on the significance of this story describing the conditions of those who deny God's revelations after they have recognized them and deviated from the line they demarcate. This is a frequently encountered state of affairs in human life. Many are those who receive religious education but turn their backs on the guidance it provides. They simply use their knowledge in order to twist the meaning of Qur'ānic revelations so that it can serve the interests of those who are in power, and consequently, their own worldly interests as they see them.

We have seen many a scholar ready to state that Islam, God's religion, adopts a certain attitude when they fully know that what they are saying is in conflict with the truth. They manipulate their knowledge in order to issue rulings that aim to support a ruler that has usurped God's authority and violated His law.

Some of these acknowledge that the authority to legislate belongs to God alone, and that whoever claims such an authority actually claims Godhead and he is, therefore, an unbeliever. They go on to state that whoever acknowledges that authority as belonging to such a person is also an unbeliever. But contrary to their knowledge of this fact, which is essentially known to all believers, such scholars are ready to include such tyrannical rulers in their prayer, describing them as Muslims and their practices as the highest form of Islam. They conveniently forget their earlier statements that classify such rulers as unbelievers. We have also seen some of these scholars writing lengthy theses on the prohibition of usury, and yet a nod is enough to make them spend long hours writing articles and theses that claim usury to be lawful. Some of them are ready to bless wanton practices and promiscuity giving it a religious guise.

What can all these be other than examples confirming the story of the person who had discarded God's revelations after having received them? Hence, Satan is able to catch up with him and push him further into error. How can such a person be described except in the terms stated by God about the original person in the Qur'ānic example: "*Had We so willed, We would have exalted him by means of those (revelations), but he clings to the earth and succumbs to his desires. He may be compared to a dog: no matter how you drive him off, he pants on away, and if you leave him alone, he still pants on.*" (Verse 176)

Had it been God's will to exalt him by means of the knowledge he had received, He would have done so, but He has not, because the person who has received knowledge of God's revelations had chosen to cling to the earth and to follow his own desires in preference to following God's teachings. He is, then, an example of everyone who turns his back on divine religion after having learnt it. Instead of following God's guidance, he pulls himself away from God's blessings in order to be a humiliated follower of Satan and ends up in the derogatory state of animals.

What about the panting that never ceases? As we understand the story and contemplate its various scenes as painted in the Qur'ān, we feel that it refers to that continuous coveting of the worldly pleasures of this life. It is for such pleasures and other trivialities of this world that people discard their knowledge of God's revelations. It is a worried coveting that is never satisfied. Whatever advice you give to such covetous people, they will continue to run after these pleasures and trivialities.

Every day we see new examples of such people everywhere and in all communities. Long periods of time may pass and we hardly see a scholar who does not follow this example. Only a small minority cling to God's guidance and refuse to succumb to Satan or follow their desires. They seek God's support in order not to covet the trifling pleasures of this world that can be bestowed by those who are in power. Hence, the example given in the Qur'ān is not limited to a single case, but occurs in every society and in every generation.

God has commanded His Messenger (peace be upon him) to tell his community, who were receiving God's revelations, of this type of person so that they may guard against falling to the same temptation. This story is meant to be in the Qur'ān so that it continues to be recited. It may, thus, serve as a warning to those who are given any amount of knowledge, so that they are aware of the need to protect themselves against ending up in such a miserable condition if they run after trivial pleasures. If they do this, they will wrong themselves in a way that no enemy can match. If they allow themselves to move towards such a miserable end, they hurt none but themselves.

In our present time, we have seen some of these imitations of the person mentioned in the Qur'ān. They appear so keen to wrong themselves and so eager to preserve for themselves a position in the depths of hell, as if they fear that their competitors may take it away from them. Every morning they come up with something that puts them firmly in their place in hell. They continue to pant on, coveting this position until they depart from this life.

In comment, we only say: Our Lord, protect us from such a situation; grant us patience and perseverance; strengthen our resolve to follow Your guidance and gather us to You at the end of our lives as true believers who submit themselves to You.

We need now to have another look at this story and how the Qur'ān relates it.

Losers by Choice

What we have here is an example of knowledge that does not provide support or protection against the pressure of desires. Therefore, the person who has such knowledge will nevertheless cling to the earth, unable to free himself from its attractions, and will thus succumb to his desires. Satan then catches up with him and leads him by a leash made of such desires.

Because mere knowledge is not sufficient for protection, the Qur'ān tries to shape Muslim souls and Islamic life on the basis of knowledge formulated into a faith that provides the motive for implementation in everyday life. The Qur'ānic method does not present the faith in the form of a theory to be studied. Such knowledge has no practical effect, either in people's consciences or in life. It does not help man to repel Satan and his schemes. Indeed, it sometimes facilitates Satan's work.

Nor does the Qur'ān present the Islamic faith in the form of a series of studies in Islamic legal or economic systems, or studies in other disciplines relating to the universe or to the human soul. It presents it as a living faith that imparts life to people's hearts and minds and makes its followers aspire to a higher standard. Once this faith is firmly established in a person's heart, it gives him the motivation to put it into practice. It alerts the system of reception and response in human nature, in order to put man back on the right track. Thus, human nature can respond to its original covenant with God. In fact, the Qur'ān draws human nature to higher concerns and aims, and gives it freedom from worldly concerns, so that it never clings to the life of this world, or to use the Qur'ānic expression, it does not cling to the earth.

The Qur'ān also presents the Islamic faith as a system for reflection and reasoning that is far superior to all human systems. It has indeed been laid down to save human beings from the defects inherent in their own systems that suffer from errors and a deliberate twisting to facilitate desire-satisfaction and surrender to Satan's temptations.

The Qur'ān also presents this religion as a criterion for the truth, putting human minds on the right course and allowing them to evaluate their thoughts, concepts and actions. Whatever is judged as correct by this criterion should be pursued, and whatever is rejected must be abandoned as erroneous.

This religion of Islam is also presented by the Qur'ān as a plan for action that leads humanity step by step along the road that climbs up it to its highest standard and noblest situation. Each step is determined by the Qur'ān itself and in accordance with its concepts and values. Through this practical action it provides human beings with a code of living, basic principles of law, as well as the foundation of an economic, social and political system. When human thinking has been moulded by the Qur'ān, people are able to formulate their own legislation, and their approaches to scientific disciplines that study the universe and human psychology, as well as all that they need in their practical lives. They approach all this from the standpoint of believing in this religion, and strengthen it with the seriousness and practicality of the Islamic law on the one hand and with the requirements of practical life on the other.

Such is the Qur'ānic approach to moulding Muslim minds and Islamic life. An academic study gives only mere knowledge that does not protect people from the temptation of desire and Satan's schemes. It simply cannot do any good for human life.[1]

The *sūrah* then makes a short pause to comment on the example provided in this scene of a person to whom God has given His revelations, but who discards them. In this comment, the *sūrah* tells us that true guidance is provided by God alone: "*He whom God guides is on the right path; whereas those whom He lets go astray are indeed losers.*" (Verse 178) God certainly guides those who make an effort to find guidance. God says in another *sūrah*: "*Those who strive for Us, We shall certainly guide along Our ways.*" (29: 69) He also says elsewhere in the Qur'ān: "*God does not change the condition of a certain people until they themselves initiate change.*" (13: 11) He further says: "*By the soul and its moulding and inspiration with knowledge of wickedness and piety. Successful is the one who keeps it pure, and ruined is the one who corrupts it.*" (91: 7-10)

Similarly, God lets go astray anyone who wishes to go astray. He allows him to turn away from the elements of guidance and pointers to the right faith, sealing his heart, ears and eyes in order that he does not hear, see or understand. The next verse in the *sūrah* states: "*We have destined for Hell many of the jinn and many human beings; they have hearts they cannot understand with, and they have eyes with which they fail to see, and ears with which they fail to hear. They are like cattle; indeed, they are even further away from the right way. They are the truly heedless.*" (Verse 179) They are described in another *sūrah* as follows: "*There is sickness in their hearts, and God has aggravated their sickness.*" (2: 10) God also says in the Qur'ān: "*Those who disbelieve and persist in wrongdoing will find that God will never forgive them,*

---

1. For further discussion, reference may be made to the Prologue of *Sūrah* 6, Cattle, in Vol. V.

nor will He guide them onto any road, except the road to hell, wherein they will abide beyond the count of time." (4: 168-169)

When we study carefully all the texts that mention guidance and going astray, relating them to one another and taking them as a whole, we find a consistent line that abandons all the controversy of the different Muslim sects or the controversies of Christian scholastic debate and the various philosophies concerning the whole question of pre-destination. God's will, which applies to human beings, is that God creates every man and woman with equal ability to follow guidance or go astray. In addition, God plants in human nature the ability to recognize the truth of the One God and to follow it, and He gives every human being a mind to distinguish guidance from error. Furthermore, He sends messengers with plain revelations to reawaken human nature when it lies dormant, and to provide guidance to the human mind when it goes astray. After all this there remains the dual susceptibility to follow guidance or error, for man has been created with this in his very nature. God's will has also determined that whoever strives for guidance shall have it. On the other hand, anyone who chooses not to use the mind God has given him, or not to use his sight and hearing in understanding the signs and pointers that are placed everywhere in the universe, and those contained in divine messages, shall be left to go astray.

Thus, in all situations, it is only God's will that is fulfilled. This means that everything happens only by God's will, not by the power of anyone else. This would not have been so, except for the fact that God has so willed. Then, in the universe there is no other will to initiate matters and events. Within the framework of this great work, man chooses his line of action and reaps the results of either following right guidance or going astray.

This is the Islamic concept, which is derived from the numerous Qur'ānic statements when taken together as mutually complementary. These statements must never be taken individually according to the prejudices of different sects. They must never be set in opposition to each other for argument and debate.

Sealing All Means of Perception

"He whom God guides is on the right path; whereas those whom He lets go astray are indeed losers." (Verse 178) This verse sets out the terms

very clearly. According to this law, which has already been explained in detail, whoever has God's guidance is truly on the right path, and will surely attain his goal. He will be able to follow guidance in order to attain success and prosperity in the hereafter. Conversely, a person whom God lets go astray, in accordance with the same law, is indeed the loser, because he has lost everything and gained nothing, no matter how much he has in this life. All this accounts for nothing. We need only to remember that such a person has lost himself. What gain can such a person have after incurring such a loss?

This explanation of this verse is supported by the next verse: "*We have destined for Hell many of the jinn and many human beings; they have hearts they cannot understand with, and they have eyes with which they fail to see, and ears with which they fail to hear. They are like cattle; indeed, they are even further away from the right way. They are the truly heedless.*" (Verse 179) Those large numbers of *jinn* and human beings are destined for hell. Why? And what for? There are two aspects to consider here. The first is that God's perfect knowledge shows that such creatures will inevitably go to hell. For God to know this does not require that actions which earn the punishment of hell actually take place. God's knowledge is absolute, free from the constraints of time, action and place. Nothing is added to God's knowledge as a result of a motion or an action that takes place in our world.

The second aspect to consider is that God's perfect knowledge does not in any way direct these creatures to go astray so as to incur the punishment of hell as a result. It is they who are just like the Qur'ānic verse describes: "*They have hearts they cannot understand with, and they have eyes with which they fail to see, and ears with which they fail to hear.*" (Verse 179) It is they who have not opened their hearts and minds to learn and understand. Proofs, signs, indications and pointers of all sorts are available throughout the universe and in the divine messages, providing guidance which can easily be understood by hearts and minds that are kept open. It is they who have chosen not to open their ears to listen to God's revelations. They have kept all these means of perception and understanding idle and unused. As a result, they live a life of wilful ignorance: "*They are like cattle; indeed, they are even further away from the right way; they are the truly heedless.*" (Verse 179)

Those who are heedless of the signs God has placed in the universe and in life itself, and choose not to reflect on the events that take place around them, and do not see God's will behind them all, are indeed further astray than cattle. Animals have natural tendencies to guide them. Human beings and *jinn* have been given hearts, minds, eyes and ears to hear, look and understand. If they choose not to open their means of perception, and prefer instead to go about life without reflecting about its meaning and aim, and without looking at its events and what they signify, or hearing its messages, they place themselves below animals who have only been given their natural tendencies. As a result, they are destined for hell. It is God's will that drives them there ever since He has given them their dual susceptibility and made the law of punishment and reward. God knows right at the beginning that their action and attitude will lead them to hell.

The *sūrah* follows this with a clear instruction to the believers to ignore those who deviate from the right path and go astray. At the time of the Prophet, those were the unbelievers who used to maintain idolatry in opposition to the Islamic message. They used to blaspheme against God's names, twist His attributes, and assign them to some of the idols they ascribe as partners to God. "*God has the finest names, so appeal to Him by these and stay away from those who blaspheme against His names. They shall be requited for all they do.*" (Verse 180)

The Arabic word in this Qur'ānic verse which is translated here as '*blaspheme against His names*' signifies also twisting and distortion. The idolaters among the Arabs distorted God's fine names and gave them to their alleged deities. They distorted the name Allah so as to call one of their idols al-Lāt, and twisted His attribute, al-'Azīz, which means the Mighty, to call another idol, al-'Uzzā. The Qur'ānic verse states clearly that these fine names and attributes belong to God alone. It instructs the believers to call Him alone by these names, without any distortion or twisting. They are also instructed to ignore the twisters who have gone far astray, and not to bother about them. They are left to God who determines their punishment. This is a very serious warning indeed.

This instruction to ignore those who blaspheme against God is not limited to that particular occasion or to those who twist and distort God's names and attributes, or who assign them to their alleged deities. It applies to all sorts of blasphemy, such as those who adopt a twisted or deviant concept of Godhead. These include those who claim that God has a son or those who allege that His will is subject to the laws of nature, or those who claim that His actions are similar to the actions of human beings, when there is no-one and nothing like Him. It also applies to those who claim that He is the deity in heaven who conducts the affairs of the universe and who determines people's destiny in the hereafter, but who negate at the same time His position as the deity on earth and in human life. Such people claim that He may not legislate for human life, because people are the ones who legislate for themselves in the light of their experience and guided by their interests, as they themselves see these interests. In this respect, the people are their own deities, or some of them are the deities of others. All this is deviation and blasphemy against God, His names and attributes. Muslims are commanded to ignore all this and not to bother about it. The blasphemers and deviants are warned here that they will receive the right punishment for what they do.

A Community with a Well Defined Purpose

The *sūrah* has so far described types of people, particularly those whom God has destined to abide in hell. These are described as ones who "*have hearts they cannot understand with, and they have eyes with which they fail to see, and ears with which they fail to hear.*" (Verse 179) A group of them are described as ones who 'blaspheme against God's names' and distort them. The *sūrah* goes on to describe other types of people, telling us about a community which holds fast to the truth and calls on people to believe in it, and implement it with determination and conscientiousness. At the other extreme there is a community of people who deny the truth and reject God's revelations. The *sūrah* tells us clearly that the first community exists without a shred of doubt. They guard the truth and hold tight to it when other people abandon it and deviate far away from it. When others reject the truth as a lie, they remain steadfast. The *sūrah* further explains that the others shall have a dreadful end, as God will punish them through His mighty schemes: "*Among those whom We have created there is a community who guide others by means of the truth and with it establish justice. As for those who deny Our revelations, We will lead them on, step by step, from whence they cannot tell; for although I may give them respite, My subtle scheme is mighty.*" (Verses 181-183)

Humanity would not have deserved any honour had it not been for the fact that there will always be, even in the worst circumstances, that community which God calls by its Islamic term, *ummah*. By definition, the *ummah* is a community which believes in the same faith that remains its basic bond, and obeys the same leadership that supervises the implementation of that faith. It is then the community that adheres to, and implements the truth, in all situations. It is the guardian of God's trust, the witness to His covenant with people, and it is the community to provide God's evidence against those who go astray turning their backs on His covenant.

The description given here of this community deserves reflection. It is a community "*who guide others by means of the truth and with it establish justice.*" (Verse 181) This community will continue to be present at all times, even though it may at certain periods be very small in number. Its main characteristic is that those who belong to it "*guide others by means of the truth*". (Verse 181) They call on people to accept the truth, and will never relinquish their task of advocating the truth. They are not happy to keep it to themselves, or to be inward looking. They try to publicize the truth they know, and guide other people to it. Thus, they have a role of leadership among those around them who have strayed away from this truth, and who have violated their covenant. They adopt a positive attitude, which is not limited to knowing the truth but goes beyond that knowledge in order to advocate the truth and guide to it.

But this is not all that they do about the truth. Their other characteristic is that they 'establish justice' with the truth. This means that they go well beyond knowing the truth and advocating it, to take positive steps to implement the truth in human life and make it the criterion for judgement in order to establish justice that cannot be based on anything other than the truth. The crux of the matter is that the truth has not been revealed only to remain a mere branch of knowledge studied by scholars, or even an admonition to point out the right path. The truth has been revealed so that people conduct their lives according to it. It should govern people's concepts so that these are moulded in accordance with it, and it should govern people's rites of worship so that these provide a practical image of the truth in as far as the relationship between human beings and their Lord is concerned. The truth has also been revealed in order to mould practical life so that all systems are in line with its principles and subject to the laws derived from it. It also shapes people's habits, traditions, moral values and behaviour, as well as their philosophical doctrines, culture and all branches of knowledge, providing the criteria to evaluate all these. When all this takes place, the truth is present in human life, and justice, which can only be based on the truth, is established. Thus, the establishment of the truth in human life is the task undertaken by this community, after having made the truth known and worked to guide other people to it.

This religion of Islam has a nature that is too plain to admit any ambiguity, and too solid to allow any equivocation. Those who stand against this faith find it exceedingly hard to force it out of its clear and solid nature. Therefore, they exert tireless efforts and mount ceaseless campaigns, utilizing all means and methods, in order to change its direction and obscure its nature. They resort to unrestrained brutality to crush the advocates of Islamic revival in any part of the world, utilizing certain regimes that they establish and support. They even utilize professional scholars to work against this faith, distorting God's words, and making lawful what God has forbidden. These professional scholars try to make God's law appear equivocal and they bless indecency and promiscuity, even giving them Islamic labels. They pat on the back those who are fascinated by materialistic culture and admire its theories and systems. Their aim is to manoeuvre Islam into imitating these theories and situations and to borrow materialistic laws and methods. The Islamic faith, which provides a system to govern all aspects of life, is described by such people as a historical event that took place in the past and cannot be brought back! At the same time, they lavish praise on this past to pacify the Muslims of today. They then tell them that Islam should remain alive today in the hearts of its followers as a set of beliefs and acts of worship, not as a law or code of living. Islam and Muslims should be satisfied with their glorious past. Alternatively, they go on, Islam should be subject to evolution, so that it submits to the realities of life, endorsing everything that people wish to adopt of concepts and laws.

To consolidate the regimes they create in the world that was Islamic, they provide theories that take the form of a faith and religion to replace the old Islamic faith. They even provide for these theories a *qur'ān* to be recited and studied so that it can replace the Qur'ān revealed by God. As a last resort, they try to change the nature of society in these countries, in the same way as they try to change the nature of this religion, so that Islam will not find receptive hearts to accept its guidance. They transform communities into human beings that are lost in the quagmire of pleasure, sex and lust, preoccupied with the necessities of life to ensure their survival, and unable to find these necessities without hard toil. Thus they ensure that after having worked hard for food and sex, people are unable to listen to any voice of guidance or to think of religion.

It is a ferocious fight against this faith and the community who guide others by means of its truth and try to establish justice with it. It is a fight where no qualms are shown about using any type of weapon, in which all means are used and for which all the forces, talents, media and international organizations and machinery are mobilized. Indeed, it is merely to sustain this fight and add to its fuel that we see certain regimes supported and patronized by world powers. Needless to say, such regimes would not survive for a day without such support.

Nevertheless, the clear and solid nature of this religion stands firm in this ferocious battle. The Muslim community that guards the truth despite its small number and poor equipment, continues to resist with success the brutal efforts that aim to crush and exterminate it. God will certainly accomplish His purpose.

Points for Reflection

"*As for those who deny Our revelations, We will lead them on, step by step, from whence they cannot tell; for although I may give them respite, My subtle scheme is mighty.*" (Verses 182-183) This is indeed the power they do not reckon with when they launch their ferocious battle against this faith and the community that follows it with conscientiousness and makes it its basic bond. Those who deny God's revelations remain always unaware of this power, and can never think that whatever means they are given are no more than something with which to lead them on, step by step. They are only given respite for a while. They do not believe in the might of God's subtle schemes. They support one another, and they only believe in the power they see with their eyes on earth. As a result, they forget about the Almighty, the One who commands all the power. But God's law in respect of those who deny His revelations remains the same. He gives them free rein, and allows them time to indulge in their excesses and disobedience. But all this only leads them along the road to ruin. A subtle but mighty scheme is being prepared for them. The question is: by whom? It is by the Almighty who has all power. While they remain unaware, the great prize is prepared for the believers who guide others by means of the truth and work for the establishment of justice on its basis.

This serious and alarming threat was directed first of all at certain people in Makkah who denied God's revelations, but Qur'ānic statements always go beyond the immediate occasion to have a more general import. It threatens these people because of their attitude towards the Muslim community, described here according to Islamic terminology as a nation or *ummah*. They are warned that they are only being given respite, and led on by a mighty scheme. This threat is followed by calling on them to use their hearts, eyes and ears, in order to spare themselves the fate of Hell. The Qur'ān also calls on them to reflect on the position of God's Messenger who explains the truth to them and guides them to it, and to consider God's dominion of the heavens and the earth and the indicators placed in this kingdom. It draws their attention to the fact that time passes and that their appointed hour is drawing near, while they remain unaware.

> *Have they not thought things over? Their companion is no madman; he is only a plain warner. Have they not considered [God's] dominion over the heavens and the earth, and all that God has created, and [reflected] that it may well be that their own term is drawing near? In what other message after this will they, then, believe?* (Verses 184-185)

The Qur'ān shakes them and wakes them up in order to rescue their nature, minds and feelings from the pressures that weigh heavily on them. It addresses their humanity with all its systems of reception and response. It does not make an academic argument, but tries to address their whole nature: "*Have they not thought things over? Their companion is no madman; he is only a plain warner.*" (Verse 184)

In their propaganda campaign against the Prophet Muḥammad (peace be upon him), the notables of the Quraysh[2] tried to deceive the public by saying that Muḥammad was a madman who uttered strange words, unfamiliar to normal human beings.

Those notables of the Quraysh were fully aware that they were lying. Numerous reports suggest that they were fully aware of the truth concerning the Prophet and his message. They could not even stop themselves listening to the Qur'ān and responding to its appeal. A

---

2. The Prophet's tribe which lived in Makkah and which was dominant in Arabia. – Editor's note.

well-known report mentions that three of them, al-Akhnas ibn Sharīq, Abū Sufyān and Abū Jahl met one another on three consecutive nights after having sat for a long while during the night listening to the Qur'ān.[3] Another well-known report describes how 'Utbah ibn Rabī'ah was deeply touched when the Prophet recited to him a long passage of *Sūrah* 41.[4] There is also a famous report describing how they held a conference as the pilgrimage season approached, to discuss what to say to pilgrims from faraway areas about the Qur'ān. Al-Walīd ibn Al-Mughīrah finally instructed them to say that the Qur'ān was the product of sorcery.[5] All these reports confirm that they were not unaware of the truth of this faith. They only adopted an arrogant attitude and feared for their authority which they felt to be threatened by the declaration that there was no deity other than God and that Muḥammad was His Messenger. That declaration constituted a threat to all types of human tyranny as it put an end to all human attempts to force people to submit to anyone other than God.

They manipulated the unique style of the Qur'ān and the fact that it was so different from all familiar human styles. They also made use of the common belief concerning a relationship between prophecy and madness that originates from the fact that a mad person may say incomprehensible words and utterances which someone close to him might interpret any way he likes, claiming that it was given him from another world. Those Arabs manipulated that legacy in order to deceive people alleging that what Muḥammad said was the product of madness.[6]

The Qur'ān calls on them to consider and reflect: they had known this companion of theirs, i.e. the Prophet Muḥammad, (peace be upon him), for a long time and they had never experienced any fault with him. Indeed, they themselves testified to his honesty, truthfulness and wisdom. They accepted him as an arbiter when a quarrel erupted between them over which tribe was to have the honour of putting the Black Stone back in its position. They accepted his judgement which spared them a potentially very costly battle. They trusted him with

---

3. Vol. III, p. 413, and Vol. V, pp. 110-111.

4. Vol. V, pp. 112-113.

5. This will be discussed in detail in our commentary on *Sūrah* 74.

6. For further discussion of the link between prophethood and madness in *jāhiliyyah* communities, see Vol. V, pp. 148-151.

their valuables which they kept in his custody until the day when he left Makkah to migrate to Madinah. His cousin, 'Alī, returned every valuable article to its owner.

The Qur'ān calls on them to consider and reflect on all this. They had known Muḥammad for a very long time and were fully aware of his character. Was he a man to experience any madness? Were any of his words or actions indicative of madness? Certainly not: "*Their companion is no madman; he is only a plain warner.*" (Verse 184) There is certainly nothing wrong with his mind or with his speech. He speaks plainly to warn people about what is awaiting them. His statements could never be confused with those of mad people and his actions were certainly the actions of a very wise person.

Reflect and Consider

And then comes this inviting question: "*Have they not considered [God's] dominion over the heavens and the earth, and all that God has created?*" (Verse 185) This serves as another deeply touching call. They are invited to open their eyes and hearts to this vast kingdom with all that it contains. Reflection with open heart and mind is sufficient to revive human nature and make it receptive to the truth underlined by God's inimitable creation and all its miraculous aspects testifying to its being the work of God, the only Creator. Reflection over anything God has created – and His creation is so greatly varied in the kingdoms of heaven and earth – is bound to leave both heart and mind in a genuine state of speechless amazement. The mind will then start to look for the origin of this creation, and the power that has made it all in such a perfect system.

Why has each creature taken its present shape and not taken an alternative form from among the countless shapes which exist in nature? Why has the system of creation followed this particular route to the exclusion of all other possible ones? Why have all creatures persisted in following this particular way, without changing it over the centuries? What is the secret behind the unity that we can detect in the nature of all creation, unless it is the result of a single will that gives practical manifestation to a consistent act of creation?

A living body, indeed a single living cell is so miraculous in its existence, make-up and behaviour. Its process of transformation continues all the time, yet it preserves its existence and has the means to give birth to new generations of its kind. Moreover, it knows its function and manages to keep it up in its successive generations. Who can reflect on the existence of a single cell and make a statement that this universe is run without God, or that God has partners to do the job with Him? Who can be rationally at ease when he makes such a statement? How can he make his nature and conscience agree with it?

The very fact that life continues through marriage and procreation is a testimony to the elaborate scheme of creation made by God, the only Creator. This should be reflected upon by every thinking human being. If it was not for God, who would guarantee that life would always enjoy the proper ratio of males and females, generation after generation, to ensure the continuity of marriage and procreation? How is it that there never comes a time when life produces only the male or the female variety? Should this ever happen, then procreation would come to an end. It is important to ask: who maintains the right balance in every generation?

Yet balance is clearly visible throughout God's dominion of the heavens and the earth, not merely in this single life phenomenon. We recognize it in the make-up of the atom, just as we see it in the constitution of the galaxy. Proper balance is also noticeable between living things and inanimate objects as well. Should this balance be tilted by a fraction one way or the other, this whole universe would instantly collapse. Who maintains this fine balance in the heavens and the earth?

The Arabs who were the first to be addressed by the Qur'ān did not have the knowledge to realize the extent of this balance and coherence in the heavens and the earth and in all God's creation. But human nature itself responds to the universe in an unspoken language that it certainly feels in its depth. It is sufficient that a human being should reflect over what he sees in the universe, with an open eye and a receptive mind in order to receive its guidance and inspiration.

When they received these signals, human beings recognized by their nature that God had created them. They were never unaware of this fact, but they were drawn to error in identifying their true Lord, until they were provided with guidance through God's messages. However, the neo-atheists, who advocate so-called 'scientific socialism', are non-entities who have corrupted their nature. Indeed, they deny their own nature and reject its consistent pointers. When one of them, an astronaut, went into space and beheld that dazzling scene of the earth looking as a ball suspended in mid-air, he cried out naturally, "Who holds it in position like that?" But when he returned to earth and remembered the tyranny of the Communist state, he said that he did not find God over there.[7] He simply suppressed the discourse of his nature as he reflected on an aspect of the kingdom of the heavens and the earth.

God who addresses man with the Qur'ān is the One who has created man and knows his nature. He concludes this invitation to reflect and consider with a reminder of death that may come suddenly taking them unawares: "*Have they not considered [God's] dominion over the heavens and the earth, and all that God has created, and [reflected] that it may well be that their own term is drawing near?*" (Verse 185) Can they tell that their term is not fast drawing to a close? Why do they prefer to remain heedless of God's reminders when they cannot fathom what God has kept hidden and when they cannot break loose from His will?

This last touch on the unknown end that may come suddenly shakes the human heart violently, so that it may wake up, think and reflect. God, who has revealed the Qur'ān and created man, knows that this emphasis is bound to re-awaken every heart and open every mind. Yet some people may still choose to deliberately deny the truth: "*In what other message after this will they, then, believe?*" (Verse 185) This message is the final one, and there will not be any following message to soften the hearts of those who choose to disbelieve.

We note how a single verse uses several ways and means to show us that when the Qur'ān addresses human nature, it does not leave any aspect of it untouched. It does not present a cold, logical argument, nor does it ignore the human intellect either. Indeed, it ensures that the mind is awakened just as the Qur'ān puts its message to the whole human being. When the human mind has been reawakened, it is invited to think, consider and reflect as life begins to send messages to it. This must remain the method of those who advocate faith. Human beings remain in their human status. They have not evolved into a different

---

7. This is a reference to the astronaut sent on the second Soviet manned space mission, when the Soviet authorities made a fuss about this statement. It is noted that the author refers to scientific socialism as the epitome of atheism. This was the trend when he was writing, particularly in Egypt which adopted such policies in the early 1960s. – Editor's note.

species. The Qur'ān remains the eternal work of God. God's address to man remains the same, even though human knowledge may have developed and greatly increased.

A Question That Needs No Answer

Now, the *sūrah* takes a short pause to restate God's law that is concerned with guidance and error. God has willed to provide guidance to everyone who seeks it and works for it. On the other hand, anyone who turns away from guidance and closes his mind and heart to the pointers to faith will be left alone to go astray. This law is restated here in connection with the situation of those people who were the first to be addressed by the Qur'ān. As we have seen, the Qur'ān makes use of a single case or a particular example in order to state a consistent law.

"*Those whom God lets go astray will have no guide; and He leaves them in their overweening arrogance to stumble along blindly.*" (Verse 186) Those who go astray do so because they choose not to consider and reflect. When people turn their minds away from the signs placed by God in the universe, they will be left to go astray. They will have none to guide them after that: "*Those whom God lets go astray will have no guide.*" (Verse 186) And whoever is so left alone in accordance with God's law that we have explained will continue with his arrogance and will, therefore, be left to stumble along blindly. There is no injustice in that. Those people have chosen to keep their eyes and hearts shut, and not to reflect on the miraculous aspects of creation and the secrets of the universe. They have decided not to listen to the testimony of everything that God has created. Wherever one looks in the universe, one is bound to find a sign or a telling message pointing one in the right direction. Whatever man looks at, either within himself, or in the world around him, he is bound to recognize God's hand and His inimitable way of creation. If he chooses to remain blind to all this, he is left in his blindness. If he chooses to adopt an attitude of arrogance and to ignore the truth, he is left to his own devices, until he finally lands himself in ruin: "*He leaves them in their overweening arrogance to stumble along blindly.*" (Verse 186)

Some of those arrogant, misguided and blind people who prefer not to see what is around them, questioned the Prophet (peace be upon him) about the final Hour, the timing of which God has chosen not to reveal. They are the same as the one who does not see what is under his feet but wants to see what lies beyond the horizon. Hence, their questioning: *"They ask you about the Last Hour: 'When will it come to pass?' Say: Knowledge of it rests with my Lord alone. None but He will reveal it at its appointed time. It will weigh heavily on the heavens and the earth; and it will not fall on you except suddenly. They will ask you further as if you yourself persistently enquire about it. Say: Knowledge of it rests with God alone, though most people remain unaware."* (Verse 187)

The call to believe in the hereafter and its related concept of punishment and reward came as a complete surprise to the idolatrous Arabs. Although this concept is fundamental to Abraham's faith, the grandfather of those idolatrous people, and also to the faith of their noble father, Ishmael, their links with the faith of submission to God preached by Abraham and Ishmael were completely severed. The concept of the hereafter had been erased from their minds and they received it again with total amazement and complete surprise. They wondered at the Prophet Muḥammad (peace be upon him) because he told them about life after death, resurrection, reckoning, punishment and reward. This is stated clearly in the Qur'ān: *"The unbelievers would say: 'Shall we point out to you a man who will tell you that [after your death,] when you will have been scattered in countless fragments, you shall be in a new act of creation? Does he attribute his own lying inventions to God, or is he a mad man?' Truly, those who deny the life to come are doomed, for they have gone far astray."* (34: 7-8)

God knows that no community may be able to assume the leadership of mankind and bear testimony against them, as is the task of the Muslim community, unless the concept of the hereafter is clear in their minds, deeply entrenched in their consciences. To think of life as only this limited period confined to this world will not raise such a community to assume such a task.

To believe in the hereafter provides broadness of concept and vision as well as a wider perspective. It also opens up life to make it go beyond this limited world. This is necessary for the formation of the human self so that it is fit to assume its great role. It is also necessary to enable human beings to control their desires and narrow ambitions. Moreover, it gives human beings the sense of broadness they need to overcome the feeling of despair when they encounter short-term adverse results, or when they have to make painful sacrifices. If believers were to despair, they would not be able to continue with the propagation of the truth and all its goodness, or to lead mankind to all that is good. All such qualities are necessary to fulfil man's great task.

Believing in the hereafter is the dividing line between the broadness and narrowness of vision and perspective. Their broadness is natural to man, while their narrowness results from concentrating only on the physical and the carnal. Adopting an animal perspective can never be suitable for assuming the leadership of humanity, or the fulfilment of God's trust given to man as the creature God has placed in charge of the earth.

For all this, strong emphasis has been laid on believing in the hereafter in all divine religions. This is brought to its climax in Islam which gives such belief in the hereafter its greatest clarity, broadness and depth. This is what makes the sense of the hereafter much stronger among the Muslim community than its sense of this world in which we actually live. That is indeed what makes the Muslim community fit to lead mankind and to make its leadership characterized by wisdom and right guidance.

The Hour That Will Come to Pass

At this point in the *sūrah* we look at the scene of the unbelievers' surprise, wonder and incredulousness towards the concept of the hereafter. This is all seen in their questioning that is given in overtones of ridicule and derision: "*They ask you about the Last Hour: 'When will it come to pass?'*" (Verse 187)

That Hour is part of a store of knowledge that God has kept to Himself and revealed to no creature. But the unbelievers questioned the Prophet about it either to test his knowledge, or to express their surprise and amusement, or to portray their contempt and derision. They ask about the time when it will take place: "*When will it come to pass?*" (Verse 187)

But the Prophet (peace be upon him) is a human being who never made any claim to know anything that lies beyond the reach of human perception. He is instructed to leave that to the Lord, and to tell people that its knowledge is part of the attributes of Godhead. As a human being, he does not make any claim to anything that goes beyond the limits of humanity. He knows only what his Lord has vouchsafed to him of divine revelations.

"*Say: Knowledge of it rests with my Lord alone. None but He will reveal it at its appointed time.*" (Verse 187) God, who alone knows the

Hour and its timing, will not reveal it until its appointed time. No one else can say anything about it with any degree of certitude.

Their attentions are turned away from asking about its time to consider its nature and to reflect on its seriousness. It is certainly a matter of great importance, and its burden is heavy indeed. Its weight is felt in the heavens and the earth. Besides, it comes suddenly when people who do not pay attention to it are still unaware of its approach: "*It will weigh heavily on the heavens and the earth; and it will not fall on you except suddenly.*" (Verse 187) Therefore, it is only wise to be prepared for it before it comes suddenly, when no precaution will be of use. Preparations and precautions must be taken well in advance, when time is ample and people still expect to live longer. No one knows when it will exactly arrive. Therefore, everyone should prepare for it now, without losing a moment or an hour, because it may come at any time.

The *sūrah* wonders at those who question the Prophet (peace be upon him) about the Hour. They do not understand the nature of the divine message or the Messenger, and they do not know the nature of Godhead, and the attribute of humility the Prophet adopts towards his Lord. "*They will ask you further as if you yourself persistently enquire about it.*" (Verse 187) They always ask about it, as if you are required to disclose its time. But God's Messenger does not ask his Lord about something when he is aware that God has chosen to keep it to Himself: "*Say: Knowledge of it rests with my Lord alone.*" (Verse 187) He has chosen to keep that information to Himself and not to reveal it to any of His creatures, "*though most people remain unaware.*" (Verse 187)

But this does not apply to knowledge of the Hour only. It applies to everything in the realm which lies beyond the reach of human perception. It is God alone who knows all that there is in that realm. He does not give knowledge of any of it, except to someone He chooses, at the time and in the measure He determines. Hence, people do not have the ability to cause themselves any benefit or harm. They may do something which they hope to be beneficial to them, but they soon discover its consequences to be very harmful. Or they may take an initiative to remove some harm but they do not reckon with its adverse results. Or they may do something reluctantly, because they are forced to do it, and then discover it to be very beneficial for them. Alternatively, they may approach something with enthusiasm, only to discover that it results in their own suffering: "*It may well be that you hate a thing although it is good for you, and love a thing although it is bad for you.*" (2: 216)

This is summed up by an Arab poet who says: "Would that someone shows me my destination before I start my journey! How could that be when one has to complete a journey to get to one's destination."[8] This is the human position in relation to what lies beyond human perception. Human beings may achieve great progress, but when it comes to what God has chosen to keep away from them, they will remain confined to the limitation of their human knowledge.

In his great position of honour and his closeness to his Lord, the Prophet (peace be upon him) is commanded to declare to mankind that when it comes to the realm that lies beyond our perception, he is only a human being who can cause himself neither benefit nor harm. This is because he is not given that knowledge, nor is he one to know the destination before starting the journey, or the consequences of actions before they take place. Hence, he cannot choose his actions on the basis of their consequences, because these are withheld from him. He has to choose his actions, and then the result takes place as God has determined: "*Say: It is not within my power to bring benefit to, or avert evil from, myself, except as God may please. Had I possessed knowledge of what lies beyond the reach of human perception, I would have availed myself of much that is good and no evil would have ever touched me. I am no more than one who gives warning, and a herald of good news to people who believe.*" (Verse 188)

With this declaration, the monotheistic faith of Islam is completely and absolutely purged of every trace of idolatry of whatever shape or form. God has His unique attributes in which no human being has any share, not even Muḥammad, God's chosen and beloved Messenger (peace be upon him). Human power and knowledge stop at the point of *ghayb*, which is the Islamic term for what lies beyond the reach of human perception. Within the limitations of humanity, God's Messenger himself stands, and his role is well-defined: "*I am no more than one who gives warning, and a herald of good news to people who believe.*" (Verse 188)

God's Messenger is indeed a warner and a bearer of good news to all mankind. But the believers alone benefit by the warnings he conveys and the good news he brings. They are the ones to understand and

---

8. Ibn al-Rūmī.

appreciate his message, and they realize what it is all about. Moreover, they are the elite of all mankind. After all, from among all mankind, they are the ones to follow God's Messenger.

A statement does not impart its true significance except to an open heart and a receptive mind. The Qur'ān does not open its treasures or give its secrets except to true believers. Some of the Prophet's companions used to say that they had faith before they were given the Qur'ān. It is that faith which enabled them to grasp the meaning of the Qur'ān so fully and understand its meanings and objectives so comprehensively. Thus they were able to scale the unscaleable in the shortest imaginable period of time.

That unique generation of the Prophet's companions found the Qur'ān so charming, enlightening and decisive to a degree that can only be appreciated by people who attain to the same standard of faith. It is true that the Qur'ān directed their souls to faith, but it was faith that opened for them in the Qur'ān treasures that could have never been opened through any other means. They lived by the Qur'ān and for the Qur'ān. Hence, they became a unique generation the like of which history has never witnessed again in the same standard and in the shape of a whole, large community. However, throughout history, there have been individuals who follow in the footsteps of that uniquely great generation. They dedicated themselves for a very long period to the Qur'ān alone. Its clear spring remained untainted by any human ideas. In addition to the Qur'ān, there was only the guidance provided by God's Messenger (peace be upon him) and that guidance drew on the same lines as the Qur'ān. Hence, that generation could easily make its remarkable achievements.

Any community of people who aspire to make similar achievements should follow in the footsteps of that generation. They should conduct their lives on the basis of the Qur'ān and live for it over a long period of time, freeing their hearts and minds from any other human ideas. Only in this way can they begin to be like that generation.

All Created From One Soul

The *sūrah* then begins a new drive to re-emphasize the question of God's oneness. It starts first with a story which describes the initial deviation within the human mind from believing in God's oneness to associating partners with Him. This story serves as a model for the deviation of the Arab idolaters from the faith of their first father, the Prophet Abraham. They are then put face to face with their own practices and the deities they associate with God. That all this is false and ludicrous is instantly apparent. Then God's Messenger is directed to challenge those pagan Arabs and the deities they worship, declaring at the same time, that, for his part, he believes in God alone, his patron and protector.

> *It is He who has created you all from a single soul, and out of it brought into being its mate, so that he might incline with love towards her. When he has consorted with her, she conceives a light burden, which she carries with ease. Then, when she grows heavy, they both appeal to God, their Lord: "Grant us a goodly child and we will be truly grateful.' Yet when He has granted them a goodly child, they associate with Him partners, particularly in respect of what He has granted them. Exalted is God above anything people may associate with Him as partners. Do they associate with Him those that can create nothing, while they themselves have been created, and neither can they give them any support nor can they even help themselves. If you call them to guidance they will not follow you. It is all the same whether you call them or keep silent. Those whom you invoke beside God are God's servants, just like you. Invoke them, then, and let them answer you, if what you claim is true. Have they, perchance, feet on which they could walk, or hands with which to grasp things, or eyes with which to see, or ears with which to hear? Say: Appeal to those you claim to be partners with God, and scheme against me, and give me no respite. My guardian is God who has bestowed this Book from on high. It is He who is the guardian of the righteous. Those whom you invoke beside Him cannot give you any support, nor can they even help themselves. If you pray to them for guidance, they will not hear you. You may see them looking at you but they do not see.* (Verses 189-198)

This whole drive explains that once people start to adopt deviant ideas and move away from believing in, and worshipping God alone, their foolishness and deviation will know no limit, and they can no longer think and reflect properly. We see how deviation that starts on a small scale takes people far away from the truth of the right path.

It is He who has created you all from a single soul, and out of it brought into being its mate, so that he might incline with love towards her. When he has consorted with her, she conceives a light burden, which she carries with ease. Then, when she grows heavy, they both appeal to God, their Lord: "Grant us a goodly child and we will be truly grateful." (Verse 189)

It is the pure nature with which all human beings are born. By nature, they turn to God, acknowledging that He is their only Lord, in situations of fear and hope alike. The example given here for human nature begins with the origin of creation and the make-up of couples and families: *"It is He who has created you all from a single soul, and out of it brought into being its mate, so that he might incline with love towards her."* (Verse 189)

It is thus a single soul and a single nature, although it has different functions for the male and the female. These differences also serve as a means to make a man incline with love towards his wife and find comfort with her. This is the Islamic outlook on the nature of man and the role of marriage. It is a complete, integrated and honest outlook stated by this religion over fourteen centuries ago when other religions that had deviated from the right path used to consider the woman as the root of human misery. She was looked on as a curse, an impurity and a tool for seduction that man should guard against as much as he could. Pagan beliefs continue even today to consider the woman as little more than an article at home, or, at best, a servant who is not to be given any status at all.

The original purpose of the meeting of a human couple is to provide love, comfort, and a settled happy life, which provides an ideal setting for the rearing of young children. It is in such a happy and loving environment that a new human generation is prepared to take over the task of promoting and adding to human civilization. The meeting of a human couple is not meant only to satisfy a fleeting desire or give a temporary pleasure. Nor is it made the basis of a quarrel, or a stage for a conflict between rules and specializations, or for a duplication of such rules and specializations. Ignorant communities, past and contemporary, have often fallen into such traps.

The story then begins, right at the first stage: *"When he has consorted with her, she conceives a light burden, which she carries with ease."* (Verse 189) The Qur'ān employs a highly refined expression, particularly in the Arabic text, when it describes the initial relationship between a married couple, "*When he has consorted with her.*" It selects such fine expressions to provide, and to impart refinement to the meeting itself so that it is not felt as merely physical. This gives human beings an impression that their approach to their physical desire has a human element that distinguishes it from the rough and physical form of animals. Conception is described as "light" in its initial stage, when a mother carries it with ease, practically unnoticed.

The second stage is then described: "*Then, when she grows heavy, they both appeal to God, their Lord: 'Grant us a goodly child and we will be truly grateful.'*" (Verse 189) Now that the pregnancy is ascertained, it gives great hopes to the parents-to-be. They now pin their hopes that the newborn will be healthy, pretty, cute, etc., bringing into reality all that parents wish to have in their children when they are still in the embrionic stage. With such hopes, pure human nature is awakened, and it turns to God acknowledging that He is the only Lord, and appealing to Him to bestow His grace. This they do because they truly feel that God is indeed the only source of strength, blessings and grace in the whole universe. Hence, they make their heartfelt appeal "*to God, their Lord: 'Grant Us a goodly child and we will be truly grateful.'*" (Verse 189)

Sophisticated Paganism

"*Yet when He has granted them a goodly child, they associate with Him partners, particularly in respect of what He has granted them. Exalted is God above anything people may associate with Him as partners.*" (Verse 190) Some reports mentioned in commentaries on the Qur'ān suggest that this is a true story that occurred to Adam and Eve, whose children used to be deformed when born. Satan came to them and persuaded Eve to call the child she was carrying 'Abd al-Ḥārith, when al-Ḥārith was the name of Satan himself. He told her that she would then ensure that her child would be healthy and would survive. She did so, persuading Adam to agree with her. Needless to say, this report can only have an Israelite origin. Distorted Jewish and Christian concepts blame Eve for all human error. This is contrary to the correct Islamic concept.

We have no need for such Israelite reports to interpret this Qur'ānic statement. The Qur'ānic account describes the stages of deviation in human beings. The idolaters at the time of the Prophet Muḥammad (peace be upon him), and prior to his time, used to pledge their children to serve their deities or be servants in temples and houses of worship. They did so in order to gain favour with God. Although at the beginning they used to turn to God alone, they then deflected from the summit of believing in God's oneness and fell into the depths of abject idolatry. In their error, they used to pledge their children to such idols and deities, hoping that by doing so their children would have a healthy life and would be protected against dangers. It is the same as some people do today when they make pledges to saints dedicating to them certain parts of their children's bodies. Some people may keep a boy's hair to grow, pledging that his first hair cut will be undertaken at the tomb or shrine of a saint, or they keep the boy uncircumcised until his circumcision is undertaken at such a tomb or shrine. Yet these people acknowledge that God is one, but follow this acknowledgement with such idolatrous practices. Human beings remain the same. "*Exalted is God above anything people may associate with Him as partners.*" (Verse 190) Rejected is all the idolatry they believe and practise.

Today we see various aspects of idolatry practised by people who claim to believe in God's oneness and say that they submit to Him. These practices provide an example of the stages of paganism depicted in the Qur'ānic verses. Today, people glorify certain gods which they may call, 'the nation', or 'the motherland', or 'the people', or a host of other names. These are no more than unshaped idols similar to the stupid forms of idols the pagans of old had. They are deities assigned a share of God's creation and to which children are pledged in the same way as they were pledged to the old idols. Sacrifices are offered to these deities on a wide scale in the same way as sacrifices used to be offered in temples.

People acknowledge God as their Lord; it is true. But they then abandon His commandments and His laws while they consider the orders and requirements of their own idols and deities as sacred. For the implementation of the latter, God's laws are contravened, and even totally disregarded. If such practices of later day *jāhiliyyah* are not to be considered as paganism, then what does constitute paganism? How are deities adopted? And how are they given a portion of people's children? Indeed, ancient paganism used to be even more polite with God. It used to acknowledge certain deities to which offerings of children, crops, fruits and sacrifices were made only as a means for them to draw closer to God. Today's *jāhiliyyah* considers the orders of its deities as having greater priority than what God commands. Indeed, it abandons His commandments altogether.

We deceive ourselves when we limit paganism to the stupid old form of having idols and statues, treating them as deities, and to the practices of worship which people used to offer to those deities, appealing to them for support. It is only the shape and form of deities and paganism that has changed, and practices of worship that have become more sophisticated, offered under different headings. The essence of paganism remains the same behind all these. We must not lose sight of this fact.

God – limitless is He in His glory – issues a clear commandment that human beings should observe chastity, dress modestly and lead a virtuous life. But the 'motherland' or 'productivity' requires women to go out revealing their beauty, all made up, and to work as hostesses in hotels in a way that is not much different from that of the geisha girls in pagan Japan. Which deity's orders are those people following? Are they abiding by God's commandments? Or by those of their false deities? God – most exalted is He – commands that people should come together with the bond of faith forming the basis of their community. But 'nationalism' or 'the motherland' orders that religion be totally disregarded and replaced by ties of race and nation. Do people then follow God's orders or those of the partners they associate with Him? Similarly, God orders that His law should be implemented, but a single human being, or a group of people reject this and claim that human beings have the authority to legislate and whatever laws they enact must be implemented. Which orders then should people follow: those of God or those of their false deities?

All these are but examples of what takes place today the whole world over. These examples show the true nature of the prevailing paganism and the nature of the idols that are worshipped in place of the old idols and statues in the old pagan days. We must never allow changing shapes and practices to blind us to the true nature of idolatry and *jāhiliyyah*.

The Qur'ān argues with those who advocated the earlier form of naïve paganism and clear ignorance. It addresses their minds so that they can abandon unbecoming naïvety and wake up to the truth. It comments on that form of *jāhiliyyah* and how paganism creeps into human beings by saying: "*Do they associate with Him those that can create nothing, while they themselves have been created, and neither can they give them any support nor can they even help themselves.*" (Verses 191-192)

It is only the Creator who deserves to be worshipped. The partners they associate with God can create nothing. Indeed, they themselves are created. How can they be raised to the status of deities? How come they assign to those deities a portion of themselves and their children? Power and authority are amongst the most essential attributes of Godhead. The One who can support His servants and protect them with His power is the One who deserves to be worshipped. All their alleged deities are powerless and without authority. How can they give them support when they cannot even help themselves? How are they to be treated as partners with God?

Hence, humanity today stands in the same old position and needs to be addressed by the Qur'ān anew. It needs someone to rescue it from its new *jāhiliyyah*, and present Islam to it; someone to take it from darkness into light and to save its hearts and minds from the new paganism and idolatry. This religion saved it the first time and it can certainly save it from the new folly into which it has sunk.

The way this Qur'ānic verse is phrased suggests that it also serves as a strong reproach to them for having adopted human deities: "*Do they associate with Him those that can create nothing, while they themselves have been created, and neither can they give them any support nor can they even help themselves.*" (Verses 191-192)

The Arabic text uses the plural form that refers only to a group which includes human beings. This suggests that there are some human beings who are considered or treated as gods. It has never been suggested that, in their pagan days, the Arabs used to have human deities whom they treated as gods or to whom they offered worship. They only gave them the position of deities in the sense that they accepted the social laws they had enacted for them and accepted their arbitration in their own quarrels, which meant that they gave them the status of Godhead. The Qur'ān refers to all this as associating partners with God. It equates it with idolatry that offers worship to statues and idols. Indeed, Islam treats both forms of paganism in the same way, just as the Qur'ān considers those who accepted the laws and verdicts given to them by rabbis and priests as polytheists, associating partners with God. They definitely did not believe that those rabbis and priests were gods or deities, and they did not offer any act of worship to them. Nevertheless, all such attitudes deviate from the concept of God's oneness, which is the cornerstone of the divine faith. That concept takes its clearest form in the declaration that "there is no deity other than God." This endorses what we have already stated, that the new forms of *jāhiliyyah* are just as idolatrous as its old form.

A Call Foolishly Turned Down

The reference in the Qur'ān to deviation from the truth starting within the human soul as represented in the story of a married couple and the birth of their baby, applies to every form of polytheism and idolatry. It is intended to alert those who are to be addressed by the Qur'ān to the absolute folly of their idolatry that leads them to believe in those deities, which can neither create anything nor support their worshippers. They are indeed created; and they are powerless, unable to help themselves. This is their state whether they are human beings or of any other type. None of them can create or provide help. Now the *sūrah* changes the mode of relating a story in order to adopt a style that fits a direct confrontation with the pagan Arabs, but it continues the previous address.

> If you call them to guidance they will not follow you. It is all the same whether you call them or keep silent. Those whom you invoke beside God are God's servants, just like you. Invoke them, then, and let them answer you, if what you claim is true. Have they, perchance, feet on which they could walk, or hands with which to grasp things, or eyes with which to see, or ears with which to hear? (Verses 193-195)

Arab paganism was, as we have already explained, too foolish by the standards of any stage of the human intellect. Hence, the Qur'ān tries to alert the Arabs' minds to their folly as they ascribed divinity to such deities. Those idols did not have feet with which to walk, hands with which to grasp, eyes with which to see, or ears with which to hear. Yet they themselves had these senses. How could they then worship statues made of stone that could not even do the things they themselves could do? Sometimes they considered these idols as symbols of the angels or of their own forefathers. Yet these were creatures like themselves who could not create anything or give support to anyone, because they themselves are created and cannot help themselves.

There was this apparent element of applying double standards in the beliefs of the pagan Arabs, vacillating between the physical idols and what they symbolized. We assume that this is the reason for the frequent change in the Qur'ānic address as it refers sometimes to these idols using the animate pronoun to point to the symbols behind them, and at others using the pronoun for inanimate objects to denote that the idols themselves are lifeless. Yet the whole concept of idolatry is apparently false by the pure standards of the simple human mind. Hence, the Qur'ān alerts our minds to the need to steer away from this unbecoming lack of awareness.

At the end of this argument, God directs His Messenger to challenge them together with all their powerless deities, and to declare his clear faith, acknowledging the patronage of God alone: "*Say: Appeal to those you claim to be partners with God, and scheme against me, and give me no respite. My guardian is God who has bestowed this Book from on high. It is He who is the guardian of the righteous. Those whom you invoke beside Him cannot give you any support, nor can they even help themselves. If you pray to them for guidance, they will not hear you. You may see them looking at you but they do not see.*" (Verses 195-198)

This is the type of challenge, which an advocate of the true faith would throw to *jāhiliyyah*. God's Messenger (peace be upon him) said it exactly as his Lord directed him, and put the challenge to all his contemporary idolaters and their alleged deities: "*Appeal to those you claim to be partners with God, and scheme against me, and give me no respite.*" (Verse 195)

He invites them to muster all their scheming powers, and those of their deities, and to strike against him without waiting for a moment. As he threw out this challenge, he was fully confident, reassured that God would protect him against all their scheming: "*My guardian is God who has bestowed this Book from on high. It is He who is the guardian of the righteous.*" (Verse 196) He thus declares what sort of support He relies on. He simply trusts to God who has revealed the Book. By this revelation, God has indicated His will that His Messenger should confront people with the truth embodied in that Book, and that He has willed that this truth will triumph over all falsehood. He has also willed to protect his righteous servants who convey His message believing in its truthfulness.

The same challenge should be thrown down by every advocate of God's message who follows in the footsteps of God's Messenger (peace be upon him). It is the same challenge everywhere and at all times: "*Say: Appeal to those you claim to be partners with God, and scheme against me, and give me no respite. My guardian is God who has bestowed this Book from on high. It is He who is the guardian of the righteous."* (Verses 195-196) An advocate of the divine faith must not rely on any earthly power, instead he must rely only on God's power. This will enable him to rise above all earthly powers. These are certainly of no substance, no matter how strong they may appear at first sight: *"Mankind, an analogy is given here; so listen to it: Those whom you invoke instead of God will never create [as much as] a fly, even though they would join all their forces for the purpose. And if a fly robs them of anything, they cannot retrieve it. Weak indeed is the seeker, and weak the sought."* (22: 73) *"Those who take beings other than God for their protectors may be compared to the spider which makes for itself a house. Surely the frailest of all houses is that of the spider, if they could only understand this."* (29: 41)

Patronage That Never Fails

An advocate of the truth relies on God. What use can other forces and masters be to him? What respect do they command, even though they may be able to cause him harm? Such harm can only be caused with God's will, and God is his patron. It is not as though God was unable to protect him, or that God lets His servants down. Far be it from God to do so. But he permits this as a test and training to His servants, and also to lead the wrongdoers on, giving them their chance before He strikes at them with force.

Abū Bakr, the Prophet's closest companion, was subjected to much harm. The idolaters hit him in the face with their shoes, and directed their strikes at his eyes, so that when they left him, his eyes were indistinguishable from his mouth. Despite this wicked assault, he kept repeating: "My Lord, how forbearing You are! How great is Your forbearance!" Deep at heart, he realized what lay behind this attack on him and how forbearing God is. He was certain that God was fully able to destroy his enemies and that He would never let His good servants down.

'Abdullāh ibn Mas'ūd, one of the Prophet's companions, went close to the pagan Arabs when they were meeting in the Ka'bah and recited the Qur'ān aloud so that they could hear it. They attacked him so badly and left him unable to stand. After this attack, he said: "By God, I had no respect whatsoever for them then." He realized that they were standing in opposition to God Himself, and he knew that whoever does this is certain to be vanquished. Hence, they could earn no respect from the advocates of God's message.

Another of the Prophet's companions, 'Uthmān ibn Maẓ'ūn, felt it unbecoming for him, a believer, to be under the protection of an unbeliever, 'Utbah ibn Rabī'ah, when some of his own brethren were tortured for no reason other than faith. Therefore, he disclaimed 'Utbah's protection. Immediately, the idolaters gathered around him, causing him physical harm and badly injuring his eye. 'Utbah offered him his protection again, but he said to him: "I am under the protection of one who is much more powerful than you." 'Utbah said to him: "My nephew, you could have spared your eye all this harm." But 'Uthmām replied: "No. By God, my other eye is eager to have the same treatment in the service of God's cause." He was absolutely certain that the protection given him by God is much more effective than that offered by human beings. He knew that his Lord would not let him down. If He allowed him to be harmed in this manner, then it was only to help him rise to such a sublime standard that enabled him to say what he did about his other eye in so far as he was eager to make that a similar sacrifice for God's cause.

These were examples of that great generation which was brought up in line with the Qur'ānic teachings, under the guidance of Muḥammad, the Prophet (peace be upon him), who fully understood his Lord's instructions as He said to him: "*Say: Appeal to those you claim to be partners with God, and scheme against me, and give me no respite. My guardian is God who has bestowed this Book from on high. It is He who is the guardian of the righteous.*" (Verses 195-196)

What happened after they had willingly tolerated all this aggression from scheming idolaters? What happened to them when they sought only the shelter of God who revealed the Book, and who is the patron of the righteous? This is well known in history. The eventual triumph and power belonged to God's servants. Defeat and misery were the lot of the tyrants. Those of them who eventually responded positively to Islam joined the Muslim community where they had a lower position than those who were ahead of them in accepting the faith and who endured all hardship with a great trust in God. The advocates of the divine faith, wherever they may be and in whichever generation they may live, will not achieve anything unless they have such trust in God and such firm resolve to serve His cause: "*My guardian is God who has bestowed the Book from on high. It is He who is the guardian of the righteous.*" (Verse 196)

God's Messenger (peace be upon him) was commanded to challenge the idolaters, and he did so. He was ordered to explain to them the powerlessness of their deities and the folly of believing in such deities, and he acted on his instructions: "*Those whom you invoke beside Him cannot give you any support, nor can they even help themselves.*" (Verse 197) Just as this statement applied to the primitive form of idols the Arabs used to have in their ancient ignorant days, it applies in equal measure to all deities claimed by modern states of ignorance, or *jāhiliyyah*.

The advocates of neo-paganism address their appeals to those who have physical power on earth, taking them as patrons instead of God. But these patrons cannot offer them any support or even help themselves when God's will is done at its appointed time. If the primitive deities of the pagan Arabs could not hear, and their eyes were made of pearls or diamonds giving the appearance of looking without actually seeing, some of the new deities are also unable to see or hear. We need only to think of the motherland, nation, national production, machines and the inevitable process of history and the rest of the endless list of alleged deities to which new *jāhiliyyah* pay homage. Human beings who are given the status of Godhead in the form of the authority to enact ultimate legislation may have seeing and hearing senses, but even these do not actually hear or see. They are among those in reference to whom God says in the Qur'ān: "*We have destined for Hell many of the jinn and many human beings; they have hearts they cannot understand with, and they have eyes with which they fail to see, and ears with which they fail to hear. They are like cattle; indeed, they are even further away from the right way. They are the truly heedless.*" (Verse 179)

An advocate of the divine faith normally finds himself confronting one of the numerous forms of *jāhiliyyah*. He must always adopt the attitude God has instructed His Messenger (peace be upon him) to adopt. He should always be ready to declare: "*Appeal to those you claim to be partners with God, and scheme against me, and give me no respite. My guardian is God who has bestowed this Book from on high. It is He who is the guardian of the righteous. Those whom you invoke beside Him cannot give you any support, nor can they even help themselves. If you pray to them for guidance, they will not hear you. You may see them looking at you but they do not see.*" (Verses 195-198) Indeed they are the same everywhere, and at all times.

11

The Road to Mercy

Make due allowance for man's nature, and enjoin the doing of what is right; and turn away from those who choose to remain ignorant. (199)

خُذِ ٱلْعَفْوَ وَأْمُرْ بِٱلْعُرْفِ وَأَعْرِضْ عَنِ ٱلْجَٰهِلِينَ ۝

If a prompting from Satan stirs you up, seek refuge with God; He hears all and knows all. (200)

وَإِمَّا يَنزَغَنَّكَ مِنَ ٱلشَّيْطَٰنِ نَزْغٌ فَٱسْتَعِذْ بِٱللَّهِ إِنَّهُۥ سَمِيعٌ عَلِيمٌ ۝

If those who are God-fearing experience a tempting thought from Satan, they bethink themselves [of God]; and they begin to see things clearly. (201)

إِنَّ ٱلَّذِينَ ٱتَّقَوْاْ إِذَا مَسَّهُمْ طَٰٓئِفٌ مِّنَ ٱلشَّيْطَٰنِ تَذَكَّرُواْ فَإِذَا هُم مُّبْصِرُونَ ۝

Their [evil] brethren try to draw them into error with unceasing determination. (202)

وَإِخْوَٰنُهُمْ يَمُدُّونَهُمْ فِى ٱلْغَىِّ ثُمَّ لَا يُقْصِرُونَ ۝

When you do not bring them a sign, they say: "Why do you not seek to have one?" Say: "I only follow what is revealed to me by my Lord: this [revelation] is a means of clear insight from your Lord, and a guidance and grace for people who will believe." (203)

وَإِذَا لَمْ تَأْتِهِم بِـَٔايَةٍ قَالُواْ لَوْلَا ٱجْتَبَيْتَهَا قُلْ إِنَّمَآ أَتَّبِعُ مَا يُوحَىٰٓ إِلَىَّ مِن رَّبِّى هَٰذَا بَصَآئِرُ مِن رَّبِّكُمْ وَهُدًى وَرَحْمَةٌ لِّقَوْمٍ يُؤْمِنُونَ ۝

When the Qur'ān is recited, hearken to it, and listen in silence, so that you may be graced with God's mercy. (204)

وَإِذَا قُرِئَ ٱلْقُرْءَانُ فَٱسْتَمِعُوا۟ لَهُۥ وَأَنصِتُوا۟ لَعَلَّكُمْ تُرْحَمُونَ ﴿٢٠٤﴾

And bethink yourself of your Lord humbly and with awe, and without raising your voice, in the morning and evening; and do not be negligent. (205)

وَٱذْكُر رَّبَّكَ فِى نَفْسِكَ تَضَرُّعًا وَخِيفَةً وَدُونَ ٱلْجَهْرِ مِنَ ٱلْقَوْلِ بِٱلْغُدُوِّ وَٱلْءَاصَالِ وَلَا تَكُن مِّنَ ٱلْغَٰفِلِينَ ﴿٢٠٥﴾

Those who are near to your Lord are never too proud to worship Him. They extol His limitless glory, and before Him alone prostrate themselves. (206)

إِنَّ ٱلَّذِينَ عِندَ رَبِّكَ لَا يَسْتَكْبِرُونَ عَنْ عِبَادَتِهِۦ وَيُسَبِّحُونَهُۥ وَلَهُۥ يَسْجُدُونَ ﴿٢٠٦﴾

Preview

This last passage of the *sūrah* contains very important directives from God to those under His patronage, i.e. His Messenger and those who have accepted His message. They were still in Makkah, facing the onslaught of the ignorant society in Arabia, supported by ignorant, or *jāhiliyyah*, societies all over the world. These directives define the attitude of the believers in their confrontation with *jāhiliyyah* and human beings who have gone astray. God's Messenger (peace be upon him) is called upon to show forbearance and to encourage everything that simple human nature can recognize as good, without any need for complication or rigidity. He is further directed to turn away from the advocates of *jāhiliyyah* and not to engage in futile argument with them. If they go beyond the limits of reason, so as to infuriate him by their obstinate attitude, and Satan stirs up this anger further, then he should seek refuge with God who alone can give him reassurance: "*Make due allowance for man's nature, and enjoin the doing of what is right; and turn away from those who choose to remain ignorant. If a prompting from Satan stirs you up, seek refuge with God; He hears all and knows all. If those who are God-fearing experience a tempting thought from*

Satan, they bethink themselves [of God]; and they begin to see things clearly." (Verses 199-201)

He is then given clear information about the nature of those ignorant people and what prompts them to go further astray. A brief reference is made to their attitude to the Prophet and how they demand miracles from him. He is then given instructions on what to say to them so that they can understand the nature of the message and the Messenger, and his relationship with his Lord: "*Their [evil] brethren try to draw them into error with unceasing determination. When you do not bring them a sign, they say: 'Why do you not seek to have one?' Say: I only follow what is revealed to me by my Lord: this [revelation] is a means of clear insight from your Lord, and a guidance and grace for people who will believe.*" (Verses 202-203)

With this reference to the Qur'ānic revelations vouchsafed to the Prophet, the believers are given relevant instructions on how to listen to the Qur'ān and the proper attitude to adopt when they remember their Lord, as they should always do. The angels who do not commit any sin are always glorifying God and prostrating themselves to Him. Human beings who are liable to slip and commit sins have better reasons to be always in remembrance of God, and to glorify Him and prostrate themselves to Him: "*When the Qur'ān is recited, hearken to it, and listen in silence, so that you may be graced with God's mercy. And bethink yourself of your Lord humbly and with awe, and without raising your voice, in the morning and evening; and do not be negligent. Those who are near to your Lord are never too proud to worship Him. They extol His limitless glory, and before Him alone prostrate themselves.*" (Verses 204-206)

When and Where to Seek Refuge

Make due allowance for man's nature, and enjoin the doing of what is right; and turn away from those who choose to remain ignorant. If a prompting from Satan stirs you up, seek refuge with God; He hears all and knows all. If those who are God-fearing experience a tempting thought from Satan, they bethink themselves [of God]; and they begin to see things clearly. (Verses 199-201)

The first directive given in this passage is to make allowances for the weaknesses of human beings and accept what is decent and easy from them. The Prophet is instructed not to require perfection or expect a very high standard of morality. He should overlook their shortfalls and weaknesses. But all that applies in personal matters, not in questions of faith or religious duties. There can be no overlooking of the essentials of faith or Islamic law. Forbearance can apply in business and personal dealings. Such forbearance is the appropriate attitude to be shown by those who are strong towards people who are weak. God's Messenger (peace be upon him) is a guide and a teacher. Hence, forbearance and forgiveness are appropriate qualities for him. Indeed, these were distinctive qualities of the Prophet Muḥammad. He never showed anger over personal matters. But if something related to the faith made him angry, then his anger was feared by all. All advocates of the divine faith are required to follow the Prophet's suit. An advocate of the divine message, who inevitably deals with human beings, must be kind and easy, but without being negligent.

"*Enjoin the doing of what is right.*" (Verse 199) This order applies to everything that is clearly good and generally accepted as such by honest people with sound, uncorrupted nature. When people get used to doing what is good, they become ready to do it voluntarily, feeling that it is no burden. Nothing stops people from doing what is good like rigidity and complication particularly in the early days of being aware of their religious duties. In the early stages, they should be given duties that are easy and common to all so that they get used to responding properly. This enables people to get ready for what requires more effort and approach it without difficulty.

"*And turn away from those who choose to remain ignorant.*" (Verse 199) As used here, ignorance may be understood as the opposite of wisdom, or the opposite of knowledge. Both meanings are closely related. Turning away from them is just to ignore them and show how petty all their ignorant actions are. One must not enter into any argument with them because that is a waste of time. Ignoring them altogether may get them to revise their attitude and soften their hearts. Argument, on the other hand, may lead to polarization and stubbornness. Even if it does not soften their hearts, they remain isolated from anyone who is good at heart. The latter will realize that the advocates of the divine message are forbearing, unwilling to enter into a slanging match while ignorant people continue with their stupid attitude. Every advocate of faith should realize the importance of this divine directive, because God knows what influences people and what may get through to them.

But God's Messenger is a human being. He may be infuriated by people's ignorance and stupidity. If he can deal with such a situation, it may be too much for his followers. When a person is too angry, Satan might find a chance to stir him up. In such a situation, he is commanded to seek refuge with God so that he will cool down and forestall Satan's design: "*If a prompting from Satan stirs you up, seek refuge with God; He hears all and knows all.*" (Verse 200) This final remark states that God hears whatever the ignorant people say and all the stupidities they may utter, and He knows what the advocates of the faith may experience as a result. That should be enough to set people's hearts at ease. It is sufficient that God hears all and knows all. When we know that God is aware of everything that happens to us, what else do we need?

The *sūrah* takes a different approach in order to emphasize to the advocates of faith that they should face all situations with resigned acceptance, and they should remember God when they are angry so that Satan will not be able to get the better of them: "*If those who are God-fearing experience a tempting thought from Satan, they bethink themselves [of God]; and they begin to see things clearly.*" (Verse 201)

This short verse is highly inspiring, pointing out some profound facts within the human soul. This is made possible only through the unique Qur'ānic style. The way the verse is concluded adds new meanings to its beginning, which are not indicated by the opening words. The conclusion, "*and they begin to see things clearly,*" suggests that Satan's thoughts can cause people to be blind, unable to see anything clearly. But fearing God and guarding against incurring His anger keeps hearts alert and reminds them of God's guidance. When they are so reminded, they begin to see things clearly. A tempting thought from Satan is, then, a cause of blindness while the remembrance of God is a cause of opening eyes and hearts. Satan's thoughts send people into darkness and turning to God gives them light. When people equip themselves with following divine guidance, Satan can have no power over them.

The Means for Clear Insight

The God-fearing, then, remind themselves of God whenever they experience an evil thought that may tempt them away from the right path. But this is given as a side issue that intervenes between the divine order to the Prophet to turn away from ignorant people and an explanation of who and what motivates them to adopt ignorance which determines all their behaviour. When the attitude of the God-fearing has been explained, the *sūrah* goes back to explaining the motivation of the ignorant: "*Their [evil] brethren try to draw them into error with unceasing determination. When you do not bring them a sign, they say: 'Why do you not seek to have one?' Say: I only follow what is revealed to me by my Lord: this [revelation] is a means of clear insight from your Lord, and a guidance and grace for people who will believe.*" (Verses 202-203)

Their brethren who try to sink them deeper into error are the satans from among the *jinn*. They may well be the satans of human beings as well. These satans never tire of driving them deeper into error. Hence they continue to act in folly, unaware of where they are being led.

The unbelievers were very persistent in demanding miracles from God's Messenger (peace be upon him). The *sūrah* quotes here some of their statements that betray their ignorance of the nature of God's message and the role of His Messenger: "*When you do not bring them a sign, they say: 'Why do you not seek to have one?'*" (Verse 203) They suggest to the Prophet that he should pray to God to give them a miracle, or they even suggest to him that he himself should perform a miracle. To them, he should be able to do so, since he claims to be a Prophet. This shows that they do not understand the Prophet's role. They certainly could not appreciate his humble attitude towards his Lord, nor that he only takes what God gives him. He does not suggest approaches or measures to his Lord, nor does he initiate matters at his own behest. God orders him to explain this to them: "*Say: I only follow what is revealed to me by my Lord.*" (Verse 203) I am not one to suggest to Him or to invent matters. I only have what is revealed to me, and I only do what I am commanded. For their part, they could only think of those impostors who claimed to be prophets in every period of ignorance. Hence, their demands.

The Prophet is also commanded to explain to them the nature of the Qur'ān that has been revealed to him. If they would only consider the plain guidance that is contained in the Qur'ān, they would certainly stop making foolish requests for signs and miracles: "*This [revelation] is a means of clear insight from your Lord, and a guidance and grace for people who will believe.*" (Verse 203) It provides clear insight and it is an aspect of overflowing blessings and grace. But that is the case only for those who believe and avail themselves of its unending blessing.

In their ignorance, the Arabs at the time of the Prophet turned away from the Qur'ān and sought to have a physical miracle like the ones given to earlier prophets. Those earlier prophets preached the divine message when humanity was still in its infancy, and were sent to certain communities, not to mankind as a whole. Their miracles could serve their purpose only at the time and place they were given, and could be appreciated only by those who witnessed them. What can be said about later generations and nations?

No physical miracle can be as superb or miraculous as the Qur'ān, no matter what type of miracle people required. Besides, it gives its message to all mankind in all generations till the end of time.

Given the importance the Arabs attached to fine, literary style, which was a source of pride for them, the artistic expression of the Qur'ān was perhaps the most immediately apparent aspect of its miraculous nature. But the Qur'ān remains a book of surpassing excellence, posing a challenge that defies human ability. God challenged the Arabs then, and the challenge continues today, to produce anything similar to it. Human beings who have the gift of fine expression and appreciate the depth of human ability in this field are the ones who can best recognize that the Qur'ānic style is uniquely superb, refined, outstanding. This applies to all people with a natural taste for fine speech, whether they believe in Islam or not. The challenge is based on objective criteria that challenge believers and unbelievers alike. In their ignorance, the elders of the Quraysh found themselves utterly powerless when faced with the Qur'ān. They hated such a position but they could not help it. The same thing is experienced today and will continue to be experienced by everyone who adopts the same attitude.

Beyond that great secret of this unique book and its excellence, there remains its overpowering attraction to human nature, once it is allowed to put its address freely to people. Even those who are hardened in their opposition to the Qur'ān often find its logic too powerful. They cannot but recognize its truth when they listen to it.

Many are those who speak out with eloquence. They may express principles, doctrines, ideas and philosophies of all sorts. But the Qur'ān has a unique and overpowering appeal to human nature in everything that it says. The elders of the Quraysh used to say to their followers, and indeed to themselves: "*Do not listen to this Qur'ān, but cut short its reciting with booing and laughter, so that you may gain the upper hand."* (41: 26) They did so because they felt that the Qur'ānic logic was irresistible. Many of those in power today try to turn people away from the Qur'ān, offering them instead their own ideas. But in spite of all this, the Qur'ān remains overpowering. Whenever a verse or passage of the Qur'ān is quoted in the context of human speech, it stands out by its rhythm and logic, appealing directly to the hearts of its audience. The rest of human speech that might have been finely composed seems, by comparison, of little use.

But beyond all this, the subject matter of the Qur'ān remains its outstanding strength. A few pages in this book cannot aspire to give justice to explaining the subject matter of the Qur'ān. Whatever we may say here is too little. Besides, how much can we say in a few pages? We can possibly give a brief outline, but a fair treatment takes volumes.

The Undeniable Appeal of the Qur'ān

The fact is that the Qur'ān has a remarkable method in presenting the truth of existence to human nature. It appeals to it as a whole, yet it addresses every one of its aspects in every single context. It goes through every opening in human nature, deals with all its thoughts and feelings. The Qur'ānic method is also remarkable as it tackles the main issues of existence, revealing certain aspects of it which are readily acknowledged both by human nature and the human intellect. They respond to these and formulate their clear vision on them. It also answers the needs of human nature, releases its potentials and puts it on the right course.

We cannot but marvel at the unique Qur'ānic approach as it takes human nature by the hand and moves up with it gently, step by step, yet with much energy and clarity of vision. It takes it to a sublime height, giving it true knowledge, definite response, firm reassurance, consistency of action and a clear and relaxed awareness of the fundamental truths of existence.

The Qur'ānic approach is unparalleled as it appeals to human nature from angles where no response could have been imagined to come. Yet we find human nature ready with its positive response. The fact is the One who has revealed the Qur'ān is the Creator of man who knows His creation. He is closer to man than his jugular vein.

So far for the approach, but what about the subject matter the Qur'ān tackles? Here we find ourselves looking at an expanse that no words can adequately describe: "*Say: If the sea were ink for my Lord's words, the sea would surely dry up before my Lord's words are exhausted, even though we were to add to it another sea to replenish it.*" (18: 109) "*If all the trees on earth were pens, and the sea were ink, with seven more seas yet added to it, the words of God would not be exhausted. God is almighty, wise.*" (31: 27)

The present author spent, by God's grace, twenty-five years with this Book as his companion, studying carefully the fundamental facts it addresses and the way it tackles various aspects of human knowledge. He has been reading at the same time what human beings have attempted to reveal in some of these aspects. He could see the great wealth and openness of the Qur'ān compared to the attempts of human beings. Compared to the great ocean of the Qur'ān, these attempts are no more than small, isolated lakes, tiny pools or even stagnant pits.

Take, if you will, the Qur'ān's holistic approach to existence, its nature, truth, aspects, origin, secrets and hidden things, as well as what it contains of living entities and potential life. Human philosophy tackles some of these aspects.

Reflect also on how the Qur'ān takes man as a complete entity, and explains his origin, potentials, fields of action, moulding, reactions and responses, as well as his different modes and inner self. Biology, psychology, sociology, education and religious studies address certain aspects of these. Consider also the unique Qur'ānic approach to the system of human life, its practical activities, areas of collaboration, renewed human needs and how these should be organized. Social, economic and political theories and doctrines may address some of these.

In all these areas a careful student of the Qur'ān is bound to find an amazing wealth of statements and directives that are comprehensive, profound, rich and truthful. Not once did I find myself in need of a single statement from outside the Qur'ān, concerning any of these fundamental issues, with the exception of God's Messenger's *ḥadīths*. These may be collectively described as an explanatory memorandum of the Qur'ān. Indeed, no other statement, correct though it may be, will appear of much value compared to what a careful student finds in this remarkable book. This is due to the practical nature of these statements. It is also the result of long reflection on, and study of, how these topics are tackled. Yet I am not attempting to praise this book. Who am I, and who are human beings to add anything to God's book by their praise?

This book, the Qur'ān, was the source of knowledge, education and proper moulding of a unique generation of human beings that was never repeated in human history. That was the generation of the Prophet's companions who brought about a greatly profound development in human history that has not yet been properly studied. This Book was responsible, by God's will, for this great miracle in human history. All supernatural miracles that testified to earlier divine messages appear small in comparison to this miracle that was practised in a human society. Indeed, that generation was an unparalleled historic phenomenon.

The society that was formed for the first time by their generation survived for more than one thousand years. It was governed by the law stated in this book and firmly based on its standards, values and directives. That very society was a human miracle. We have only to compare it to other human societies which, as a result of human material progress, surpassed it in material abilities, but could not come near to it in human civilization.

Nowadays, in modern *jāhiliyyah* societies, people seek to satisfy their own needs as well as the needs of their communities in isolation of the Qur'ān. People in ignorant Arabia used to require miracles other than the Qur'ān. Their naïve outlook, profound ignorance and their various interests prevented the old Arabs from appreciating the great miracle represented by this remarkable book. The people of contemporary *jāhiliyyah* have different obstacles preventing them from appreciating the miracle of the Qur'ān. These include the arrogance derived from their superior material knowledge, their sophisticated organization of human life, its apparent progress and maturity, which all come naturally with the accumulation of experience of one generation after another and with more complex and sophisticated needs. But they are also prevented from appreciating the Qur'ān by the die-hard Zionist and imperialist opposition that has continued to scheme and plot against this faith and its revealed message for fourteen centuries. They continue with their unceasing attempts to divert Muslims away from the Qur'ān and its directives. This is because the Zionists and the imperialists have learnt through long experience that they cannot be a match for the Muslims as long as they adhere to the Qur'ān in the same way as the first generation of Muslims did. It is not sufficient that Muslims continue to pay lip service to the Qur'ān while they conduct their lives in a fashion that is in conflict with it.

Such scheming continues today with more resolve and wickedness. The final outcome of this scheming is the sort of societies in which people who claim to be Muslims live today, when they cannot be truly Muslims unless they implement Islamic law. We see the outcome of this scheming in various attempts all over the world to remove every trace of Islam, putting in place of the Qur'ān some other sort of constitution, giving it the status of ultimate arbiter in all disputes and on all issues of life. True Muslims refer only to God's book in all such matters.

The Qur'ān is ignored today by its people who know it only as hymns to be chanted and charms to be worn. They have been diverted away from it for centuries and driven deep into a state of *jāhiliyyah* that corrupts minds and hearts. The people of old *jāhiliyyah* used to divert the masses away from the Qur'ān, demanding physical miracles. The people of modern *jāhiliyyah* try to divert the masses away from the Qur'ān by putting in its place a false bible which they promote through all mass media and information channels. Yet it is the Qur'ān that is described in these words by God who knows all: "*This [revelation] is a means of clear insight from your Lord, and a guidance and grace for people who will believe.*" (Verse 203) It is then a means of clear insight, providing true guidance and abounding grace and blessings for true believers. It is only those who truly believe that find all this in the Qur'ān.

Mercy Through Listening to the Qur'ān

Because the Qur'ān is such, the believers are given an express directive: "*When the Qur'ān is recited, hearken to it, and listen in silence, so that you may be graced with God's mercy.*" (Verse 204) This verse comes towards the end of the *sūrah* which begins with a clear reference to the Qur'ān: "*This is a book that has been bestowed on you from on high – so do not entertain any doubt about it – in order that you may warn people with its message, and admonish the believers.*" (Verse 2)

There are various reports suggesting different situations when the order applies to listen attentively and in silence to Qur'ānic recitation. Some scholars are of the view that it applies in obligatory prayer when the imām reads aloud. An authentic *hadīth* related by Imām Aḥmad as well as Abū Dāwūd, al-Tirmidhī, al-Nasā'ī and Ibn Mājah mentions a report by Abū Hurayrah that one day, on finishing a prayer in which he recited aloud, the Prophet said: "Has any of you read something of the Qur'ān while I was reading?" A man said: "Yes, Messenger of God!" The Prophet said: "I was wondering why the Qur'ān was being pulled away from me." From that day, people stopped reading the Qur'ān in prayer when the Prophet was reading aloud. Another report mentions that 'Abdullāh ibn Mas'ūd, a leading scholar among the Prophet's companions, was praying when he heard some people in the congregation reading the Qur'ān with the imām. When he finished, he said: "When will you understand? When will you use your reason? You must do as God has commanded you: *When the Qur'ān is recited, hearken to it and listen in silence.*" (Verse 204)

Other scholars say that this was a directive to the Muslims so that they do not do like the unbelievers who used to come to the Prophet when he stood for prayer and would say to one another in Makkah: "*Do not listen to this Qur'ān. Cut short its recital with booing and laughter, so that you may gain the upper hand.*" (41: 26) In reply to them, God revealed this verse: "*When the Qur'an is recited hearken to it and listen in silence.*" (Verse 204) Al-Qurṭubī mentions this and says that it was revealed in relation to prayer.

Another reason for revealing this verse is mentioned by Ibn Jarīr al-Ṭabarī who quotes 'Abdullāh ibn Mas'ūd as saying: "Some of us used to greet others in prayer, but then the Qur'ānic verse was revealed which says, "*When the Qur'ān is recited, hearken to it, and listen in silence, so that you may be graced with God's mercy.*" In his commentary on the Qur'ān, al-Qurṭubī mentions a report by Muḥammad ibn Ka'b al-Quraẓī who says, "When God's Messenger used to read the Qur'ān aloud in prayer, those in the congregation read with him. When he said, 'In the name of God, the Merciful, the Beneficent,' they would say likewise, until he finished reading the Fātiḥah and another *sūrah*. The situation continued like that for some time until the verse was revealed which says, "*When the Qur'ān is recited, hearken to it, and listen in silence, so that you may be graced with God's mercy.*" This suggests that the order to listen attentively to the Qur'ān means to stop reading it aloud with the Prophet when he recited it in prayer.

Al-Qurṭubī also mentions a report by Qatādah concerning this verse, which says: "A man may come when a prayer is in progress and ask people in the congregation: 'How many *rak'ahs* have you completed? How many are left?' Then God revealed this verse: '*When the Qur'ān is recited, hearken to it, and listen in silence, so that you may be graced with God's mercy.*'" Mujāhid also mentions that they used to speak in prayer, and then God ordered them to listen so that they may be graced with mercy.

Those who consider this verse to apply only to recitation in prayer quote a report mentioned by al-Ṭabarī which mentions that a man named Ṭalḥah saw 'Aṭā' ibn Abī Rabāḥ, a leading scholar, talking to 'Ubayd ibn 'Umayr when a man was reading the Qur'ān. Ṭalḥah said to them: "should you not be listening to the recitation so that you receive what has been promised? (i.e. referring to God's mercy which is promised to those who listen attentively to the Qur'ān). They looked at me, and continued their conversation. I repeated what I said, and they looked at me and said: that relates to prayer." In his commentary on the Qur'ān, Ibn Kathīr also mentions that Sufyān al-Thawrī, a leading scholar of the early period of Islam, also mentions that this verse applies to prayer only. Several scholars are of the view that if a man is reading the Qur'ān in any situation other than prayer, then people may speak if they wish.

Other scholars, such as Sa'īd ibn Jubayr, 'Amr ibn Dīnār, Yazīd ibn Aslam and 'Abdullāh ibn al-Mubārak suggest that the Qur'ānic verse applies to recitation in prayer and in sermons that are given on Fridays and on weekdays. Al-Qurṭubī says that such a suggestion "is not practically sound, because the Qur'ān constitutes only a small portion of such sermons, when people are required to listen to all the sermon. Besides, this verse is a Makkan revelation, when there was no sermon or Friday prayer held in Makkah."

Al-Qurṭubī mentions in his commentary on the Qur'ān a report by al-Naqqāsh who says: all commentators on the Qur'ān are unanimous that listening attentively to the Qur'ān in obligatory and voluntary prayer is a binding duty. Al-Naḥḥās says: from the linguistic point of view, this attentive listening must apply in all situations, unless we have cause to believe that it is restricted.

For our part, we do not feel that any of the causes for the revelation of this verse restricts it to recitation in prayer, whether obligatory or voluntary. The verse mentions a general statement that need not be restricted by the cause of its revelation. It is more appropriate to say that this is a general statement, unrestricted in application. Whenever the Qur'ān is recited, listening attentively to it is the proper course of action, because it demonstrates people's respect of the Qur'ān, the word of God the Almighty. When God speaks, it behoves human beings to listen attentively. Besides, this listening is in the hope of being graced with mercy. What restricts that to prayer only? Whenever the Qur'ān is recited, and people listen attentively to it, they may understand and respond to it. This puts them in a position which may bring them mercy in this life and in the life to come as well.

People incur a great loss that cannot be compensated when they turn away from the Qur'ān. At times, listening to one verse of the Qur'ān brings about remarkable interaction, response, clear insight, appreciation, reassurance together with an enlightened understanding that can only be appreciated by a person who has had a similar experience. When the Qur'ān is listened to carefully, not merely heard for enchantment and pleasure by its recitation, it provides the listener with a clear, penetrative insight, reassurance, knowledge, energy and a firmly positive attitude that cannot be produced by any other means.

To view the fundamental facts of existence and the basic realities of life, through the Qur'ānic description, and to view human life itself, its nature and needs, through Qur'ānic statements, is of immense value. It provides clear and accurate insight that helps man to approach life in a totally different spirit from that provided by all human philosophies and doctrines. All that invites God's mercy. It can take place in prayer and in other situations as well. We do not find any reason to restrict this general Qur'ānic directive to prayer only, as mentioned by al-Qurṭubī and others.

Staying Permanently Close to God

The *sūrah* then gives a final directive: "*And bethink yourself of your Lord humbly and with awe, and without raising your voice, in the morning and evening; and do not be negligent. Those who are near to your Lord are never too proud to worship Him. They extol His limitless glory, and before Him alone prostrate themselves.*" (Verses 205-206)

In his commentary on the Qur'ān, the famous scholar, Ibn Kathīr says: "God gives this general order that we should remember Him often at the beginning and end of each day, just as He ordered that we should worship Him at these two times, when He says: '*Extol your Lord's limitless glory and praise before the rising of the sun and before its setting.*' (50: 39) This used to be the case before the daily prayers were made obligatory during the Prophet's night journey." This present verse was revealed in Makkah. Here God says that we should remember Him *'in the morning and evening'*, and this should be done humbly, and with awe, without raising our voices; this is the best way to remember God, not to address Him loudly. The Prophet's companions asked him: "Is our Lord near to be addressed softly, or distant so that we should appeal to Him aloud?" In reply God revealed the Qur'ānic verse: "*When My servants ask you about Me, well, I am near. I answer the prayer of the supplicant when he calls to Me.*" (2: 186) Both al-Bukhārī and Muslim relate in their *Ṣaḥīḥ* collections on the authority of Abū Mūsā al-Ash'arī: "Once on a journey, people raised their voices when they made their supplication. The Prophet (peace be upon him) said to them: 'People, watch what you do. You are appealing to someone who is neither deaf nor far away. The One whom you are calling hears all that is said, and He is close at hand. Indeed, He is closer to each one of you than the neck of his camel.'"

Ibn Kathīr does not accept the interpretation of Ibn Jarīr al-Ṭabarī and others who say that this statement is an order to anyone who is listening to the Qur'ān to remember God in this particular fashion. He says that this view has not been endorsed. What is meant here is to emphasize the importance of people remembering God at all times, particularly in the morning and evening, so that they may not be among the negligent. The angels are praised because they glorify God at all times, without hesitation or slackening. Hence, they are described here as follows: "*Those who are near to your Lord are never too proud to worship Him. They extol His limitless glory, and before Him alone prostrate themselves.*" (Verse 206) Their action is praised here so that people can follow their suit in their worship and obedience of God.

We feel that what Ibn Kathīr says and the *ḥadīths* he quotes show how the Qur'ān and the Prophet's guidance were able to give the Arabs true knowledge of their Lord and the nature of the universe around them. From their questioning and the reply given to them we recognize how far they were brought by means of the glorious Qur'ān and the Prophet's instructions. They were far removed from their past, and in this they recognized God's blessings and mercy.

God's remembrance is not the mere mentioning of His name verbally; it can only be achieved when both heart and mind are brought into it. It is the type of remembrance that makes hearts tremble and minds respond. Unless it is coupled with a feeling of humility and awe, it will not be true remembrance of God. Indeed, it could border on impoliteness towards God. When we remember God, we should think of His greatness, fear His punishment and hope for His mercy. Only in that way, can we achieve spiritual purity. When we mention His name as we remember His greatness, and we join the physical action with the spiritual, we must show our humility, speaking in a low voice, without singing or showing off.

"*And bethink yourself of your Lord humbly and with awe, and without raising your voice, in the morning and evening.*" (Verse 205) This is to ensure that our hearts remain in contact with God at both ends of the day. Remembering God is not limited to these two times; indeed it must be present all the time. We should be constantly on our guard against slipping into error. But in these two particular periods we can observe the clear change that takes place in the universe as the night changes into day, and the day changes into night. Human hearts feel in touch with the universe around them, as they witness how God accomplishes this transition of day and night and the great change that takes place as one gives way to the other.

God – limitless He is in His glory – knows that at these two particular times, human hearts are most likely to be impressed and to respond positively. There are frequent directives in the Qur'ān to remember God and glorify Him at the time when the whole universe appears to interact with the human heart, sharpen its impressions, and motivate it to remain in touch with God Almighty: "*Bear with patience whatever they may say, and extol your Lord's limitless glory and praise before the rising of the sun and before its setting; and in the night too, extol His glory, and at every prayer's end.*" (50: 39-40) "*Extol His glory, too, during the hours of the night as well as during the hours of the day, so that you may attain a state of contentment.*" (20: 130) "*Bear in mind your Lord's name early in the morning and before sunset, and during some of the night, and prostrate yourself to Him, and extol His limitless glory throughout the long night.*" (76: 25-26)

There is no need to say that this order to remember God at this particular time was before the daily prayers were made obligatory at their appointed times, because this may give the impression that these obligatory prayers have superseded this order. The fact is that this remembrance of God is wider than obligatory prayers. Its timing and its form are not limited to obligatory prayer. It may be a remembrance in private, or something in which both heart and mouth share without the movements that prayer includes. It is indeed wider than that, because it involves constant remembrance of God's Almightiness, when one is alone or with people, before any action, large or small, and before resolving to do anything. However, the early morning, the end of the day as the sun begins to set, and the depth of the night are mentioned because these are times that have special appeal to human hearts. God who has created man and who knows his nature is fully aware of all this.

"*Do not be negligent*". (Verse 205) This is a reference to people who neglect to remember God, not by word of mouth, but in their hearts and minds. It is the remembrance that keeps the heart alive to deter man from doing anything or following any course in which he feels embarrassed to be seen by God, and who watches God before doing anything. This is the type of remembering God that is ordered here. Otherwise, it would not be true remembrance of God if it does not lead to obeying Him and implementing His orders.

Do not let yourself be negligent of remembering God and watching your actions. Man needs to remain in constant touch with his Lord so that he is able to resist the temptation that Satan may place before him: "*If a prompting from Satan stirs you up, seek refuge with God; He hears all and knows all.*" (Verse 200) In its early part, the *sūrah* painted a panoramic scene of the battle between man and Satan. Throughout, it showed the procession of faith as the satans from among the *jinn* and human beings tried to force it out of its way. Satan was also mentioned in the story of the person to whom God gave His signs, but he pulled himself away from them, and chose to remain in error. At its end, it mentions the temptations of Satan and how people should seek shelter from him with God, who hears all and knows all.

Here we see a constant line that concludes with the instruction to remember God humbly and with awe, and not to be among the negligent. This order comes as part of the divine instruction to the Prophet to "*make due allowance for man's nature, and enjoin the doing of what is right; and turn away from those who choose to remain ignorant.*" (Verse 199) Thus it adds to the landmarks along the way which God approves. It also equips those who follow His guidance with what enables them to overcome all difficulties that they encounter along the way.

God then gives the example of angels commanding a high position. They do not entertain any tempting or evil thought, because Satan has no influence on their nature. They have no overpowering desire or fleeting whim. Nevertheless, they constantly glorify God and extol His praises. They are never too proud to worship Him. Man has a much more pressing need to remember God, glorify Him and worship Him. He has a difficult road to cover. By nature, he is susceptible to Satan's temptation. Negligence may lead him to ruin. He has a limited ability which can only be increased through worshipping God and glorifying Him: "*Those who are near to your Lord are never too proud to worship Him. They extol His limitless glory, and before Him alone prostrate themselves.*" (Verse 206)

Worship and the remembrance of God constitute a basic element in the practical application of this religion. Its method does not rely on theoretical knowledge or philosophical argument. It adopts a practical approach aiming to bring about a drastic change in human society which, inevitably, has rules that are well established in people's minds and practices. Changing this situation into the type which God wants people to follow is a difficult task that requires sustained efforts and much perseverance. With the limited ability human beings have, an advocate of this religion can only approach this difficult task if added strength is granted to him by his Lord. Knowledge on its own does not provide such strength, unless it is coupled with proper worship and with seeking God's help.

This *sūrah* begins with an address by God to His Messenger: "*This is a book that has been bestowed on you from on high – so do not entertain any doubt about it – in order that you may warn people with its message, and admonish the believers.*" (Verse 2) The *sūrah* also gives glimpses of the procession of faith, led by God's messengers, and the impediments placed in its way through the scheming of Satan and his helpers from among the *jinn* and human beings, as well as arrogant people and tyrants who try to exercise absolute power. This last directive points out the proper equivalent for those who want to join this noble procession along its hard way.

Index